The IDG Books Bible Advantage

The *Windows NT Workstation 4.0 Bible* is part of the Bible series brought to you by IDG Books Worldwide. We designed Bibles to meet your growing need for quick access to the most complete and accurate computer information available.

Bibles work the way you do: They focus on accomplishing specific tasks — not learning random functions. These books are not long-winded manuals or dry reference tomes. In Bibles, expert authors tell you exactly what you can do with your software and how to do it. Easy to follow, step-by-step sections; comprehensive coverage; and convenient access in language and design — it's all here.

The authors of Bibles are uniquely qualified to give you expert advice as well as insightful tips and techniques not found anywhere else. Our authors maintain close contact with end users through feedback from articles, training sessions, e-mail exchanges, user group participation, and consulting work. Because our authors know the realities of daily computer use and are directly tied to the reader, our Bibles have a strategic advantage.

Bible authors have the experience to approach a topic in the most efficient manner, and we know that you, the reader, will benefit from a "one-on-one" relationship with the author. Our research shows that readers make computer book purchases because they want expert advice on a product. Readers want to benefit from the author's experience, so the author's voice is always present in a Bible series book.

In addition, the author is free to include or recommend useful software in a Bible. The software that accompanies a Bible is not intended to be casual filler but is linked to the content, theme, or procedures of the book. We know that you will benefit from the included software.

You will find what you need in this book whether you read it from cover to cover, section by section, or simply one topic at a time. As a computer user, you deserve a comprehensive resource of answers. We at IDG Books Worldwide are proud to deliver that resource with the *Windows NT Workstation 4.0 Bible*.

Brenda McLaughlin

Senior Vice President and Group Publisher

YouTellUs@idgbooks.com

Windows NT®
Workstation 4.0
Bible®

Windows NT® Workstation 4.0 Bible®

by Allen L. Wyatt

IDG Books Worldwide, Inc.
An International Data Group Company

Foster City, CA ◆ Chicago, IL ◆ Indianapolis, IN ◆ Dallas, TX

Windows NT Workstation 4.0 Bible®
Published by
IDG Books Worldwide, Inc.
An International Data Group Company
919 E. Hillsdale Blvd., Suite 400
Foster City, CA 94404
www.idgbooks.com (IDG Books Worldwide Web Site)

Library of Congress Catalog Card No.: 96-78777
ISBN: 0-7645-8011-6

Printed in the United States of America
10 9 8 7 6 5 4 3 2 1
1B/QW/SS/ZW/FC

Distributed in the United States by IDG Books Worldwide, Inc.

Distributed by Macmillan Canada for Canada; by Contemporanea de Ediciones for Venezuela; by Distribuidora Cuspide for Argentina; by CITEC for Brazil; by Ediciones ZETA S.C.R. Ltda. for Peru; by Editorial Limusa SA for Mexico; by Transworld Publishers Limited in the United Kingdom and Europe; by Academic Bookshop for Egypt; by Levant Distributors S.A.R.L. for Lebanon; by Al Jassim for Saudi Arabia; by Simron Pty. Ltd. for South Africa; by Pustak Mahal for India; by The Computer Bookshop for India; by Toppan Company Ltd. for Japan; by Addison Wesley Publishing Company for Korea; by Longman Singapore Publishers Ltd. for Singapore, Malaysia, Thailand, and Indonesia; by Unalis Corporation for Taiwan; by WS Computer Publishing Company, Inc. for the Philippines; by WoodsLane Pty. Ltd. for Australia; by WoodsLane Enterprises Ltd. for New Zealand. Authorized Sales Agent: Anthony Rudkin Associates for the Middle East and North Africa.

For general information on IDG Books Worldwide's books in the U.S., please call our Consumer Customer Service department at 800-762-2974. For reseller information, including discounts and premium sales, please call our Reseller Customer Service department at 800-434-3422.

For information on where to purchase IDG Books Worldwide's books outside the U.S., please contact our International Sales department at 415-655-3172 or fax 415-655-3295.

For information on foreign language translations, please contact our Foreign & Subsidiary Rights department at 415-655-3021 or fax 415-655-3281.

For sales inquiries and special prices for bulk quantities, please contact our Sales department at 415-655-3200 or write to the address above.

For information on using IDG Books Worldwide's books in the classroom or for ordering examination copies, please contact our Educational Sales department at 800-434-2086 or fax 817-251-8174.

For authorization to photocopy items for corporate, personal, or educational use, please contact Copyright Clearance Center, 222 Rosewood Drive, Danvers, MA 01923, or fax 508-750-4470.

is a trademark under exclusive license to IDG Books Worldwide, Inc., from International Data Group, Inc.

ABOUT IDG BOOKS WORLDWIDE

Welcome to the world of IDG Books Worldwide.

IDG Books Worldwide, Inc., is a subsidiary of International Data Group, the world's largest publisher of computer-related information and the leading global provider of information services on information technology. IDG was founded more than 25 years ago and now employs more than 8,500 people worldwide. IDG publishes more than 275 computer publications in over 75 countries (see listing below). More than 60 million people read one or more IDG publications each month.

Launched in 1990, IDG Books Worldwide is today the #1 publisher of best-selling computer books in the United States. We are proud to have received eight awards from the Computer Press Association in recognition of editorial excellence and three from *Computer Currents'* First Annual Readers' Choice Awards. Our best-selling *...For Dummies®* series has more than 30 million copies in print with translations in 30 languages. IDG Books Worldwide, through a joint venture with IDG's Hi-Tech Beijing, became the first U.S. publisher to publish a computer book in the People's Republic of China. In record time, IDG Books Worldwide has become the first choice for millions of readers around the world who want to learn how to better manage their businesses.

Our mission is simple: Every one of our books is designed to bring extra value and skill-building instructions to the reader. Our books are written by experts who understand and care about our readers. The knowledge base of our editorial staff comes from years of experience in publishing, education, and journalism — experience we use to produce books for the '90s. In short, we care about books, so we attract the best people. We devote special attention to details such as audience, interior design, use of icons, and illustrations. And because we use an efficient process of authoring, editing, and desktop publishing our books electronically, we can spend more time ensuring superior content and spend less time on the technicalities of making books.

You can count on our commitment to deliver high-quality books at competitive prices on topics you want to read about. At IDG Books Worldwide, we continue in the IDG tradition of delivering quality for more than 25 years. You'll find no better book on a subject than one from IDG Books Worldwide.

John Kilcullen
President and CEO
IDG Books Worldwide, Inc.

Eighth Annual Computer Press Awards ≥1992

Ninth Annual Computer Press Awards ≥1993

Tenth Annual Computer Press Awards ≥1994

Eleventh Annual Computer Press Awards ≥1995

Credits

**Senior Vice President &
Group Publisher**
Brenda McLaughlin

Senior Acquisitions Editor
John Osborn

Marketing Manager
Jill Reinemann

Managing Editor
Andy Cummings

Administrative Assistant
Laura J. Moss

Editorial Assistant
Timothy J. Borek

Production Director
Andrew Walker

Supervisor of Page Layout
Craig A. Harrison

Production Associate
Christopher Pimentel

Development Editor
Susan Pines

Copy Editors
Kerrie Klein, John C. Edwards

Technical Reviewer
Ron Nutter

Project Coordinator
Katy German

Graphics & Production Specialists
Mario F. Amador
Vincent F. Burns
Stephen Noetzel
Mark Schumann
Elsie Yim

Quality Control Specialist
Mick Arellano

Proofreader
Jon Weidlich

Indexer
Ty Koontz

Cover Design
Liew Design

About the Author

Allen L. Wyatt

Allen L. Wyatt, an internationally recognized expert in small computer systems, has been working in the computer and publishing industries for almost two decades. He has written more than 35 books and numerous magazine articles explaining many different facets of working with computers. His books have covered topics ranging from programming languages to using application software to mastering operating systems. Through the written word, Allen has helped millions of readers learn how to better use computers.

Besides writing books, Allen has helped educate thousands of individuals through seminars and lectures about computers. He has presented seminars and lectures throughout the United States, as well as throughout Mexico and Costa Rica. His books, which often form the basis of his presentations, have been translated into many languages, including Spanish, French, Italian, German, Greek, Chinese, and Polish.

Allen is the president of Discovery Computing Inc., a computer and publishing services company located in Sundance, Wyoming. Besides writing books, he helps further the computer book industry by providing consulting and technical development services. He lives with his wife and children on a 390-acre ranch just outside of town, on the edge of the beautiful Black Hills. In his spare time he tends his animals, has fun with his family, and participates in church and community events.

You can learn more about DCI and Allen at http://www.dcomp.com.

The Publisher would like to give special thanks to Patrick J. McGovern,
without whom this book would not have been possible.

Contents at a Glance

Table of Contents

Introduction

Welcome to *Windows NT Workstation 4.0 Bible*. This book is designed to provide the information you need to not only use this latest version of Windows NT, but to use it effectively.

The information in this book cannot be garnered by reading any other single source. You certainly can't find it in the Microsoft documentation; that has been shrinking for the past several years, even as the operating system grows more complex.

You can't find it in the on-line documentation, because in some areas that contains less information than the printed documentation. And most other books on the market do not focus on those areas where you can maximize your use of the operating system, putting it to work right away.

Exactly what is *Windows NT Workstation 4.0 Bible*, then? It is the culmination of working for years not only with the Windows NT betas, but with previous versions of Windows NT and with Windows 95, on which the new Windows NT interface is based.

The reference information, tutorial helps, tips, hints, notes, and secrets represent the information you need to increase your knowledge of Windows NT, regardless of where you presently view your understanding.

What You Should Know

Every author makes assumptions about the readers of his or her books. What, then, are the assumptions I have made about you?

- You are not a neophyte. You have been around computers for a while, and you understand some of (but perhaps not all about) how they work. You may be viewed as the "computer expert" in your office, or you may be fortunate enough to have someone else who wears that title.

- You know how to do run-of-the-mill tasks, such as click a mouse or move a window. You may not, however, know every nitty-gritty detail of configuring your system to reflect your tastes and work habits.

- You already have Windows NT Workstation 4.0 installed on your system. You know how to log in and start your system, and you are ready to dive in and learn how to really put the many features of Windows NT Workstation to work for you.

■ You are using Windows NT Workstation as just that — a workstation. You probably belong to a network, and you interact with others across that network.

■ You are running a number of general purpose programs, but you also use some type of specialized software to get your work done. For instance, you might use specialized multimedia software or CAD/CAM programs on your workstation.

■ You are looking for a way to get an edge on using your computer. You are not the type to settle for "good enough." You are self-motivated, and you typically learn by jumping in the deep end of the pool. You may be over your head for a while, but you quickly regain your bearings and set out toward your objective.

What Is in This Book?

Windows NT Workstation 4.0 Bible is chock-full of valuable information you can put to work right away. The book's parts each focus on a different aspect of the operating system. The sections are further broken down into 18 chapters addressing specific features, tools, or concepts you need to know.

Part I

Part I, "Understanding Your Windows NT System," provides you with the basic information you need to effectively use Windows NT Workstation on a daily basis. It is composed of five chapters that cover everything from the interface to managing disks and files to printing.

Chapter 1, "Understanding the Interface," teaches you all about the new design used for this version of Windows NT. The focus is on the desktop, how you can use the Taskbar, and how to access the various aspects of the Help system. When you are through with this chapter, you will know your way around the block like an old pro.

Chapter 2, "Controlling Your Environment," helps you learn your way around the various parts of your system. You learn how to access local and network resources, how to use the new Explorer, why properties are such a big deal in Windows NT, how to successfully use shortcuts, and understand user profiles.

Chapter 3, "Customizing Your System," guides you through modifying your desktop to reflect your personal tastes. Here you learn about changing the appearance of the desktop, modifying the sounds used in your system, changing the Start menu, and how your customization can affect the performance of your workstation.

Chapter 4, "Managing Disks and Files," covers the fundamentals of controlling your disk drives and their contents. You learn how disk drives are organized, what filing systems are supported by Windows NT, how long filenames are best used, how to manage your drives and the files contained on them, and how to access files over the network.

Chapter 5, "Printing," teaches you everything you need to know to master printers, both local printers and those shared over the network. Here you learn about the Printers folder, how to control the print server built into your workstation, how to manage individual printers, and how to handle print jobs once they are created.

Part II

Part II, "Your Hardware and Software," examines the intricacies of working with both hardware and software. Through the course of four chapters you learn the ins and outs of how Windows NT interacts with the two most important components of any computer system.

Chapter 6, "Managing Hardware," takes a look at how Windows NT utilizes the hardware in your system. Here you find out how to add hardware, develop hardware profiles, and change input devices on your system.

Chapter 7, "Using Accessories," gives a whirlwind tour of the most basic of Windows NT software — the accessories that are provided with the operating system. You learn which ones are installed by default, as well as which ones can be installed later. A hands-on approach leads you through the key features of most of the accessories. (Others are covered in different sections of the book.)

Chapter 8, "Controlling Your Software," looks at how Windows NT provides a stable platform for your applications software. Here you learn about the different facets of the environment, the subsystems provided as part of the operating system, how software is added, how you can control the DOS program environment, and how best to remove your software.

Chapter 9, "Using the Command Window," teaches you how to best use the command-line environment provided as a part of Windows NT. You even have a great guide to those commands that are different under DOS, Windows 95, and Windows NT, as well as detailed descriptions of all the unique command-line commands in Windows NT.

Part III

Part III, "Moving Beyond the Basics," leads you into territory not covered in most books about Windows NT. In six chapters you learn about such important topics as the Registry, advanced disk use, networking, and communications — even the Internet.

Chapter 10, "Understanding the Registry," provides the information you need to make sense of the single most important set of files in Windows NT. Here you learn not only why the Registry is so important, but how it is organized, how to edit it, and how to recover from a damaged Registry.

Chapter 11, "Advanced Disk Topics and Tools," picks up where Chapter 4 left off. Here you learn about the fault-tolerant support in Windows NT, how to implement those features in your workstation, how disk compression can be performed on a file-by-file basis, how to check your system for disk errors, and why making backups is important.

Chapter 12, "Effective Networking," presents the information you need to round out your knowledge about networking under Windows NT. In other chapters you learned how to access and manage network resources. In this one you learn the networking paradigm used in Windows NT, how to manage network components, and how to search for computers in a large network.

Chapter 13, "Controlling Communications," guides you through the sometimes bewildering world of data communications. Here you learn the fundamentals behind communicating, how Windows NT works with a modem, the basics of telephony, how to use Dial-Up Networking to contact remote networks, and how you can use Remote Access Server to provide dial-in capability on your workstation.

Chapter 14, "Using Tools for the Internet," discusses the support Windows NT Workstation provides for Internet connectivity. Here you learn about the command-line and Windows interface tools that allow you to reach out and touch computers around the world. You even learn about Peer Web Services, which allow you to publish information that others can access.

Chapter 15, "Personal Communications Tools," teaches you how to use the three major communications accessories provided with Windows NT Workstation. You learn how to use the Phone Dialer, put HyperTerminal to work, and use Microsoft Exchange for electronic mail.

Part IV

Part IV, "Making the Most of Your System" provides the information you need to move into guru territory. The information, which builds on topics discussed earlier in the book, provides the tools you need to optimize your use of Windows NT Workstation.

Chapter 16, "Establishing Security," focuses on the ways in which you can make your workstation (and the data it contains) more secure. Here you learn different security strategies, how to use the User Manager, how to establish account policies, why you need to be concerned with user rights, how to manage file and folder permissions, how to enable auditing on your system, and finally how you can manage the log files generated by Windows NT.

Chapter 17, "Automating Tasks," teaches you how to make your computer use a little less mundane and repetitive. You first learn about starting programs when you start Windows NT, then progress to writing batch files, and finally to scheduling programs for execution at a specific time.

Chapter 18, "Improving Performance," is the final chapter in *Windows NT Workstation 4.0 Bible*. Here you learn how to keep your workstation running at peak efficiency. You learn about the different aspects of performance, how to measure it, and how to correct the major problems you may uncover.

Part V

Finally, the appendix at the back of the book describes what is included on the companion CD-ROM. Here you learn how to access, use, and (in some cases) register the software.

All in all, *Windows NT Workstation 4.0 Bible* presents a tour de force in gaining complete control over your workstation and this powerful operating system.

How to Use This Book

Windows NT is a complex, complicated operating system that provides more features than any one person may ever take full advantage of. You may use a few features this month, try out a new one next month, and finally add a couple more later this year. Some features you may never use.

Because the uses to which Windows NT Workstation is put are so diverse, and the implementation so varied from system to system, this book is not necessarily intended to be read sequentially.

While everyone can probably benefit from reading Part I, "Understanding Your Windows NT System," in sequential order, beyond that, all bets are off. You should look for those subjects which interest you, and which you need to know about at the time. The other chapters or sections can safely be ignored — for now. Later, you can read them as the need arises.

Over the years, I have discovered another tactic which is always beneficial to learning. When you are implementing a Windows NT feature, read the chapter you need in order to make the feature work properly. Once you have learned the concepts and have been using the feature for three or four weeks, go back and reread the chapter — you'll be surprised what tidbits you pick up the second time through.

Editorial Devices

An *editorial device* is a publishing term for a book element that is designed to accomplish a specific purpose. *Windows NT Workstation 4.0 Bible* includes several editorial devices that are designed to draw your attention to important, unique, or little-known information. You can recognize these special elements by the icons that periodically appear in the margins.

The various elements include the following:

Note

This icon indicates something that is particularly noteworthy and deserves your attention. These items help you understand either the topic at hand better, or correlate the information with related topics.

Tip

This icon points out information that can save you time or effort. When you learn the tip, you become more familiar with how to use Windows NT effectively and productively.

Caution

This icon draws your attention to information that is important to your data, programs, or system as a whole. If you heed the caution, you are less likely to damage the information in your computer.

Secret

This icon highlights information that is either not widely known, not documented, or seldom thought about in the context in which it is used. Secrets, when learned and used, set you apart from other users; they truly make you the master of your system.

In some places you will also notice special sidebars. Sidebars are essentially extended notes, covering multiple paragraphs, that are treated as a whole unit. While there aren't very many of these editorial devices, sidebars provide special information which is related to the main text, but which deserves its own treatment.

How to Contact the Author

One of the primary ways I make my living is as a professional author. As such, I enjoy hearing from people who have found my books of value. If you find this book of value, or if you have a question, I would love to hear from you.

My e-mail address is:

awyatt@dcomp.com

While I cannot guarantee I will answer every piece of e-mail, I do read it all. I take helpful, constructive criticism well and appreciate a kind word every now and again. (Don't we all.) However, if you have a gripe or you find something wrong, you can still write me; I need these things pointed out as well.

Note

There is one thing I should mention about the CD-ROM in the back of this book. While I did pick the software included on it, I did not write the software.

If you have a problem with the software, be sure to examine the documentation files provided with the software. Typically there will be information on how you can get more help. You might as well go straight to the experts — the people who wrote the software.

With all that said, I hope you enjoy this book and wish you well as you set out to learn with the *Windows NT Workstation 4.0 Bible*.

Understanding Your Windows NT System

Chapter 1

Understanding the Interface

In This Chapter

Before you can begin to effectively use any operating system, you need to learn how to use its interface; Windows NT Workstation 4.0 is no exception. If you are an expert user of Windows 95, using the new Windows NT Workstation 4.0 interface may seem like "old hat." There are subtle differences, however, which you can use to make the most of your NT experience.

This chapter introduces the core elements of the user interface; when you have learned those (including the more subtle parts of the interface), you have laid a groundwork that is necessary for everything else you do with Windows NT. The following items are covered in this chapter:

▶ How the new interface design results in a cleaner desktop

▶ How you can recognize, understand, and use the objects on your desktop

▶ Why the Taskbar is such a powerful feature of the new NT interface

▶ How you can use task buttons to switch between active tasks

▶ How to understand the Windows NT menu system

▶ The subtle (and not so subtle) differences between windows and dialog boxes

▶ How you can use tips, on-line Help, and Wizards to find out more information about using Windows NT

▶ The different ways in which you can end your Windows NT session

A New Design

Windows NT Workstation 4.0 puts a brand new face on an old friend. The interface used in version 4.0 is similar to the interface made popular in Windows 95. Adopting the Windows 95 interface (code-named Indy by the folks at Redmond) may seem like a step backward to some people. After all, Windows NT is much more robust than Windows 95. Remember, however, that I am only talking about the interface. Everything behind the scenes remains at the industrial-strength level that you have come to expect from Windows NT.

In previous versions of Windows NT, the interface relied on the familiar Program Manager and various icons. For instance, Figure 1-1 shows an example of a typical desktop in Windows NT Workstation 3.51.

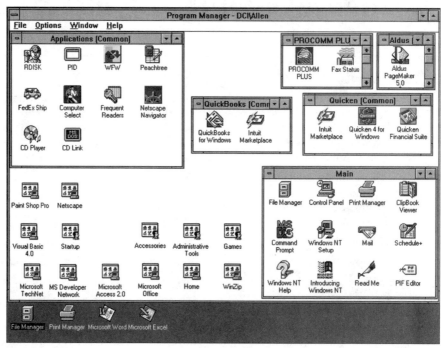

Figure 1-1: The traditional Windows NT interface relies on the Program Manager approach to management.

When you start Windows NT Workstation 4.0, you notice an immediate difference in the way your desktop appears. Figure 1-2 shows an example of the new interface that is used in this version of NT.

As you can tell by comparing Figure 1-2 with Figure 1-1, the new 4.0 desktop looks quite different from the traditional desktop. The biggest differences are that the new 4.0 desktop looks much less cluttered and that the Program Manager is missing. Under the 4.0 interface, everything is done directly from the desktop without the need for a Program Manager.

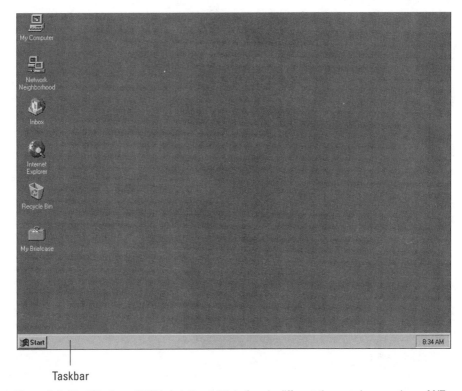

Taskbar

Figure 1-2: The Windows NT Workstation 4.0 interface is different than previous versions of NT.

If you look back at Figure 1-2, you can see that there are numerous elements to the 4.0 desktop:

- My Computer icon
- Network Neighborhood icon
- Inbox icon
- Internet Explorer icon
- Recycle Bin icon
- My Briefcase icon
- The Taskbar

These elements are present in a full Windows NT Workstation 4.0 installation but can vary from system to system. For instance, you may not see the Network Neighborhood icon if your workstation is not connected to a network.

If you have installed additional software on your system, you may see other elements on the desktop. The next several sections describe each of the standard desktop elements.

My Computer icon

The My Computer icon provides a way for you to examine the resources available on your PC. If you double-click on this icon, a window displaying your resources is displayed, as shown in Figure 1-3.

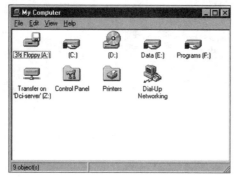

Figure 1-3: The My Computer window displays the resources that are available on your local PC.

Notice that this window contains icons for each of the disk drives on your system as well as the Control Panel, Printers Folder, and a Dial-Up Networking folder. It is highly possible that all of these icons are not available on your system; again, their presence varies from system to system.

The meaning of each type of resource icon is as follows:

 This icon indicates a floppy disk drive. There is no difference in the appearance of the icon for 3 $\frac{1}{2}$-inch or 5 $\frac{1}{4}$-inch drives.

 This icon indicates a local hard disk drive.

 This icon indicates a CD-ROM drive.

 This icon indicates a disk drive that is remote. These drives result from mapping a remote directory to a local disk drive letter. (Drive mapping is covered in Chapter 4).

This folder icon represents the Control Panel, which is used in configuring Windows NT Workstation.

 This folder icon represents the Printers subsystem of NT. How you use this subsystem is covered in Chapter 5.

 This icon represents the Dial-Up Networking (DUN) portion of NT. DUN replaces the older Remote Access System (RAS) of previous NT versions. DUN is covered in Chapter 13.

The My Computer icon is primarily used to browse the contents of your local PC system. For instance, if you double-click on a disk drive, the contents of that drive are displayed in another window. Browsing is covered in more depth in Chapter 2.

Network Neighborhood icon

The Network Neighborhood icon is visible on your desktop only if you have installed a network adapter for your system. While networking is discussed in depth in a later chapter (Chapter 12), you should understand that, unless you are connected to a network, the Network Neighborhood icon does not appear on your desktop.

If the Network Neighborhood icon is visible on your desktop, you can double-click on it to begin browsing through the network to which you are connected. Figure 1-4 shows an example of what you may see if you double-click on the Network Neighborhood icon.

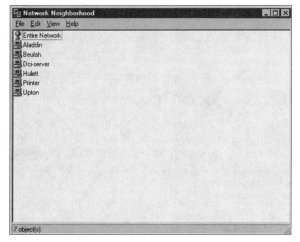

Figure 1-4: The Network Neighborhood window displays the resources that are made available by other workstations or servers on your network.

Because all networks are different, it should go without saying that the contents of your Network Neighborhood window can vary from what is shown in Figure 1-4. Again, you can browse through the network by selecting resources and double-clicking on them.

The Inbox icon

If your computer is attached to a network, you may see the Inbox icon on your desktop. This icon enables you to quickly access the Microsoft Exchange e-mail program. In reality, the program provides much more than just e-mail. For instance, you can also use Exchange to send or receive faxes.

Once you have set up Microsoft Exchange, you double-click on the Inbox icon to view your messages. Figure 1-5 shows an example of what the Microsoft Exchange Inbox looks like.

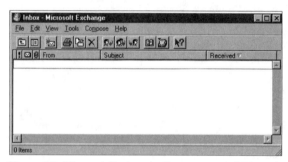

Figure 1-5: Microsoft Exchange allows you to quickly and easily control your e-mail and faxes.

More information about Microsoft Exchange (and the Inbox icon) is provided in Chapter 15.

The Internet Explorer icon

The Internet is all the rage these days, and Windows NT Workstation 4.0 includes a tool which allows you to take advantage of the World Wide Web. The Web is the multimedia portion of the Internet, and the tool provided is called Internet Explorer. This is a good example of a classification of pro-grams known as Web browsers.

If the network of which you are a part is connected to the Internet, or if you establish a dial-up connection to the Internet through a modem, then you can use the Internet Explorer. When you double-click on the icon, you see the program window shown in Figure 1-6.

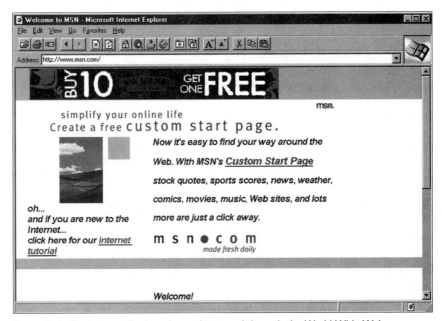

Figure 1-6: The Internet Explorer is used to travel through the World Wide Web.

Secret

The version of Internet Explorer provided with Windows NT Workstation 4.0 is Version 2.0. The latest version of Internet Explorer is Version 3.0. You can download this latest version for free from `http://www.microsoft.com`.

You can find more information about the Internet, the World Wide Web, and the Internet Explorer in Chapter 14.

The Recycle Bin icon

As initially installed by NT, the Recycle Bin looks like a wastebasket with an ecological recycling symbol on the front of it. The Recycle Bin is something new in Windows NT Workstation 4.0; it represents a way for you to manage your deleted files. If you double-click on the Recycle Bin, you see a window similar to Figure 1-7.

Figure 1-7: The Recycle Bin
contains files that were deleted
from a disk drive.

As you delete files during the course of your normal work, the files are not
really deleted. Instead, they are transferred to a special area of the disk
known as the Recycle Bin. The files remain here until either the bin is full or
you explicitly delete them. If you need to recover a file that you previously
deleted, it is still probably in the Recycle Bin and can be recovered.

Take another look at the Recycle Bin icon shown in Figure 1-2. If the Recycle
Bin looks empty (as it does in the figure), then it contains no deleted files. If,
on the other hand, the Recycle Bin looks like the following, then it contains
files.

Exactly how you control the Recycle Bin is covered in Chapter 4.

My Briefcase icon

One of the common tools installed by Windows NT Workstation 4.0 is
known as the Briefcase. This tool is used to synchronize files between two
computers, using regular floppy disks. You save files in the Briefcase, and
then copy the Briefcase from your system to a floppy disk.

You can then take the disk to another computer to work on the files. (This
is a great help if you take work home from the office.) When you return the
disk with the Briefcase to your system, the files are compared to those still
on the original computer.

If the files have changed, then they are copied from the Briefcase to your
original system. You access the Briefcase tool by double-clicking on the My
Briefcase icon. Figure 1-8 shows what the Briefcase window looks like.

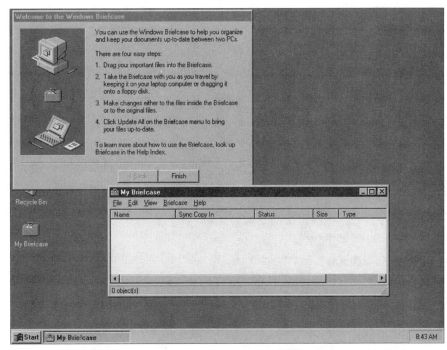

Figure 1-8: The Briefcase is used to synchronize files between two computer systems.

The Taskbar

If you are familiar with using Windows 95, you should also be familiar with the use of the Taskbar. This special control center, now included with Windows NT Workstation 4.0, allows you to quickly switch between different applications that are running on your system. The Taskbar appears at the bottom of your desktop, as shown in Figure 1-9.

Figure 1-9: The Taskbar enables you to quickly control programs that are running on your system.

When you first start Windows NT, the most prominent feature of the Taskbar is the Start button, located at the left side of the Taskbar. (The Start button is easily picked out in Figure 1-9.) The Start button is used to access the menu system used in Windows NT Workstation 4.0 and is discussed shortly.

The status area

At the right side of the Taskbar is the status area. This area indicates limited information about what is going on in your system. At a minimum, the status area indicates the time of day. There may also be other icons in the status area, such as a speaker, modem, or printer.

If present, each of these icons represents a device that is currently active in your system. If you double-click on any of the items in the status area, you can access the controls for that item.

For example, if you double-click on the time, you see the Date/Time Properties dialog box, as shown in Figure 1-10.

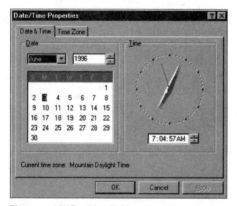

Figure 1-10: Double-clicking on an item in the status area of the Taskbar allows you to modify controls associated with the item.

The Date/Time Properties dialog box allows you to change the system date or time that is used by your PC. Properties dialog boxes are intrinsic to changing how NT interacts with devices in your system. These special dialog boxes are discussed more fully in Chapter 2.

Task buttons

The majority of the Taskbar (the area between the Start button and the status area) is used to display a series of task buttons. Each of these buttons represents an active task that is running within your system, or an open window.

For instance, if you double-click on the My Computer icon on your desktop, this action not only opens a window showing your system resources, but it also adds a button to the Taskbar (see Figure 1-11).

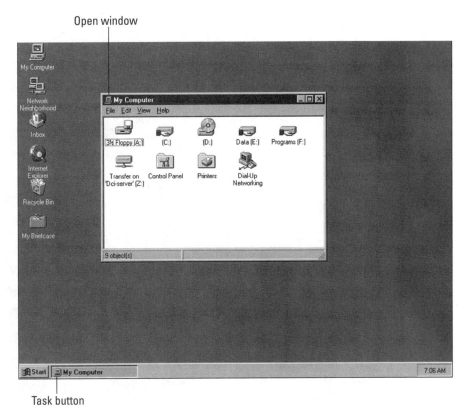

Figure 1-11: Opening a window adds a button to the Taskbar.

The purpose of the task buttons is to allow you to quickly and easily switch between different tasks that are running in your system. This may not seem like such a big deal if you have only a single program or two running, but it can be a real time-saver if you have multiple programs running and windows open at the same time.

As you start new programs or open new windows, task buttons are added to the Taskbar. As programs are ended or windows closed, the task button that is associated with that program or window is removed from the Taskbar.

If you open more tasks (or windows) than can fit across the Taskbar, the buttons for all the tasks are made smaller so that they can fit. For instance, Figure 1-12 shows the Taskbar with quite a few tasks running.

Figure 1-12: The Taskbar can contain many task buttons.

As you continue to open tasks, you reach a point where NT can no longer fit any more task buttons on the Taskbar. In this case, an extra line is added to the Taskbar (even though only one line is displayed), and a set of scroll controls appears at the right side of the task button area, as shown in Figure 1-13.

Figure 1-13: When necessary, the Taskbar can consume more than a single line, although only one line is displayed. Note the scroll controls at right.

When you reduce the number of active tasks, the size of the Taskbar again shrinks to one line, and the scroll controls disappear.

Windows NT menus

In older versions of Windows NT, you started programs by double-clicking on icons located in the Program Manager. While version 4.0 still contains a few icons on the desktop, most programs are now initiated through a series of menus.

These menus are accessed by using the Start button, located at the left side of the Taskbar. Clicking on the Start button displays the Start menu, which consists of a series of fundamental choices that you can make about what you want to do with your system. Figure 1-14 shows an example of the Start menu.

Figure 1-14: Clicking on the Start button displays the Start menu.

The choices that are available on the Start menu can vary, depending on how you have customized your system. When you first install Window NT Workstation 4.0, the Start menu contains the following fundamental choices:

- **Programs.** Selecting this menu option displays another menu, most often referred to as the Programs menu. In reality, this menu is constructed on the fly from the contents of the Programs folder.

  The menu is your gateway to standard Windows NT programs, accessories, and utilities.

- **Documents.** Selecting this menu option displays the names of data files that you have recently worked with. The menu is used to provide a quick way to access your most recently used documents.

  When you select one of the documents, the program that is used to work with the document is also automatically loaded.

- **Settings.** Selecting this menu option displays another menu that allows you to select the major configuration areas of NT 4.0. You use the Settings menu choice to access the Control Panel, the Printers folder, and the Taskbar configuration.

- **Find.** This menu option is used to locate files, folders, or resources, either on your local system or over the network. Exactly how you use the Find tool is discussed fully in Chapter 4.

- **Help.** This menu option is used to access the Windows Help system. The Help system is discussed later in this chapter.

- **Run.** Choosing this option allows you to quickly run a program without needing to open an MS-DOS command window. This option is essentially the same as the Run command in the File menu of the Program Manager in previous version of Windows NT.

- **Shut Down.** This option allows you to either log off your system or shut it down entirely. Later in this chapter, you learn more about ending your NT session.

Remember that these are the basic choices available from the Start menu. In Chapter 3, you learn how you can modify your system, including the Start menu. If you take another look at the Start menu, you can notice something else about it.

Each choice on the menu can appear in one of three ways. To the right of some menu choices is a triangle, while others contain three dots (ellipses); still others have no triangles or ellipses.

Menu choices with triangles

In Windows NT Workstation 4.0, menus are constructed from the contents of directories (folders) on your hard drive. If a menu choice has a triangle to the right of it, this means that the choice is a folder, and selecting the choice leads to more choices, which are the contents of that folder. (This point is critical to understanding how you can modify the contents of the menu system, as you learn later.)

For instance, the Programs option on the Start menu has a triangle to the right of it. To view the additional choices that are represented by the triangle, simply move the mouse pointer over the Programs option on the Start menu. Shortly another menu appears, as shown in Figure 1-15.

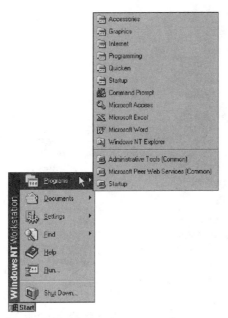

Figure 1-15: Moving the mouse pointer over a menu choice with a triangle to the right of it displays more menu choices.

Menu choices with ellipses

If you move the mouse pointer over a menu choice that has ellipses, no more choices appear. Instead, you must click (just once) on the menu choice. The ellipses mean that selecting the menu choice displays a dialog box.

For instance, on the Start menu, notice that the Run option has ellipses after it. Clicking on this option displays the Run dialog box, as shown in Figure 1-16.

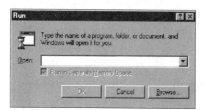

Figure 1-16: Menu choices with ellipses display dialog boxes when selected.

Regular menu choices

If a menu choice has no triangles or ellipses, then choosing it runs the program that is associated with the menu choice. Similarly, if the menu choice actually represents a document (such as under the Documents menu), then selecting it runs the program that is associated with the document represented by the menu choice.

Browse through the menus on your system, paying attention to the number of regular menu choices. As you get further into the menu system, you see more regular menu choices and fewer of the other types. It is the regular menu choices that get the work done under Windows NT.

Context menus

There is one type of menu that is a bit different from those discussed so far. The menus you have learned about to this point are all accessible through the Start button, and they follow a logical pattern. The other type of NT menu — a context menu — is a bit different.

A context menu, sometimes called a pop-up menu, is used to display a series of options that are applicable to a particular object. You display a context menu by using the mouse to point to an object (such as an icon, the desktop, a menu item, a title bar, or a window), and then click on the right mouse button.

For instance, Figure 1-17 shows the context menu that is displayed when you right-click on the desktop. You can try this on your system; simply right-click on any part of the desktop. Make sure it is the desktop itself and not a window or other object residing on the desktop.

Context menu

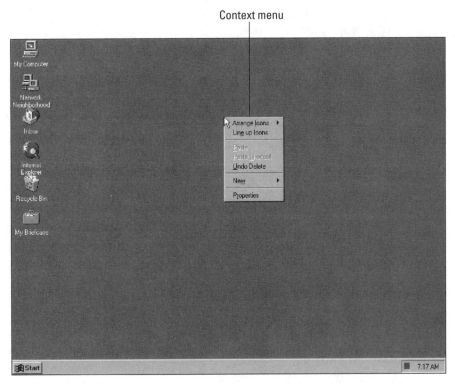

Figure 1-17: Context menus display tasks you can perform that are related to specific objects.

Once a context menu is displayed, you can use it just as you would any other menu. The trick is to right-click to get the menu displayed. You learn more about context menus and how you can use them to simplify your use of NT as you work through this book.

Controlling Windows

By now you have probably already noticed that the actual windows displayed in Windows NT Workstation 4.0 are different from their predecessors in older versions of Windows NT. Most of these changes are cosmetic in nature; this can lead to a momentary sense of disorientation as you first use the new NT. This quickly passes, however, and you are shortly faced with more substantial changes.

There are two types of windows that you need to examine. The first type is the regular windows — those used for the majority of your work. The other is the trusty dialog box, which has changed quite a bit under NT 4.0.

Regular windows

The majority of the substantive changes are visible in the title bar of any window. Gone are the old-version window-control buttons. In their place are new window-control buttons at the right side of the title bar, as shown in Figure 1-18.

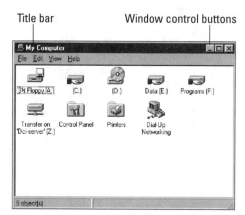

Figure 1-18: The window-control buttons in Windows NT Workstation 4.0 have changed.

Notice that there are three window-control buttons visible. One looks like a bar, another like a window, and the third contains an X. The button that contains a bar serves the same purpose as the minimize button in older versions of Windows NT.

Instead of minimizing the window to an icon, however, it instead minimizes the window to a spot on the Taskbar. To again see the window, you then click on the task button on the Taskbar, and the window is restored to its current size.

The window button serves the same purpose as the maximize and restore buttons in older versions of Windows. If the window does not currently occupy the entire screen, clicking on this button maximizes it so that it is as large as possible. If the window has already been maximized, then clicking on the window button restores the window to an open, but less-than-full-screen, size.

Finally, the button that contains an X is used to close the window. This button is new in NT version 4.0, and it is a welcome addition. Clicking on the X button has the same effect as double-clicking on the control menu icon — it closes the window.

If there was a program running in the window, the program is ended. If, instead, the window contained a data file, then the file is closed. (Depending on the program you are using, you may be prompted to save the data file before the window is closed.)

While the new window-control buttons may appear different at first, they do offer greater and more intuitive functionality than was available in older versions of Windows NT. You should be able to get used to them within a day of starting to use Windows NT Workstation 4.0.

Folder windows

Folder windows are the same as regular windows, but they display the contents of a folder (a directory, in pre-4.0 verbiage). There are a couple of standard items regarding folder windows that should be discussed, however; namely, display types and how you can sort the information in a folder window.

Display types

Windows NT allows you to control how information is displayed in a folder window. You can select any of the following display methods:

- Large icons
- Small icons
- List
- Details

You switch between window display types by choosing one of the display options from the View menu in the folder window. In addition, you can set display types for each open folder window, independent of the setting in other folder windows.

The default display method is large icons; this is how information is displayed in Figure 1-18. An icon is one of several types:

 This icon represents a document file that has been associated with a program. (You learn how to associate documents with programs in Chapter 4.) These icons look the same as the icons for the programs that the documents use.

 This icon represents a document file that has not been associated with a program, or a program file for which an icon was not available.

 This icon represents a program file for which an icon was available. (Typically these are Windows programs, and the icon definitely varies.)

 This icon represents a command-prompt batch file.

 This icon represents a folder.

The icons may vary slightly, but by and large you can determine what the icon represents by the icon that is used in the folder window.

If you choose to display the contents of a folder using small icons, the display changes a bit. Under this format, the information that is displayed is more tightly packed, but icons are still shown. Figure 1-19 shows an example of a folder window using small icons.

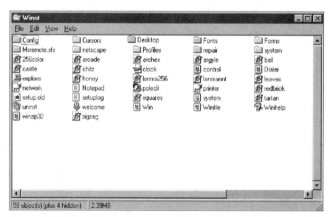

Figure 1-19: Small icons allow more information to be displayed in the same window space.

The acceptability of using small icons often depends on the size of the monitor that you are using. If you are using a large monitor, you may find the large icons display to be overpowering, whereas the small icons may be just about right. Try out both options to see which one you like best.

The list display type is essentially the same as the small icons display type, except that the orientation of the list is different. Whereas the small icons display lists files from left to right and then top to bottom, the list display type does it in the reverse order: from top to bottom and left to right. This display type is shown in Figure 1-20, which you should compare with Figure 1-19.

Figure 1-20: The list display type lists your folder contents in columns.

Notice that the information is listed in columns; if you don't like the number of columns that you see on the screen at one time, you can adjust the width of your window to display just the right amount of information for your tastes.

Finally, the details display type lists the most information of any of the display types. Using this you can see all of the information that you would normally see in a command-prompt directory listing. Figure 1-21 shows an example of this type of directory listing.

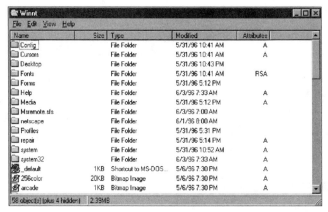

Figure 1-21: The details display type lists a great deal of information about your folder contents.

When using the details display type, each folder item is listed on its own line. If your window is not wide enough, you may need to make it wider to see all of the information about a file.

Sorting folder windows

Windows NT allows you to sort how files are displayed in a folder window. Sorting can be done using any of the following criteria:

- **Name.** Sorting is done alphabetically by the name of the file.

- **File type.** Sorting is done alphabetically, first by the file type (determined by the filename extension) and then by the filename itself.

- **File size.** Sorting is done based on the size of the file, in ascending order.

- **Date.** Sorting is done based on the date that the file was last modified.

You can change the sorting order by choosing Arrange Icons from the View menu and then picking a sorting type. Sorting types can be changed independently for each folder window that you have open.

Tip

If you are using the details display type for your folder window, you can control sorting by simply clicking on the column headings at the top of the folder window. For instance, if you take a look back at Figure 1-21, clicking on the Type column heading (in the gray area) sorts the display by file type.

Dialog boxes

Dialog boxes have perhaps changed more than regular windows. Dialog boxes are used to display options or to gather input for the current program. Many of the dialog boxes that were previously used in Windows NT are now streamlined and take advantage of a new feature called *tabs*. Figure 1-22 shows an example of a dialog box with tabs.

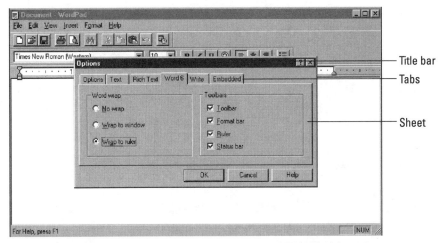

— Title bar

— Tabs

— Sheet

Figure 1-22: Dialog boxes have changed under Windows NT Workstation 4.0.

Tabs are designed to mimic the tab dividers used in an index card file. They are used to logically organize a large amount of information in a dialog box. If you want to see the information related to a tab, you simply click on the title of the tab.

From a referential standpoint, the entire dialog box is referred to by the name in the title bar, while the information displayed after clicking on a particular tab is often called a *sheet*. Thus, in Figure 1-22, the Options dialog box contains six tabs, which are as follows:

- Options
- Text
- Rich Text
- Word 6
- Write
- Embedded

When you click on the Write tab, you see information in the Write sheet.

Often the number of tabs in a dialog box can be imposing. Most dialog boxes are limited to two, three, or four tabs. Some dialog boxes can contain quite a few more, as shown in Figure 1-23.

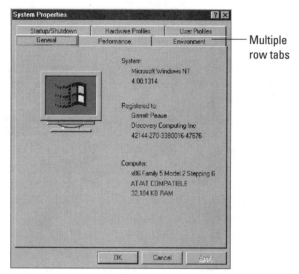

Multiple
row tabs

Figure 1-23: Tabs can appear in multiple rows
in a dialog box.

The only thing different in this example is that the tabs now appear stacked
across the top of the sheets in the dialog box. You access the information
that is associated with a tab in the same manner — by clicking on the tab.
Understanding how dialog boxes work under Windows NT 4.0 is essential to
effectively using the operating system.

The Help System

Windows NT Workstation 4.0 includes an in-depth Help system that offers
greater ease-of-use than previous versions of NT. Not only has the Help system been redesigned, but it contains more information, and there are more
ways that you can receive help.

The help that is available from Windows NT Workstation 4.0 is presented
using the following features:

■ Tips

■ On-line Help

■ Wizards

Each of these ways of getting help is discussed in the following sections.

Tips

The simplest way to get help in Windows NT is through *tips*. These are often called FastTips by the people at Microsoft. To see a tip, simply move the mouse pointer over an object on your desktop, or a button on a toolbar, and then hold the pointer there for a short time. If a tip is available, it appears in a small yellow box, as shown in Figure 1-24.

This is a tip

Figure 1-24: Tips appear right under the mouse pointer when using Windows NT Workstation 4.0.

The information provided in the tip is designed to jog your memory about the purpose of the object to which you are pointing. Moving the mouse pointer makes the tip disappear. You can then move the pointer to another object to see the tip that is associated with that item.

In reality, tips are nothing new in Windows NT Workstation 4.0. They have been around for some time in different applications. For instance, they have been rather pervasive in full-featured applications such as Microsoft Word or Excel.

What is new is the degree to which tips have been integrated into the operating system itself. If you remember that there are tips, there is a good chance you can get the "whack in the head" that you need to figure out what an object does.

Note

Tips are only available if they have been designed into the program that is responsible for an object. For instance, if you use an older program under Windows NT Workstation 4.0, it probably does not contain tips. This is because it was not fashionable to include tips when the program was first created.

On-line Help

On-line Help has been a part of Windows for several generations now. Unfortunately, the Help system has sometimes been less than helpful. Windows NT Workstation 4.0 features a new and improved on-line Help system that uses an entirely new user interface and includes an expanded amount of information.

The easiest way to access the on-line Help system is to choose Help from the Start menu; you can also access it by pressing F1 at any point while you are using Windows NT (this is sometimes known as the *help key*). Regardless of the method that you use, you shortly see the window that is shown in Figure 1-25.

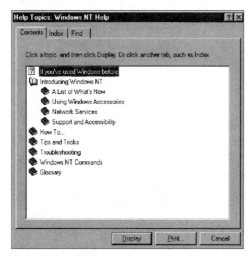

Figure 1-25: The on-line Help system allows you to quickly gain assistance on a topic of your choice.

The information in a Help window is pulled from a help file on disk. The help file displayed at any given point depends on how you accessed the on-line Help system. For instance, if you selected Help from the Start menu, then the displayed help file is the main Windows NT help file.

If, instead, you accessed the Help system from within an application, then the help file displayed is unique to that application. From a user standpoint, however, the interface used is exactly the same.

Note

Help files, stored on disk, have a filename extension of HLP. Normally the root filename is the same as the application with which the help file is associated. For instance, the name of the program that is used for the Notepad accessory is NOTEPAD.EXE. The help file that is associated with this program is NOTEPAD.HLP. (Both of these files can be found in the Windows NT program directory.) Developing help files is the responsibility of application developer.

Notice that the Help window contains three tabs: Contents, Index, and Find. Each of these represents different ways that you can access information in the on-line Help system.

The Contents tab

When you select the Contents tab, you can view the major help topics that are available in the particular Help file that you are viewing. There are three types of icons that can be used in the Contents sheet:

- **Closed book.** Double-click on the closed book to see more detail on the topic. You can also click on the topic and select the Open button.

- **Open book.** Double-click on the open book to show less detail on the topic. You can also click on the topic and select the Close button.

- **Document.** Double-click on the document icon (it has a question mark on it) to display the actual help information. You can also select the topic and click on the Display button.

The Contents tab is supposed to be an electronic version of a table of contents, similar to what you would find in any reference book. The difference is that, since the Contents tab is electronic, you can view as little or as much detail as you like by simply clicking on the icons on the sheet.

The Index tab

While you can select a general help topic from the Contents sheet, it is often more productive to jump directly to the topic that you want to view. This is done by first clicking on the Index tab. When you do, the on-line Help window appears, as shown in Figure 1-26.

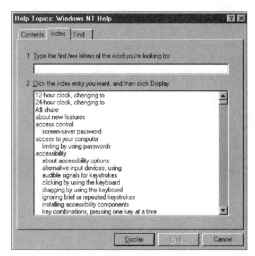

Figure 1-26: The Index sheet allows you to quickly zero in on the information that you want.

With the Index tab selected, the on-line Help window is divided into two sections. In the top section, you can type the name of the subject about which you want information. The bottom section contains a list of topics that are covered in this particular help file.

There are two ways that you can use the Index sheet. First, you can scroll through the topics listed at the bottom of the sheet. To do this, just use the scroll bar at the right side of the list. To view the information related to a topic, simply highlight the topic and click on the Display button. (You can also double-click on the topic in the list.)

The other way to use the Index sheet is to select the field at the top of the sheet. Start the name of a topic that you want to view. As you type, the information in the topic list at the bottom of the sheet changes. For instance, if the first letter you type is E, then the topic list displays all topics beginning with E.

Typing the second letter, perhaps D, displays all topics beginning with ED. You can continue in this manner until the list of topics at the bottom contains those you want to see. You can then highlight the topic that you want in the bottom list, and click on the Display button. (Again, you can also double-click on a topic.)

The Find tab

Both the Contents and Index tabs allow you to quickly find your way through the headings in a help file. There are times, however, when the headings just won't do — instead you want to go directly to all of the words in a help file.

For instance, you may want to look at documents that contain all occurrences of a particular word or phrase — and that word or phrase is not included in a major topic heading. This detailed search capability is provided by the Find tab. When you click on this tab, what you see depends on whether you have used the Find tab before for this particular help file.

If you have not used the Find tab before, then Windows NT needs to make a detailed index of the words in all of the topics in the help file. This can take a while, as indicated in Figure 1-27.

In most instances, you want to use the default choice (Minimize database size). Click on the Next button, and then click on Finish. The Help system files are accessed, and the necessary index is compiled. Shortly you see the Find tab, which you use to locate words, as shown in Figure 1-28.

Figure 1-27: When the Find tab is first used, Windows NT needs to make a detailed index of the help file.

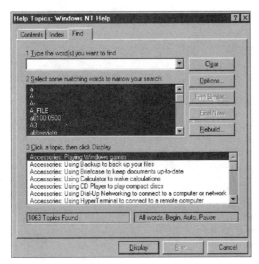

Figure 1-28: The Find sheet is used to search by any word in a help file.

The Find sheet is divided into three sections. In the top section, you can type the word or words that you want to locate, while the second section contains indexed words, and the bottom section contains help file topics.

To use the Find sheet, simply start typing the word that you want to find. As you type, the information in the second section of the sheet changes to match what you are typing. (This is the same process that you used in the Index sheet.) When you have sufficiently narrowed the list of available words, use the mouse to highlight a word.

This modifies what is shown in the third portion of the Find sheet, which is all of the help file topics that contain the selected word (or words). When you see a desired topic displayed, highlight it and click on the Display button, or simply double-click on the topic.

Viewing Help documents

Regardless of how you locate the topic that you want displayed (using the Contents, Index, or Find tab), when you finally locate the topic on which you want help, Windows NT displays a document containing the help information. These documents are displayed in a Help window, as shown in Figure 1-29.

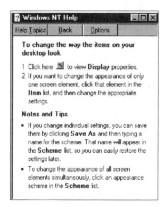

Figure 1-29: The Help window is used to display information about a topic.

The Windows NT Help window is much simpler than those used in earlier versions of Windows. It contains only three choices on the button bar: Help Topics, Back, and Options.

- **Help Topics.** This first button displays the same sheet that you used to access this topic in the first place (either Contents, Index, or Find).

- **Back.** The second button (when available) allows you to step back through previous Help screens that you have viewed.

- **Options.** The final button is used to change how the Help screen is displayed or to print the information in the Help window.

Notice, as well, that the information in the Help window also contains *hyperlinks* to additional information. These links can be identified because they typically look like small buttons or blocks (there is one such link in the first item in Figure 1-29). If you click on a link, you can view the help file information related to that topic.

Wizards

A Wizard is the name used to identify a step-by-step procedure that accomplishes a task. Wizards have been used for some time in Windows programs such as Excel. They are a way to lead you through what may otherwise be a complex set of steps. In Windows NT, several Wizards have been provided for your use.

For instance, the process of creating a Find tab index in the on-line Help system (as described in the previous section) uses a Wizard. You can see another example of a Wizard if you select Settings from the Start menu and then select Printers. This opens the Printers folder, as shown in Figure 1-30.

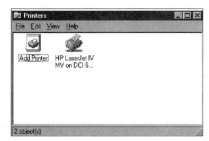

Figure 1-30: The Printers folder contains information about printers defined in your system.

Notice the icon entitled Add Printer. You can't tell by looking at the icon, but when you double-click on it, a Wizard is started. Go ahead and start it now; you then see the window for the Add Printer Wizard, as shown in Figure 1-31.

Figure 1-31: The Add Printer Wizard helps you define a new printer for your system.

Wizards always have a series of buttons that control the steps that you perform. (You can use these buttons to help identify a Wizard.) These buttons, located at the bottom of the window, are fairly standard, regardless of the Wizard.

They include the following items:

- **Hint.** Displays a hint about what can be done at the current time within the Wizard.

- **Cancel.** Ends the task without making any changes.

- **Back.** Backtrack to the previous step of the task.

- **Next.** Proceed to the next step of the task.

- **Finish.** Complete the task using the information provided so far, along with default information for the steps not yet completed.

To use a Wizard effectively, all you need to do is answer the question posed on the present screen or make a selection when prompted, and then click on the Next button. If you make a mistake and you don't realize it until you have clicked on Next, you can then click on Back to return to the previous step.

The exact steps that are presented in a Wizard depend on the purpose of the Wizard. Working through concise steps in this manner, however, allows you to complete tasks that otherwise have the potential of being difficult to perform.

Ending Your NT Session

When you are done with your Windows NT Workstation session, it is generally a good idea to log off the system. This is particularly true when your workstation provides access to a network. If you leave your system connected to the network (logged in), then you become a security risk to the network as a whole.

To end your session, click on the Start button, and then choose the Shut Down option from the Start menu. When you choose this option, you are provided with four more options, as shown in Figure 1-32.

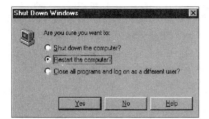

Figure 1-32: There are multiple ways that you can end your Windows NT Workstation session.

The three shutdown choices result in the following actions:

■ **Shut down the computer.** This shuts down all your files, closes all your devices, and disconnects all network connections. You then see a message indicating that it is safe to turn off your computer.

■ **Restart the computer.** This accomplishes the same steps as the Shut down the computer option, but instead of displaying a message, the system is rebooted. This is essentially the same as (but safer than) pressing the reset button on your system.

■ **Close all programs and log on as a different user.** This closes all of the programs that you were using and then logs you off. The system is left at the log-in screen (where the user must press Ctrl+Alt+Del), which means you or another user can log in.

You should choose the option that best describes the type of shutdown that you want to perform and then click on the Yes button.

Tip

If you choose Shut Down by mistake, you can stop the shutdown process by choosing the No button from the shutdown dialog box.

Summary

The Windows NT Workstation 4.0 interface is a huge improvement over previous versions of Windows. In this chapter, you have learned the following items:

▶ The new user interface does away with the Program Manager and removes program groups from the desktop. Instead, you do your work directly from the desktop using a simpler, cleaner design.

▶ When you first install Windows NT Workstation 4.0, there are several standard icons on the desktop. These include My Computer, Network Neighborhood, Recycle Bin, and the InBox.

▶ The Taskbar is your Windows NT command post. It allows you to not only access the menu structure but to switch between active tasks and to control common devices in your system.

▶ The Windows NT menu system is at the heart of the operating system. By clicking on the Start button on the Taskbar, you can access the menus and select which programs you want to use.

▶ Design changes in both windows and dialog boxes provide a cleaner look and easier-to-use controls. Program windows include controls to close the window, and dialog boxes often include tabs for logical groupings of information.

▶ Windows NT Workstation 4.0 includes many ways that you can get help with the operating system or with programs that you use on the system. These methods include tips (sometimes called FastTips), on-line Help, and Wizards.

▶ When you are done working with NT, you can use the Shut Down option from the Start menu to choose how you want to end your session.

Chapter 2

Controlling Your Environment

In This Chapter

Windows NT Workstation 4.0 provides many ways in which you can control your environment. Don't confuse control with configuring or customizing, however. Customizing is covered in the next chapter, while this chapter introduces the solid information and expert tips and shortcuts you need to take advantage of everything Windows NT has to offer.

In this chapter you learn the following items:

▶ How you can navigate through your system directly from the desktop

▶ How you can access networked computers by browsing

▶ How folder windows can be managed easily and efficiently

▶ Why the new Explorer is a great upgrade to the older File Manager

▶ How properties are used and accessed in Windows NT

▶ How shortcuts can be created and managed

▶ How the new, improved Task Manager can be used to control programs and processes

▶ How user profiles are stored on the disk, and how you can make changes to those profiles

Taking a Browse

In Chapter 1, you learned how the Program Manager, which was so prevalent in previous versions of Windows, has gone away. Instead, you do all of your work directly from the desktop.

Two of the icons on the desktop are used to access the resources of your system, but you can also use them to browse through your system. These icons, My Computer and Network Neighborhood, work in pretty much the same way, and if you learn to use one of the icons, you won't be lost in using the other.

Browsing your computer

Double-click on the My Computer icon on your desktop. This should display a window similar to what you see in Figure 2-1.

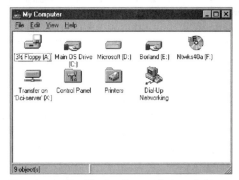

Figure 2-1: The My Computer window displays the resources available from your local computer.

Notice that there are many different icons in the My Computer window. In general, these icons represent different resources that are available to your system. If you want to examine a resource, you can double-click on it.

For example, if you wanted to see what was on your C drive, you simply double-click on the C drive's icon. Figure 2-2 shows what happens when you open this window.

Notice that NT opened another window, this one containing the contents of the C drive. If you wanted to see the contents of another folder or of another resource, just double-click on the object, and a new window is opened to display the contents of the resource. This repetitive process of double-clicking on objects and viewing their contents is referred to as browsing.

In Windows NT Workstation 4.0, browsing is one of two ways you can examine what is available on your system. (The other is to use the Explorer, which is covered in the next section.) Windows NT allows you to browse to your heart's content, and this feature provides a great way to quickly access your resources.

Secret

To open multiple folder windows, hold Ctrl as you select your set of folders, and then double-click on the last item to be added to the set. For instance, if you wanted to open windows for folders called Folder1, Folder2, and Folder3, you would select Folder1, then hold Ctrl as you select Folder2, and hold Ctrl as you double-click on Folder3.

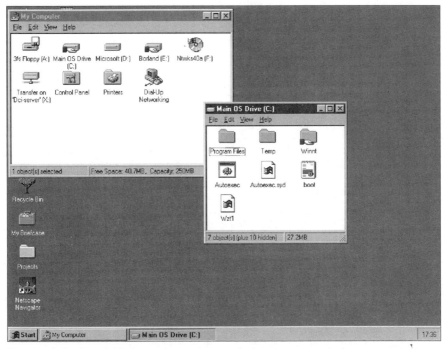

Figure 2-2: Double-clicking on a resource opens that resource to your view.

Tip

With multiple folder windows open on your screen, you can use the mouse to move objects from one folder to another. This is covered in more depth in Chapter 4.

When you opened the contents of the C drive, you noticed that Windows displayed a second window on your screen. Also, if you look back at Figure 2-2, notice that there are two task buttons on the Taskbar.

Each button is related to the windows on the screen. Because Windows NT opens a new window every time you double-click on a resource, your desktop can quickly get cluttered unless you close each window that you no longer need.

Some people find this open/close process rather tiring and instead only want a single window open on their desktop at any given time. If you fall into this category, you can instruct Windows NT to do this by following these steps:

STEPS

Turning multiple windows off and on

Step 1.   In an open folder window, choose Options from the View menu. This displays the Options dialog box, as shown in Figure 2-3.

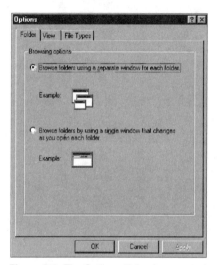

Figure 2-3: The Options dialog box controls what is displayed in folder windows.

Step 2.   Choose the second option on the Folder sheet; Browse folders by using a single window that changes as you open each folder.

Step 3.   Click on OK.

After turning off multiple windows, NT reuses the previous folder window to display the contents of a new window. This feature keeps your desktop less cluttered. With it turned off, however, there may be times when you want to see another window for a folder. For instance, you may want to compare contents or move items from one folder to another.

Secret

To display a separate window for a resource when you have multiple windows turned off, or to reuse the same window when you have them turned on, hold Ctrl as you double-click on an object.

Browsing the network

The Network Neighborhood icon allows you to quickly and easily browse the contents of your network, instead of just your local system. There are some differences, however, in how Windows NT displays local resources as opposed to network resources. Figure 2-4 shows what you see when you first double-click on the Network Neighborhood icon on your desktop.

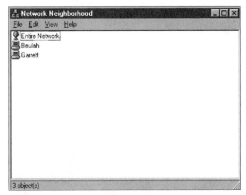

Figure 2-4: The Network Neighborhood window displays all of the network resources to which you are connected.

Notice that the Network Neighborhood window displays only those computers in your neighborhood, which in this case means your domain. A domain is a logical grouping of computer resources and is controlled by your system administrator. In Figure 2-4, you can see that there are three icons listed: one labeled Entire Network and the others representing individual computers.

The computers listed are all those currently available within your domain. If you double-click on the Entire Network icon, you can see the other networks that you can reach from your machine.

This is analogous to jumping from your street, where you can see only the houses on your block, to an elevation of 10,000 feet, where you can see all the cities for miles around. Figure 2-5 shows an example of what is displayed when you double-click on the Entire Network icon.

The example in Figure 2-5 shows that there is only one network available to you. If you are a member of a complex network, you could have many more options. The next step in browsing, however, is to double-click on the network that you want to view.

Figure 2-5: The Entire Network view shows you all of the networks to which you are connected.

This displays the domains within that network. Returning to the analogy, this action jumps from the 10,000-foot level down to a 2,000-foot level, where you can see all the neighborhoods within a single city. Figure 2-6 shows an example of what you see when you double-click on a network icon.

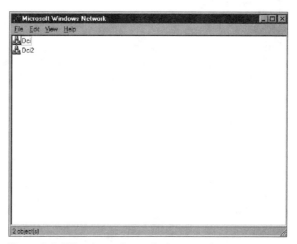

Figure 2-6: When browsing a single network, you can see all of the domains within that network.

The example in Figure 2-6 shows all of the domains (in this case, two) within the larger Microsoft network. If you wanted to browse further, you could double-click on a domain to see the resources that are available in that domain.

Working with folder windows

Regardless of whether you are browsing your local resources (My Computer) or the network (Network Neighborhood), Windows NT provides you with quite a few options for how you can work with the information that is presented in a folder window. If you look at any of the folder windows presented thus far in this chapter, notice that there is a menu at the top of each window.

What you may not know, however, is that there is also a toolbar available, and that you can control how information is displayed. Each of these areas is fully discussed in the following sections.

Folder window menus

At the top of every folder window is a menu, which is composed of four choices. This menu functions in the same manner as menus in other Windows programs. For instance, if you want to select a menu, click on the menu name. This presents a list of choices from which you can make additional choices. The following menu choices are available from a folder window menu:

- **File.** This menu allows you to take actions on files that you may have selected, as well as creating new folders, renaming existing folders or files, and closing the window.

- **Edit.** This menu allows you to perform standard editing functions, such as copying, cutting, and pasting.

- **View.** The options in this menu control the amount of information that is displayed in the window, as well as how that information is displayed.

- **Help.** This menu allows you to access the Windows NT Help system.

Using the toolbar

Secret

Believe it or not, you can add a toolbar to your folder windows. This toolbar is not visible by default, but you can turn it on by selecting the Toolbar option from the View menu. (This option is a toggle; select it again, and the toolbar disappears.) Figure 2-7 shows an example of the toolbar.

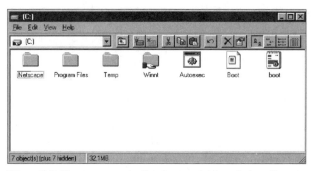

Figure 2-7: You can use a toolbar in your folder window if you desire.

The tools on the toolbar provide a quick way to access most of the functions that are available through the menus, plus a few extras. At the left side of the toolbar is a drop-down list that indicates what is displayed in the window.

Clicking on the drop-down arrow at the right side of the list displays a tree of system resources from which you can select. Only items at a drive level or higher are shown in the tree. If you select a resource in the tree, then the information in the window is changed to show the contents of that resource.

Note

The resource tree that is used in a folder window has a limited resolution. This means that you can only view items down to a disk-drive level. If you want to view individual folders in a tree, you must use the Explorer, as described later in this chapter.

Just to the right of the drop-down list are the actual tools on the toolbar. The 13 tools are divided into six groups, with each group divided by a space. The groups are, from left to right, as follows:

- **Tree Movement.** This group consists of a single tool with an upward-pointing arrow on it. This tool allows you to move up through the object hierarchy. (This is the hierarchy that is shown when you use the drop-down object list.) Clicking on the tool moves you up one level in the hierarchy.

- **Drive Mapping.** This group consists of two tools that are used to map drives and to remove drive mappings. These tools should look familiar if you used the File Manager in previous versions of Windows NT.

  The drive mapping functions are available only on the toolbar; they are not available from the menus.

- **Editing.** This group consists of three tools that are standard in many Windows applications. The tools allow you to cut, copy, and paste information or objects (such as folders or files).

- **Undo.** This group consists of a single tool that allows you to undo your previous action.

- **Miscellaneous.** This group consists of two tools. The left-most tool, with a stylish X on it, is used to delete the object that is selected in the window. For instance, if you click on a file and then click on the delete tool, then the file is moved to the Recycle Bin.

  The other tool is used to display the properties of the selected object. (Properties are discussed later in this chapter.)

- **Viewing.** This group consists of four tools that are used to control how information is displayed in the window, as discussed in the following section.

Changing views

Exactly how information is displayed in a folder window is controlled by the selections you make in the <u>V</u>iew menu or by using one of the tools at the right side of the toolbar. You can display information in one of four ways. Each of the following items corresponds to a choice in the <u>V</u>iew menu:

- **Large Icons.** Information is displayed using large icons with identifying text under each icon.

  An example of this type of display is shown in Figure 2-8.

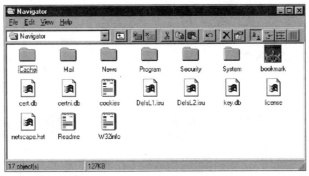

Figure 2-8: The Large Icons view makes objects easy to work with in the folder window.

■ **Small Icons.** Information is displayed using small icons with identifying text to the right of each icon. Files and folders are organized from left to right and then top to bottom, as shown in Figure 2-9.

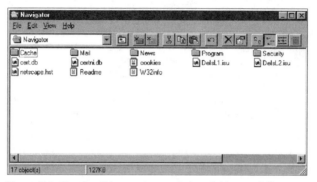

Figure 2-9: The Small Icons view organizes folders and files horizontally.

■ **List.** Information is displayed in the same way as the Small Icons choice, except files and folders are organized from top to bottom and then left to right. An example of this is shown in Figure 2-10.

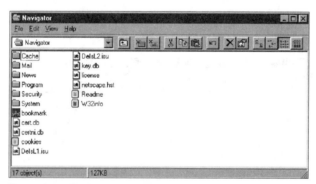

Figure 2-10: The List view organizes folders and files vertically.

■ **Details.** Information is displayed using small icons with identifying text and full information to the right of each icon. Each file or folder occupies a separate line in the window. Figure 2-11 shows an example of this type of view.

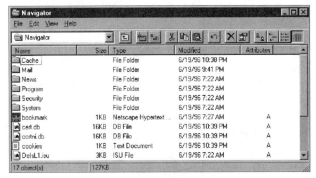

Figure 2-11: The Details view displays full information on each file and folder.

To a large degree, the type of view that you choose determines how you work with the objects in the folder window. For instance, if you select one of the icon views (large or small), then you can move icons around in the window.

For example, you can drag a file icon from one area of the window to another. When you move icons, they stay where you put them until you use one of the sorting commands or use the Auto Arrange feature, as described later in the chapter.

If you use one of the list views (List or Details), then you cannot drag items from place to place in the window. If you use the Details view, you can adjust the width of the columns displaying information about the files. If you look back at Figure 2-11, notice that the Details view includes a header at the top of the file list.

This header consists of gray blocks, each containing labels such as Name, Size, Type, and so on. If you move the mouse pointer over one of the division lines between these blocks, it changes to a two-headed pointer. At this point, you can click and drag to adjust the width of the columns.

Sorting information

Windows NT enables you to easily change the order in which information is presented in a folder window. Normally, the order in which files and folders appear is dictated by the type of view that you are using.

If you are using either the Large Icons or Small Icons views, objects are, by default, displayed at whatever position you drop them. In either the List or Details views, information is displayed in alphabetical order, according to the name of the file.

If you choose Arrange Icons from the View menu, you can quickly change how the information in the window is sorted. There are four different sorting orders that you can use:

- **Name.** Objects are sorted in alphabetical order based on their name, regardless of the view being used.

- **Type.** Objects are sorted first by file extension (DOC, GIF, BMP, EXE, etc.) and then by name.

- **Size.** Objects are sorted in ascending order based on file size. (All directories, which have no file size, are placed at the beginning of the list.)

- **Date.** Objects are sorted by when they were last modified, with the most recently modified files listed first.

You can use the sorting commands regardless of which view you are using for the window. Sorting only has a temporary effect, however. When you make changes to the items in a folder, the changes are not automatically arranged in sorted order.

For example, if you rename a file, then it does not assume its new position in the window based on its new name. To see the list sorted again, you must again choose the sorting option.

If you are using the Details view, you can also sort information by clicking on one of the gray buttons that make up the column headings. For instance, if you wanted to sort by file size, you could click on the Size column header. Because there are quite a few columns in the Details view, you can actually sort in more ways than you can by using one of the sort commands from the menus.

Arranging icons

As you work with icons in a folder window, you may have noticed that the icons do not arrange themselves well. As you move icons and resize windows, it is easy for the icons to start "piling up." Granted, you can sort the icons using the methods that were outlined in the previous section, but if you make many changes, this can get very tiresome.

One way that you can straighten up the icons in a window is to choose the Line up Icons option from the View menu. This causes icons to be moved, as necessary, to fit a grid pattern within the window. The icons are not sorted; they are just moved slightly so that they are not on top of each other, which means that they are all visible.

If you regularly make changes to folders and you use either the Large Icons or Small Icons views, you may want to consider turning on the Auto Arrange feature. With this feature turned on, the icons in a folder window are automatically arranged so that the maximum number of icons is available on the screen at once.

Thus, if you copy a file to the folder, it doesn't appear on top of another icon. Likewise, if you change the size of the folder window, the icons are rearranged to fit into the window. To turn on the Auto Arrange feature, follow these steps:

STEPS

Turning Auto Arrange on and off

Step 1. Select the Arrange Icons option from the View menu. This displays a submenu of choices.

Step 2. Select the Auto Arrange option. If a check mark appears next to the option, then Auto Arrange is enabled; if there is no check mark, it is turned off.

Understanding persistence

Persistence is a general term that refers to how long a certain characteristic is maintained. When you work with folder windows, certain characteristics are maintained indefinitely, and others are not.

Some characteristics are remembered for a window. This means that even if you close a window, the next time you open it, those characteristics are present.

Thus, if you open a window for the C drive, make changes to its appearance, and then close the window, it looks the same the next time you open it.

The following characteristics have persistence for a single window:

- Toolbar
- View (Large Icons, Small Icons, List, or Details)
- Auto Arrange
- Window size
- Window position

Other characteristics, such as the way in which a folder is sorted, do not have persistence.

Using the Explorer

In previous versions of Windows NT, the File Manager was a trusted member of the family. You used the File Manager to manipulate files and access resources. In the previous section, you learned that you can now do quite a bit of browsing directly from the desktop, which was a function previously limited to the File Manager. Desktop browsing does not allow you to do everything that you previously did in the File Manager, however.

Under Windows NT Workstation 4.0, the File Manager has been replaced by the Explorer. This tool allows you to view, change, and manage the contents of your disk drives. If you have the proper security permissions, you can do the same functions over the network; Explorer makes very little distinction between local and remote resources.

Starting the Explorer

There are several ways that you can start the Explorer:

- Open the My Computer or Network Neighborhood icon, and then choose a drive or folder. Then choose Explore from the File menu.

- Open the My Computer or Network Neighborhood icon, and then hold Shift as you double-click on a drive or folder.

- Choose the Programs option from the Start menu, and then choose Windows NT Explorer.

Regardless of how you choose to start the Explorer, you shortly see the Explorer window, as shown in Figure 2-12.

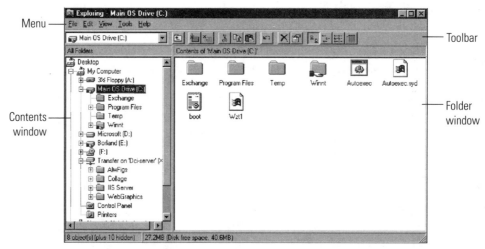

Figure 2-12: The Explorer allows you to work with different resources that are available to you.

The four main parts of the Explorer (menu, toolbar, Folder window, and Contents window) are discussed in the following sections.

The menu

If you look back at Figure 2-12, notice that the Explorer has five menu choices that are available at the top of its window. The menus that these choices represent are very similar to the menu choices that are available in a folder window when you are browsing on your desktop.

The menu choices available include the following:

- **File.** This menu enables you to take actions on files that you have selected, as well as creating new folders, renaming existing folders or files, and exiting the Explorer.

- **Edit.** This menu enables you to perform standard editing functions, such as copying, cutting, and pasting.

- **View.** The options in this menu control the amount of information that is displayed by the Explorer as well as how that information is displayed.

- **Tools.** This menu enables you to find files or folders, or to control the mapping of network drives.

- **Help.** This menu enables you to display information about Explorer through the Help system.

If you look through the Explorer menus, notice that some of the choices may look familiar, particularly if you are familiar with older version of Windows NT. While the Explorer is different in many ways from the older File Manager, many of the menu choices it uses are a carryover from the File Manager.

The toolbar

The toolbar that is used in the Explorer is exactly the same as the toolbar that is available when you browse your desktop, as discussed earlier in the chapter. There is a major difference in how the toolbar is used, however.

In the Explorer, you can work in either the Folder window or the Contents window. (Both of these windows are covered shortly.) When you use one of the tools from the toolbar, you affect any object that is selected in the Folder window or the Contents window.

The Folder window

At the left side of the Explorer is the Folder window. You should not confuse the Folder window with a folder window (notice the capitalization). The Folder window is a portion of the Explorer, whereas a *folder* window is a window that you open when browsing your desktop. The Folder window is used to show the organization of the resources that are available to you.

Adjusting window size

Depending on the complexity of your resource tree (shown in the Folder window), you may from time to time need to adjust how much of the Explorer window is devoted to the Folder window and how much is devoted to the Contents window. You do this by moving the mouse over the vertical bar that divides the Folder and Contents windows.

As you do, notice that the mouse pointer turns into a double-headed arrow. This means that you can click and drag the border so that either window (Folder or Contents) is the size that you require. When you release the mouse button, the border stays where you left it until you explicitly change it again.

The old File Manager, in previous versions of NT, displayed only directories in the current drive. The tree that is used in the Folder window of the Explorer is much more than that. In fact, you can think of the Folder window as displaying a complete outline of your system resources, not just drives and folders.

Take some time to scroll through the Folder window. Note that the tree shows all of the drives on your system, as well as any mapped network drives, and any other computers that are available to you on your network. Also visible are special areas of your computer, such as the Control Panel, the Printers folder, and the Recycle Bin.

Secret

If a red X appears through an item in the Explorer, it simply means that the item is not currently available. Typically, this means the item is on a different computer in the network, but Windows NT has detected that the computer cannot be currently reached for some reason.

If you examine the tree that is displayed in the Folder window, notice that at each branch of the tree, there may be a small box that contains a plus or minus sign. This box controls the amount of detail that is displayed for this particular branch.

If the box contains a plus sign and you click on it, then the branch is expanded, thereby displaying more detail of what the branch contains. If the box contains a minus sign and you click on it, then the branch is collapsed, thereby hiding the detail of the branch.

Secret

The branches of a tree are not the only places where plus signs appear. When you first use the Explorer, there is a plus sign beside both the A and B drives of your computer, even if you don't have disks in those drives. This is because there could be additional information in those drives. Windows NT doesn't actually check them unless you choose them. It then removes the plus sign if it detects that there is no information on the disk in the drive.

Another way to select items in the Folder window is by using the drop-down list at the left side of the toolbar. Using this list, you can select disk drives or other major resources that are available to your system.

The Contents window

To the right side of the Folder window is the Contents window. This area of the Explorer is used to show the contents of the item that is selected in the Folder window. While the information in the Folder window stays fairly static, the information in the Contents window can change quite a bit as you are using Explorer.

For instance, if you click on a folder in the Folder window, then the Contents window changes to reflect the folder. If you open a different folder, then the Contents window changes again.

In many ways, the Contents window is just like a window you may use when browsing from your desktop. Information can be presented in the same manner, meaning that you can move icons, pick the same four views, sort the icons or listings, etc. Because of this, you may wonder what advantage there is in using the Explorer as opposed to browsing.

The answer is that you can use the Contents window in conjunction with the Folder window. For instance, it is very easy to drag a file from the Contents window and drop it in another folder that is visible in the Folder window. This is not easily done from the desktop, unless you open two folder windows that represent your source and destination for the move.

Using Properties

Windows NT Workstation 4.0 uses the concept of *properties* in relation to objects in the operating system. These properties are the characteristics that control how the object behaves when used or how it is treated by other objects. The exact properties that are associated with an object depend on the nature of the object.

For instance, a file's properties include such items as filename, date created, size, and type. Conversely, the properties for a printer may include the printer driver used, the printer model, and other capabilities.

Fortunately, Windows NT gives you excellent control over object properties. To access the properties of an object, just right-click on the object and choose Properties from the Context menu. Figure 2-13 shows an example of the Properties dialog box for a file.

Figure 2-13: Objects within Windows NT possess properties that you can change.

Virtually everything that you can think of in Windows NT has properties that are associated with it. Items such as files, folders, shortcuts, printers, modems, networks, the desktop, the Taskbar, and literally any device all have properties.

If you want to change how something behaves, simply change its properties. Depending on the object, the changes could be implemented immediately, although some objects require you to restart Windows NT before the changes can take effect. (In this latter case, you are notified of the need to restart.)

Before changing the properties of an object, you may want to make note of what they were originally. This provides you with a way to change properties back in case of error.

Using Shortcuts

Windows NT Workstation 4.0 features a new concept in program management that was first introduced in Windows 95 — shortcuts. *Shortcuts* are nothing more than links to programs, documents, or folders.

When you click on the link, the program that is associated with the shortcut is executed, or the document or folder is opened. Shortcuts can be used anywhere within your system, including on the desktop.

The big advantage of shortcuts is that they provide multiple references to the same program or document without consuming valuable resources. For instance, you can create a shortcut to your accounting program. One shortcut can run the program using one set of data files and another can run it using a different set.

You don't need to make a copy of the program or data files to do this. Instead, you simply create a shortcut and then edit the shortcut to reflect how you want the program run. Multiple copies of the program file would have consumed valuable disk space. The shortcut, on the other hand, consumes only a miniscule amount of disk space.

The easiest way to create a shortcut is to follow these steps:

STEPS

Creating a shortcut

Step 1. Browse your desktop or through the Explorer until you find the program, folder, or document for which you want a shortcut created.

Step 2. Right-click on the item. This displays a Context menu for the object.

Step 3. Select the Create Shortcut option. This creates a shortcut for the object in the same folder in which the object is located.

Step 4. Drag the new shortcut to the place where you want it. For instance, you can drag it to the desktop.

You can always identify a shortcut by the appearance of its icon. Shortcut icons have a small arrow in the lower-left corner of the icon. For instance, Figure 2-14 shows an example of both a shortcut icon and the program to which it is related.

Shortcut   Original
icon   icon

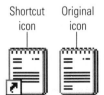

Figure 2-14: Shortcut icons have a small arrow in the lower-left corner.

Technically, a shortcut is a file with an extension of either LNK or PIF. The special PIF extension is used only for shortcuts to DOS programs, while LNK is used for all other shortcuts. These shortcut files are generally less than 500 bytes, which is why they can save disk space when compared to larger programs.

Editing shortcuts

Because a shortcut is nothing but a pointer to a file, program, or folder, you may want to change the command line that is used by the shortcut. For instance, you may have a shortcut that starts the Notepad accessory, but you want it to start with a billing file that is already loaded. Another shortcut to the Notepad accessory may be used to load your daily journal.

To edit a shortcut, simply right-click on the shortcut icon, and choose Properties from the Context menu. This displays the Properties dialog box for the icon. You then click on the Shortcut tab, and the dialog box that is shown in Figure 2-15 appears.

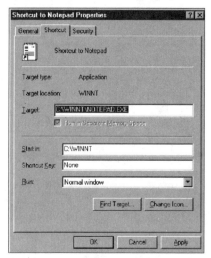

Figure 2-15: The Properties dialog box for a shortcut controls how the shortcut works.

You can change the contents of the Target field to anything you desire. Thus, if you want to use the shortcut to launch the Notepad accessory for use with your billing file, you may change the Target field to something like NOTEPAD C:\BILLING.DAT.

Adding this filename as a parameter to the command line causes Notepad to load the file when it is started. Similar shortcuts could be created for many other special needs.

Renaming shortcuts

After creating a shortcut, you may want to rename it to create a more descriptive name. For instance, if you look back at Figure 2-14, you can see that the shortcut is named Shortcut to Notepad. While this is true, it can be a bit unwieldy. To rename the shortcut, use the same procedure that you would use to rename any other object:

STEPS

Renaming a shortcut

Step 1. Right-click on the shortcut icon. This displays a Context menu.

Step 2. Select the Rename option. The text below the icon is activated, allowing you to make changes.

Step 3. Use the keyboard to rename the shortcut as desired.

Step 4. Press Enter to save your new shortcut name.

Tip

It is a good idea to use a different name for your shortcut than what you used for the original object. If both the original object and the shortcut have the same name, it is easy to confuse the two.

Deleting shortcuts

If you no longer need a shortcut, you can delete it by simply selecting the shortcut icon and pressing Delete. Once deleted, the shortcut is moved to the Recycle Bin, the same as any other file.

It is important to realize that if you delete a shortcut, you only delete the link to the file, folder, or document. You don't actually delete the item with which the link was associated. If you want to delete the actual item (after deleting the shortcut), you must either delete it manually or use the uninstall program that was provided with the application.

Ending Tasks

There are two ways that you can end a task; one way is natural, and the other uses what I like to call brute force. The natural way of ending a task is to use the task itself. For instance, if you are using Word for Windows, you end the task by choosing Exit from the File menu or by closing the program window using the X button in the upper-right corner of the window.

The brute force method of ending tasks is necessary if the program is not behaving as you expect. You would use this method of ending a task if it seems that a program is no longer responding to commands.

To display the Task Manager, right-click on the Taskbar and then choose Task Manager from the Context menu. An example of the Task Manager is shown in Figure 2-16.

Figure 2-16: The Task Manager is used to control individual tasks.

The Task Manager is much more versatile and robust than under previous versions of Windows NT, and it does more than the Task Manager in Windows 95. The different tabs in the Task Manager allow you to monitor different aspects of your system as follows:

- **Applications.** This tab allows you to control entire programs.

- **Processes.** This tab allows you to control individual threads of different programs.

- **Performance.** This tab allows you to quickly monitor the performance of your system. (The tab is discussed fully in Chapter 18.)

The first tab, Applications (shown in Figure 2-16), is used to control individual programs. To end a program, select the program name in the Task list, and then click on the End Task button.

At this point, you may be prompted to confirm that you really want to end the program. If you answer Yes, then the program is ended, and the resources that were previously used by the program are made available to other programs running on your system.

If you click on the Processes tab, the Task Manager appears, as shown in Figure 2-17. Using the information on this tab, you can control individual threads or processes that are running on your system. As you learn in Chapter 8, individual programs can run multiple processes under Windows NT.

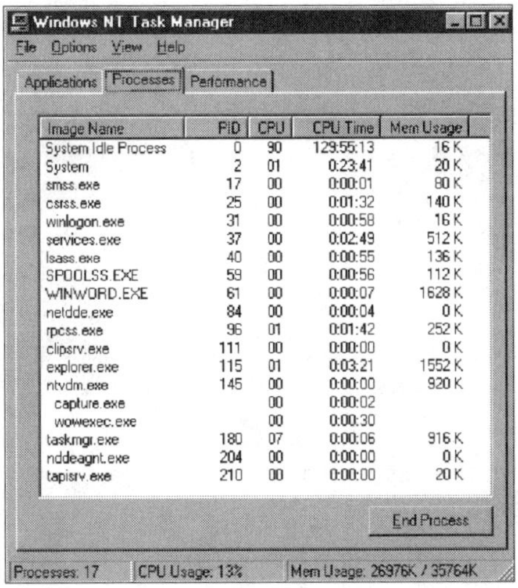

Figure 2-17: The Task Manager enables you to control individual processes.

For instance, if you are running a spreadsheet application, one process may monitor the keyboard, another can look for changes on embedded information from a remote source, and a third can update the calculations in the spreadsheet.

The ability to access and control individual processes is a big improvement in Windows NT Workstation 4.0. In the past, if a program "crashed" and exited, it may have meant that there were individual processes of the program that remained in memory. This could have caused problems if you tried to reload the program that had crashed, and it always meant that precious system resources were no longer available for other purposes.

With this new feature of Task Manager, however, you can select individual processes and terminate them. You do this in the same way that you end entire programs — you select the process in the Image Name list, and then click on the End Process button.

Understanding User Profiles

You probably already know that multiple people can use a Windows NT workstation. Each person may have his own likes and dislikes, his own programs, and his own way of using the computer. Windows NT Workstation automatically creates user profiles whenever you create a new user on your system.

As an example, consider that Bob and Martha both work for the same company, but they work different shifts. Bob uses the computer during the day, and Martha uses it during the evenings. Both have their own accounts on the workstation, meaning that they have their own user IDs and passwords.

When Bob signs in, his desktop pops up with all of the programs, settings, and icons that he is used to using. Similarly, when Martha sits down at the machine, her system looks just as she left it, even though Bob used it earlier in the day.

Secret

Whenever you create a new user at the log-in screen or by using the User Manager, Windows NT automatically adds a new profile to the system. This profile results in changes to the Registry (covered in Chapter 10) and the file system.

The effects on the file system are easiest to understand, so open the Explorer and display the contents of the Winnt/Profiles folder. At a minimum, you should see the following folders:

- Administrator
- All Users
- Default User

These are the default account profiles that were created by Windows NT. If you have additional folders in Winnt/Profiles, then they each represent specific users on your workstation. The names of the folders are the names of the users. In the scenario previously discussed, one folder would be called Bob and another Martha.

The profile folders contain the individualized information that creates a tailored system for the user. If you browse through some of the folders, you can see additional folders, such as Application Data, Desktop, Favorites, Start Menu, and a few others. As the user makes changes to his environment, these changes are saved in the appropriate profile folders.

There is not a one-to-one correlation between the Winnt/Profiles folders and the accounts that you may establish with the User Manager (see Chapter 12). The Administrator folder corresponds to the Administrator account that you established when you installed Windows NT Workstation, but the other two may require some explaining.

The All Users folder contains information on applications that are available to all users; these are called *common* applications. Whether an application is common or specific to an individual user is determined by the application's installation program.

The other folder, Default User, is used as a "starting point" for any new user profile that is added to the system. It contains the settings and configuration information that are necessary to establish a new user. Once the settings in Default User are copied to the new user's profile, they can be changed without disturbing the starting point for other new users.

The upshot of all this is that if you understand the directory structure, you can modify which programs are available to which users. Look through the folders; you may want to make some accessories available only to the Administrator account but not to individual users. (In a serious work environment, the games that are available with Windows NT Workstation come to mind as candidates for limitation.)

As an example, you may want to move some of the administrative tools so that they can only be used by the Administrator. By default, the administrative tools are available to all users (common programs), so they are stored in the All Users/Start Menu/Programs/Administrative Tools (Common) directory.

If you create the same directory under the Administrator path, then you can move files from the All Users area to the Administrator area. These tools are then only available for the Administrator, not for all other users.

Summary

Learning your way around Windows NT Workstation 4.0 can be disconcerting at first, but once you learn the "lay of the land," you find yourself in charge of a powerful, stable, and secure operating system.

In this chapter, you have learned how to control your environment and more specifically the following items:

- ▶ You can use the My Computer icon to begin browsing through your local resources (those connected to your computer).

- ▶ You can also use the Network Neighborhood icon to easily browse through the networks to which you have access.

- ▶ Information that is derived from browsing is presented in windows (which is quite appropriate). You can move, resize, close, or delete these windows in any manner or order that you desire.

- ▶ There are four general ways to view information in folder windows, each of which can be selected from menus or a toolbar. The viewing methods include Large Icons, Small Icons, List, and Details. Each type of view has its particular strengths.

- ▶ The new Explorer is the successor to the older File Manager. It provides an overview of your system in a Folder window and content detail in the Contents window. The Contents window can be used and managed in much the same way as the folder windows that appear when browsing the desktop.

- ▶ Windows NT keeps track of properties for virtually every object that you encounter. These properties control how the object is treated by the operating system, how the object behaves on your system, or what you can do with the object. Many properties can be changed by right-clicking on the object and selecting the Properties option from the Context menu.

- ▶ Shortcuts provide a quick link to programs, folders, or documents. You can use them to place "access points" to these objects wherever you want.

- ▶ Windows NT includes a new, improved Task Manager. This robust control can be used to manage programs or individual processes that are created by programs.

- ▶ User profiles are stored in the Windows NT directory structure. Understanding the directory structure can help you better tailor your machine for all system users.

Chapter 3

Customizing Your System

In This Chapter

One of the strong points of Windows has always been its ability to be configured and customized to match the work habits and preferences of users. In this chapter, you learn the information necessary to configure how Windows NT appears during use. In particular, you learn the following items:

▶ How your video mode settings affect your desktop

▶ How you can change the appearance of your desktop

▶ How you can control the behavior and appearance of the Taskbar

▶ How you can change the sounds that are associated with common system events

▶ How you can change the Start menu structure

▶ Why every customization change that you make has an impact on the performance of your system

Changing the Desktop

The desktop is synonymous with your screen. Whatever you see on your computer screen resides on your Windows desktop. Under Windows NT Workstation 4.0, you have quite a bit of control over how your desktop appears; all you need to do is change the properties relating to the portion of the desktop that you want to have modified.

Most desktop characteristics are changed by modifying the display properties. To access this dialog box, simply right-click on the desktop. (Make sure that you actually right-click on the desktop itself, not on an icon, window, or the Taskbar. These are simply items that are displayed on your desktop.)

As with virtually any other right-click in Windows, you should see a Context menu. Choose the Properties option, and shortly you see the Display Properties dialog box, as shown in Figure 3-1.

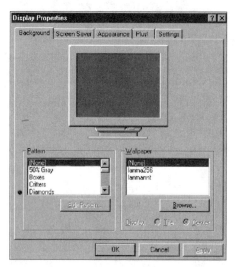

Figure 3-1: The Display Properties dialog box is used to control the appearance of Windows.

Quite a few options are available from the Display Properties dialog box. The next several sections describe each of the major areas that you can modify.

The basics: Your display settings

There is one display property that affects every other display property that you can think of — this is the resolution and color depth of your display. This area is intimately tied to your hardware, meaning the capabilities of your video card and monitor.

To change these settings, click on the Settings tab of the Display Properties dialog box. The dialog box should then appear as shown in Figure 3-2.

When you first installed Windows NT Workstation 4.0, it attempted to determine what type of video card you were using in your system. This information was stored in the Registry and is used by Windows to control everything that you see on your screen.

You can check to see which video card you are using by clicking on the Display Type button in the lower-right corner of the dialog box. This displays a dialog box similar to Figure 3-3.

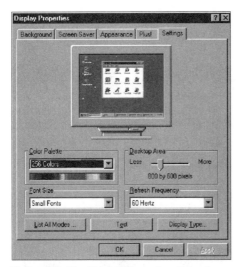

Figure 3-2: The Display Properties dialog box with the Settings tab selected.

Figure 3-3: The Display Type dialog box shows you how your video hardware is configured.

The Display Type dialog box is divided into three sections. At the top of the dialog box, you can see the type of adapter that Windows NT believes is installed in your system, whereas the middle portion shows the video driver being used, and the bottom gives information about the adapter.

You can click on the Change button to manually select a different type of video adapter, or you can click on the Detect button to have Windows NT automatically detect which video card you are using.

Note

You should never need to use the Detect button. Normally, Windows NT checks whenever it boots to see which video card is installed. If you changed the card, then that should already have been detected and the proper drivers loaded. The exception to this is that Windows NT may not automatically detect switching video cards if both your old and new card use the same chip set (referring to the video controller chips). In this case, you may need to either force a detection or manually pick another video card type.

When you are finished looking at which hardware is in your system, you can click on the Cancel button to return to the Display Properties dialog box.

When Windows NT understands which video card is installed in your system, you can begin to configure Windows NT for how you want the card to be used. Most video cards allow you to choose any of several different display modes. These display modes are defined by three major characteristics:

■ **Resolution.** This refers to the number of *pixels* (picture elements, or individual dots) that can be displayed on the screen at the same time. Common resolutions are 640 × 480, 800 × 600, and 1024 × 768 pixels, where the first number is the horizontal resolution and the second is the vertical. Although these are common resolutions, they are not the only ones. Many video cards support quite a few additional, higher resolutions — all the way to 1600 × 1200 pixels.

■ **Color depth.** This refers to the number of colors that can be displayed on the screen at the same time. Different cards provide different color capabilities, and the number of colors that you can use often varies based on the resolution that you have selected. (This is directly related to memory availability, as described shortly.) Common color depths are 16 colors (4 bits per color), 256 colors (1 byte per color), 65,536 colors (2 bytes per color), and 16,777,216 colors (3 bytes per color).

■ **Refresh rate.** This refers to how many times per second the video card can redraw the screen. Again, different cards can refresh the screen at different rates, and the rates may vary based on the resolution that you are using. Refresh rates are specified in *hertz* (Hz), which means cycles, or times, per second. Common refresh rates are 60, 72, or 76 Hz. The higher the refresh rate, the higher the quality of the image being produced by the video card.

The first two characteristics (resolution and color depth) depend on how much memory is installed on your video card. The higher the resolution, the more memory is required to represent your screen. For instance, in a 640 × 480 screen, there are 307,200 pixels on the screen. At a color depth of 256 colors, it takes 1 byte of storage (8 bits) to represent each pixel. Thus, it takes 307,200 bytes of memory to display that screen.

If you increase the resolution, say to 1024 × 768, then the memory requirements jump to 786,432 bytes, simply because there are so many more pixels displayed on the screen. If you increase the color depth on top of that — for instance, to 65,536 colors — then you double the memory requirements, because it takes 2 bytes for every pixel on the screen.

You can see which video modes are valid for your video card by clicking on the List All Modes button at the bottom-left corner of the Display Properties dialog box. When you do, a list appears, detailing all the valid combinations of the three display mode characteristics. This type of list is shown in Figure 3-4.

Figure 3-4: The Detected Adapter dialog box lists the possible video modes for your video card.

The length of the display modes for your video card can vary from what is shown in Figure 3-4. Remember that these modes depend on the type and capabilities of the video card that you have installed.

Using the Settings tab of the Display Properties dialog box (Figure 3-2), Windows allows you to change all three characteristics of your video card. The first setting you should change is the resolution, which is controlled by the Desktop Area slider in the right-central part of the dialog box. You can click and drag the slider on the "less-to-more" scale to change the resolution.

As you make changes in this, you may notice that your color depth (the Color Palette drop-down list) and refresh rate (the Refresh Frequency drop-down list) may change automatically. This is because the capabilities of your video card dictate what color depth and refresh rates are available at different resolutions. After you have selected a resolution, you can then check to see what color depths and refresh rates are available and make your choices accordingly.

As you make your choice in terms of resolution, notice that the sample screen shown in the dialog box changes to reflect the new size. As you increase the resolution, the apparent size of the information in the sample decreases. This is because, at higher resolutions, you can cram more information on the screen at once.

The Settings tab also contains a drop-down list that allows you to modify the size of the fonts used on the desktop. These fonts are used for icons and listings, such as directory listings in the Explorer, or as you are browsing.

There are only two options in the drop-down list — small fonts and large fonts. When you are using a lower resolution, it makes more sense to use the smaller fonts. For higher resolutions, use the larger fonts.

Secret

If you are familiar with Windows 95, you may notice something missing from the Settings tab in Windows NT. Under Windows 95, you can specify what type of monitor you are using; this is not a choice under Windows NT. Under Windows 95, you can specify the monitor type so that automatic choices for your refresh rate and resolution are available. Under Windows NT, you are required to figure this out for yourself.

If you change your display settings, you should click on the Test button to see if your selected options work. This button is useful in determining if your video card settings work properly with your monitor. Many times you may be able to use a high-powered setting of the video card, but the monitor cannot support the same resolution or refresh rate that you have chosen.

When you click on the Test button, a test pattern is displayed for 5 seconds. If the test pattern appears OK, then your changes work fine. If the test pattern does not appear properly, then you must downgrade your settings just a bit so that you can see the information on the monitor.

When you are done changing your display settings, click on the OK button to close the Display Properties dialog box. If you changed your display settings, you may be informed that you need to restart your system. Typically, you are only asked to restart if you change the color depth that you are using.

Modifying Windows' appearance

When most people think about customizing Windows, they think about changing the appearance of the operating system. The most sweeping changes in the appearance of Windows NT can be made by selecting the Appearance tab from the Display Properties dialog box, as shown in Figure 3-5.

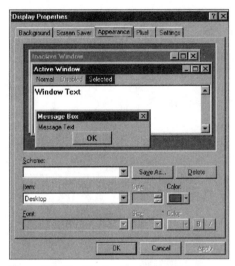

Figure 3-5: The Display Properties dialog box with the Appearance tab selected.

If you look at the contents of the Appearance tab, you notice at once that it looks rather complex. It is not as complex as it may at first appear, however. Basically, the dialog box is divided into two parts. The top half of the screen (with all the windows and text) serves two purposes.

First, it allows you to see the effects of the changes that you make in the bottom part of the screen. Second, it allows you to pick the elements that you want to change in the bottom half. This explanation is not meant to sound circular but to reflect the symbiotic relationship between the two halves of the dialog box.

Working with schemes

The best place to start when changing the appearance of Windows is to select one of the predefined schemes that are available from the Scheme drop-down list. Windows NT comes with 27 schemes, which are nothing more than named profiles of how you can make your desktop look.

The predefined schemes are as follows:

- Brick
- Desert
- Eggplant
- High Contrast Black
- High Contrast Black (extra large)
- High Contrast Black (large)
- High Contrast White
- High Contrast White (extra large)
- High Contrast White (large)
- Lilac
- Lilac (large)
- Maple
- Marine (high color)
- Plum (high color)
- Pumpkin (large)
- Rainy Day
- Red, White, and Blue (VGA)
- Rose
- Rose (large)
- Slate
- Spruce
- Storm (VGA)
- Teal (VGA)
- Wheat
- Windows Standard
- Windows Standard (extra large)
- Windows Standard (large)

After picking a scheme, the sample display changes to show what the scheme does to your desktop. If you don't like the way that a scheme appears, you can modify individual parts of the scheme as desired.

Tip

Before modifying an existing scheme, it is always a good idea to save the scheme under a new name and then make changes to the copy. This leaves the original in case you want to use it later. To save a scheme under a new name, click on the Save As button. Windows asks you for the name of the new scheme, offering the current scheme name as a default. If you simply click on OK, the changes you have made overwrite the current scheme. If, however, you supply a new name, then it is saved as a new scheme and appears in the scheme list.

Changing item appearance

You can use either of two methods to change the appearance of an item. First, you can select the item from a drop-down list (labeled, appropriately enough, Item), or you can simply use the mouse to click on the item in the sample display at the top of the dialog box. Windows lets you modify the size and color of many screen elements, and on some items may allow you to change the font and its characteristics. Table 3-1 details the different desktop items and what you can change.

Table 3-1   Items that you can change on your desktop

Item	Size	Color	Font Size	Font Color
3D Objects		√		√
Active Title Bar	√	√	√	√
Active Window Border	√	√		
Application Background		√		
Caption Buttons	√			
Desktop		√		
Icon	√		√	
Icon Spacing (Horizontal)	√			
Icon Spacing (Vertical)	√			
Inactive Title Bar	√	√	√	√
Inactive Window Border	√	√		
Menu	√	√	√	√
Message Box			√	√
Palette Title	√		√	

(continued)

Table 3-1 *(continued)*

Item	Size	Color	Font Size	Font Color
Scrollbar	√			
Selected Items	√	√	√	√
ToolTip		√	√	√
Window		√		√

As you can see from Table 3-1, you cannot modify all aspects of every desktop item. After you have selected the object that you want to modify (in the Item drop-down list), you can modify the desired attribute by using the appropriate controls:

- To modify the item size, use the Size control
- To modify the item color, use the Color drop-down list
- To modify the font used for the item, use the Font drop-down list
- To modify the font size, use the Size drop-down list
- To modify the font color, use the Color drop-down list
- To modify the font style (bold or italics), use the bold and italics tools at the right side of the font name

Other appearance details

If you click on the Plus! tab of the Display Properties dialog box, you can modify a few items that affect the appearance of Windows NT. The contents of the tab are shown in Figure 3-6.

Each item on this tab affects your display in some way. At the top of the dialog box, you can modify the icons that are used for the four standard desktop items: My Computer, Network Neighborhood, and the full or empty Recycle Bin.

To make a change, select the icon that you want to change, and then click on the Change Icon button. This displays the available icons from which you can choose, or you can provide a different icon filename to select different icons.

At the bottom of the dialog box, you can specify other characteristics of your desktop as follows:

- **Large icons.** Choosing the first check box allows you to specify that large icons are used on the desktop. This can be helpful if you are using a high resolution for your screen.

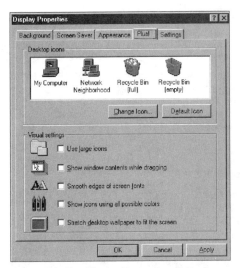

Figure 3-6: The Display Properties dialog box with the Plus! tab selected.

- **Active dragging.** When you normally drag a window across the desktop, Windows only displays an outline of the window until you release the mouse button. With this check box selected, the window is displayed as it is dragged, instead of only using an outline.

- **Font smoothing.** If you are using a high-resolution screen, with large fonts, individual letters may appear a bit jagged. (This is particularly true when looking at diagonal strokes in letters.) If you select this option, then Windows uses aliasing techniques to make the fonts appear smoother. This does not change the resolution but simply changes how the edges of letters are displayed on the screen.

- **Icon colors.** Icons are typically displayed using only a few colors. Windows, however, tracks quite a bit of additional color information about each icon, even though it is not used. If you want the icons to be displayed in full color and if you have set your color depth to 256 colors or above, you can select this check box.

- **Wallpaper stretching.** This option affects how your wallpaper is displayed on the screen. (Wallpaper is discussed in the following section.) With the option selected, your wallpaper is stretched to fit the dimensions of your screen.

Once you have selected the items that you want Windows to use, click on the OK button to save your changes. The desktop is updated, and you can continue using your system as normal.

Setting background characteristics

By default, Windows NT displays a bland cyan (blue-green) desktop. This desktop color is defined in the Windows Standard scheme, as discussed earlier in this chapter. If you have picked another scheme or changed the desktop color, then your desktop may appear differently.

To spice up your desktop, Windows allows you to use either patterns or wallpaper. In addition, you can select different screen savers for use on your system. Each of these areas is covered in the following sections.

Patterns and wallpaper

Patterns are nothing more than a block of dots that, when displayed in succession, appear as a pattern. Each block consists of 64 dots in an 8 x 8 square. Windows places the first block in the upper-left corner of the screen, the next block just to its right, and so on, until the entire screen is filled.

Wallpaper, on the other hand, is a bitmap image (a graphic). Wallpaper can be displayed in the center of the desktop (as a single image), tiled, or stretched to fit the screen. To select a pattern or wallpaper image, click on the Background tab of the Display Properties dialog box (see Figure 3-7).

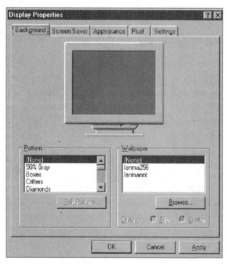

Figure 3-7: The Display Properties dialog box with the Background tab selected.

At the left side of the dialog box, you can select the pattern that you want. Windows provides 13 different, predefined patterns that you can use. When you click on a pattern name (from the Pattern list), the sample display at the top of the dialog box is changed to show what the pattern looks like.

If you don't like the patterns that are provided with Windows NT, you can click on the Edit Pattern button to make changes to a pattern that you have selected. The Pattern Editor dialog box is shown in Figure 3-8.

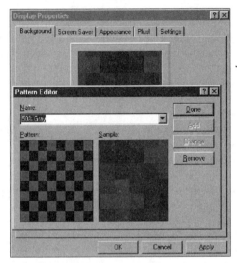

Figure 3-8: The Pattern Editor dialog box is used to change background patterns.

To change a pattern, simply click on a position in the Pattern window. Your modification is made by changing the condition of the pixel at that position. Clicking on a dot turns it off; clicking again turns it on. Your changes are also reflected in the Sample window of the Pattern Editor.

When you are done making changes, you can click on the Done button. If you have changed the pattern or the pattern name, you are asked if you want your changes saved. If you choose to save the pattern under a new name, the name is shown in the Pattern list of the Background tab.

At the right side of the Background tab is the Wallpaper list. This list shows different wallpaper files that are stored in the WINNT folder. You can display the wallpaper files in a different folder by clicking on the Browse button. Wallpaper files are nothing but graphic image files stored in the BMP format. If you have a favorite graphic and you save it in BMP format (any paint program should do just fine), then you can use the file as your wallpaper.

As you pick different wallpapers from the list, the change is reflected in the sample display at the top of the Display Properties dialog box. You can also click on the Tile or Center option at the bottom of the dialog box.

If you choose Tile, then the wallpaper image is displayed over and over again, over the entire screen. If you choose Center, then the image appears as a single, centered image on your desktop. You can also use an option on the Plus! tab to stretch a centered wallpaper file so that it fills the entire screen. (The Plus! tab was discussed in the previous section.)

When you choose a pattern, the pattern appears over the top of whatever your background color is. Your wallpaper then appears over the top of the pattern. Because of this, it doesn't make much sense to select some items in conjunction with other items.

For instance, it doesn't make sense to have a pattern selected if you later choose to use a tiled or stretched wallpaper file. Why? Because the wallpaper overlays the pattern. If the wallpaper takes the entire screen, then there is no room for patterns.

Screen savers

It used to be true that if an image were displayed continuously on your monitor, it would physically burn that image into the screen's phosphors — allowing you to see the image even if the screen were turned off. (This effect can be seen on some older, dedicated video games, like those at an arcade. If the video game were left on around the clock, the image was burned into the screen.)

Although the burn-in danger is not prevalent today because of advances in monitor technology, the use of screen savers is increasing. Reasons for their popularity are that they're fun to watch, some people like to show off for their friends, and others need to protect what was previously displayed on the screen from casual observers.

The operation of screen savers is simple; after a set period of time, the screen saver appears. If you press a key or move the mouse while the screen saver is visible, the previous screen appears. Windows NT comes with 12 built-in screen savers that you can use.

To select a screen saver, click on the Screen Saver tab of the Display Properties dialog box. The Display Properties dialog box then appears, as shown in Figure 3-9.

At the top of the dialog box is a sample screen that shows what your selected screen saver looks like. In the Screen Saver drop-down list, you can select any of the screen savers that you want. Some screen savers allow you to select the Password check box, which means that you can specify a password for canceling the screen saver and redisplaying the regular video screen.

At the bottom-right corner of the dialog box is the Wait field. This field is used to indicate how long your system should remain unused (no mouse movement or keys pressed) before the screen saver is activated. The default is 15 minutes, although you can pick any value between 1 and 60 minutes.

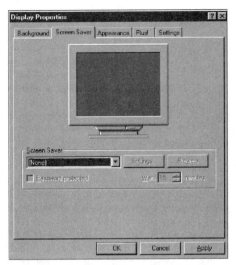

Figure 3-9: The Display Properties dialog box
with the Screen Saver tab selected.

The screen saver that you select most likely also has its own properties that
you can change. This is done by clicking on the Settings button after you
have selected a screen saver.

The exact properties that are available for each screen saver depend on the
screen saver itself. For instance, Figure 3-10 shows the Starfield Simulation
Setup dialog box, which is displayed after picking the Starfield Simulation
screen saver and clicking on the Settings button.

Figure 3-10: Different screen savers
have different properties that you
can modify.

Once you pick a screen saver, you should play around with the settings to
configure the screen saver to your liking. You can always change them back,
or to some other value, until you are satisfied.

Controlling the Taskbar

In Chapter 1, you learned about the Taskbar. This feature of Windows NT is quite nice, allowing you to easily switch between different tasks that are running on your system. Many people like the Taskbar to always be visible, but others may find it distracting — for instance, when using a full-screen graphics program.

Fortunately, Windows NT allows you to easily control the Taskbar to reflect how you want to work with it. You can resize, move, or hide the Taskbar altogether.

Resizing the Taskbar comes in handy when you are working with quite a few tasks on your system. Normally, a scroll bar appears at the right side of the Taskbar when you have too many task buttons to fit within the Taskbar.

If you move your mouse over the top edge of the Taskbar, notice that it changes to a double-headed arrow. This means that you can click on the top edge and drag it in either direction. When you release the edge, it remains there. The task buttons are then resized to fit the available space.

If you want to move the Taskbar, you can also do that. Normally, the Taskbar is located (by default) at the bottom of the desktop area. If you click and drag the Taskbar itself, you can move it to any of the other three sides of the desktop. For instance, Figure 3-11 shows what your desktop looks like with the Taskbar along the right edge of the screen.

With the Taskbar on different edges of your desktop, you can still adjust its size by dragging the exposed edge of the Taskbar. To move the Taskbar back to another position, simply click and drag to the new side of your desktop.

You can also configure the appearance and behavior of the Taskbar by right-clicking on it and then choosing the Properties option from the Context menu. This displays the Taskbar Properties dialog box, as shown in Figure 3-12.

Three of the four check boxes at the bottom of the dialog box control how the Taskbar is configured. The first option, Always on Top, controls how the Taskbar is displayed in relation to other windows. When selected, the Taskbar is always visible, regardless of what else is on the screen. (This is the normal behavior of the Taskbar.)

If you clear the check box, then the Taskbar can be hidden by other windows. The only way to again display the Taskbar (if it is covered) is to move the windows, close or minimize them, or click on a part of the Taskbar, if any part is exposed.

Tip

If the Taskbar is hidden, you can also switch between tasks by pressing Alt+Tab repeatedly until the task that you want is highlighted.

Figure 3-11: You can move the Taskbar to any edge of the desktop that you desire.

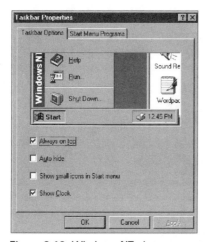

Figure 3-12: Windows NT gives you complete control over how the Taskbar is displayed.

The Auto Hide check box in the Taskbar Properties dialog box allows you to have the Taskbar be hidden when you are using other programs or windows, but still have easy access to the Taskbar. When this option is selected, the Taskbar disappears when you are using other windows.

To redisplay the Taskbar, you simply move the mouse pointer to the side of the desktop where it is located. For instance, if the Taskbar is located along the bottom of the desktop, you just move the mouse pointer to the bottom edge of the desktop — voilà; the Taskbar appears.

The final option of the Taskbar Properties dialog box allows you to control whether the time-of-day clock is displayed in the status area (right side) of the Taskbar. With the check box selected, the time appears; with it unselected, the time is not visible.

Changing Sounds

If you have a sound card installed in your system, Windows NT emits a sound for various events that occur while you use your computer. For example, when Windows NT first starts you may hear chimes or a "ta-da" sound. These are wave files (the filename extension is WAV) that are played by Windows NT because they have been associated with different events.

To modify sound events, open the Control Panel and double-click on the Sounds applet. This displays the Sounds Properties dialog box, as shown in Figure 3-13.

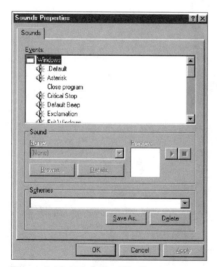

Figure 3-13: Windows NT allows you to associate different sounds with different events.

At the top of the dialog box is a list of different events. If a speaker icon appears to the left of an event name, then a sound file is associated with the event. Notice, as well, that events are organized according to the group in which they belong. When you first install Windows NT, the groups and events detailed in Table 3-2 are established automatically.

Table 3-2   Sound categories and events

Category	Event	Meaning
Windows	Default	The default beep — another name for the Default Beep event
Windows	Asterisk	Produced when a generic, informational dialog box is displayed
Windows	Close program	Produced when you close (exit) an application
Windows	Critical Stop	Produced when a dialog box appears that has a stop sign in it
Windows	Default Beep	The default beep
Windows	Exclamation	Produced when a warning dialog box (one containing an exclamation mark) appears
Windows	Exit Windows	Produced when you shut down Windows
Windows	Incoming Call	Produced when you are running any communications software in the background and the phone line rings
Windows	Maximize	Produced when you maximize a window
Windows	Menu command	Produced when you select a menu command
Windows appears	Menu pop-up	Produced when a Context or other pop-up menu
Windows	Minimize	Produced when you minimize a window
Windows	Open program	Produced when you start a new program
Windows	Outgoing Call	Produced when you are running any communications software in the background and a scheduled outgoing call is occurring
Windows	Program error	Produced when a program encounters an error during operation
Windows	Question	Produced when a dialog box appears that has a question mark in it

(continued)

Category	Event	Meaning
Windows	Restore Down	Produced when you restore a window from its maximized condition
Windows	Restore Up	Produced when you restore a window from its minimized condition
Windows	Start Windows	Produced when Windows is started
Explorer	Empty Recycle Bin	Produced when you empty the Recycle Bin
Media Player	Close program	Produced when you close (exit) the program
Media Player	Open program	Produced when you start the program
Sound Recorder	Close program	Produced when you close (exit) the program
Sound Recorder	Open program	Produced when you start the program

Table 3-2 *(continued)*

If you examine the events that are defined for your system, you may notice that you have some events that are not listed in Table 3-2. This is because your programs, as they are installed, can add events to this list.

To assign a sound to an event, simply select the event in the Events list, and then select a sound from the Name drop-down list. By default, the sound files that are contained in the c:\winnt\media directory are displayed in the Name list. You can select sounds from different directories by clicking on the Browse button. When you have a sound file selected, you can view information about it by clicking on the Details button, or you can click on the speaker icon to actually hear the sound.

After you have defined the sounds that are associated with different events on your system, you can save them in schemes. These schemes are essentially the same as those used when you customized your desktop. Clicking on the Save As button allows you to save the sound-to-event associations under a name that you specify. You can later change to a scheme by again selecting it from the Schemes drop-down list.

Modifying the Start Menu

The Start menu is the heart of everything you do in Windows NT. When you click on the Start menu, you have access to all of the programs that are installed on your system. To make the Start menu easier to use, you may want to customize it to reflect how you use it.

This change is possible, and very easy, once you realize that the Start menu is nothing but a reflection of what you have stored in different directories of your system. If you change the contents of the directories, you change what is displayed in the Start menu.

As an example, you may use the Calculator accessory quite a bit, so you would want to make it available directly from the Start menu. This customization makes your menus more reflective of how you work.

Instead of going through three menus to find the Calculator, you only need to go through one, the Start menu. The easiest way to add the Calculator to the Start menu is to follow these steps:

STEPS

Adding a program to the Start menu

Step 1. Either by browsing or by using the Explorer, locate the Calculator accessory program. (It should be located in the c:\winnt\system32 directory. The program name is CALC.EXE.)

Step 2. Create a shortcut for the Calculator accessory, and move it to the desktop.

Step 3. Rename the shortcut to a meaningful name, such as *Start Calculator.*

Step 4. Right-click on the Start button. This displays a Context menu.

Step 5. Choose the Open option from the Context menu. This displays a folder window for the Start menu that is defined for your profile. (User profiles are discussed in Chapter 2.)

Step 6. Move the newly created shortcut to the folder window.

Step 7. Close all windows and programs used in these steps.

This series of steps may look very similar to steps that you learned in Chapter 2 for adding programs to the Startup folder. In reality, the steps are very similar. The only difference is that the target of these steps is the Start

Menu folder, whereas in Chapter 2 it was the Startup folder. The concepts
are the same and are possible because Windows NT relies so heavily on the
contents of special folders to accomplish special needs.

When you next see the Start menu, it should look similar to Figure 3-14. Notice
that the Start Calculator choice has been added to the top of the Start menu.

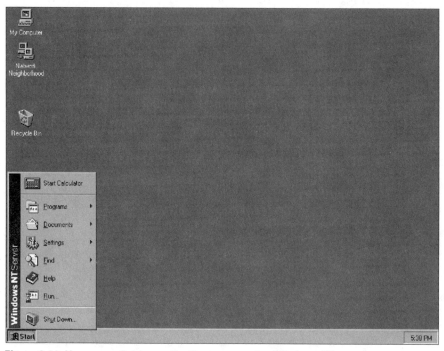

Figure 3-14: You can easily change the Start menu using Windows NT.

Tip

This exercise illustrates an important point: Anything that you place in the
Start Menu folder appears at the top of your Start menu. With this understanding, you may be tempted to start placing programs in the folder, left
and right. This presents a problem, however. If you place actual programs in
the folder, you typically need to place all of the program data files in the
folder as well. This would cause the data files to also show up as part of the
Start menu — probably an undesired condition. A better approach is to
place a shortcut in the Start Menu folder — one that points to your program
that resides in a different directory. In this way, you can keep your Start
menu uncluttered.

Another way to organize your menus is to create your own submenu off the
Start menu. This is done by simply placing a folder in the Start Menu folder.
For instance, if you want to create a submenu called Internet Tools which is
accessible from the Start menu, follow these steps:

STEPS

Adding a submenu to the Start menu

Step 1. Right-click on the Start button. This displays a Context menu.

Step 2. Choose the Open option from the Context menu. This displays a folder window for the Start menu that is defined for your profile.

Step 3. Choose the New option from the File menu in the folder window. This displays a menu of new items that you can create; you should choose Folder.

Step 4. Rename the new folder Internet Tools.

Step 5. Close all windows and programs used in these steps.

After completing these steps, if you display the Start menu, it should appear as shown in Figure 3-15. Notice the triangle to the right of the Internet Tools menu item. As you already know, this means that selecting the item displays additional choices. At this point, there are no additional choices available, because you have not added those choices. You can now add items to the new Internet Tools directory, and they then appear in your submenu.

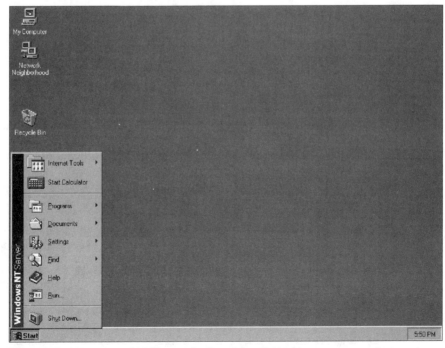

Figure 3-15: When you add folders to the Start Menu folder, they appear as submenus in the Start menu.

Secret

If you have an existing folder, program, or shortcut that you want added to the Start menu, you can drop and drag it there. Simply use the mouse to drag the object to the Start menu button. When you drop the item on the button, it appears in the Start menu.

Performance Considerations

Everything that you do to customize your system has an impact on the performance of your system. This may sound like a sweeping statement, but nonetheless, it is true.

Before you can make an informed decision on which customization features you want to take advantage of, you need to know the effects on the overall performance of your system.

If you have been around computers for a while, you probably already know that system performance is determined, to the largest extent, by the following items:

- CPU speed
- Amount of memory
- Video speed
- Hard drive speed

Anything that affects these items adversely affects the performance of your system. For instance, if you have a relatively slow video card and the program that you are using places heavy demands on your video system, then your overall performance will be below par. Likewise, if something requires quite a bit of hard drive access and you have a slower hard drive, then performance will suffer.

To see a general overview of how different configuration choices affect the different elements of system performance, refer to Table 3-3. Remember that the information in the table is generalized, but it provides a good starting point. Also, the information in the table reflects the impact on an average system, not on a top-notch, top-speed system. If your system "pushes the envelope," then you can adjust the impact information in the table downward.

Table 3-3   Impact of configuration choices on system elements

Item	CPU	Memory	Video	Hard Drive
Video resolution	Heavy	Moderate	Heavy	None
Color depth	Low	Moderate	Heavy	None
Background pattern	Low	Low	Moderate	None

Item	CPU	Memory	Video	Hard Drive
Wallpaper	Moderate	Moderate	Heavy	Low
Screen saver	Heavy	Heavy	Heavy	Low
Desktop schemes	Low	Low	Moderate	None
Font smoothing	Low	None	Moderate	None
Show windows during drag	Low	Low	Heavy	None
High-color icons	Low	Low	Moderate	None

Secret

While most of the information in Table 3-3 is self-explanatory, it may help to provide a little more background on a few of the items. Perhaps the biggest resource hit you can take is from some of the screen savers that are provided with Windows NT. This may sound strange, but some of the screen savers were devised to show how cool the OpenGL specification, as implemented in Windows NT, really is.

OpenGL is a specification, primarily intended for games developers, that allows graphics to be controlled quickly and easily under Windows. These screen savers have the nomenclature "OpenGL" included in the name of the screen savers so that you can tell which ones use this technology.

Note that if you have the Task Manager displayed while you are trying out screen savers (from the Display Properties dialog box), when you display the 3D Maze screen saver (which uses OpenGL), the CPU usage jumps from 4 to 5 percent to over 50 percent, and when you click on the Preview button, CPU usage jumps to 100 percent! (Using the Task Manager for this purpose is covered in Chapter 18.)

This may not seem like that big of a deal; after all, you aren't using your machine when your screen saver kicks in. However, if your machine is being used as a print server (you are sharing a printer), the print processing times are much slower when the screen saver is in use. This means that your performance has seriously degraded simply by using an OpenGL screen saver.

The next biggest problem occurs if you have an average video card and you use a lot of customization features that increase your video requirements. For instance, you add wallpaper and turn on full-window dragging.

Both of these items require your screen to be redrawn much more often than is otherwise necessary. The bottom line is that, because more redraws are necessary, you are taxing your video system more, and it has a greater chance of becoming a bottleneck.

As you customize your system, make sure that you think about the performance impact of your choices. You may want to check out actual performance results on your system by applying the skills that you learn in Chapter 18.

Summary

While Windows NT Workstation 4.0 is a handsome operating system (in case anyone ever asks you), there is nothing like making changes so that your computer interface matches your preferences more closely. In this chapter, you have learned how to customize Windows NT.

In particular, you have learned the following items:

▶ For Windows NT to be customized properly, you must modify your display settings within the limits imposed by your video card. Windows NT allows you to take full advantage of the capabilities of your video system.

▶ Windows NT allows you to change virtually every aspect of your desktop appearance. You can choose from predefined desktop schemes or develop your own schemes to suit your taste.

▶ As in earlier versions of Windows NT, you can choose different background patterns, wallpaper, and screen savers to help customize the look of your workstation.

▶ The Taskbar can be moved to any side of your desktop to fit the way you work. In addition, you can modify how it behaves by using the Taskbar Properties dialog box.

▶ Windows NT allows you to associate sound files with different system events. When those events occur, the sound file is played through your sound card.

▶ The Start menu and all subservient menus reflect a directory structure on your hard drive. If you change the contents of the related directory, you change the options on the menu.

▶ You can add items (programs, shortcuts, or folders) to the Start menu by adding them to the Start Menu directory. This directory is contained within the path that defines your user profile.

▶ Customization typically adds features that use resources. The use of precious system resources can have a negative effect on system performance. It is a good idea to think through the effects of your customization efforts before completing them.

Chapter 4

Managing Disks and Files

In This Chapter

It makes sense that an operating system would allow you to manage disks and files. After all, this has been the case since the earliest days of MS-DOS. Windows NT provides many unique tools and integral features that allow you to quickly become the master of your hard drive.

In this chapter, you learn about the tools that are available and how you can put them to work right away. In particular, you learn the following items:

▶ How disk drives are organized under Windows NT

▶ How Windows NT supports different disk filing systems

▶ How long filenames work within the Windows NT environment

▶ How you can manage your disk drives using the Disk Administrator

▶ How the Find feature can be used to find the proverbial needle in a haystack

▶ Why file associations are so powerful in Windows NT 4.0

▶ How you can view the contents of a file without the need for the file application

▶ How the Send To command can save you time

▶ Why you should review the size that is allocated to your Recycle Bin

▶ How to use several different methods to access remote information

Disk Organization

Your disk drive is physically made up of a magnetic medium that allows you to store information. You cannot store information on the drive, however, until you decide how that information should be stored.

The first step is to decide how you want your disk drives organized at a "low level." This typically means how you want your disk drives partitioned.

A *partition* is nothing more than a logical portion of a disk drive. For instance, if you have a 2GB disk drive, you may want it partitioned into smaller, more manageable pieces; these pieces are the partitions. Partitions can be formatted using a filing system, as described later in this chapter.

Disks can have up to four partitions: three primary and one extended, or four primary. A *primary* partition is the portion of a physical disk that can be used by an operating system; it can be used to boot your system.

An *extended* partition is used exclusively for data storage and can be divided into multiple logical drives. (A primary partition can only be treated as a single logical drive; it cannot be subdivided.)

Windows NT also allows you to create other types of logical organizations on your disk drive besides partitions. These include volume sets, disk mirroring, and disk striping.

- **Volume sets.** These are partitions from separate physical disk drives that have been combined into a single logical drive. This is helpful if you have a small disk drive and you need more space than you can get from the one drive.

- **Disk mirroring.** This organization allows you to use partitions on two separate drives to store identical information. The information that is written to the partition on the primary disk is also written to the mirror partition on the other disk. If one disk fails, the system is able to use the data from the other disk.

- **Disk striping.** This allows portions of your data to be written to partitions on separate disk drives. Thus, if your stripe set is made up of partitions on five drives, your data are broken into five pieces, with each piece being written to a different drive.

  You can also implement disk striping with parity, which uses an additional partition to store error-correction information for your data.

Of these three organizational methods, the last two are considered *fault-tolerant technologies,* meaning that they are used for data integrity and security. You learn more about how Windows NT uses them in Chapter 11.

Understanding Disk Filing Systems

A disk filing system is the organization structure that is used to store information on a disk. The majority of personal computer systems in use today use one of three types of filing systems: FAT, HPFS, or NTFS. Windows NT Workstation 4.0 supports two of these types, but all three are worth discussing in the following sections.

The FAT filing system

The FAT filing system is the most common operating system. It originated in 1981 with the introduction of MS-DOS, and it is used on any system that uses DOS, Windows, or Windows 95. This filing system is also supported by Windows NT.

The name FAT is an acronym for *file allocation table*, which describes how the filing system does its work. The disk is divided into a series of sectors and tracks, which I am sure that every reader is already familiar with. Depending on the size of the hard drive, another organizational unit is a cluster.

These units reference groups of sectors; on some systems, a cluster may be two sectors; on others, it may be four or more. Each cluster is sequentially numbered and is tracked by an entry in the file allocation table. Thus, a FAT entry exists for every cluster on the disk.

The directory for the disk is nothing more than a database that contains information about the files that are stored on the disk. Each record in the directory includes information such as the name of the file, when it was created, the length of the file, and the starting cluster number. This last part, the cluster number, indicates which cluster starts the file.

This point is where the operating system can start loading the file. However, the entry for the file in the FAT indicates the second cluster used, and the second cluster entry indicates the third cluster used, and so on.

This arrangement and the use of the FAT is illustrated in Figure 4-1.

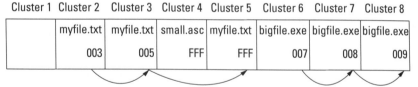

Figure 4-1: The FAT organization allows quick chaining of disk storage areas.

Figure 4-1 illustrates a situation where there are three files stored on the disk. The directory entry for the first file (myfile.txt) has a starting cluster number of 002. The FAT entry for that cluster then contains the number of the next cluster that is used by the file (003), and that entry contains the next cluster number (005).

This final cluster number contains the value FFF (hexadecimal), which indicates that there are no more clusters used by the file. The next file, small.asc, has a starting cluster number of 004, but that cluster entry contains a next cluster value of FFF. This means that small.asc is contained within a single cluster (004).

The FAT structure works very quickly and allows fast access to information. It wastes space, however, for small files that may consume less than a full cluster. (This is because the FAT is used to allocate entire clusters, even if the file being stored doesn't require an entire cluster.)

The HPFS filing system

In 1990, when OS/2 was first introduced, IBM also debuted the HPFS filing system. This system is designed for larger hard disks than FAT, and it works very efficiently for large data files. HPFS, which is an acronym for *high-performance file system,* is used only on systems that use OS/2.

HPFS does not use a file allocation table as was done in the FAT system. Instead, it divides the disk space into bands. Each band is no more than 8MB in size and includes a 1K bitmap at either the beginning or the end of the block.

This bitmap is used to mark whether sectors in the adjoining band are occupied or available. Each bit in the bitmap corresponds to a 512-byte sector in the band. This arrangement is depicted in Figure 4-2.

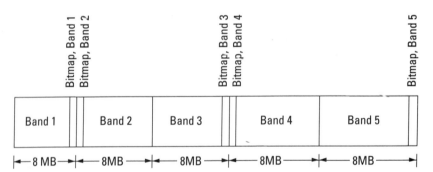

Figure 4-2: HPFS uses bitmaps to manage data that are stored in different bands on the disk.

The performance of HPFS is greatly enhanced, particularly on large volumes, by the use of B-trees in organizing directories. *B-trees* are structures that have long been used in the computing industry for organizing long lists of information.

The primary feature of this type of structure is that you can find any item in the tree with only a couple of comparisons. When used in a directory structure, this means that any file can be located much quicker than with a regular directory structure in which every record is examined sequentially.

Before Windows NT Workstation 4.0, the HPFS filing system was supported. This meant that you could access HPFS drives, and read or write the data with no problem.

Beginning with Version 4.0, however, Microsoft decided to drop support for HPFS. Thus, if you are upgrading to Windows NT 4.0 from an earlier version and you have an HPFS-formatted disk, you need to change to a different filing system for that disk.

The NTFS filing system

The filing system that is native to Windows NT is referred to as NTFS, or *new-technology filing system*. This filing system, introduced when NT was first introduced, features outstanding performance for a wide range of filing needs. NTFS works great with regular, mundane files, but it also works well with large files and large volumes as well.

When storing files on an NTFS drive, each file has a record in what is called the master file table (MFT). This is a special file that is used to keep tabs on the other files on the drive.

The first record of the MFT describes the MFT file itself, and the second record describes a mirror file, which is made as an automatic backup to the primary MFT.

Secret

Each file record in the MFT contains either an index to where the file information is stored on disk, or if the file is less than approximately 1,500 bytes long, the actual file data itself. This organization allows for very fast file accessing under NTFS.

In addition to excellent performance, NTFS also features outstanding security provisions. This means that you have more control over who has access to an NTFS file than under any other filing system.

This also allows for greater accountability on files, meaning that you can track who has had access to them. Windows NT provides means for you to implement such security measures, as described more fully in Chapter 16.

Converting to NTFS

When you first format a disk, you are essentially overlaying the disk with the organization imposed by the filing system that you have chosen. Thus, when you use the FORMAT command from DOS, you are choosing to use the FAT filing system on the disk being formatted. To convert a disk to another filing system typically involves reformatting the disk, which means that you lose the data that you stored on the disk.

Windows NT, however, provides a way that you can convert from another filing system (FAT or HPFS) to NTFS. This program is called (oddly enough) CONVERT, and it is run exclusively from the command prompt.

To convert your drive, follow these steps:

STEPS

Converting a drive to NTFS

Step 1. Choose the <u>P</u>rograms option from the Start menu. This displays the Programs menu.

Step 2. Click on the Command Prompt option in the Programs menu. This opens a command prompt window.

Step 3. At the command prompt, enter the following command, substituting for *drive* the letter of the drive that you want to convert:

```
convert drive: /fs:NTFS
```

Step 4. Answer any questions, as appropriate, when prompted.

Step 5. When the conversion is done, restart your system.

Understanding Long Filenames

Windows NT supports long filenames, meaning that you can use descriptive names for your files; these names can be up to 255 characters long. With all the hype about Windows 95, you may be led to believe that Windows 95 and Windows NT use the same filenaming system for their files; this is not true.

Secret

Windows NT has allowed long filenames for much longer than Windows 95, and it supports long filenames on both FAT partitions and NTFS partitions. Windows 95 supports long filenames, but only on FAT partitions. Also, the encoding method that is used to store the long filenames is different under Windows 95 than it is under Windows NT. It is important for you to understand how long filenames are used by Windows NT.

Filename aliases

To remain compatible with older operating systems that rely on a limited "eight-dot-three" (DOS) file system, Windows NT maintains two names for every file that it saves. First, it stores the full, long filename, and then it stores a truncated filename that complies with the DOS standard.

This shortened filename, referred to as an *alias,* is created automatically by Windows NT, in the following manner:

- Characters that are not allowed in DOS filenames (except spaces) are replaced with underscores.

- Spaces are removed to pack the name together.

- The name is truncated at six characters.

- The characters ~1 are appended to make an eight-character filename.

- The filename is converted to uppercase characters.

- The first three characters appearing after the last period in the original name are appended as the filename extension.

- The filename is checked against existing aliases. If there is a conflict, the ~1 in the filename is incremented until there is no conflict. (That is, ~2, ~3, etc.)

The alias is then stored with the file information. When an older program or operating system (such as DOS) requests the file, it always works with the alias. As an example of how creating aliases works, consider the following filename, which is perfectly legal in Windows NT:

```
May, 1997 original materials for monthly report.source
```

Because this is a legal filename in Windows NT, it is stored, as is, with the file. Windows NT then creates the following alias:

```
MAY_19~1.SOU
```

Note that, according to the previous conversion guidelines, the underscore replaced the comma, not the space. Now consider if there is also a file with this name:

```
May, 1997 working draft for monthly report.source
```

In this case, when the alias is created, there is a conflict with the first alias. Windows NT increments the alias counter by one, and the alias becomes this:

```
MAY_19~2.SOU
```

Finally, consider the following filename:

```
May, 1997 original materials for monthly report.source.doc
```

In this case, the only difference between this and the first filename is the appending of the doc extension. However, there are two periods in the filename (which is still legal under Windows NT). In this case, the following alias is created:

```
MAY_19~1.DOC
```

Remember that the filename extension is always created based on the position of the last period in the original filename.

Using long filenames

If you are using the Windows NT interface, then you can use long filenames with no change in the way that you do your work. This is because you typically point at and click objects, rather than typing in filenames. In those instances where you must type a filename, you should be able to do so with no problem.

If you are working with long filenames at the command prompt, then you must remember to surround the long filename with quotation marks. For instance, consider the same filename that you used in the previous section:

```
May, 1997 original materials for monthly report.source
```

If you wanted to move this file to the D drive, and you were using the MOVE command at the command prompt, you would enter the following:

```
move "may, 1997 original materials for monthly report.source" d:
```

Notice that uppercase and lowercase characters don't matter when entering command-prompt commands. If you forget to use the quotation marks, then you get an error. As an alternative to typing the entire command, you could always use the filename alias in the command.

If you want to see what aliases have been created by Windows NT, then you can enter the following at the command prompt:

```
dir /x
```

There are some command-prompt commands that you need to be careful with. It is not uncommon to use the wildcards (the question mark and asterisk) to affect multiple files with a single command.

For instance, assume that you have the following files in your directory:

```
May, 1997 original materials for monthly report.source
May, 1997 final report.doc
Figures.txt
Day, John senior, resume.doc
May bring this report to the committee.doc
Mayberry Town Financials.doc
```

If you wanted to delete the file Mayberry Town Financials.doc, you may be tempted to enter the following at the command line:

```
del mayb*.doc
```

After all, this saves typing the quotation marks, it saves a lot of typing over using the entire filename, and the file specification is long enough that it isn't confused with the May 1997 files. The only problem is that this single command deletes both final files on the list.

The reason is that command-prompt commands search both primary filenames (the long ones) and aliases (the short ones). The result is that the wildcard matches the final file, as you expected, but it also matches the alias for the next-to-the-last file, which works out to be the following:

```
MAYBRI~1.DOC
```

Managing Disk Drives

Windows NT includes quite a few tools to help you manage your disk drives quickly and efficiently. Whether you know it or not, you already know quite a bit about managing your disk drives.

In essence, however, there are two levels at which your disk drives can be managed: the file level and the disk level. The following two sections examine both of these management levels.

File-level management

At the file level, you use such features as the Explorer or desktop browsing to work with files. For instance, take a look at the folder window that is shown in Figure 4-3. This window is essentially no different than the Contents window that is used in the Explorer. Both allow you to view objects (files and directories) and to manipulate them.

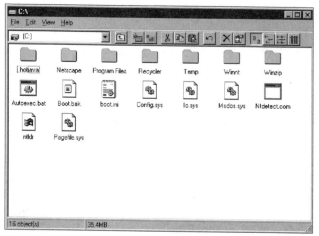

Figure 4-3: A folder window displays the contents of a folder or disk drive.

Using a folder (or Contents) window, you can perform any of the following management tasks:

- **Create folders.** You accomplish this task by choosing the New option from the File menu and then choosing Folder. Once created, you must provide a name for your new folder.

- **Delete files or folders.** You accomplish this task by selecting the file or folder (clicking on it once) and then either pressing Delete, choosing Delete from the File menu, or dragging the item to the Recycle Bin on the desktop. You can also delete by right-clicking on the item and choosing Delete from the Context menu.

  If you are deleting an entire folder, you may be asked to verify some of your deletions because you are deleting not only the folder but the files in the folder.

- **Move files or folders.** You can accomplish this task by clicking on the file or folder and dragging it to a new location. If you are moving the item to the same disk drive, then you can just click and drag. If you are moving it to a different disk drive, then you must hold Shift as you move the item.

  You can also right-click and drag the item to its new location. When you release the item, a Context menu appears; choose the Move Here option.

- **Rename files or folders.** You can accomplish this task by right-clicking on the item and then choosing Rename from the Context menu. You can also rename the item by selecting it (clicking once) and choosing the Rename option from the File menu.

- **Open files or folders.** You accomplish this task by double-clicking on the item, by clicking on it once and choosing Open from the File menu, or by right-clicking on the item and choosing Open from the Context menu.

  If you are opening a file, then either the program is started (if the file is a program file) or the program associated with the file is started (if the file is a data file). If you are opening a folder, then either a new folder window is opened for the folder or the current folder window is changed to reflect the contents of the opened folder.

- **Copy files or folders.** You can accomplish this task by right-clicking on the item and choosing the Copy option from the Context menu. You can also use the mouse to drag and copy the item. If you right-click and drag, then a Context menu appears when you release the item; choose Copy Here from the menu.

  If you drag using the left mouse button, hold Shift if you want the copy on the same drive. If you want the copy on a different drive, simply drag it there.

Disk-level management

Disk-level management is done without regard to the files, folders, or filing system on the disk drive. Instead, you work with partitions, organizational items (such as volume or stripe sets), or entire drives. In Windows NT Workstation, this type of management is done with the Disk Administrator.

To access the Disk Administrator, follow these steps:

STEPS

Starting the Disk Administrator

Step 1. Choose the Programs option from the Start menu. This displays the Programs menu.

Step 2. Choose Administrative Tools (Common) from the Programs menu. This displays a menu of tools.

(continued)

STEPS *(continued)*

Starting the Disk Administrator

Step 3.   Choose Disk Administrator from the tools menu. Shortly you see the Disk Administrator window, as shown in Figure 4-4.

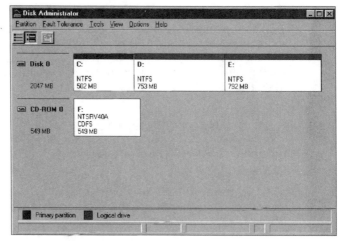

Figure 4-4: The Disk Administrator is used to manage logical sections of your disk drives.

Caution

Your changes affect disk structure, and thus it is easy to erase data on your disk drives. Make sure that you really want to take any potential action before you take it.

The contents of your Disk Administrator may differ from what is shown in Figure 4-4, because it represents the logical organization of your drive. There are two ways that you can view the information in the Disk Administrator.

The first way is the Disk view, which is what is shown in Figure 4-4. The other way is called the Volume view, which is shown in Figure 4-5.

You can use either view; it basically boils down to a your preferences. (You select different views by using the choices from the View menu.) Most people do their work in the Disk view, although the Volume view displays information a bit more concisely.

The management tasks that you can accomplish with the Disk Administrator are discussed in the next several sections.

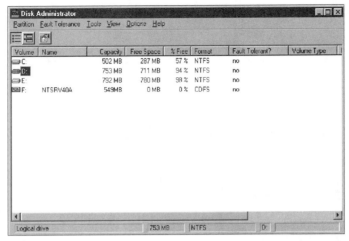

Figure 4-5: Information about your drives can be displayed in Volume view.

Disk Administrator commands dealing with fault tolerance are not discussed in this chapter. For information on these commands, refer to Chapter 11.

Creating or deleting a partition

When a disk drive has not been logically organized, the Disk Administrator treats the unorganized portion as free space. For instance, Figure 4-6 shows an example of a disk drive that has two partitions (formatted as drives C and E) and a large block of free space.

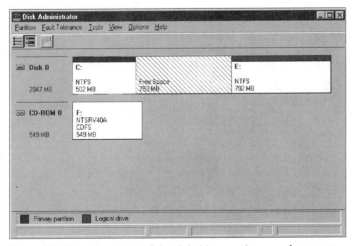

Figure 4-6: Unused portions of the disk drive are shown as free space.

To use free space, it must be partitioned. When you are ready to create a partition, you simply select the free space (by clicking on it) and then choose Create from the Partition menu.

As an alternative, you can right-click on the free space and then choose Create from the Context menu. This displays the Create Logical Drive dialog box, as shown in Figure 4-7.

Figure 4-7: When setting up a partition, you can specify how large the partition should be.

Using the control in the center of the dialog box, you can specify a size (in MB) for the partition, which is referred to here as a logical drive. The information at the top of the dialog box indicates the minimum and maximum sizes for the partition.

When you have made your selection, click on the OK button. The partition is created, and the next available logical drive letter is used for your new partition.

To delete a partition, simply click on the partition and then choose Delete from the Partition menu, or right-click on the partition and choose Delete from the Context menu. Either way, Windows NT checks to see if the partition had been previously formatted.

If so, then you are asked to make sure that you really want to delete the partition. After confirming your action, the partition is removed. Once a partition is deleted, it is depicted as unused space on the drive, as shown earlier in Figure 4-6.

After you have changed or deleted partitions, you need to commit your changes to disk. This writes the information to the partition table and enables you to further prepare the partitions by formatting them.

Creating or enlarging a volume set

A *volume set* is a logical grouping of partitions so that they appear as a single drive to the user. You can create volume sets when it would be unwise to repartition your entire hard drive. For instance, take a look at Figure 4-8. In this instance, there are three areas of free space on the drive, interspersed with partitions that are being used.

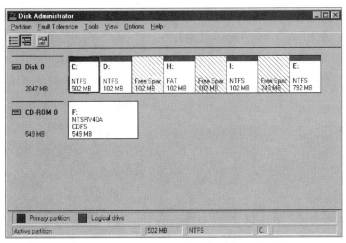

Figure 4-8: It is possible, under some circumstances, for drive partitions to appear fragmented.

In this case, it may be advantageous to create a volume set using two or more of your free-space areas. To do this, simply click on the first free-space area and then hold Ctrl while you click on the others.

Then you can choose Create Volume Set from the Partition menu. This displays the Create Volume Set dialog box, as shown in Figure 4-9.

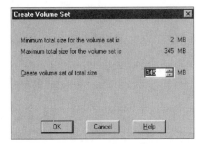

Figure 4-9: The Create Volume Set dialog box allows you to specify how large your volume set should be.

The Create Volume Set dialog box looks very similar to the dialog box that you used to create partitions. At the top of the dialog box is information that indicates the minimum and maximum sizes for the volume set.

In the control, you can specify the size that you want and then click on the OK button. The volume set is created, and the Disk view appears as shown in Figure 4-10.

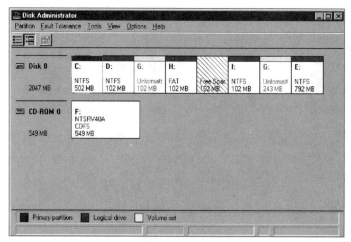

Figure 4-10: A volume set uses the same drive letter for two noncontiguous partitions.

Notice that the volume set is shown with a yellow stripe on the screen, and both partitions have the same drive letter (in this case, drive G). After a volume set is created, you can delete it the same as you would any partition, and it must be formatted before you can use it.

After it is created, a volume set is treated by the Disk Administrator and the operating system as a complete unit. This means that if your volume set appears in the Disk view as two or three pieces, you cannot perform operations on individual pieces, only on the entire volume set.

You can also enlarge a volume set using the same technique that you used to create it in the first place. Just select an existing volume set or partition, and then hold Ctrl as you click on the free space. When you choose the Extend Volume Set option from the Partition menu, you see the same dialog box as that shown in Figure 4-9.

You can only use partitions that are formatted with the NTFS filing system in your volume sets. The FAT filing system does not support volume sets.

Formatting a drive

Once a partition or volume set has been created, it must be formatted before it can be used to store data. *Formatting* uses the filing system that you choose to create the logical disk structures necessary to later accept the information that you want to store. The Disk Administrator allows you to format a partition using either the FAT or NTFS filing system, as described earlier in this chapter.

Note

If you just finished partitioning a portion of your disk, you cannot format the new partition until you commit your changes. Make sure that you use the Commit Changes Now option from the Partition menu before formatting new partitions.

To format a drive, simply click on the partition and choose Change Format from the Tools menu, or right-click on the partition and choose Format from the Context menu. This displays the Format Drive dialog box, as shown in Figure 4-11.

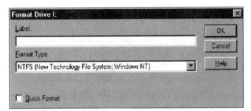

Figure 4-11: When formatting a drive, you have
the opportunity to select the filing system that you
want to use.

Caution

Do not confuse the Change Format option on the Tools menu with the CONVERT command that was described earlier in this chapter. The choice of terminology for the menu option is unfortunate, as it implies that any data on the drive may be retained; this is misleading. The Change Format command only reformats a drive, without regard to any existing data.

You can fill in the Label field, but this is optional. You do, however, need to specify a filing system choice in the Format Type drop-down list. You have two options: NTFS and FAT. Make your selection, and then click on the OK button to format the partition.

You are asked to confirm your action, and then the partition is finally formatted. Depending on the size of the partition, formatting could take a while to complete.

When done, you see a dialog box informing you of the results of the operation. At this point, you can use the disk the same as you would any other disk drive.

Checking for errors

If you are experiencing problems using your hard drive, you may periodically want to check your drives for errors. You initiate this process by clicking on the drive that you want to check and then choosing Check for Errors from the Tools menu. This displays the Check for Errors dialog box, as shown in Figure 4-12.

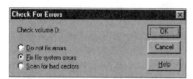

Figure 4-12: The Disk Administrator allows you to check a disk partition for errors.

The choices in the Check for Errors dialog box allow you to specify how Disk Administrator should do its work. The choices are reminiscent of the ScanDisk tool used in Windows 95. You can either have the program notify you of errors, fix the errors, or scan for bad sectors. Make your choice, and then click on the OK button.

As Disk Administrator checks the disk, it keeps you informed of its progress. If you asked to be notified of errors, then the program stops and displays a dialog box after each error is detected. When the program is complete, a dialog box is displayed that details the findings of the program (see Figure 4-13).

Figure 4-13: When done checking, the Disk Administrator provides a status report of what it found.

Changing drive letters

Secret

Windows NT is very liberal on how it allows you to assign drive letters. In other operating systems, you typically have to use the next sequential drive letter when you are creating a new drive. To the contrary, Windows NT allows you to assign any drive letter to any drive at any time. The drive letters do not need to be sequential, nor does changing a drive letter destroy the data on the hard drive. The only exception to this is that drive letters A and B are reserved for floppy disk drives.

To change a drive letter, select the drive whose letter you want to change, and then choose the Assign Drive Letter option from the Tools menu. As an alternative, you can right-click on the drive and choose Assign Drive Letter from the Context menu. Either way, you see the Assign Drive Letter dialog box, as shown in Figure 4-14.

Figure 4-14: Windows NT allows you to assign any drive letter to a disk drive.

You can choose to either have a drive letter assigned, which you can select from the drop-down list, or you can choose to not assign a drive letter. It is unclear exactly why you would not want to assign a drive letter, however, because you cannot access the drive if there is no way to address it.

When you are done, click on the OK button. Your changes are immediately changed, and you can begin accessing the drive using your new drive letter.

Viewing drive properties

As you have already learned, everything in Windows NT Workstation 4.0 uses the concept of properties. Your logical disk drives are no exception.

You can view and change the properties that are associated with a disk drive at any time. Simply right-click on a drive in the Disk Administrator, and then choose the Properties option from the Context menu.

Note that you can also display drive properties by right-clicking on a drive icon in the My Computer window. When you choose Properties from that Context menu, you also see a drive properties dialog box, but it is a bit different from the one that you see in the Disk Administrator. Figure 4-15 shows what both properties dialog boxes look like.

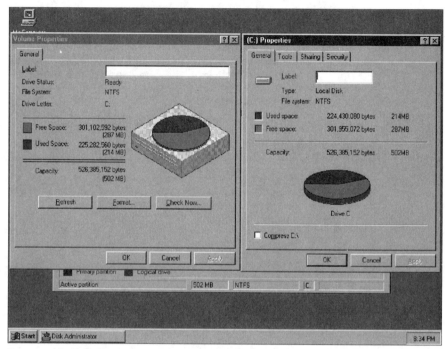

Figure 4-15: Windows NT provides two different types of disk properties displays.

Both dialog boxes show you the same information, although it is organized a bit differently. The Volume Properties dialog box (which is on the left and accessed through the Disk Administrator) provides buttons that allow you to format and check the drive, as previously discussed.

When you are finished viewing the properties of your drive, click on the OK button to close the dialog box.

Using File Tools

Windows NT includes quite a few unique tools that allow you to manage your files. Many of these tools are new with this version of NT, and all of them can help you use your system better.

These tools allow you to find files, associate files with different programs, quickly view the contents of a file, send the file to your desired destination, and recycle your discarded files. Each of these areas is covered in the following sections.

Finding files

It happens to all computer users at one time or another — you prepare a report or memo, file it on your disk drive, and promptly forget about it. Two months later, you are frantically searching your hard disk, looking for that file that you know is somewhere on your system.

To make such a task easier, Windows NT Workstation includes a handy feature that allows you to search for files anywhere on your hard drive or on any network drive to which you have access. To access this tool, simply choose the Find option from the Start menu.

This displays a small submenu which indicates that you can search for either of two items: Files or Folders, or a Computer system. You will probably use the Files or Folders option the most.

Note

Searching for computer systems is discussed in Chapter 12.

When you choose the Files or Folders option, you see the Find dialog box, as shown in Figure 4-16.

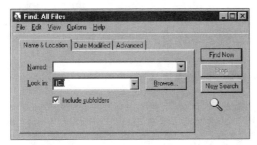

Figure 4-16: The Find dialog box is used to find files or folders on a disk drive.

The Find dialog box uses three tabs, each of which allows you to specify criteria to be used in your search. Each of those tabs is discussed in the following sections, along with additional ways that you can make your search criteria more specific.

The Name & Location tab

As you can see in Figure 4-16, the Name & Location tab contains two fields and a check box. The Named field allows you to specify the name (or partial name) of the file for which you are looking.

You can use wildcard characters in this field, the same as you would from the command prompt. Valid wildcards include the question mark (?), which represents any single character, or the asterisk (*) which represents any multiple characters.

If you click on the Look In drop-down list, notice that it contains three items:

- All of your local drives, individually

- All of your mapped network drives, individually

- A special entry for all of your local hard drives, collectively

You can pick any of these as the drive on which to search for the file. In addition, if you click on the Browse button, you can specify that specific folders be used as the starting point for the search.

You should also pay special attention to the Include Subfolders check box at the bottom of the dialog box. If this is selected (the default), then everything in the directory tree under the current folder is searched; if it is not selected, then only the single folder is searched.

The Date Modified tab

This tab allows you to specify the age of a file that you are looking for or to specify when the file was last changed. When you click on the Date Modified tab, the Find dialog box appears, as shown in Figure 4-17.

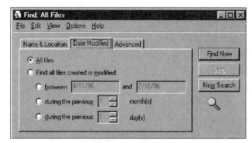

Figure 4-17: The Date Modified tab allows you to limit your search to specific file dates.

The default setting for this tab is for the first radio button (All Files) to be selected. With this option selected, there are no limits based on file dates. You can also look for files with any of the following criteria:

- Created between two dates

- Created during the previous X number of months (valid ranges are 0 to 999 months)

- Created during the previous X number of days (valid ranges are 0 to 999 months)

The Advanced tab

This tab allows you to specify the type of file that you are looking for, the size of the file, or some text that the file contains. When you click on the Advanced tab, the Find dialog box appears, as shown in Figure 4-18.

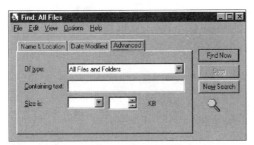

Figure 4-18: The Advanced tab is very useful in finding word processing documents.

The Advanced tab is perhaps the most useful of all of the Find dialog box tabs. The first field (the Of Type drop-down list) allows you to search only specific types of files. If you use the drop-down list at the right side of the field, notice that there are quite a few file types listed.

These file types are garnered from files that have been associated with programs, as discussed elsewhere in this chapter. You can only select from associated file types; you cannot enter your own file extension for an unassociated file type.

The Containing Text field is a big boon for finding wayward documents. You can enter any text from your document here, and it is used as a criterion for searching. For instance, you could enter "1996 growth," and only files containing those exact letters, in that sequence, would be matched.

If you use the Containing Text field, you can also choose the Case Sensitive selection on the Options menu if you want what you type to be exactly matched. Without this option selected, then "growth" would also match "Growth" or "GROWTH" or even "GrOwTh." If you select the option, then "growth" would match only the all-lowercase version of the word.

Secret

Even though the Advanced tab can be very helpful in finding word process-ing documents, it may not work properly with all word processors. Some programs intersperse text with formatting information, which can make matching impossible. If this is the case for your word processor, then you may not be able to match all text — unless, of course, you enter the proper formatting control codes to enable such a match.

At the bottom of the dialog box, you can specify a target size for the file for which you are searching. There are two fields here; the drop-down list allows you to pick a qualifier for the file size.

There are two qualifiers provided: At least, which means that your size spec-ification represents the smallest size of the file, and At most, which means that your size represents the largest size. Once the qualifier is selected, then you can specify a file size. (The valid size range is from 0 to 32,767K.)

Initiating a search

With your search criteria specified, you are ready to begin the search. Searching is done by clicking on the Find Now button at the right side of the dialog box. Your system is searched, and you can see information about the progress of the search in a status bar that appears at the bottom of the Find dialog box.

If you want to cancel the search for some reason, you can click on the Stop button. (For instance, if there are too many files being located and you decide to change your search criteria.)

As the search progresses, a list of files appears at the bottom of the Find dia-log box (see Figure 4-19). When the search is complete or when you stop the search, you can work with these files the same way that you would in the Explorer or the desktop browser.

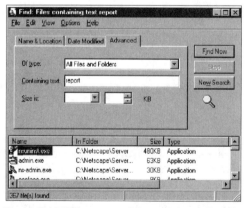

Figure 4-19: When a search is complete, a list of matching files is displayed at the bottom of the Find dialog box.

For instance, if you scroll through the list of files and you find one that you want to open, you can either double-click on the filename or you can drag the file to an open application window.

Tip

You can sort the file list by clicking on the headers at the top of each column. For instance, if you click on the Size column header, then the selected files are sorted based on their size.

Saving your search criteria

Because the Find tool provides such a wide assortment of criteria that you can use in constructing your search, it is possible to develop a very complex search. If you develop such a search and want to save your search criteria, you can do so by selecting the Save Search option from the File menu. When you do this, a search definition is saved and placed on your desktop.

Your new search definition acts the same as a shortcut (it allows you to quickly access Find using your criteria), but it is not quite the same. The biggest difference is that the definition's icon does not look like a regular shortcut icon; it does not have the arrow in the lower corner of the icon.

To use the definition, simply double-click on it and the Find dialog box again appears, but this time it has all of your criteria already filled in. You can then initiate the search by clicking on the Find Now button.

Associating files

As in earlier versions of Windows NT, the newest version allows you to establish associations between data files and the programs that are used to control them. You do this by indicating the type of files that are created by the application, and then Windows NT assumes that all files of that type can be manipulated by that application.

For instance, you could associate all files having an .XLS association with Microsoft Excel, all files having a .TXT extension with Notepad, and all files using a .PCX extension with your favorite graphics program. As a matter of point, many associations are automatically created when you install Windows NT, and other associations are added as you install different applications.

To establish new or change existing file associations, follow these steps:

STEPS

Setting or editing file associations

Step 1. Open the Explorer or open a folder window.

(continued)

STEPS *(continued)*

Setting or editing file associations

Step 2. Choose <u>O</u>ptions from the <u>V</u>iew menu. This displays the Options dialog box.

Step 3. Click on the File Types tab. The Options dialog box should now appear, as shown in Figure 4-20.

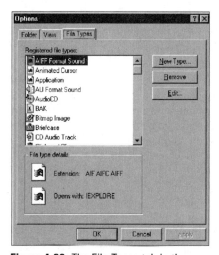

Figure 4-20: The File Types tab in the Options dialog box allows you to alter file associations.

The Registered file <u>t</u>ypes list represents those associations that currently exist on your system. The list shows the icon that is associated with the file type and the name of the file type.

If you want to edit an association, you can do so by selecting the existing file type and then clicking the <u>E</u>dit button. This displays the Edit File Type dialog box, as shown in Figure 4-21.

Figure 4-21: The Edit File Type dialog box is used to change what is done with a file.

The Edit File Type dialog box has three main parts. At the top of the dialog box, you can specify the icon that is used for this type of file.

If you click the Change Icon button, you can select a different icon. Remember, the icon that you choose here is used every time a file with this extension is displayed on your system.

The second part of the dialog box is the Description of Type field. This is simply a name used to describe the association. You can change this to anything you want; it only shows up when you click the File Types tab in the Options dialog box.

The third and most important part of the editing dialog box is the Actions list. By using the four buttons that appear under the Actions list (New, Edit, Remove, and Set Default), you can change what appears in the list. *Actions* are nothing more than a definition of what can be done with the file.

Actions are basically an extension of the traditional idea of file associations, but they are much more versatile. Actions allow you to define a wide range of functions that can be performed on a file. Once defined for a file type, actions then appear in the Context menu anytime that you right-click on a file that has that type.

As an example of how actions are used, assume that you want to create a new action for a particular type of file. With the Edit File Type dialog box visible, click on the New button. This displays the New Action dialog box, as shown in Figure 4-22.

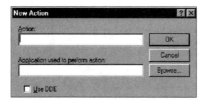

Figure 4-22: The New Action dialog box
is used to define actions for a file type.

In the Action field, enter the name of the action that you are defining. This
can be any name that you want, such as print, enlarge, delete, or process;
there are no preset actions, so what you enter is entirely up to you.

You could even use multiple words in the Action field, such as Convert to
Text. The actions that you enter are shown in the Context menu when you
right-click on a file of the type that you are editing.

In the next field, Application Used to Perform Action, enter the complete
command line that should be used to achieve the action (when the action is
selected from the Context menu). When you're satisfied with the action and
the command used to carry out the action, click on OK. The new action then
appears in the Actions list of the Edit File Type dialog box.

The other buttons under the Actions list allow you to Edit an existing action
or Remove an action from the list. Actions are shown in the Actions list
alphabetically.

By default, the first action listed is used to control the icon that is displayed
for the file type, so if you change the program that is used in the first action,
you change the icon (unless, of course, you override the icon by clicking on
the Change Icon button).

The final button in the Edit File Type dialog box is Set Default. This is the
button that is used to establish what we traditionally think of as a file association. When you select an action and then click on the Set Default button,
the action is shown in bold type.

This is the action that is automatically selected whenever someone double-
clicks on the icon that is used for this type of file. Normally, the default is set
to the open action, but you can set it to any action that you deem advisable.

Secret

At the bottom of the Edit File Type dialog box is a check box entitled Enable
Quick View. This check box, when selected, results in the Quick View option
being listed in the Context menu for the file type. It is not a good idea to
start selecting these check boxes capriciously.

As mentioned in the next section, Quick View relies on the presence of filters to define how a file can be viewed. If you select this check box and no filter is present, then a default filter is used, and the result is garbage displayed in the viewer.

Quick View

Windows NT Workstation includes a new feature known as Quick View. This feature allows you to view the contents of a file without starting the application. The Quick View program was originally developed by a company called Systems Compatibility Corp., which was recently acquired by Inso Corp. This program uses special filters that allow you to simply and quickly look at the contents of a file without needing the actual application.

Quick View is available from virtually anyplace that you can select a file. For instance, if you are browsing through your desktop and you see a file that you are curious about, you can right-click on the file and select Quick View from the Context menu. (If the Quick View option is not present, then a filter for that type of file is not present on your system.) Figure 4-23 shows an example of using Quick View to look at a file.

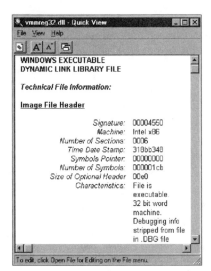

Figure 4-23: Quick View can be used to examine the contents of a file.

Not all files have the Quick View option available to them. As mentioned earlier, Quick View works based on the presence of filters that define how a file can be examined. Filters are contained in DLL files that are stored in your winnt\system32 directory. Table 4-1 details the types of files for which Quick View filters are supplied.

Table 4-1   File types supported by Quick View

Extension	File Type	DLL File
ASC	ASCII files	vsasc8.dll
BMP	Bitmap image	vsbmp.dll
DLL	Dynamic link libraries	vsexe2.dll
DOC	Microsoft Word documents	vsw6.dll
DOC	WordPad documents	vsword.dll
DOC	WordPerfect 5 documents	vswp5.dll
DOC	WordPerfect 6 documents	vswp6.dll
DRW	Micrographix Draw files	vsdrw.dll
EXE	Executable files	vsexe.dll
INF	Setup information	vsasc8.dll
INI	Configuration settings	vsasc8.dll
MOD	Multiplan files created	vsmp.dll
PPT	PowerPoint version 4 files	vspp.dll
REG	Registry files	vsexe2.dll
RTF	Rich Text Format files	vsrtf.dll
TIF	TIFF graphic files	vstiff.dll
TXT	Text documents	vsasc8.dll
WKS	Lotus 1-2-3 files	vswks.dll
WKS	Microsoft Works 3 files	vswork.dll
WMF	Windows metafiles	vswmf.dll
WPD	WordPerfect document files	vswpf.dll
WRI	Write documents	vsmsw.dll
XLC	Excel chart files	vsxl5.dll
XLS	Excel spreadsheet files	vsxl5.dll

Additional Quick View filters may be available on your system. You can get additional filters from Inso Corp., or a filter may have been installed with some of your applications.

Using Send To

You may have noticed an option called Se_n_d To on your Context menus, from the _F_ile menu in the Explorer, or in a folder window. This is a special menu option that allows you to quickly copy a file from one location to another. The great thing about this command is that you can easily add destinations to the menu.

Using the desktop browser, look around until you find the SendTo folder. This folder is available in the following directory:

```
c:\winnt\profiles\username\sendto
```

Because the SendTo folder can vary based on the user, replace _username_ in the preceding with your user ID. If you look in the folder, it probably appears as shown in Figure 4-24.

Figure 4-24: Your SendTo folder
probably contains only two shortcuts.

Secret

These two shortcuts may look familiar; they are the same two choices that you see whenever you highlight the SendTo option on a menu. This means that you can modify the SendTo menu by simply adding items to the SendTo folder.

For instance, you may want to add the following shortcuts:

- A shortcut to a printer, which would send the file to the printer

- A shortcut to a mapped network drive, which would copy the file to the remote drive

- A shortcut to Notepad, which would open the file in the text editor

- A shortcut to your graphics programs, which allows you to choose which program should open the file

The possibilities are almost endless, but if you think through them well, the Send To feature of Windows NT can be a real time-saver.

The Recycle Bin

By now, you probably regard the Recycle Bin as a valued addition to Windows NT Workstation 4.0. As described in Chapter 1, the Recycle Bin is a way station for your files; it is a stopover point between the time you delete them and the time that they are removed from your system. However, there are file-management considerations to the Recycle Bin as well.

If you need to recover a file that you accidentally deleted, the Recycle Bin is invaluable. However, the Recycle Bin can also waste precious disk resources without your knowledge.

You can check this out by right-clicking on the Recycle Bin and then choosing Properties from the Context menu. This displays the Recycle Bin Properties dialog box, as shown in Figure 4-25.

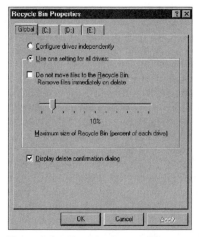

Figure 4-25: Even the Recycle Bin has properties in Windows NT Workstation 4.0.

This dialog box contains a tab for every hard drive on your system and one titled Global. Each tab contains the same controls, except the Global tab includes an option to allow the Recycle Bin on each drive to be configured independently. If you select this radio button, then you can change settings for each drive; with it unselected, only the Global tab has any significance.

Besides the control that was already described, there are three other controls that have meaning in the dialog box. The first is a check box near the top of the dialog box. This check box, when selected, effectively turns the Recycle Bin off.

With this check box selected, when you delete a file, it is gone for good, bypassing the Recycle Bin altogether. Unless you are running very low on disk space or if you never make mistakes(!), you should leave this check box cleared.

The slider control in the middle of the dialog box allows you to specify how much of your hard drive space should be consumed by the Recycle Bin before it starts throwing out the trash. The default value for this control is 10%, but on many drives this can be quite large.

For instance, if you have a 500MB hard drive, then 10% is a whopping 50MB — just for the trash can! If you can get by with less space for the Recycle Bin, you free resources and speed your system performance just a bit.

At the bottom of the dialog box is a check box that controls whether Windows NT checks with you before moving something to the Recycle Bin. If this check box is cleared, then you are not asked for confirmation.

Accessing Remote Information

In previous versions of Windows NT, if you wanted to access information that other people on your network have made available, you needed to map their folder to a drive letter on your system.

In this way, you could access that remote folder as if it were a local drive. Under Windows NT Workstation 4.0, you can still map drives, but you don't have to map them all the time.

A temporary solution

If you want to quickly access information that is on a remote folder, you can do so using your desktop browser. For instance, consider that Marcel is another user on your network, and you need to transfer a file from a folder that he has shared on the network.

You don't need to create a permanent mapping to his folder, as you only need this one file. In this case, you should browse through the Network Neighborhood icon until you locate the folder on Marcel's system.

As you learned in Chapter 2, browsing like this leaves a folder window (of the remote system) open on your desktop. You can then drag items from that folder to your local drives to access the files. When you close the window for the remote folder, the connection between your system and Marcel's is broken.

Using a UNC specification

If you are using a program, you already know that you can access a file on your own system by using the path name to that file. This path name provides a unique address for the location of the file on your hard drive.

Many applications, particularly those developed for Windows NT, allow you to use a UNC (universal naming convention) path to specify a remote file. The UNC can be viewed as nothing more than a path, across the network, to a remote file. The syntax for a UNC is as follows:

`\\servername\sharename\path\`

Notice that the UNC begins with double backslashes and that each level of the UNC is separated by a single backslash. The different parts of the UNC are as follows:

- **servername.** This is the name of the server on which the resource resides. Essentially, it is the name of the computer that is making the resource available.

    Thus, if you want to access a file on John's computer and his computer ID is JohnW, then the servername would be JohnW or johnw.

- **sharename.** This is the name under which the resource was published on the remote system; it is the name that you see when browsing through the Network Neighborhood.

- **path**. This is optional and refers to a path starting at the remote resource.

As an example, consider browsing through your Network Neighborhood; here you view the contents of a remote system called Hulett. As shown in Figure 4-26, a folder is available on that system called DOWNLOAD. The UNC to this resource would be the following:

`\\hulett\download`

Notice that there is no path used in this UNC. If you wanted to access the report.doc file within the reports folder of DOWNLOAD, then the UNC would be as follows:

`\\hulett\download\reports\report.doc`

Mapping a drive

Many times, you need more permanent access to remote data. In this case, it is advantageous for you to map the remote folder to a drive letter on your system.

The way that you do this is quite easy, and there are two ways it can be accomplished. The first way is to use a UNC (as discussed in the previous section), and the second is by browsing through the network.

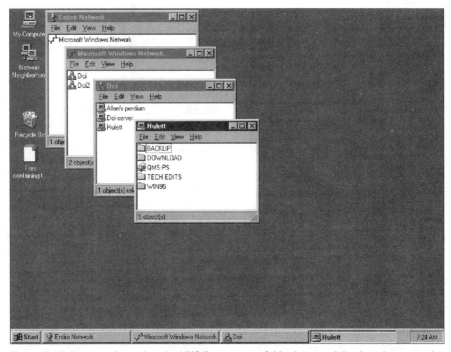

Figure 4-26: You can determine the UNC for a remote folder by examining how it appears in the desktop browser.

Mapping with a UNC

If you know the UNC of a remote folder, you can easily map it to a drive letter on your system. To do this, simply right-click on either the My Computer or Network Neighborhood icon on your desktop.

This displays a Context menu from which you should select the Map Network Drive option. This displays the Map Network Drive dialog box, as shown in Figure 4-27.

Figure 4-27: The Map Network Drive dialog box is used to establish a link between your system and a remote folder.

In the Drive drop-down list, you can select an unused drive letter on your system. (The default for the drop-down list is the first unused drive letter on your system.) The next field, Path, is where you enter the UNC for the remote folder.

Secret

You can also use a DNS domain name in the Path field. For instance, you could use \\dcomp.com\transfer as the network path. DNS names are used on TCP/IP networks, such as the Internet. See Chapter 14 for more discussion on DNS names.

At the bottom of the dialog box is a check box that controls whether this mapping is *persistent.* If you want the mapping to be established every time you start Windows NT, then select the check box. If you only need it for this NT session, then make sure that the check box is cleared.

Just below the Path field is the Connect As field. This field is used to specify a different user account to be used when connecting to this remote folder. When you leave this field blank, you are connected using the user name that you used when you logged in to the workstation. If you want to use some other log-in name for this connection, then you can supply it in the Connect As field.

When you click on the OK button, the connection is established between your system (using the drive letter that you specified) and the remote folder. The mapped drive then appears every time you browse your system using the My Computer icon.

Mapping by browsing

If you don't know the UNC for a remote folder, you can simply browse until you find the resource. Perhaps Garrett, another user on your network, has shared a folder that you want to map.

Use the Network Neighborhood to browse until you see Garrett's folder displayed as a folder icon. (Don't open his folder into its own window; leave it as a folder icon.) Right-click on the folder icon, and a Context menu appears. Select the Map Network Drive option, and you see the Map Network Drive dialog box, as shown in Figure 4-28.

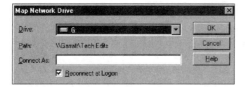

Figure 4-28: When browsing, the Path field of the Map Network Drive dialog box is already filled in.

This is the same dialog box that you learned about in the previous section. The only difference is that the Path field is already filled in. You can select the field, but you cannot change the value contained there.

You should, however, fill in the other fields as discussed in the previous section. When you are done, click on the OK button to establish the drive mapping.

Disconnecting a mapped drive

How a mapped drive is disconnected depends on whether you made the mapping persistent. When you established the connection, the check box at the bottom of the Map Network Drive dialog box controlled whether the connection was persistent. If it is not persistent (the check box was cleared), then the mapping is automatically disconnected whenever you restart your system.

If the mapping was persistent or if you want to break the connection before logging off, then you need to explicitly disconnect. You can do this by first opening the My Computer icon on your desktop.

Right-click on the mapped drive that you want to disconnect, and then choose Disconnect from the Context menu. The drive is disconnected and disappears from the My Computer window.

As an alternate method, you can simply right-click on the My Computer or Network Neighborhood icon. This displays a Context menu, from which you should choose the Disconnect Network Drive option. You then see the Disconnect Network Drive dialog box, as shown in Figure 4-29.

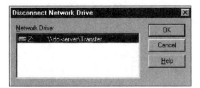

Figure 4-29: The Disconnect Network Drive dialog box allows you to select a drive that you previously mapped.

In the Network Drive list, select the mapped drive that you want to disconnect. When you click on OK, the connection is broken. If you later want to re-establish a connection, you must again map the remote folder to a local drive letter.

Summary

Before you can become proficient at managing your workstation, you need to become comfortable with the tools that are at your disposal. This chapter has discussed not only the tools available to you under Windows NT Workstation 4.0 but also the underlying concepts that allow you to make sense of how Windows NT does its work.

In particular, you have learned the following items:

▶ Disk drives are logically organized into partitions. These partitions are typically assigned drive letters, but you can create special organizational structures under Windows NT. These include volume sets, stripe sets, and mirror sets.

▶ The three most common filing systems used today are FAT (file allocation table), HPFS (high-performance file system), and NTFS (new-technology filing system). Windows NT supports both the FAT and NTFS filing systems.

▶ Long filenames allow you to attach meaningful names to your files. To remain compatible with older filing systems, such as DOS, Windows NT always creates a short filename alias that can be used in the more limited naming convention of DOS.

▶ When using long filenames from the command prompt, you should surround any filename containing spaces with quotation marks.

▶ The Disk Administrator is a robust tool that gives you complete control over the logical organization of your disk drives. You can use it to control partitions, volume sets, stripe sets, and mirror sets.

▶ The Find command, available from the Start menu, gives you precise control over searching for files on your disk drives. You can specify a wide range of search criteria and save your criteria for use at a later time.

▶ Under Windows NT 4.0, you can associate specific actions with types of files and then tie different programs to each action. This is much more powerful than the traditional file associations that were used in previous versions of Windows NT.

▶ The Quick View feature allows you to easily view the contents of common file types. You can select the Quick View command from the Context menu of a file.

▶ The Send To command can save you time by providing a quick link to common file destinations.

▶ When you install Windows NT Workstation 4.0, the Recycle Bin is configured to use up to 10% of your disk space. On large hard drives, it makes sense to change this amount to a more reasonable, lower setting.

▶ You can access remote information by either browsing the Network Neighborhood, using the UNC for the resource, or by mapping a remote folder to a local drive letter.

Chapter 5

Printing

In This Chapter

Creating printed output is one of the most common tasks performed with a computer. You may remember the talk in the mid-1980s about the "paperless office." Many people talked about computers as if they were going to greatly reduce the paper that we process in our offices. The truth is, computers make printing so easy that we generate even more paper than before.

Windows NT provides outstanding support for a wide variety of printers. In this chapter, you learn how you can create your own printer definitions, control the information that you send to the printer, and control how the printer processes that information.

In broad terms, you learn the following items:

▶ How to use the new Printers folder

▶ How to manage the print server that is built into Windows NT Workstation

▶ How to manage individual printers

▶ How to manage print jobs that you have created

Using the Printers Folder

In previous versions of Windows NT, you used the Printer Manager and the Control Panel to manage your printing. In Windows NT Workstation 4.0, all printer management takes place in the Printers folder.

There are several ways that you can access the Printers folder:

■ Double-click on the My Computer icon, and then double-click on the Printers folder.

■ Choose Settings from the Start menu, and then choose Printers.

■ Open the Control Panel, and then double-click on the Printers shortcut.

Regardless of how you choose to access the Printers folder, you soon see a folder that looks like virtually any other folder in Windows NT. Figure 5-1 shows an example of the Printers folder.

Figure 5-1: The Printers folder is where you manage your printers.

Like any other folder window, the Printers folder contains icons that refer to objects. One icon is used to add printers to your system, and other icons are used to represent existing printer definitions. Your Printers folder could have quite a few icons; the one in Figure 5-1 contains only two icons, including a definition for a single printer.

The Printers folder also contains a menu, and the choices should look familiar to you. The choices are as follows:

- **File.** This menu allows you to control a selected printer or modify the properties that are assigned to your print server. (You learn more about print servers shortly.)

- **Edit.** This menu is the same as the Edit menu in other folder windows. It allows you to cut, copy, and paste objects in the Printers folder, as well as to undo your previous editing action.

- **View.** This menu is the same as the View menu in any other folder window. It allows you to arrange icons, choose how information is displayed, and indicate exactly what is displayed in the window.

- **Help.** This menu is used to get general Windows NT help, the same as you get when you choose Help from the Start menu.

When you work with the Printers folder, you are typically accomplishing tasks in relation to printers or documents. These tasks can be broken down into three broad categories: tasks that affect the server, those that affect a printer, and those that affect documents. Each of these areas is covered in the following sections.

Managing Your Print Server

Windows NT implements the concept of a *print server*. This server allows you to make global choices that affect all printing through your system. It may sound strange to think that you have a print server on your workstation, but that is exactly what you have. This is especially true because you can share your printers with others on your network.

To manage your server, you need to display the Print Server Properties dialog box. This is done by choosing Server Properties from the File menu. This displays the dialog box shown in Figure 5-2.

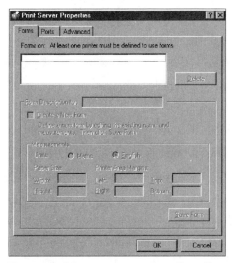

Figure 5-2: Print server properties affect all printers on your system.

This dialog box contains three tabs that allow you to manage your entire print server. Believe it or not, you should use the tabs in the reverse order of what they are shown. (I believe Microsoft put the tabs in the order shown because after you have configured your server, you are more likely to use the Forms tab most often.)

Setting print spooler properties

If you have used Windows for any length of time, you already know what a print spooler is. In older versions of Windows, the Print Manager was the print spooler. The purpose of the spooler is two-fold: to free your program so that you can continue working and to manage the transfer of information to the printer. The spooler can accept information just as fast as your program can send it.

It then doles out the print job to the printer at the speed that the printer can handle it. Any print job that you send to your printer is automatically spooled (placed in a queue) and printed in the background while you continue to work. For most users, this is a very efficient way to print.

In Windows NT Workstation 4.0, the print subsystem has been reorganized to provide better performance. From a user's perspective, the print spooler appears as shown in Figure 5-3.

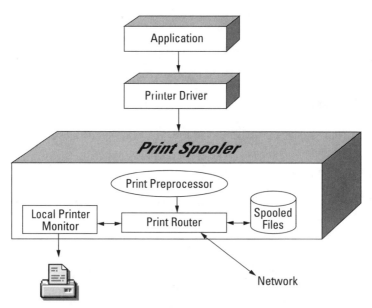

Figure 5-3: The print spooler is made up of many components.

When you print something from an application, the printer driver prepares the job for the print spooler. The job is then handed to the print preprocessor, which in turn works with the print router to determine where the job should be sent.

If the job is to be handled on a local printer, it is either sent to the printer or to a spooling file (if the printer is busy or the job is large). If the job is destined for a printer across a network, then it is routed over the network where the spooler at the remote site takes care of managing the printer.

When you are configuring your print server, you have the opportunity to specify several important items about the print spooler. Click on the Advanced tab, and the Print Server Properties dialog box appears, as shown in Figure 5-4.

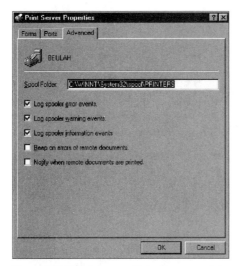

Figure 5-4: The Advanced tab allows you to configure spooler settings.

Secret

At the top of the dialog box, you can indicate where you want your spooler files stored. If you do a great deal of printing, it is a good idea to choose a drive that is quite fast. Also, you should always choose a local drive. Choosing a network drive puts you at the mercy of the network; if the network is down, then you can't print.

The check boxes in the rest of the dialog box allow you to control how your print server interacts with your print spooler as well as with remote print spoolers. The first three choices allow you to specify which type of spooler messages should be recorded in your event log. (The event log is discussed in Chapter 16.) The other two check boxes are used to indicate how you want to be notified of messages from network printers.

Controlling ports

There is a good chance that you already know what a *port* is — it is a communication channel between two computer devices. Your print server, in order to function properly, needs to know what ports are available from your system. These ports can either be local ports (such as LPT1 or COM2) or they can be ports that are accessible through the network.

To configure your ports, click on the Ports tab. The Print Server Properties dialog box now appears, as shown in Figure 5-5.

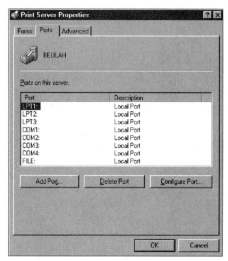

Figure 5-5: The Ports tab is used to define and configure printer ports.

As you can see from the list of ports, quite a list is automatically defined by Windows NT. These are of three types: LPT, which are your parallel ports; COM, which are your serial ports; and FILE, which is a special port that allows you to print to a file. (You learn more about printing to a file later in this chapter.)

In most instances, you do not need to configure your ports. If you decide that you need to configure them or if you just want to review how they are currently configured, simply select a port from the list and then click on the Configure Port button.

For instance, if you choose to configure a serial port, you see the Ports dialog box, which again provides a listing of serial ports. Select (again) the one that you want to configure, and click on the Settings button. This displays the Settings dialog box, as shown in Figure 5-6.

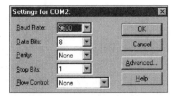

Figure 5-6: When configuring a serial port, you need quite a few pieces of information.

The five drop-down lists in the Settings dialog box allow you to specify how communication should occur over the serial port. In-depth information on serial communications is a bit beyond the scope of this book, but the following provides a quick idea of what each drop-down list means:

- **Baud Rate.** This refers to how fast your printer can accept information. Most serial printers operate at 9600 bps (bits per second), but you should check your printer manual to make sure of what yours accepts.

- **Data Bits.** Information sent over a serial connection is sent in packets, which contain a certain number of data bits. These data bits represent the information to be printed. Normally, PC-based equipment uses eight data bits.

- **Parity.** Some serial connections include a parity bit in the information packets that are transmitted. This bit provides rudimentary error detection. Possible settings are Even (parity is based on whether there are an even number of data bits set to 1), Odd (opposite of Even), None (parity is not used), Mark (parity bit is always set to 1), or Space (parity bit is always set to 0). The default (None) is appropriate for most PC-based equipment.

- **Stop Bits.** An information packet also contains stop bits that mark the end of the packet. You can select from 1, 1.5, or 2 stop bits. (Most equipment uses the default of 1 stop bit.)

- **Flow Control.** This determines how the flow of information over the communications link is managed. The default of Xon/Xoff means that a software signal is used by the printer to indicate when to start and stop sending information. Hardware flow control means that dedicated wires in the serial cable are used for the same signals.

Finally, if None is selected, then information is sent to the printer without pausing. You should check your printer manual to see which type of flow control your printer uses. (Xon/Xoff is the most common, but Hardware is the most efficient.)

When you are done configuring your ports, you can use the Add Port button on the Ports tab of the Print Server Properties dialog box to add additional ports if required for your network. Some networks use specialized printer equipment that allows communication over the network without intervening print servers. Typically you need a driver disk from the printer manufacturer to add these specialized kind of ports.

Managing forms

If you have local printers defined for your print server, you can also define different forms that are available at your site. The Forms tab of the Print Server Properties dialog box is the first form displayed when you open the dialog box, as shown in Figure 5-7.

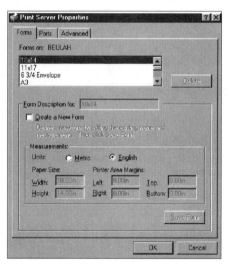

Figure 5-7: You can create custom forms definitions for your print server.

A number of different forms are defined automatically by Windows NT. These forms outline the physical characteristics of the paper (or other media) on which you print. If you select a form in the top section of the dialog box, you can see the specifications for the form in the lower portion.

If you decide that you need to create your own forms, you can do so by clicking on the Create a New Form check box. This effectively allows you to edit the form that you previously picked in the top of the dialog box, but you can give the form a new name so that you don't overwrite the original form definition.

Tip

When you think of forms, you probably think of preprinted forms. This is not what Windows NT means by forms. It is better to think of paper sizes rather than forms. You should carefully examine how you use paper in your environment, and then make sure that there is a form definition for every piece of paper that you use with your printers.

The forms that are defined for your print server can be used by any printer at your server. (This is why you needed to have a local printer defined before you could work with forms.) Later in this chapter, you learn how you can assign different forms to different types of printers.

Managing Your Printers

If you look back at your Printers folder, notice that printers appear as objects within the folder. These objects are nothing more than printer definitions that control how Windows NT communicates with the physical printer. There are many aspects to managing a printer, but perhaps the best place to begin is at the beginning — how to add a printer.

Adding a new printer

When we think of printers, we often think of the physical devices sitting near our desks or down the hall in the printing room. This is one way to look at printers, but Windows NT views them a bit differently.

Instead of physical printers, Windows NT deals with *logical* printers. Logical printers are defined by specifying the rules by which the physical printer should be treated. Each of the printer icons that appears in the Printers folder represents a logical printer definition.

Secret

If you think about this concept, it means you can create multiple logical definitions for the same printer; this is very powerful. As an example, assume that you have a single printer attached to your system. You can create one definition that allows the printer to be treated one way and another definition that uses a different set of rules. When you print to one logical printer, the job is handled one way, and printing to the other causes the job to be handled entirely differently.

For instance, let's say that you have a physical printer attached to your computer, and that you create three logical definitions that use the printer. One definition may print to the printer using a higher priority than the other two definitions. The second definition may print two copies of each print job, and the final definition may only allow printing between the hours of 6:00 pm and 7:00 am.

The first printer definition could be used for your local print jobs, the second for special jobs that demand an extra copy, and the final definition could be shared on the network, allowing others to print to your printer during off hours.

As you consider adding printers to your system, you need to think through how you do your work and how you want your printer to do its work. This allows you to create flexible printer definitions that make you more productive.

The one icon that is always available in the Printers folder is the Add Printer icon. This icon, when opened, starts the Add Printer Wizard, which walks you through the process of defining a printer. The first dialog box that is used by this Wizard is displayed in Figure 5-8.

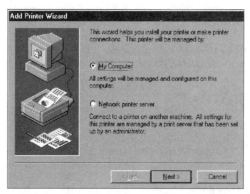

Figure 5-8: The Add Printer Wizard helps you define a printer.

This dialog box is where you specify the most fundamental issue about printing under Windows NT — where is the printer located. There are two choices from this dialog box:

■ **My Computer.** Choose this option (the default) if the printer is physically connected to your computer via one of your parallel or serial ports or if you are printing to a disk file.

■ **Network Printer Server.** Choose this option if the printer is connected to a different computer that you can access through a network or if the printer is connected directly to your network.

You should make your selection and then click on the <u>N</u>ext button. Based on the type of printer that you are installing, you see different steps in the rest of the Wizard. The next section details how to add a local printer, whereas the following one treats the topic of adding a network printer.

Adding a local printer

When adding a local printer, you are first asked how the printer is connected. You learned a bit about printer ports earlier in this chapter, and the Add Printer Wizard displays a dialog box (Figure 5-9) that allows you to pick the port that you want to use.

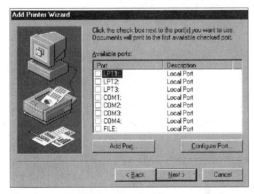

Figure 5-9: To define a local printer, you need to specify a local printer port.

You should select the check boxes beside the printer ports to which you want to print. Notice that you can pick more than one port. This is helpful if you have multiple printers and you tend to keep them very busy.

If you select multiple ports, Windows NT attempts to print to the first port that you have selected; if it is busy, Windows NT prints to the next port that you have selected. In this way, you can define your own *printer pool* to receive the output that you generate.

Note

You can use the Add Port and Configure Port buttons to control the ports that are visible. These buttons work the same way as they do when you are managing your print server. The use of these buttons is described earlier in this chapter.

When you are ready to continue, click on the Next button. This displays the next Add Printer Wizard dialog box, as shown in Figure 5-10. This dialog box lists all of the printers that are supported by Windows NT Workstation 4.0.

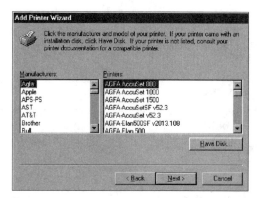

Figure 5-10: Windows NT supports a wide range of printers.

In the <u>M</u>anufacturers list (at the left side of the dialog box), select the manufacturer of your printer. As you select different manufacturers, the information in the <u>P</u>rinters list changes automatically. When you have selected your printer manufacturer, select the model of the printer that you are installing.

When you pick a printer manufacturer and model, you are informing Windows NT of the type of printer driver that you need to have installed. Even though Windows NT provides drivers for hundreds of different printers, it is possible that your brand-new printer is not listed.

In such a case, you should get a disk from the printer manufacturer that has Windows NT printer drivers on it. If the manufacturer did not supply such a disk, contact its technical support department. Many times you can download the required drivers from a bulletin-board service or from the Internet. After you have the drivers, you can click on the <u>H</u>ave Disk button and install your drivers.

If the printer manufacturer does not yet provide a printer driver for Windows NT 4.0, you may be able to select a compatible printer driver from those listed in the Add Printer Wizard. For instance, you may select a driver of an older model of your printer. In addition, the following information may be helpful in determining which alternate printer driver to use:

■ If your laser printer is compatible with Hewlett-Packard's Printer Control Language (PCL) codes, choose HP as the manufacturer and HP LaserJet Plus as the printer.

■ If your PostScript laser printer has support for 35 or more built-in fonts or it emulates PostScript, choose Apple as the manufacturer and Apple LaserWriter Plus v38.0 as the printer.

- If you have a color PostScript laser printer, select QMS as the manufacturer and try several of the QMS ColorScript printers until you find one that supplies all the features that you need.

- If your 9-pin dot-matrix printer is IBM compatible, select IBM as the manufacturer and IBM ProPrinter as the printer. You can also choose Generic as the manufacturer and Generic IBM Graphics 9-pin or Generic IBM Graphics 9-pin Wide as the printer.

- If your 9-pin dot-matrix printer is Epson compatible, select Epson as the manufacturer and Epson FX-80 as the printer.

- If your 24-pin dot-matrix printer is IBM compatible, select IBM as the manufacturer and IBM ProPrinter X24 as the printer.

- If your 24-pin dot-matrix printer is Epson compatible, select Epson as the manufacturer and Epson LQ-1500 as the printer.

After selecting your printer, click on the Next button. This displays the dialog box shown in Figure 5-11.

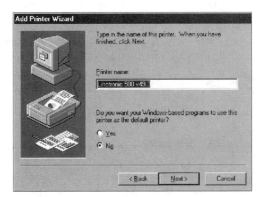

Figure 5-11: You can provide any name that you like for your printer.

Here you can enter a name for your printer. You can enter any printer name that you want, up to 241 characters in length. At the bottom of the dialog box, you can specify whether you want this printer to be the default printer for your system.

When you are ready to continue, click on the Next button. This displays a dialog box that allows you to share your printer over the network (see Figure 5-12). To share the printer, click on the Shared radio button, and then provide a name under which the printer is to be shared.

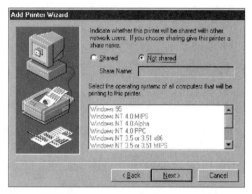

Figure 5-12: You may want to share your printer with others on your network.

Secret

If you enter a shared name ending in a dollar sign, other workstations on your network cannot see your printer when browsing. The printer name is visible from a server but not from a workstation. People can still connect to your shared printer, however, as long as they explicitly enter the name instead of simply browsing to it.

If you decide to share your printer, you need to pick the types of computers that are to be printing to your printer. This is done so that Windows NT can load the proper printer drivers for the different computer systems. When you click on the Next button, you see the final dialog box for the Add Printer Wizard, as shown in Figure 5-13.

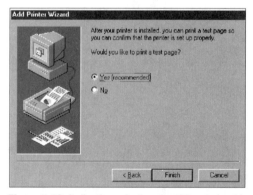

Figure 5-13: Indicating whether the Wizard should print a test page is the final step in adding a printer.

In this dialog box, you can indicate whether or not you want Windows to print a test page. If the printer that you are installing is connected to a port on your system, you should click on Yes. On the other hand, if your printer output is directed to a file, select No. (There is no real need to print a test page to a file.)

After you click on the Finish button, the necessary printer drivers are loaded. You may be asked at this point to supply the Windows NT CD-ROM. When the driver installation is finished, the test page is generated, if you chose to print one.

When you have completed your printer installation, you are given the chance to change the properties of the printer. Exactly how you modify the properties depends on what you want to accomplish by modifying them.

Modifying properties is discussed in many places in the remainder of this chapter; for now you can close the properties dialog box. You should notice that an icon appears in the Printers folder for your new printer. You can use this new icon to manage the printer, as described shortly.

Adding a network printer

When adding a network printer, you are first asked to indicate where the printer is located. You do this by using a network browser, similar to what you use when browsing the Network Neighborhood. (This is shown in Figure 5-14.)

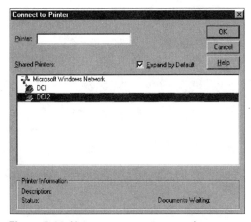

Figure 5-14: You can connect to any printer shared on your network.

You should browse around your network until you find the printer that you want to be connected to. As an alternative, you can type the UNC (universal naming convention) for the printer in the Printer field at the top of the dialog box. When you are done, click on the OK button. This loads the printer drivers for the network printer (if necessary) and then displays the final screen of the Add Printer Wizard (shown in Figure 5-15).

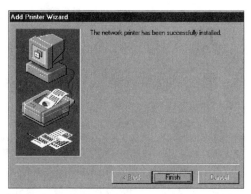

Figure 5-15: Adding a printer over the network is fast and easy.

To finish the installation, click on the Finish button. The newly defined printer should appear in the Printers folder. You can tell that this printer is accessed through the network because the printer icon has a small network cable running under it.

Note

You are not given the opportunity to print a test page when you connect to a network printer. It would appear that Microsoft feels there is less to go wrong when connecting to a network printer.

Removing a printer definition

It makes sense that hardware configurations change over time. For instance, you may add new printers and need to delete old printers, or a printer that you previously had access to through your network is no longer available to you. Windows NT makes it easy to delete a printer definition.

Just follow these steps:

STEPS

Removing a printer

Step 1. Open the Printers folder so that you can see the icon for the printer that you want to delete.

Step 2. Click on the printer that you want to delete. (Make sure that you only highlight the printer icon; don't open it.)

Step 3. Press Delete or choose Delete from the File menu.

Step 4. When asked to confirm your action, click on the Yes button.

Once deleted, the printer icon is removed from the Printers folder. There is no way to undo this action. Instead, you must add the printer again, as described earlier in this chapter.

Note

When you remove a printer definition and the definition was for a network printer, your action does not make the printer inaccessible to other people on the network. If, however, you have a local printer that you were sharing over the network, and you delete the definition for that printer, then no one else on the network can access your printer.

Changing printer settings

Windows NT provides you with quite a bit of control over how your printer is controlled. This is done from the Device Settings tab of the printer's Properties dialog box. Many options can appear in this dialog box, depending on the type of printer that you have defined. Figure 5-16 shows an example of the Properties dialog box with the Device Settings tab selected.

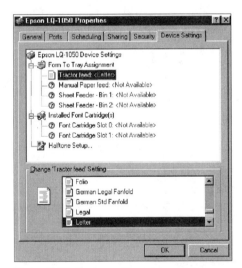

Figure 5-16: Device settings for a printer are highly dependent on the capabilities of the printer itself.

The example shown in Figure 5-16 is from an Epson LQ-1050, which does not have many device options. The device settings available are shown in a hierarchical layout, meaning that you can select either individual options to change, or you can select entire groups.

When you select an option in the upper part of the dialog box, you can then change the setting for that option in the bottom portion. The way that you make changes depends on the option being changed, but the controls that you use are the same controls that you have used in similar dialog boxes in other parts of Windows.

As an example, if you look back at Figure 5-16, you can see that the Tractor feed option is selected in the top of the dialog box. This option is within the Form To Tray Assignment group, so you can tell that you are assigning a form to be used with the tractor feed. (Forms are defined on a print-server level and were covered earlier in this chapter.)

At the bottom of the dialog box, you can select the form that is being used in the tractor feed. For instance, if you scroll through the forms, you may pick a wider form, one that reflects the wide, continuous paper in your printer.

When you are done making changes to one option, you can then make changes to others. The number of available options depends on the printer that you are configuring. For instance, Figure 5-17 shows the same tab setting for the QMS ColorScript 1000 printer, which you can tell right away has more options.

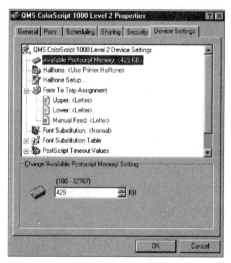

Figure 5-17: Different printers have different numbers and types of available options.

In all likelihood, you need to set your printer options only once — when you first install your printer. After that, unless you make changes in the way that you use your printer, you don't need to change these options again. When you are done making changes, click on the OK button to close the Properties dialog box.

Understanding print processors

The Windows NT printing system uses a print processor to prepare information to be printed; you learned a bit about this earlier in the chapter. Windows NT enables you to control which print processor is used for a particular printer.

When a printer is created, NT installs the winprint print processor. This is the default print processor, but you may have special applications that install additional print processors.

Most of the time, you should not need to change the print processor that you are using or the default data type that is used by the processor. When configuring your printer, Windows NT allows you to make modifications to this area. You can access the print processor configuration area by following these steps:

STEPS

Changing the print processor

Step 1. Open the Printers folder so that you can see the icon of the printer that you want to configure.

Step 2. Right-click on the printer icon. This displays a Context menu.

Step 3. Choose the Properties option from the Context menu. This displays the Properties dialog box for the printer; a sample is shown in Figure 5-18.

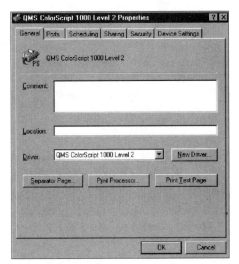

Figure 5-18: The Properties dialog box for a printer allows you to set many different options.

(continued)

STEPS *(continued)*

Changing the print processor

Step 4.   Click on the Print Processor button. This displays the Print Processor dialog box, as shown in Figure 5-19.

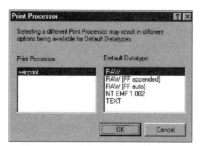

Figure 5-19: You can change the print processor that is used by Windows NT.

On the left side of the dialog box is a list of print processors that are available for the printer. On the right side is a list of data types that can be specified for the print processor that is chosen on the left side. For the winprint print processor, you can select several different data types. These include the following types:

■ **NT EMF.** Information is stored in a metafile format (an intermediary format) that conserves disk space and results in faster print times.

■ **NT JNL.** Information in the print job is stored in an intermediary file format that relies on the Windows GDI interface to process the information in the job. Information is stored in the print job partially processed which allows the application to finish faster. The print processor then calls on the GDI routines to finish processing the file in the background before it is sent to the printer.

■ **PSCRIPT1.** This data type is used when you have services for the Macintosh installed. This data type instructs the print processor to convert the print job from Level 1 PostScript (native output from the Macintosh) to a monochrome bitmap, which can be printed on a non-PostScript printer.

■ **RAW.** Information destined for the printer is stored in the format native to the printer. It is passed directly from the printer driver to the print router without alteration by the print processor.

- **RAW [FF appended].** This is the same as the RAW format, except that the print processor appends a form feed at the end of all print jobs. This data type should be used if you have problems getting the final page of your job to print when the RAW format is selected.

- **RAW [FF auto].** This is the same as the RAW format, except that the print processor appends a form feed at the end of the print job if it does not see one there already.

- **TEXT.** Information is assumed to be regular ANSI text. The print processor formats the file using the standard codes that are necessary for the target printer. Thus, if the target is a PostScript printer, this data type prints a text file correctly, which normally doesn't happen with PostScript.

The data types that are visible in the Print Processor dialog box also depend on the type of printer that you are configuring.

Using separator pages

In a networked environment, where a printer is shared among many people, it is often beneficial to use separator pages between print jobs. Windows NT Workstation allows you to define separator pages for each of your printers. Thus, you could have one style of separator page for your dot-matrix printers and another for your laser printers.

There are three sample separator pages supplied with Windows NT Workstation:

- **SYSPRINT.SEP.** This file works with PostScript printers and prints a single separator page between each print job.

- **PCL.SEP.** This file works with PCL printers and prints a single separator page between each print job.

- **PSCRIPT.SEP.** This file works with PostScript printers, but it does not print a separator page. It simply switches the printer to PostScript mode in preparation for the incoming print job.

These files are located in the c:\winnt\system32 directory. If you want to create your own separator pages, you can copy one of these files and then modify it to fit your needs. For instance, the following list shows the contents of the PCL.SEP file:

```
\
\H1B\L%-12345X@PJL ENTER LANGUAGE=PCL
\H1B\L&l1T\0
\H34
\B\S\N\4
\I\4
\U\D\4
\E
```

This short file actually does quite a bit, but it uses special commands that are understood by the Windows NT print system. In this file, the commands begin with the backslash (\) character. Table 5-1 shows the meanings of the different commands that you can use in a separator file.

Table 5-1   Commands that are used in separator files

Command	Meaning
\	This single character must be the first line of the separator file; it defines the delimiter character to be used in the rest of the file.
\W*nn*	Sets the width of the separator page to *nn* characters. The default is 80 characters, and the maximum is 256.
\N	Prints the user name that is associated with the print job.
\I	Prints the document ID number from the print spooler.
\D	Prints the date that the document was created.
\T	Prints the time that the document was created.
\L	Prints literal text, which is everything following \L, until the next command is encountered.
\F*filename*	Copies the contents of the specified file to the printer. The *filename* parameter can include a full path.
\B\S	Turns on single-width block printing.
\B\M	Turns on double-width block printing.
\U	Turns off block printing.
n	Skips *n* lines on the printout (n may be 0 through 9).
\H*nn*	Sends a hexadecimal value to the printer. Used primarily for sending control codes to the printer. This is very printer-specific; refer to your printer manual for the available control codes.
\E	Ejects the page.

Based on the information in Table 5-1, you can deduct exactly what the PCL separator page is doing. It first sets the delimiter character (which is required in the first line of the file) and then switches the printer to PCL language. The third line sends printer control codes to set up the printed page, as does the fourth. The fifth line turns on single-width block printing, after which the user's name is printed and four lines are skipped.

Then the print-job ID is printed, and another four lines are skipped. Block printing is then turned off, the date of the print job is printed, and another four lines are skipped. Finally, the page is ejected.

The PostScript separator page (SYSPRINT.SEP) is a bit more complex than the PCL page. This file does not use the backslash as the command delimiter; it uses the at sign (@):

```
@
@Lerrordict begin /handleerror { $error begin newerror { /newerror
false
@Ldef showpage 72 72 scale /x .25 def /y 10 def /Helvetica findfont
.2
@Lscalefont setfont x y moveto (PostScript Error Handler)
@Lshow /y y .2 sub .2 sub def x y moveto
@L(Offending Command = ) show /command load { dup type /stringtype
ne { (
@Lmax err string ) cvs } if show } exec /y y .2 sub def x y moveto
(Error
@L= ) show errorname { dup type dup ( max err string ) cvs show ( :
) show
@L/stringtype ne { ( max err string ) cvs } if show } exec /y y .2
sub def
@Lx y moveto (Stack =) show ostack { /y y .2 sub def x 1 add y
moveto dup
@Ltype /stringtype ne { ( max err string ) cvs } if show } forall
showpage
@L} if end } def end
@L% Pull off the job specific values:
@L%————————
@L/name (@N@L) def
@L/jobid(@I@L) def
@L/date (@D@L) def
@L/time (@T@L) def
@L% Get the page limits
@L%————————
@Lnewpath clippath closepath pathbbox
@L/ymax exch def
@L/xmax exch def
@L/ymin exch def
@L/xmin exch def
@L/PrintWidth xmax xmin sub def
@L/PrintHeight ymax ymin sub def
@L% Define some handy procedures and values
@L%————————
@L/inch {72 mul} def
@L/White 1 def
@L/Black 0 def
@L/Gray .9 def
@L/CenterString {
@L     /str exch def /width exch def
@L     width str stringwidth pop sub 2 div 0 rmoveto
@L     str
@L} def
@L% Print the printers logo (if any)
@L%————————  --
@L/SysPrint where
```

```
@L{
@L      pop
@L      SysPrint
@L}{
@L      /Times-Roman findfont .5 72 mul scalefont setfont
@L      PrintWidth 2 div 6 72 mul moveto
@L      (\\\\server\\name) dup stringwidth pop 2 div neg 0 rmoveto
show
@L      PrintWidth 2 div 5 72 mul moveto
@L      (PSCRIPT Page Separator) dup stringwidth pop 2 div neg 0
rmoveto show
@L}ifelse
@L% Set some standard parameters
@L%————————--
@L100 0 {dup mul exch dup mul add 1 exch sub} setscreen
@L2 setlinewidth 2 setmiterlimit
@L% Clear and outline the title area
@L%————————--
@Lnewpath
@Lxmin ymax moveto
@Lxmax ymax lineto
@Lxmax ymax 1.5 inch sub lineto
@Lxmin ymax 1.5 inch sub lineto
@Lclosepath
@Lgsave
@Lcurrentgray 1 setgray fill setgray
@Lgrestore
@Lcurrentlinewidth 1 setlinewidth stroke setlinewidth
@L% Add the label header
@L%————————-
@L/Helvetica findfont .2 inch scalefont setfont
@L% Date ————————
@Lxmin .25 inch add ymax .2 inch sub moveto
@L(Date: ) show date show
@L% Time
@LPrintWidth 1.5 inch sub ymax .2 inch sub moveto
@L(Time: ) show time show
@L% Job Number
@LPrintWidth 2 div ymax .2 inch sub moveto
@Ljobid stringwidth pop
@L( : ) stringwidth pop
@Lname  stringwidth pop
@Ladd add 2 div
@Lneg 0 rmoveto
@Ljobid show ( : ) show name show
@L% Underline label header
@Lnewpath
@Lxmin ymax .3 inch sub moveto xmax ymax .3 inch sub lineto
@Lclosepath
@Lstroke
@L% Add the username
@L%————————--
```

```
@L/Helvetica-Bold findfont 1 inch scalefont setfont
@Lnewpath
@Lxmin ymax 1.25 inch sub moveto
@LPrintWidth name CenterString true charpath
@Lclosepath
@Lgsave
@LGray setgray fill
@Lgrestore
@Lstroke
@Lshowpage
@E
```

In this file, each line begins with @L, except for the last line, which begins with @E. Remember that the at sign (@) is the same as the backslash, which is used in Table 5-1.

Thus, @L is the same as \L, which means that literal text is being sent, and @E is the same as \E, which means that the page is ejected. In the case of this file, the literal text being sent is composed entirely of PostScript commands.

Although explaining PostScript is beyond the scope of this book, there is some information that you can pull from the file. The most important is near the beginning of the file, where a couple of other delimited separator-file commands are used:

```
@L/name (@N@L) def
@L/jobid(@I@L) def
@L/date (@D@L) def
@L/time (@T@L) def
```

These lines set up PostScript definitions, assigning @N (the user's name) to the variable *name,* @I (the print job ID) to the variable *jobid,* @D (the print date) to the variable *date,* and @T (the print time) to the variable *time.* These variables are then used later in the file to produce the output.

After you have a separator page created, you can use it in your print jobs. You do this by following these steps:

STEPS

Adding a separator page

Step 1. Open the Printers folder so that you can see the icon of the printer for which you want to assign a separator page.

Step 2. Right-click on the printer icon. This displays a Context menu.

Step 3. Choose the Properties option from the Context menu. This displays the Properties dialog box for the printer.

(continued)

STEPS *(continued)*

Adding a separator page

Step 4.   Click on the Separator Page button. This displays the Separator Page dialog box, as shown in Figure 5-20.

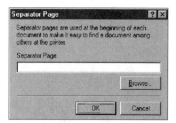

Figure 5-20: The Separator Page dialog box allows you to specify a file to print between jobs.

Step 5.   In the Separator Page field, enter the full filename (including the path) for the separator page file that you want to use.

Step 6.   Click on the OK button.

Step 7.   Close the Properties dialog box and the Printers folder.

Tip

If your printers are expensive to operate — for instance, a color laser printer or a dye-sublimation printer — you may not want to use separator pages. Print jobs on these types of printers tend to be small, and by using separator pages, you may increase your operational costs by 50 to 100 percent.

Sharing your printer

Windows NT Workstation allows you to share any of your local printers; this means that you can make them available to other people on the network. After you have successfully installed your printer and can use it for your local work, you are ready to share it on the network.

Before assuming that you must share your printer (unless your boss says you need to), you should consider how sharing a printer can affect the use of your system and your printer. If you have a shared printer that is attached to your local system, you should expect the following:

- **Delays.** If other people are using your printer, you cannot print your work. In fact, your work becomes just another job in the queue, behind whoever else is already there.

- **Interruptions.** If your printer is located in your office (as printers typically are), then you often suffer interruptions as people come to get their print jobs.

- **Service.** With more work going through your printer, it will need toner, ribbons, ink, paper, and other consumables more often than if you were using it by yourself.

Just because there are potential problems, however, does not mean that you should not share your printer. In many environments, it makes economic sense to share expensive printers. You can share your printer by following these steps:

STEPS

Sharing a printer

Step 1. Open the Printers folder so that you can see the icon of the printer that you want to share.

Step 2. Right-click on the printer icon. This displays a Context menu.

Step 3. Choose the Properties option from the Context menu. This displays the Properties dialog box for the printer.

Step 4. Click on the Sharing tab. The Properties dialog box now appears as shown in Figure 5-21.

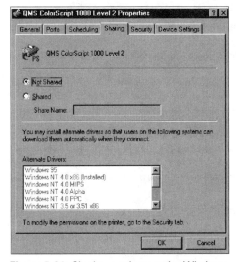

Figure 5-21: Sharing a printer under Windows NT is easy.

(continued)

STEPS *(continued)*

Sharing a printer

Step 5.   Click on the Shared radio button.

Step 6.   In the Share Name field, enter the name that you want others to see for your printer.

Step 7.   Click on the OK button.

Step 8.   Close the Printers folder.

Once these steps are completed, your printer is immediately available for other people to use. If you look back at Figure 5-21, notice that enabling the shared printer is not the only thing that you can do on the Sharing tab of the Properties dialog box. In fact, even though sharing is quite easy, there are some other considerations that you may need to look into when you share your printer. These are covered in the following sections.

Secret

Windows NT allows you to use long names for printers and then share them over the network. If you use a long printer name (more than eight characters), and the printer is accessed from a Windows 95 system, you could run into some software problems. Some older 16-bit software, running under Windows 95, will generate GPF errors (and crash wonderfully) when trying to print to a network printer with a long name.

Understanding alternate drivers

Windows NT, in implementing a print server, supports the concept of alternate printer drivers. This recognizes the fact that not all computers attached to a network may be the same.

For instance, you may have several different versions of Windows running on the various workstations on your network. Unfortunately, not every version of Windows uses the same printer drivers.

To get around this, Windows NT allows you to specify additional printer drivers that can be loaded on your server and then used when a system using another version of Windows tries to print through your shared printer. Windows NT allows you to load the following types of printer drivers:

- **Windows NT 3.1.** You can load printer driver versions for Intel, MIPS, and DEC Alpha systems.

- **Windows NT 3.5.** You can load printer driver versions for Intel, MIPS, and DEC Alpha systems.

- **Windows NT 3.51.** You can load printer driver versions for Intel, MIPS, DEC Alpha, and Power PC systems.

- **Windows NT 4.0.** You can load printer driver versions for Intel, MIPS, DEC Alpha, and Power PC – based systems.

- **Windows 95.**

In all, there are twelve different types of printer drivers that you can install. To add these additional printer drivers, you must first make sure that the printer has been shared (as discussed in the previous section) and then follow these steps:

STEPS

Picking alternate printer drivers

Step 1. Open the Printers folder so that you can see the icon of the printer that you want to share.

Step 2. Right-click on the printer icon. This displays a Context menu.

Step 3. Choose the Properties option from the Context menu. This displays the Properties dialog box for the printer.

Step 4. Click on the Sharing tab. The Properties dialog box now appears, as shown earlier in Figure 5-21.

Step 5. In the Alternate Drivers list at the bottom of the dialog box, select the printer drivers that you want to install. You can select additional drivers by holding Ctrl as you click on each driver name.

Step 6. Click on the OK button.

Step 7. Close the Printers folder.

Setting security permissions

If you don't want to give full printer access to everyone on the network, then you can use the permissions feature of Windows NT to make limitations. As the name implies, security permissions are a part of the Windows NT security system. Even though you learn the most about security in Chapter 16, here are some tips to limit access to your printer right now.

To change permissions on who can access your printer, use the following steps. If you need more information on security in general, refer to Chapter 16.

STEPS

Setting permissions for your printer

Step 1. Open the Printers folder so that you can see the icon of the printer that you want to share.

Step 2. Right-click on the printer icon. This displays a Context menu.

Step 3. Choose the Properties option from the Context menu. This displays the Properties dialog box for the printer.

Step 4. Click on the Security tab. The Properties dialog box changes to display three buttons that are related to security.

Step 5. Click on the Permissions button. This displays the Printer Permissions dialog box, as shown in Figure 5-22.

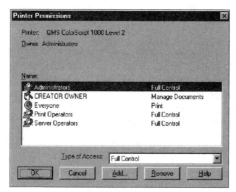

Figure 5-22: Windows NT Workstation provides you with complete control over who can access your resources.

Step 6. Review the list of users and groups that have access to your printer. Then use the Add and Remove buttons to manipulate the list.

Step 7. If desired, select a user or group and use the Type of Access drop-down list to specify how much access that user or group should have.

Step 8. Click on the OK button.

Step 9. Close the Properties dialog box and the Printers folder.

Setting availability and printing priorities

One of the helpful tools that you have at your disposal when managing printers is the ability to define the availability of a printer. Windows NT allows you to specify what time of day a printer is available. This means that you can define a printer and then make that printer available only during certain hours.

For instance, you may have a single printer that is connected to your system. You could actually define two printers, both of which control the same physical printer, with the following characteristics:

- **Full.** This printer definition allows high-priority access to the printer around the clock.

- **Limited.** This printer definition allows lower-priority access to the printer only between 9:00 p.m. and 6:00 a.m.

You would use the first printer for all of your work and allow access to the second printer over the network. Then, when people print to your printer, their jobs are queued until 9:00 p.m., when they start printing. In addition, if you have a large job that can wait, you can also print to the second printer. The result is better use of your printer with less interruption of your normal work day.

To adjust the scheduling of a printer, follow these steps:

STEPS

Setting availability and priority for your printer

Step 1. Open the Printers folder so that you can see the icon of the printer that you want to share.

Step 2. Right-click on the printer icon. This displays a Context menu.

Step 3. Choose the Properties option from the Context menu. This displays the Properties dialog box for the printer.

(continued)

STEPS *(continued)*

Setting availability and priority for your printer

Step 4.   Click on the Scheduling tab. The Properties dialog box now appears, as shown in Figure 5-23.

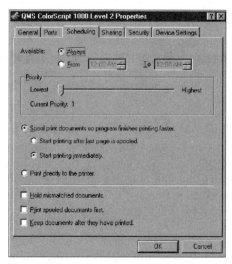

Figure 5-23: You have complete control over when your printer is available.

Step 5.   Click on the From and To radio buttons to limit the hours during which this printer is available. In the two time fields, indicate a beginning and ending time, respectively.

Step 6.   Using the Priority control, slide the marker to indicate the importance of the print jobs that are sent to this printer.

In addition, you can use the different check boxes and radio buttons at the bottom of the dialog box to control how individual print jobs are treated on the printer. For instance, you can indicate whether the jobs should be spooled or sent directly to the printer without spooling. If you are spooling the jobs (the default), you can also indicate when printing should begin.

Caution

Although printing directly to the printer without spooling provides the fastest printout possible, it is not necessarily the most productive. While the application is printing to a direct-printer definition, you cannot do anything else with it. You can work on other applications under Windows NT, but the application that is printing remains busy until the print job is completed.

Managing Your Print Jobs

Once your printers are correctly installed and configured, you are ready to use Windows NT to create your printed output. Creating print jobs is only half the story, however.

Through effective use of the Printers folder you have complete control over how your jobs are printed under Windows NT. The ins and outs of managing your print jobs are covered in the following sections.

Creating a print job

Print jobs are created by the various applications. As you work with your software, you periodically click on the Print button or choose the Print command from the File menu. The application then works with the printer driver to create a print job and submit it to the Windows NT spooler. Before you print from your application, you should check the following items:

- Make sure that you have selected the proper printer. Most full-featured applications allow you to select which printer you want to use for your output.

- Make sure that you have defined the proper page characteristics. Many applications allow you to specify paper size, margins, printing order, number of copies, and so on.

- Make sure that you have selected the proper paper source. Many printers support multiple sources for paper, such as different trays or manual feed.

- Make sure that the printer is turned on and is available for use. If the printer is not turned on, you may not get part of your print job, or the job could end up at a different printer (if you have a printer pool set up).

If the application that you are using is very simple (that is, it does not provide a great deal of control over the printer), then you may need to specify the default printer outside of the application. For instance, most of the accessories that are supplied with Windows NT print only to the default printer and don't give you the capability of changing destinations from within the program. To change the default printer, follow these steps:

STEPS

Setting the default printer

Step 1. Open the Printers folder so that you can see the icon of the printer that you want to share.

(continued)

STEPS (continued)

Setting the default printer

Step 2. Click on the printer that you want to be the default.

Step 3. Choose the Set As Default option from the File menu. A check mark should then appear beside this option.

Step 4. Close the Printers folder window.

Working with the printer queue

You learned earlier in this chapter that one of the jobs of a print spooler is to maintain print jobs in a queue until a time that they can be handled by the printer. Windows NT provides you with a great deal of control over the printer queue.

Even though the spooler maintains only a single printer queue, you manage the jobs based on which printer was used to place the job in the queue. Thus, to view the print jobs in the queue for a specific printer, you simply double-click on that printer's icon in the Printers folder. This displays a window similar to Figure 5-24.

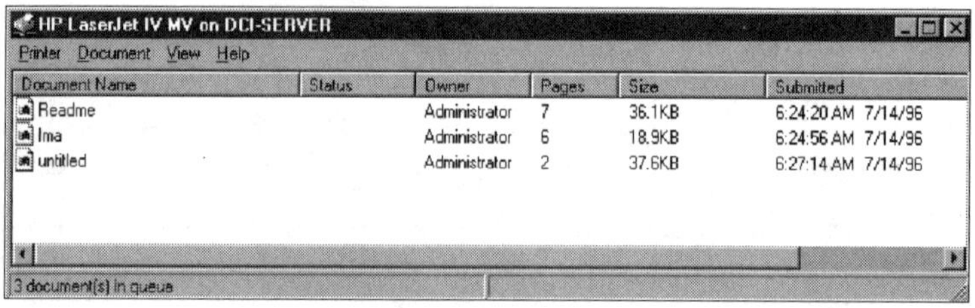
HP LaserJet IV MV on DCI-SERVER
Printer Document View Help
Document Name
Status
Owner
Pages
Size
Submitted
Readme Administrator 7 36.1KB 6:24:20 AM 7/14/96
Ima Administrator 6 18.9KB 6:24:56 AM 7/14/96
untitled Administrator 2 37.6KB 6:27:14 AM 7/14/96
3 document(s) in queue

Figure 5-24: A print queue window shows the different print jobs that are waiting at a printer.

The printer queue window lists the various print jobs that are being worked on by the spooler, for the printer being viewed. The information that is displayed for each print job includes the following:

- **Document Name.** When you print a document from an application, the application creates a name for it. Typically this is some combination of the application name and the name of the document.
- **Status.** The status of the print processor in relation to this job. Typically this is a single word, such as Spooling, Printing, or Error.

- **Owner.** The user ID of the person who submitted the job to the printer.

- **Pages.** An approximate page count for the file being printed. Sometimes the print processor does a great job counting pages; other times, this figure can be off by quite a bit.

- **Size.** The number of bytes that are left in the file. As jobs are sent to the printer, you can watch the size decrease.

- **Submitted.** The date and time that the print job was created.

- **Port.** If you specified multiple ports for a particular printer definition, the port being used is indicated here.

If there are quite a few print jobs in the queue (there could be if the printer is a heavily used network printer), you may want to sort the jobs in different ways. You do this by clicking the column header (the gray area above a column) by which you want to sort. Thus, if you want to view the print jobs by who created them, click on the Owner column header.

Pausing and resuming the printer

There may be times when you need to stop sending jobs to a particular printer. For instance, you may need to change paper, restart or reset the printer, or perform some other maintenance task. To do this, simply follow these steps:

STEPS

Pausing the printer

Step 1.   Open the Printers folder so that you can see the icon of the printer that you want to pause.

Step 2.   Right-click on the printer that you want to pause. This displays a Context menu for the printer.

Step 3.   Choose the Pause Printing option from the Context menu. A check mark should then appear beside this option; the printer is now paused.

Step 4.   Close the Printers folder window.

When you pause a printer, the printing may not stop immediately. Two things have to happen first:

- The current print job must finish printing.

- The buffer in the printer itself must be emptied.

Once these items are complete, the printer stops printing, and all jobs in the queue continue to "stack up" until you resume the printer. To start printing again, make sure that the printer is turned on and is on-line, and then repeat the same steps that you used to pause the printer in the first place.

Pausing and resuming a print job

Besides stopping the printer itself, you can also pause individual jobs that are destined for the printer. You may want to pause a print job if it is quite large and you prefer to wait before it is printed. Or, you may need to run to the printer to make sure that the proper paper is installed. For any reason, you can pause a print job by following these steps:

STEPS
Pausing a print job

Step 1.   Open the Printers folder so that you can see the icon of the printer that is to process the job that you want to pause.

Step 2.   Double-click on the printer whose queue contains the job that you want to pause. This displays the queue window for the printer.

Step 3.   Right-click on the name of the document that you want to pause. This displays a Context menu for the document.

Step 4.   Choose the Pause option from the Context menu. The word Paused appears in the Status column for the print job.

Step 5.   Close the printer's queue window, and then close the Printers folder window.

While a print job is paused, the effect depends on whether the job was being processed when you paused it. If the job was waiting in the queue but processing had not begun, then it isn't processed until you release it.

Other print jobs can still be processed by the printer, however. If you pause a job that was being printed, then printing is immediately paused.

Because the print spooler was in the middle of printing the job, no other jobs are sent to the printer. (This avoids two jobs getting mixed up with each other.) If you leave the job paused too long, the printer will probably time out, and you must delete the print job and start printing again.

When you want to resume printing, simply repeat the steps for pausing. The only difference is that you choose Resume from the Context menu instead of Pause.

Deleting a print job

There are two ways that you can delete print jobs, depending on the scope that you want to use. If you want to delete all of the print jobs in the queue for a particular printer, you can follow these steps:

STEPS

Deleting all print jobs for a printer

Step 1.   Open the Printers folder so that you can see the icon of the printer whose print jobs you want to delete.

Step 2.   Right-click on the printer icon. This displays a Context menu.

Step 3.   Choose the Purge Print Documents option from the Context menu.

Step 4.   Close the Printers folder window.

The other way that you can delete documents is not so radical. There may be times when you just want to delete a single document. For instance, I delete documents all the time when I realize that I printed something prematurely. To delete a single document in the queue, follow these steps:

STEPS

Deleting a single job for a printer

Step 1.   Open the Printers folder so that you can see the icon of the printer that is processing the print job that you want to delete.

Step 2.   Double-click on the printer icon. This displays the queue window for the printer.

Step 3.   Click on the name of the print job that you want to delete. This highlights the job.

Step 4.   Press Delete. The job status (in the Status column) changes to Deleting, and then the print job disappears from the queue.

Step 5.   Close the printer's queue window, and then close the Printers folder window.

Secret

If you delete a print job that is already being printed, it could have strange effects on your printer. Depending on the capabilities of your printer, it could either mean you get a garbled page of text or the printer could hang completely. This is because the printer doesn't know that you deleted the print job — it was just doing its job when the data stopped coming. In some cases, you may need to restart or reset your printer to put everything back on an even keel.

Changing print job properties

When you first create a print job, the file is assigned priorities based on the default priorities of the printer for which it is destined. As the job is waiting in the queue, you can modify the properties that are associated with the document.

For example, you may look at the print queue and see that your print job is about sixth in line. If you want the job to be handled more quickly, you can give it a higher priority by changing the properties of the document.

Tip

It is generally a good idea to only change the properties of print jobs that have not begun printing. If you need to, pause the print job before it starts printing. After you change the properties, you can release the print job so that it is processed by the spooler.

To display the Properties dialog box for a document, simply right-click on the document name in the queue. This displays a Context menu from which you should choose the Properties option. This displays the Properties dialog box, as shown in Figure 5-25.

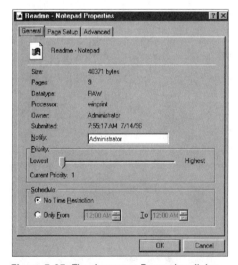

Figure 5-25: The document Properties dialog box allows you to modify how a document is treated by the print spooler.

This dialog box contains three tabs, which you can use to modify the characteristics of the document. The information in each tab can be used in the following ways.

- **General.** This tab allows you to review and set general processing parameters.

- **Page Setup.** This tab allows you to modify a limited set of document characteristics. These settings are only available if your application allowed them to be set in the first place. (Thus, you can't change these for print jobs that are created with many of the Windows NT accessories.)

- **Advanced.** This tab allows you to change how the document takes advantage of printer-specific features. For instance, you can change the forms that are used for the document, how the graphics are processed, and so on. These features are highly printer-specific and very similar to the tabs that you used to control printer features when you first defined the printer.

You probably should not change many of these properties once you have sent the job to the printer. After all, it may be easier to just delete the job and print it again, rather than changing from portrait to landscape mode on the Page Setup tab, for example.

There is one exception to this, and that is the information contained in the General tab. In particular, you can change both the printing priority and the schedule for the job.

When you change the printing priority, you change how your job is printed in relation to other print jobs that are pending. The default priority, based on information in the printer definition that was used to create the job, is 1 — the lowest.

Priorities can go up to 99; those with the higher priorities are printed first by the spooler. Thus, if you were sixth in the queue, you can be processed sooner if you move your priority up a few notches.

The other item that you may want to examine is the Schedule area of the dialog box. This is set according to the availability of the printer, as you defined it when you first added the printer.

If you later decide that this job can wait, you can click on the Only From radio button and then set the times when this job can print. This is helpful if you realize that you just printed a huge job that is not particularly pressing and you don't want to tie up the printer for a long period of time.

When you are done changing the properties of the print job, click on the OK button.

Summary

Windows NT Workstation 4.0 provides unparalleled and unprecedented control of your printing needs. You have the power to define the paper that you use in your printers as well as the printers themselves. Windows NT helps you to work with logical printers, processing the print jobs according to the rules that you establish.

In this chapter, you have learned how to control your printers. In particular, you have learned the following items:

▶ Windows NT Workstation 4.0 enables you to control the print server portion of the operating system. This includes setting print spooler characteristics, defining ports that are used by your printers, and setting up forms that are used by your printer definitions.

▶ You can add either local or network printers to your workstation. Local printers are those that are physically connected to your system, while network printers are those that you access through your network.

▶ As part of a printer definition, Windows NT maintains an extensive inventory of printer capabilities and features. You have complete control over how Windows NT takes advantage of these printer features.

▶ Print processors, and their associated data types, enable you to define how the print spooler processes your print jobs.

▶ Separator pages can be used as delimiters between individual print jobs. Windows NT provides three sample separator pages and provides a way for you to create custom pages.

▶ You can share a local printer with other people over the network. When you do so, you have complete control over how and when the printer is accessed.

▶ After a print job is created, you have control over how and when it prints. You can pause, resume, and delete print jobs as you see fit.

▶ You can modify the properties of a print job. This enables you to exercise last-minute control over how a job is processed by the print spooler.

Your Hardware and Software

PART

◆ ◆ ◆ ◆

In This Part

◆ ◆ ◆ ◆

Chapter 6

Managing Hardware

In This Chapter

Your computer hardware is the starting point for everything that you do with your system. Windows NT provides many different ways that you can interact with your hardware. Through the use of specialized device drivers, you can customize Windows NT to match the hardware that you want to use. In this chapter, you learn how you can control the relationship between Windows NT Workstation and your hardware.

In particular, you learn the following items:

▶ How Windows NT interacts with your hardware

▶ How you can add hardware to your system and make Windows NT aware of it

▶ How you can control your Windows NT configuration through hardware profiles

▶ How to change and control your input devices

How Windows NT Interacts with Hardware

Windows NT is designed to work with a wide variety of computer hardware. This latest release of the operating system includes support for more devices than ever before. To understand how you add hardware to your system, it is helpful to understand a bit about your own system from a hardware level.

In the next couple of sections, you learn about the resources that are available in your system, how Windows NT stores hardware information, and how it communicates with your hardware.

System resources

In the broadest sense of the term, resources can be just about anything in your computer system. For instance, hard disk space could be a resource as could your video system. At a nuts-and-bolts level, however, system resources refer to fundamental communications channels and memory areas of your system.

From the perspective of adding a hardware device, resources consist of the following items:

- IRQs
- I/O ports
- DMA channels
- Memory addresses

A proper understanding of these resources is critical to configuring Windows NT to work with your hardware. Each of your primary resources is discussed in the following sections.

Interrupt request lines (IRQs)

An *interrupt request line* is used by a hardware device to signal the CPU that it needs attention. These lines are implemented through a series of physical wires on the motherboard. When a device needs attention, it sends a signal across one of the wires. This signal is received by the CPU, which then services the device, thereby fulfilling its request for attention.

Note

You may wonder why the acronym IRQ does not match the first letters of the words that it stands for (interrupt request line). This is a good question, and the actual reasons may be lost in the arcane corners of computer history. The best answer is that IRQ was borrowed from the name of the electrical signal line on the first CPUs in which IRQs were implemented. These lines were simply labeled IRQ on all the drawings and technical documents.

In the majority of PC systems, there are 16 IRQs. These are assigned a number, 0 through 15, with the lower-number interrupts having the highest priority. Each IRQ can be used by a single device that is installed in your system. This limitation is imposed because of how the hardware in your system is implemented. If you have two devices that use the same IRQ line, then confusion results, and the CPU doesn't know which device should be serviced when the interrupt occurs.

The 16 IRQs in today's PCs are implemented through the use of two special-ized programmable interrupt controllers (PICs) on your computer's mother-board. These controllers are connected to each other through IRQ 2. Table 6-1 details the common uses of the 16 PC interrupts.

Table 6-1   Standard PC IRQ line assignments

IRQ	Use
0	System timer
1	Keyboard controller
2	Second IRQ controller
3	Serial port 2 (COM2)
4	Serial port 1 (COM1)
5	Parallel port 2 (LPT2)
6	Floppy disk controller
7	Parallel port 1 (LPT1)
8	Real-time clock
9	Available
10	Available
11	Available
12	MousePort connector
13	Math coprocessor
14	Hard disk controller
15	Available

Notice from Table 6-1 that only a certain number of IRQs (9, 10, 11, and 15) are available for use. This is a bit deceiving, as some of the other IRQs may also be available in your system. For instance, IRQ 5 is used for LPT2, but your system may not have a second parallel port. In this case, you can safely use IRQ 5 for any other purpose.

I/O ports

It is essential for your hardware devices to be able to communicate with the rest of the world — at least the world within your computer system. For instance, your serial ports must be able to communicate with the CPU. Likewise, the audio card must be able to communicate with your system.

Communication between hardware devices and the CPU occurs through an I/O port address. The address is located at a very low memory address, which enables the communication to occur very quickly at a reserved location. Each hardware device in your system must have its own I/O port address; if two devices share the same address, the CPU (and, by extension, the operating system) cannot reliably communicate with either device.

The number of "standard" I/O port addresses in a PC is very limited. This is not to say that the number of potential I/O port addresses is limited; on the contrary, quite a few are available. But those addresses on which you can rely have developed because the devices with which they are associated are fairly standard. Table 6-2 details the I/O port addresses that are used in a normal PC.

Table 6-2   Standard PC I/O port address assignments

Address	Use
0x3F8	COM1
0x2F8	COM2
0x3E8	COM3
0x2E8	COM4
0x3BC	LPT1
0x378	LPT2
0x278	LPT3

Because most hardware devices that you install in your system must use one (or more) I/O port addresses, you must make sure that these devices do not conflict with each other. You do this by making sure that a new card does not overlap or use the address that is used by the standard devices, and that it does not use any of the addresses that are being used by your other devices.

DMA channels

DMA is an acronym for *direct memory access*. These special communication channels are used by some devices to improve the speed at which information is transferred from the device to the CPU or vice versa. Devices such as sound cards, network adapters, and some disk drives typically use DMA channels.

There are a limited number of DMA channels in your PC, but a redeeming factor is that very few of those are used by the system. Table 6-3 details the eight DMA channels that are used in your PC.

Table 6-3   Standard PC DMA channel assignments

Channel	Use
0	Available
1	Available
2	Floppy disk controller
3	Available
4	First DMA controller
5	Available
6	Available
7	Available

As with the interrupt controllers, there are two DMA controllers in your system. These controllers are connected to each other through DMA channel 4. You can assign more than one device to the same DMA channel. The caveat is that you cannot use the two devices at the same time.

Thus, if you used DMA channel 1 for your sound card and for your network card, you could use either card as long as you were not using the other. Because this approach is hard to keep straight, it is best to use devices that allow you to select which DMA channel to use.

Memory addresses

Many hardware devices use memory in your system. This used to present more of a problem than it does with newer devices, because the memory used was part of the upper memory of the PC itself. When this occurred (and it still may, if you have older cards), you needed to be concerned with which memory areas are being used. You want to make sure that no two devices are using the same memory areas.

The biggest user of memory addresses is your video controller. Most video cards use memory areas starting somewhere near 0xC000 or 0xD000 and going upward. The exact memory areas that are used depend on the type of video card that is installed in your system as well as the model of video card.

Hardware properties

Most hardware items in your system are treated as objects by Windows NT; this means that there is typically an icon for the object, or at least a "line item" in some dialog box. The upshot is that, as with other objects, you can set properties for individual hardware items. These properties control either the device itself or how Windows NT relates to the device.

You learned about two examples of this concept in previous chapters. Your video system's properties, which rely on your video card (a hardware device), can be modified by right-clicking on the desktop, choosing Properties, and then clicking on the Settings tab. The result is shown in Figure 6-1.

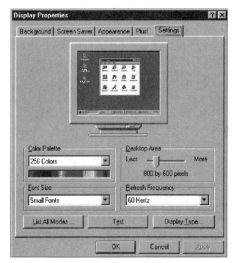

Figure 6-1: The information in the Settings tab of the Display Properties dialog box reflects the properties of a hardware device — your video card.

As you make changes in the Settings tab, you make changes in which video mode is used by the video card. At the same time and through the same changes, you also make modifications in how Windows NT internally maintains information about your video system.

Similarly, you can view the properties of other hardware devices and make changes in their configuration, performance, or behavior. Later in this chapter, you learn how to do this for two common hardware devices: your keyboard and mouse.

The information about how a hardware device is configured is stored in the Windows NT Registry. When you display the properties for a device, you are actually displaying the contents of that device's entry (or entries) in the Registry. As you make changes in the properties of a device, your changes are stored in the Registry. You learn more about the Registry in Chapter 10.

Device drivers

When you first installed Windows NT Workstation, the Setup program detected, as much as possible, the hardware that was installed in your system. The program then installed various device drivers that were specifically necessary for your hardware. *Device drivers* are used to allow Windows NT to communicate with the device. The concept of device drivers is not new with Windows NT, but it has been refined a bit.

Windows NT is very modular in its approach to device drivers. Whenever you change hardware, you typically change the device drivers that are installed on your system. In this way, NT knows how to communicate with the new device without the need to reinstall the whole operating system. In fact, you could look at Windows NT's organization as follows: The base operating system understands how to work with the CPU and memory; everything else is handled through device drivers.

Whether or not you realized it, in Chapter 5 you learned how to add device drivers to your system. The Add Printer Wizard allowed you to pick a manufacturer and a model of printer. Windows NT then took care of determining the proper driver to use to support that printer.

While not every type of device has a Wizard to aid in your installation, most Properties dialog boxes for hardware devices include some sort of change or install capability that allows a new device driver to be installed.

For example, Figure 6-2 shows the Multimedia Properties dialog box with the Devices tab selected. At the bottom of the dialog box are Add and Remove buttons. When you use these buttons to add or remove devices, you are actually adding and removing device drivers that are used by Windows NT to control those devices.

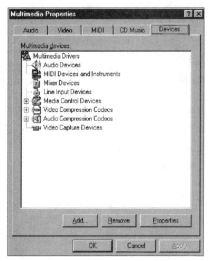

Figure 6-2: The Multimedia Properties dialog box allows you to control the multimedia device drivers that are installed in your system.

This is not the only example of how you can control different device drivers. The ability to change and control different hardware devices in your system is at the heart of Windows NT. As you work through different sections of this book, you learn how to add and remove the drivers that make that heart function properly.

Adding Hardware

Very few of us ever have what can be called a "static system." Instead, our computers tend to be dynamic, changing over time as we add new gadgets, tweak some settings here or there, and generally try to make the system evolve as our needs change. It is inevitable that you will, at some time, want to add hardware to your system. The following sections walk you through what you should do when adding devices to your Windows NT system.

Before installing

Before you install your new hardware, you need to think about its impact on your present Windows NT configuration. In the majority of cases, adding the new hardware may not mean much of a change. For instance, if you add a new printer, it doesn't hurt to leave your old printer drivers installed on your system. There are other devices, however, for which it pays to make changes ahead of time.

A word on Plug and Play

If you are familiar with Windows 95, you may be familiar with the much-touted Plug and Play feature that it includes. Plug and Play (PnP) allows you to quickly and easily add hardware to your system. In fact, for hardware that is compliant with the PnP specification, you simply need to install it in the computer, and Windows 95 takes care of everything else. Because Windows NT adopted the Windows 95 interface, you may think that it also includes support for Plug and Play.

Unfortunately, Windows NT Workstation 4.0 does not support the PnP standard. While there is no problem using PnP hardware under Windows NT, the special configuration capabilities of the hardware are not used. Microsoft has indicated that Plug and Play will be included in a future release of Windows NT, most likely in late 1997.

Perhaps the best example of this is your video system. If you are adding a new video card (replacing your old one), you don't want to just pull out your old card and put in the new one. In many cases, this is a sure way to end up with a system that doesn't work.

This is because you only have one video driver installed in your system. If that driver is designed to work with a different chip set than what is in your new video card, then the driver won't work with the new video card. To circumvent this problem, you should do use following steps before installing the new card:

1. Open the Display Properties dialog box, and select the Settings tab.

2. Click on the Display <u>T</u>ype button.

3. Click on the <u>C</u>hange button.

4. Choose (Standard display types) as the manufacturer and VGA compatible display adapter as the display.

5. Click on OK, and return to the Display Properties dialog box.

6. Reduce the number of colors to 16 and the desktop area to 640 x 480.

7. Close the Display Properties dialog box.

The noted driver (as specified by the manufacturer and display) is generic, meaning that it works with any video card for Windows NT. After you install your new video card, you can then install the drivers that it needs. This process of returning to the "least common denominator" is most critical in the video area, but you can also use it in other hardware areas for your system.

Tip

Before you install your hardware, it is a good idea to make sure that it works with Windows NT Workstation 4.0. You can determine this either by checking the official Microsoft hardware compatibility list (included with your copy of NT) or by checking on-line at http://microsoft.com. You can also contact the manufacturer to determine compatibility.

Determining resource usage

Many of the hardware devices that you install in your NT workstation require you to configure them. This configuration is required so that the device can use the same resources that the computer has reserved for it to use. Before you can configure the device, however, you need to know which resources your system is already using.

To determine which resources Windows NT is using, you can follow these steps:

STEPS

Reviewing resources used

Step 1. Choose the Run option from the Start menu. This displays the Run dialog box.

Step 2. In the Open field, enter the name winmsd.

Step 3. Click on the OK button. This runs the winmsd diagnostic program.

Step 4. Click on the Resources tab. The program window now appears, as shown in Figure 6-3.

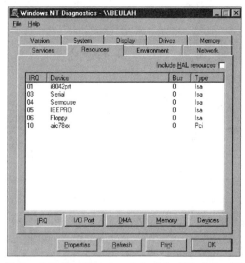

Figure 6-3: The Resources tab of the Windows NT Diagnostics program is useful for determining which resources are available.

Step 5. Using the buttons at the bottom of the tab area (IRQ, I/O Port, DMA, Memory, and Devices), review the different resources that are used on your system.

Step 6. Compare the resources used with those that are available (as discussed earlier in the chapter). The differences are the resources that you can use for your new hardware device.

Step 7. If desired, click on the Pri_n_t button, and choose to print a _S_ummary report. This provides a printed report on what resources are in use in your system.

Step 8. Close the diagnostics program window.

When you know what is available, you can compare this information to the information in the documentation for the hardware device that you are installing. Check to see which resources are used and how you can configure the card to use them.

Installing the drivers

After the hardware is installed in your system, you should start Windows NT and proceed to install the drivers for your new hardware. This is done by accessing the section of NT that is designed to manage that device, and then typically using the _A_dd or _C_hange button from the appropriate dialog box. Windows NT allows you to install any number of devices:

- **Hard drive.** Use the Disk Administrator. You access this tool by choosing Programs from the Start menu, selecting Administrative Tools (Common), and finally Disk Administrator.

- **Tape drive.** Open the Control Panel, and then open the Tape Devices applet. Click on the Drivers tab, and choose the _A_dd button.

- **Network card.** Open the Control Panel, and then open the Network applet. Click on the Adapters tab and then the _A_dd button.

- **SCSI adapter.** Open the Control Panel, and then open the SCSI Adapters applet. Click on the Drivers tab and then the _A_dd button.

- **Video card.** Right-click on the desktop, and then choose P_r_operties. Click on the Settings tab and then on the Display _T_ype button. Finally, click on the _C_hange button.

- **Printer.** Open the Printers folder, and double-click on the Add New Printer icon.

- **Sound card.** Open the Control Panel, and then open the Multimedia applet. Click on the Devices tab and then the Add button.

- **Modem.** Open the Control Panel, and then open the Modems applet.

- **Keyboard.** Open the Control Panel, and then open the Keyboard applet. Click on the General tab and then the Change button.

- **Mouse.** Open the Control Panel, and then open the Mouse applet. Click on the General tab and then the Change button.

If, while installing the drivers for your new device, you cannot find a listing for the device in the appropriate dialog boxes or Wizards, you may need to contact the device's vendor to determine the appropriate drivers to use.

Secret

After the drivers are installed, you must still configure the device to use the proper resources and to function the way that you require. (Remember that, in reality, you are configuring the driver that you just installed.) Information on how you can configure many of the devices just mentioned is included elsewhere in this book, and you should refer to those sections for detailed configuration information.

Testing the installation

After you have installed the hardware and the drivers for the hardware and configured it the way you require, you may need to restart your system (Windows NT lets you know). After restarting, it is always a good idea to test your new device to make sure that it is working properly.

The first thing you should do is to just start using the device. You can run it through its paces and see if it works as you expect. If it doesn't, you can use the winmsd diagnostics program to check if the device is actually using the intended resources (the driver should have taken care of reserving the resources for your device).

Tip

If not, then you know something is not right, and you have some detective work to do. The following ideas may be helpful in tracking down the problem:

- Check the switch settings on the card (if any), and make sure that they match your configuration settings in Windows NT.

- Make sure that the adapter card is firmly seated in the motherboard.

- Make sure that all cable connections to the adapter card (if any) have been made and are secure.

- Restart your system if you had not restarted it before. Sometimes this can help reinitialize related areas of the operating system.

- Make sure that any software necessary to use the device is installed and configured properly. For instance, if you installed a sound card, you need additional software that takes advantage of the sound card.

- Check the documentation for the device. Many times, it contains a section on troubleshooting an installation. (This can be very helpful, as it should be specific to the device that you just installed.)

If all else fails, write down exactly what is happening (if anything), and then call the tech-support hotline for the device's manufacturer. The technicians there have probably heard of your problem before and can walk you through how to correct it.

Using Hardware Profiles

Windows NT Workstation provides you with the capability to define hardware profiles. A *hardware profile* allows you to define different configurations for your system and to then pick one of those configurations when you first boot. For instance, hardware configurations are helpful under the following circumstances:

- **Portable user.** You have a portable computer that has Windows NT Workstation 4.0 installed on it. This computer can be used by itself, or it can be plugged into a docking station or a port replicator at your office. Each potential use is a natural for a hardware configuration.

- **Roaming hardware.** In your office environment, you have several high-cost peripherals that can be moved from system to system (for example, a tape backup unit, a CD-ROM burner, or a high-end color laser printer). When you have one or more of these items plugged into your system, you need to have your hardware configured differently.

- **Test system.** You have a hard drive that has Windows NT Workstation 4.0 installed on it. This hard drive is your "base unit." You physically move the hard drive from system to system for the purpose of testing hardware. Each system, however, falls into one of five standard configuration categories. You set up five different hardware profiles to accommodate your tests on the five different types of machines.

These are just a few of the many ways in which hardware profiles can be used. You develop and manage hardware profiles as part of your system properties. You can display the appropriate dialog box by right-clicking on the My Computer icon on your desktop and then choosing Properties from the Context menu.

This displays the System Properties dialog box, from which you should choose the Hardware Profiles tab. The System Properties dialog box then appears as shown in Figure 6-4. In the next several sections, you learn how you can use the controls in this dialog box to develop and use hardware profiles on your system.

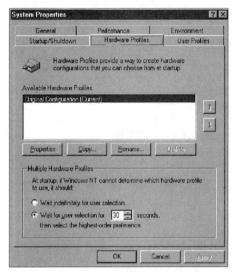

Figure 6-4: Windows NT Workstation allows you to develop hardware profiles for your system.

Creating a hardware profile

Before you create your hardware profile, it is helpful to understand exactly what you expect the profile to accomplish. This means that you need to look at your different reasons for implementing profiles and then write down how the profiles differ from each other.

For instance, you may determine that you need two profiles, and that one includes a network card and the other does not. When you write down information like this ahead of time, it makes creating the profiles much easier.

When you have a clear idea of what you want to accomplish, creating a hardware profile is relatively easy. To create a hardware profile, follow these steps:

STEPS

Adding a hardware profile

Step 1. Right-click on the My Computer icon on your desktop. This displays a Context menu.

Step 2. Choose the Properties option from the Context menu. This displays the System Properties dialog box.

Step 3. Click on the Hardware Profiles tab. The System Properties dialog box now appears, as shown earlier in Figure 6-4.

Step 4. In the Available Hardware Profiles list, click on the hardware profile that is closest to the one that you want to create.

Step 5. Click on the Copy button. The Copy Profile dialog box appears, as shown in Figure 6-5.

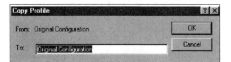

Figure 6-5: You must supply a name for your new hardware profiles.

Step 6. In the To field, enter the name by which you want this new profile known.

Step 7. Click on the OK button to close the Copy Profile dialog box. The new profile now appears in the list of Available Hardware Profiles.

At this point, you are ready to make changes to the profile. The first changes that you can (and should) make are in the properties of the new profile. You do this by selecting the new profile from the list and then clicking on the Properties button. This displays the dialog box that is shown in Figure 6-6.

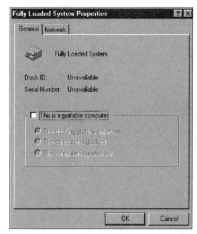

Figure 6-6: You can change properties of your new hardware profile.

There are two tabs in this Properties dialog box. With the General tab showing, you can indicate whether this profile refers to a portable computer. If it does (and you select the check box), you can also indicate the docking status of the system. If Windows NT can recognize whether your PC is docked, you can't change the status radio buttons; instead, they are controlled by the operating system itself.

If you click on the Network tab, you can modify whether Windows NT uses any network information under this hardware profile. The Properties dialog box, with the Network tab selected, is shown in Figure 6-7.

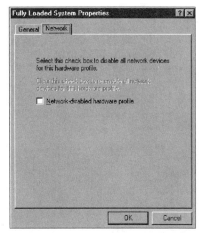

Figure 6-7: You should make changes to the networking control under some circumstances.

Secret

It is not unusual to find systems that have network interface cards (NICs) installed but are not connected to a network. (This often happens with portable computers.) If your system has an NIC and you are developing this hardware profile for those times when the system is not connected to a net-work, then you should select the check box on this tab.

Caution

If you still plan on using your portable computer with RAS (Remote Access Service) or DUN (Dial-Up Networking), then you should not select this check box. Although you may still be able to connect, you can't use the networking capabilities of your system with this check box selected.

Note

RAS and DUN are essentially different names for the same type of service. Both allow you to establish a network link over a modem connection. These services are discussed in more detail in Chapter 13.

When you are finished setting properties, you can click on the OK button to save your changes. You can then close the System Properties dialog box by clicking on its OK button.

Changing the profile

After you have defined a new hardware profile, you need to make changes to the profile to ensure that it does what you want it to. You do this by opening the Control Panel and then double-clicking on the Devices applet. This displays the Devices dialog box, as shown in Figure 6-8.

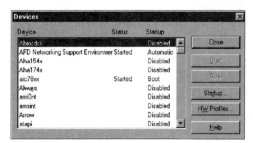

Figure 6-8: Using the Devices dialog box, you can control which device drivers are used by Windows NT.

The Devices dialog box is used to control device drivers, which you learned about earlier in this chapter. Normally, the Devices dialog box is used to enable or disable different device drivers as needed. If you are working with multiple hardware profiles, however, you can also control device drivers for different profiles.

You do this by first selecting the device driver from the list and then clicking on the HW Profiles button. This displays the Device dialog box (different from the Devices dialog box), as shown in Figure 6-9.

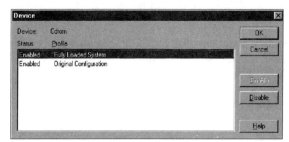

Figure 6-9: The Device dialog box indicates how a device is treated by different hardware profiles.

Notice that there are two buttons in the Device dialog box. The first, Enable, is used to "turn on" a device for the selected hardware profile, whereas Disable is used to turn it off. By default, all devices are enabled for all hardware profiles.

You customize the profiles by selecting the devices to be disabled from a profile and then turning them off. When you are finished, click on the OK button to save your changes.

Changes to booting

When you log in to your Windows NT system, and if you have multiple hardware profiles defined, NT attempts to determine which profile best matches the current hardware configuration of the system.

If NT can figure this out, it automatically uses that hardware profile. If it cannot, then NT presents a text menu that allows you to specify which profile to use. (See Figure 6-10.)

```
        Hardware Profile/Configuration Recovery Menu

    This menu allows you to select a hardware profile
    to be used when Windows NT is started.

    If your system is not starting correctly, then you may
    switch to a previous system configuration, which
    may overcome startup problems.

    IMPORTANT:  System configuration changes
    made since the last successful startup will be discarded.


            Original Configuration
            Fully Loaded System




    Use the up and down arrow keys to move the highlight
    to the selection you want.  Then press ENTER.
    To switch to the Last Known Good configuration, press `L´.
    To Exit this menu and restart your computer, press F3.

    Seconds until highlighted choice will be started automatically:  20
```

Figure 6-10: When using hardware profiles, you can select the profile to be used during booting.

This screen shows the various hardware profiles that you have defined for your system. When you select an option, that hardware profile is used for booting. You can exercise a bit of control over how the startup process works by using the Hardware Profiles tab of the System Properties dialog box. Go ahead and display this dialog box (as shown earlier in Figure 6-4), and notice the area at the bottom of the dialog box, in the Multiple Hardware Profiles area.

Here you have the option of specifying how Windows NT should start. If you select the first option, then NT waits at the screen shown in Figure 6-10 until you specify a profile to use. If you select the second option, then you can select a number of seconds that Windows NT waits for you to make a choice. If you don't make a choice in that time, then NT automatically selects the first choice in the profiles list.

Tip

You can control which profile is used as the default by using the up and down arrows to the right of the Available Hardware Profiles list. Make sure that, if you have specified a default startup selection time, your default profile is positioned at the top of the profiles list.

Removing a hardware profile

As you change the uses for your system, you may need to periodically delete hardware profiles that you have defined. To delete a hardware profile, follow these steps:

STEPS

Deleting a hardware profile

Step 1.   Right-click on the My Computer icon on your desktop. This displays a Context menu.

Step 2.   Choose the Properties option from the Context menu. This displays the System Properties dialog box.

Step 3.   Click on the Hardware Profiles tab. The System Properties dialog box now appears, as shown earlier in Figure 6-4.

Step 4.   In the Available Hardware Profiles list, click on the hardware profile that you want to delete. (You cannot delete the profile that is currently in use, that is, the one marked as current.)

Step 5.   Click on the Delete button. After you confirm your action, the profile is removed from the list.

Step 6.   Close the System Properties dialog box by clicking on the OK button.

Changing Input Devices

Your keyboard and your mouse are the most elemental pieces of hardware. These devices account for the majority of your interaction with Windows NT, yet they are often taken for granted. You may be interested in knowing that NT does not take them for granted; instead, you can make changes in the configuration of both devices.

These changes can help you mold both the keyboard and the mouse to your way of working. In the following sections, you learn how to control both of these devices.

Your keyboard

The keyboard that you use with your computer is most likely a direct descendant of the keyboard used on the very first manual typewriters. Despite this direct lineage, the PC keyboard is adaptable in many ways. For instance, you can change the speed at which the keyboard responds to your typing or modify the language that is used with the keyboard. These are all properties that you can control.

The properties associated with your keyboard are controlled by the keyboard driver that you have installed. If you install a fancy, special-purpose keyboard, you may need to install a special driver to take advantage of it. You can change your keyboard driver by following these steps:

STEPS

Changing your keyboard driver

Step 1. Choose the Settings option from the Start menu. This displays the Settings menu.

Step 2. Choose the Control Panel option from the Settings menu. This opens the Control Panel.

Step 3. Double-click on the Keyboard applet in the Control Panel. This displays the Keyboard Properties dialog box.

(continued)

STEPS *(continued)*

Changing your keyboard driver

Step 4. Click on the General tab. The Keyboard Properties dialog box now appears, as shown in Figure 6-11.

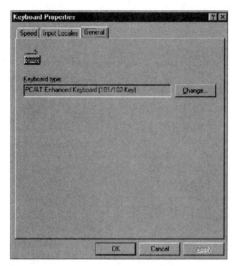

Figure 6-11: You can change the driver that is used to control your keyboard.

Step 5. Click on the Change button. This displays a list of compatible devices (from the viewpoint of Windows NT).

Step 6. Click on the Show All Devices radio button. All of the potential keyboard device drivers are listed in the dialog box.

Step 7. Click on the name of the keyboard driver that you want to use.

Step 8. Click on OK to save your choice. You again see the Keyboard Properties dialog box.

Step 9. Click on the OK button to close the Keyboard Properties dialog box.

Step 10. Restart your system.

Because the properties of your keyboard may be dependent on the driver that you have installed, it is impossible to cover every possible property that you can change. The following sections, however, discuss properties that should be common to all keyboards. If you have a special keyboard, you may want to refer to your documentation to learn how to control the special features that it includes.

The speed settings

One of the most common properties of the keyboard is the speed at which it reacts to you, the typist. When you press a key, the operating system manages receiving the character that is associated with the key that you pressed. Believe it or not, Windows NT tracks when you press the key and when you release it.

If you don't release it right away but instead hold it down for a while, Windows NT assumes that you want the character to be repeated. You can control the time period after which Windows NT repeats the character, and you can control how fast the actual characters are repeated once that time period has passed.

In general, you should tailor the repeat delay to how fast you can type. If you are a "touch typist," then you probably want the repeat delay to be pretty short. If you are a beginning typist or you just have heavy fingers, you may want the delay to be longer. To make changes in the repeat delay or the repeat rate, follow these steps:

STEPS

Adjusting the keyboard speed

Step 1. Choose the Settings option from the Start menu. This displays the Settings menu.

Step 2. Choose the Control Panel option from the Settings menu. This opens the Control Panel.

(continued)

STEPS (continued)

Adjusting the keyboard speed

Step 3.   Double-click on the Keyboard applet in the Control Panel. This displays the Keyboard Properties dialog box, as shown in Figure 6-12.

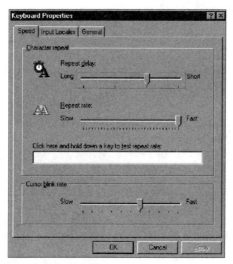

Figure 6-12: Windows NT allows you to change several characteristics that are related to the speed of your keyboard.

Step 4.   Using the Repeat Delay control, adjust the slider from Long to Short. The farther toward the right that you position the control, the shorter the delay before repeating begins.

Step 5.   Using the Repeat Rate control, adjust how quickly (from Slow to Fast) the characters should repeat after you exceed the repeat delay time. The farther toward the right that you position the control, the faster the characters repeat.

You can click in the test area to try out your settings. Just hold down a key, and see how long it takes to repeat. You can keep making changes to the repeat properties until you are satisfied with the behavior of the keyboard.

Secret

Many newer computer systems include, as part of the CMOS setup routines, the capability to change the keyboard repeat rate. You may need to do some testing between CMOS and NT settings to make sure that you have the proper mix for your preferences.

Notice, as well, that at the bottom of the dialog box, you can adjust the rate at which the cursor blinks on-screen. It is interesting that Microsoft decided to put this control in the Keyboard Properties dialog box, because it would at first appear that the cursor blink rate has nothing to do with the keyboard. The reason for including it here, however, is that the cursor rate is controlled most often by the keyboard input routines of a program.

The cursor blink rate is a matter of personal preference. You can adjust the setting, from Slow to Fast, using the provided control. When you are finished making changes, click on the OK button to close the Keyboard Properties dialog box and save your changes.

Setting a keyboard language

Windows NT is an international operating system. This means that you can configure it to work using languages other than English. Part of that capability is the ability to change which language the keyboard uses. It makes sense that keyboards around the world have been adapted to the locality in which they are used.

Window NT Workstation 4.0 allows you to specify any of 78 international localities for your keyboard. In addition, many of those localities include multiple keyboard layouts.

The steps that you use to modify your keyboard language are as follows:

STEPS

Changing the keyboard language

Step 1. Choose the Settings option from the Start menu. This displays the Settings menu.

Step 2. Choose the Control Panel option from the Settings menu. This opens the Control Panel.

(continued)

STEPS *(continued)*

Changing the keyboard language

Step 3.   Double-click on the Keyboard applet in the Control Panel. This displays the Keyboard Properties dialog box, as shown earlier in Figure 6-12.

Step 4.   Click on the Input Locales tab. The Keyboard Properties dialog box now appears, as shown in Figure 6-13.

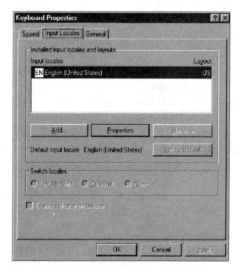

Figure 6-13: Windows NT supports a wide variety of international keyboard layouts.

Step 5.   In the Input Locales list, select the locale that you want to use. If the locale is not visible, click on the <u>A</u>dd button. This displays the Add Input Locale dialog box.

Step 6.   In the Input Locale drop-down list, choose from the 78 locales that are available. Most languages have more than one permutation, so select the one that matches what you want to use.

Step 7.   Click on the OK button to save your new locale. It should now appear in the Input Locales list on the Keyboard Properties dialog box.

Step 8.   With your desired locale selected, click on the <u>P</u>roperties button. This displays the Input Locale Properties dialog box.

Step 9. In the <u>K</u>eyboard Layout drop-down list, select a layout for your keyboard.

Step 10. Click on the OK button to save your layout. This returns you to the Keyboard Properties dialog box.

Step 11. In the Switch Locales area of the dialog box, select the key combination that you want to use to signal a switch between locales.

Step 12. Make sure that the check box at the bottom of the dialog box is selected if you want an indicator to be displayed in the status area of the Taskbar. (The indicator looks like the symbol to the left of the locale name in the Input Locales list.)

Step 13. Click on the OK button to save your layout.

Your mouse

The mouse is one of the most important tools that you use in Windows NT. Without the mouse, it would be virtually impossible to efficiently use the operating system. In fact, some operations require the use of a mouse, and the keyboard cannot be used for these operations. Just as you could customize your use of the keyboard, Windows NT also allows you to control how the mouse is used.

There are many types of mice that you can install in your system. Some have one button, most have two, and a few even have three or more. The way in which your mouse interacts with Windows NT is controlled by the mouse driver. You can change your mouse driver by following these steps:

STEPS

Changing your mouse driver

Step 1. Choose the <u>S</u>ettings option from the Start menu. This displays the Settings menu.

Step 2. Choose the <u>C</u>ontrol Panel option from the Settings menu. This opens the Control Panel.

Step 3. Double-click on the Mouse applet in the Control Panel. This displays the Mouse Properties dialog box.

(continued)

STEPS *(continued)*

Changing your mouse driver

Step 4. Click on the General tab. The Mouse Properties dialog box now appears, as shown in Figure 6-14.

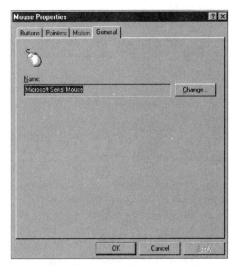

Figure 6-14: The mouse driver controls how you use your mouse.

Step 5. Click on the Change button. This displays a list of mice that are compatible with what Windows NT thinks you have installed in your system.

Step 6. Click on the Show All Devices radio button. All of the potential mouse device drivers are listed in the dialog box.

Step 7. Click on the name of the mouse model (driver) that you want to use.

Step 8. Click on OK to save your choice. You again see the Mouse Properties dialog box.

Step 9. Click on the OK button to close the Mouse Properties dialog box.

Step 10. Restart your system.

Each mouse driver is a bit different, but there are some common characteristics. The following sections discuss properties that should be common to all mice. If your mouse has special features, you should refer to your mouse documentation to find out how to use or enable those features.

Controlling the buttons

Windows NT allows you to control how the buttons on your mouse are used. In particular, if you have a two-button mouse, you can switch the purpose of the left and right buttons. This is particularly important for left-handed computer users. If your mouse has more than two buttons, you should also be able to control the use of any additional buttons on the mouse.

To configure Windows NT for how you want the mouse buttons used, follow these steps:

STEPS

Changing your mouse driver

Step 1. Choose the Settings option from the Start menu. This displays the Settings menu.

Step 2. Choose the Control Panel option from the Settings menu. This opens the Control Panel

Step 3. Double-click on the Mouse applet in the Control Panel. This displays the Mouse Properties dialog box, as shown in Figure 6-15.

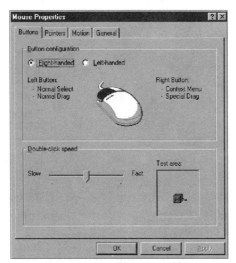

Figure 6-15: You can control how the buttons are used on your mouse.

Step 4. At the top of the dialog box, indicate whether you are left- or right-handed. Selecting a radio button switches the purpose of the buttons on the mouse.

(continued)

STEPS *(continued)*

Changing your mouse driver

Step 5.   Using the slider control at the bottom of the dialog box, indicate how fast you want the mouse to be clicked in succession for your actions to be considered a double-click. Moving the slider control toward the right means that you need to click the button faster than if the control is toward the left.

Step 6.   In the Test Area at the right of the dialog box, test your new double-click speed by double-clicking on the icon of the Jack-in-the-box.

Step 7.   Click on the OK button to close the Mouse Properties dialog box and save your changes.

Changing mouse pointers

As a part of customizing your system, Windows NT Workstation allows you to change the mouse pointers that you use. The array of mouse pointers that are used by Windows NT is collected into schemes, the same as color schemes or other types of schemes on your desktop.

You can pick a scheme by following these steps:

STEPS

Changing the mouse pointers

Step 1.   Choose the Settings option from the Start menu. This displays the Settings menu.

Step 2.   Choose the Control Panel option from the Settings menu. This opens the Control Panel.

Step 3.   Double-click on the Mouse applet in the Control Panel. This displays the Mouse Properties dialog box, as shown earlier in Figure 6-15.

Step 4.   Click on the Pointers tab. The Mouse Properties dialog box now appears as shown in Figure 6-16.

Figure 6-16: You can select different mouse pointer schemes to use with your system.

Step 5. At the top of the dialog box, select the mouse collection that you want to use from the Scheme drop-down list. (There are 12 schemes, including None.)

Step 6. Click on the OK button to save your scheme and close the Mouse Properties dialog box.

Adjusting the pointer speed

Different mice use different resolutions, meaning that some can detect finer movements of the mouse over your mousepad or desktop. For some people, the amount of mouse movement compared to how much the mouse pointer moves may seem wrong.

You can adjust the mouse movement to your own preference by following these steps:

STEPS

Changing the mouse pointer speed

Step 1. Choose the Settings option from the Start menu. This displays the Settings menu.

(continued)

STEPS *(continued)*

Changing the mouse pointer speed

Step 2.   Choose the Control Panel option from the Settings menu. This opens the Control Panel.

Step 3.   Double-click on the Mouse applet in the Control Panel. This displays the Mouse Properties dialog box, as shown earlier in Figure 6-15.

Step 4.   Click on the Motion tab. The Mouse Properties dialog box now appears as shown in Figure 6-17.

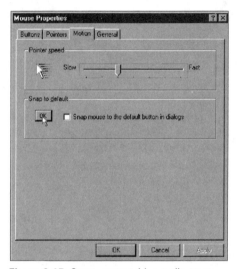

Figure 6-17: Some mouse drivers allow you to control the rate at which the mouse pointer moves.

Step 5.   At the top of the dialog box, use the slider control to specify how fast the mouse pointer should move in relation to your physical movement of the mouse. If you move the slider toward the right, the mouse pointer moves relatively faster.

Step 6.   Use the Snap to Default check box to indicate if the mouse pointer should be automatically positioned over the default button when a dialog box is displayed.

Step 7.   Click on the OK button to save your scheme and close the Mouse Properties dialog box.

Summary

If you learn how Windows NT interacts with hardware and how to control that interaction, you have progressed a long way toward truly making your system your own. Windows NT gives you complete control over the hardware in your system, and you can configure the way that Windows NT acts in relation to that hardware.

In this chapter, you have focused on the fundamentals of controlling your hardware. In previous chapters, you have learned about configuring your system, and it is understandable that those skills rely a bit on controlling your hardware. In this chapter, however, you have learned the basis on which hardware control is founded.

In particular, you have learned the following items:

▶ Windows NT allows you to identify, use, and manage system resources for specific hardware devices. These resources include IRQs, DMA channels, I/O port addresses, and memory areas.

▶ You can configure hardware devices (and how Windows NT interacts with those devices) by using Properties dialog boxes. This approach is consistent with all the other ways that NT provides for customizing your system.

▶ Through the use of device drivers, Windows NT allows you to customize your computer system for your particular hardware requirements.

▶ When you add hardware to your system, you need to identify the system resources that are to be used by the device, install it in your system, configure Windows NT for its presence, and test your installation.

▶ You can use hardware profiles to easily define different collections of hardware that you can use with your system. These profiles, when used, alter the way in which you start Windows NT.

▶ The two most common computer devices are your keyboard and your mouse. Windows NT allows you to completely adapt both the keyboard and the mouse to the way that you do your work.

Chapter 7

Using Accessories

In This Chapter

Consistent with previous versions of Windows, Windows NT Workstation 4.0 provides a variety of accessories that you can use to accomplish simple tasks. Some of these accessories are new with version 4.0, whereas others have a long history. In this chapter, you learn how to use the accessories.

The information that is provided here is not meant to be the answer to every question that you may have about accessories but rather to provide a whirlwind tour of what you can do using the accessories, as well as to provide the secrets and tips that can make the accessories immediately productive.

In this chapter, you learn the following items:

▶ What accessories are provided with Windows NT

▶ How the Calculator accessory can provide quick, convenient calculations

▶ How the new Unicode Character Map can help you access any character of any font in your system

▶ Why the Clipboard Viewer is really a misnomer

▶ Why the Clock accessory provides redundancy in Windows NT

▶ How you can use the Imaging accessory to scan images and make modifications to them

▶ How the multimedia accessories help enliven your use of Windows NT

▶ How the Notepad accessory can be used to edit small text files

▶ Why Paint makes a good choice as an entry-level graphics program

▶ Why WordPad could suffice as a word processing program for those with minimal word processing needs

What Are the Accessories?

Accessories are programs supplied with Windows NT that are not part of the base operating system, but are provided as minimalist tools to help accomplish certain tasks. This is not to say that the accessories are worthless; to the contrary, for many people they may be more than adequate to accomplish what they need to do. Because the accessories are "extras," you can easily choose not to install them, or you can ignore them once they are installed.

Depending on how you installed Windows NT Workstation, you could have any number of accessories installed on your system. Some accessories are installed by default, and others are installed only by explicitly choosing to install them.

The following accessories are most commonly installed with Windows NT Workstation:

- Calculator
- CD Player
- Character Map
- Clipboard Viewer
- Clock
- Imaging
- Media Player
- Notepad
- Paint
- Sound Recorder
- Volume Control
- WordPad

Each of these accessories is discussed in this chapter. This is not all of the accessories that you can have installed, however. Indeed, there are others that you may find installed on your system.

The following accessories are *not* discussed in this chapter:

- **Chat.** This tool is used for real-time communication between two work-stations. Chat is discussed in Chapter 15.

- **Games.** Windows NT Workstation allows you to install four different games: Freecell, Minesweeper, Pinball, and Solitaire. Anyone who has been using Windows for any amount of time probably knows how to use these games, so they are not covered in this book.

- **HyperTerminal.** This tool is used to communicate with other computers via a modem. The tool is also discussed in Chapter 15.

- **Internet Explorer.** This tool is used to browse the World Wide Web. The browser is discussed in Chapter 14.

- **Phone Dialer.** This tool uses your modem to dial voice calls. The Phone Dialer is also discussed in Chapter 15.

Using the Calculator

The Calculator accessory is a tool that has been available since the earliest days of Windows. It is a general-purpose accessory that lets you perform mathematical calculations, the same as you would with a hand-held calculator.

The handy part about the Calculator is how you can copy and paste answers from the Calculator into any Windows application. To start the Calculator, follow these steps:

STEPS

Starting the Calculator

Step 1.   Choose the Programs option from the Start menu. This displays the Programs menu.

Step 2.   Choose the Accessories option from the Programs menu. This displays the list of accessories that are installed on your system.

Step 3.   Click on the Calculator option. This starts the Calculator, as shown in Figure 7-1.

Figure 7-1: The Calculator accessory looks like a hand-held calculator.

If you've used a hand-held calculator, then using the Calculator accessory is very intuitive. Simply use the keys on your numeric keypad, or click on the on-screen numbers with your mouse. As you enter numbers, they appear in the Calculator's display area. The buttons on the calculator are defined in Table 7-1.

Table 7-1   Calculator button definitions

Button	Meaning
+	Add
−	Subtract
*	Multiply
/	Divide
=	Equals
C	Clear
CE	Clear the displayed value
Back	Delete the last digit in the number that you are entering
%	Percent
+/−	Switch the displayed value between positive and negative
sqrt	Square root
1/x	Reciprocal
MC	Clear memory
MR	Recall the value in memory (the value is not cleared)
MS	Save the displayed value to memory
M+	Add the displayed value to the value in memory

Tip

If you want to see what a Calculator key does, right-click on the key, and choose What's This from the Context menu.

Secret

The percent key (%) does not work like you may expect. You are supposed to click on a number, click on the multiplication key (*), click on a second number, and then the click on the percent key. For instance, if you click on 3 * 5 %, you get 0.15; this is the correct answer. If you click on 3 + 5 %, or 3 − 5 %, however, you get the same answer — 0.15. The percent key overrides any operator that you use in your equation.

There are actually two ways to use the Calculator. The mode displayed in Figure 7-1 is called standard view. You can also use the more powerful scientific view by choosing Scientific from the View menu. This expands the Calculator, as shown in Figure 7-2.

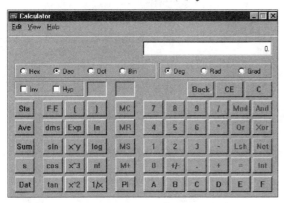

Figure 7-2: You can also use the Calculator in its scientific view.

The scientific view is much more complex than the standard view, but it also allows you to perform quite a few additional functions. Many of the functions may look familiar if you have used scientific calculators before. The scientific view allows you to work with numbers in decimal, octal, binary, and hexadecimal notations.

Depending on the numbering system that you choose, the input type, just below the Calculator display, changes. When you are working in decimal notation, then the input type allows you to use either degrees, radians, or gradients. If you are using one of the other notational forms, then you can specify input types of dword (double word, 32 bits), word (16 bits), and byte (8 bits).

All of the keys from the standard view are visible in the scientific view, with the exception of the % and sqrt keys. In addition, quite a few other keys and controls are available, as you can see from Table 7-2.

Table 7-2   Additional Calculator buttons in the scientific view

Button	Meaning
And	Bitwise AND.
Xor	Bitwise XOR.
Not	Bitwise inverse.
Int	Truncates the displayed value at the decimal point. Only works in decimal notation.
Lsh	Shifts the binary equivalent of the displayed value a certain number of places to the left. After using Lsh, you must click on a value representing the number of places to move left.
Or	Bitwise OR.
Mod	Returns the modulus (remainder) of an integer division.
PI	Returns the value of pi.
ln	Returns the natural logarithm of the displayed value.
log	Returns the common logarithm of the displayed value.
n!	Calculates the factorial of the displayed value.
Exp	Signifies that you want to enter the exponent part of a number in scientific notation. Only works in the decimal numbering system.
x^y	Raises a number to another number's power. Enter the first number, click on the x^y key, and then enter the power (value) that you want the number raised to.
x^3	Returns the cube of the displayed value.
x^2	Returns the square of the displayed value.
F-E	Switches the display from scientific notation to normal. Only works in the decimal numbering system.
dms	Converts the displayed number to degree-minute-second notation.
sin	Returns the sine of the displayed value.
cos	Returns the cosine of the displayed value.
tan	Returns the tangent of the displayed value.

Button	Meaning
Sta	Displays the statistics dialog box and activates the Ave, Sum, s, and Dat keys.
Ave	Returns the mean of the numbers in the statistics dialog box, entering it in the Calculator display.
Sum	Returns the sum of the numbers in the statistics dialog box, entering it in the Calculator display.
s	Returns the standard deviation of the numbers in the statistics dialog box, entering it in the Calculator display.
Dat	Adds the number in the Calculator display to the statistics dialog box.
Inv	Signals that you want to use the inverse of the next key that you select. Works with the sin, cos, tan, PI, x^y, x^3, x^2, ln, log, Ave, Sum, and s keys.
Hyp	Signals that you want to use the hyperbolic function of the sin, cos, or tan keys.

When you work in hexadecimal, octal, or binary notations, you can only use whole numbers. If the value in the display has anything to the right of the decimal point, then it is automatically truncated when you switch from decimal to one of the other numbering systems.

In addition, the keys that perform functions based on a value to the right of a decimal point do not work properly. For instance, you cannot use the sin, cos, or tan functions (outside of decimal notation format) and get meaningful results.

Tip

To copy a number from the Calculator's display to another program, simply use the Clipboard. Press Ctrl+C or select the Copy option from the Edit menu in the Calculator, and then paste the number in your other program.

Using the Character Map

The Character Map accessory has grown over the years, and the latest version supports the Unicode character format that is native to Windows NT Workstation 4.0. The accessory is used for three main purposes:

- To review characters in different fonts
- To access and use characters that do not appear on your keyboard
- To determine the keystrokes that are necessary to create a character

To use the Character Map accessory, follow these steps:

STEPS

Starting the character map

Step 1.   Choose the Programs option from the Start menu. This displays the Programs menu.

Step 2.   Choose the Accessories option from the Programs menu. This displays the list of accessories that are installed on your system.

Step 3.   Click on the Character Map option. Shortly you see the Character Map window, as shown in Figure 7-3.

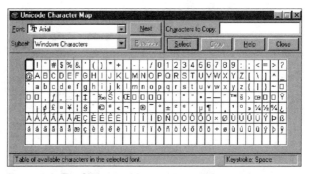

Figure 7-3: The Character Map accessory displays font information in a grid pattern.

The majority of the Character Map window is used to display the characters that are used in the font being displayed. At the top of the window, using the Font drop-down list, you can select the font that you want to have displayed in the window. You can display the contents of any TrueType or system font that is installed on your computer.

As previously mentioned, the Character Map supports the use of Unicode. Under ASCII, up to 255 different characters can be defined. This number is determined by the fact that ASCII is stored in an 8-bit code.

Unicode, on the other hand, can represent up to 65,535 characters, because it uses 16 bits for each character. Most fonts that are on the market do not support the extended character capabilities of Unicode, but some do.

If you have a Unicode font, you can view the different subsets of the font by using the Subset drop-down box. As an alternative, you can step through the subsets using the Next and Previous buttons.

If you see a character that you want to copy to the Clipboard, you can do so by clicking on the character in the main part of the window and then clicking on the Select button. This places the character in the Characters to Copy field, at the top-right of the Character Map window. When the field contains all of the characters that you want to copy, click on the Copy button to transfer them to the Clipboard.

Secret

You can only select characters from a particular font. When you change to a different font, all of the characters in the Characters to Copy field also change to the new font.

As you look through a font with the Character Map, you can also view the keystroke that it takes to create the character. This only works with the first 255 characters (in the ASCII range), but when the character is selected, the right side of the Character Map status bar shows the keystroke that creates the character. Some characters are created by pressing regular keyboard keys, and others are created by holding Alt while you enter a four-digit code on the keypad.

Using the Clipboard Viewer

The Clipboard is that special area of Windows NT that makes it possible to cut, copy, and paste. When you cut or copy something, it is placed in the Clipboard. When you later paste the item, it is copied from the Clipboard. Without the Clipboard, using the same data in different applications (and even in the same application) would be much more difficult.

The Clipboard Viewer is the accessory that allows you to view the contents of your Clipboard. However, the accessory actually allows you to do much more than just work with the Clipboard. To start the Clipboard Viewer, follow these steps:

STEPS

Starting the Clipboard Viewer

Step 1.   Choose the <u>P</u>rograms option from the Start menu. This displays the Programs menu.

Step 2.   Choose the Accessories option from the Programs menu. This displays the list of accessories that are installed on your system.

Step 3.   Click on the Clipboard Viewer option. Shortly you see the window that is shown in Figure 7-4.

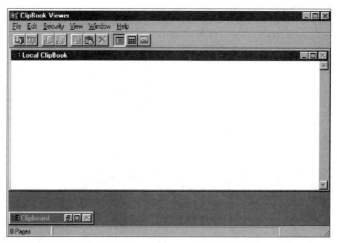

Figure 7-4: The Clipboard Viewer is used to display information saved from the Clipboard.

The first thing that you should notice is that the Clipboard Viewer is actually a misnomer. The title bar on the accessory window tells the real story —

choosing to start the Clipboard Viewer accessory actually starts the ClipBook Viewer. There is a distinct difference between a ClipBook and a Clipboard.

The Clipboard is stored and used on your local machine. The ClipBook, on the other hand, can be shared with other people across your network. You can also store multiple pages in the ClipBook, which makes it much more powerful and versatile than the Clipboard.

At the top of the ClipBook Viewer window, you can see the contents of your local ClipBook; at the bottom of the window is the minimized appearance of your Clipboard. You can enlarge the Clipboard, and view its contents, using the window control buttons on the minimized Clipboard.

The toolbar and menus at the top of the ClipBook Viewer window allow you to control what is displayed in the ClipBook window as well as how it is displayed. Most of the menu options (and their tool counterparts) deal with two things:

- **Format.** Because the ClipBook can contain multiple pages, you can control how those pages are displayed. For instance, the choices from the View menu allow you to specify how many pages you want displayed at the same time.

- **Network.** Because the ClipBook can be used over the network, there are options that allow you to connect to another computer and view that ClipBook. In addition, you can assign security permissions to your ClipBook so that you can control who gets to use it.

Using the Clock

The Clock accessory is a holdover from previous versions of Windows. This accessory displays, in a dialog box, a simulation of either a digital or analog clock. (Analog clocks have a dial with hands that indicate the time.) To start the Clock accessory, follow these steps:

STEPS

Starting the Clock

Step 1. Choose the Programs option from the Start menu. This displays the Programs menu.

(continued)

Step 2. Choose the Accessories option from the Programs menu. This displays the list of accessories that are installed on your system.

Step 3. Click on the Clock option. Shortly you see the Clock accessory appear, as shown in Figure 7-5.

Figure 7-5: The Clock accessory tells you the current time.

In earlier versions of Windows, the Taskbar was not a feature. In Windows NT Workstation 4.0, the Taskbar can be used to always view the current time. Although you can continue to use the Clock accessory, there is little need to still do so. The Clock accessory will most likely be dropped from future versions of Windows.

Using Imaging

The Imaging accessory is brand new with the introduction of Windows NT Workstation 4.0. This tool allows you to grab information from your scanner and manipulate it. For the accessory to work with your scanner, the scanner must understand and use TWAIN drivers.

This is a device driver specification that allows many different types of scanners to use the same basic drivers. Most scanners sold today understand TWAIN, but older scanners may use their own proprietary drivers; these do not work with the Imaging accessory.

To start the Imaging accessory, follow these steps:

STEPS

Starting the Imaging accessory

Step 1. Choose the Programs option from the Start menu. This displays the Programs menu.

Step 2. Choose the Accessories option from the Programs menu. This displays the list of accessories that are installed on your system.

Step 3. Click on the Imaging option. Shortly you see the Imaging window appear, as shown in Figure 7-6.

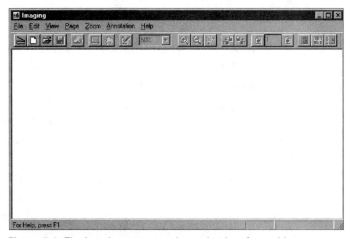

Figure 7-6: The Imaging accessory is used to interface with scanners.

The work area in the Imaging window looks like the work area in the Paint accessory, and many of the tools on the toolbar look the same. Don't confuse the Imaging accessory with a drawing program, however. It is intended primarily for scanning images and then manipulating those images in a couple of ways.

Assuming that you have a TWAIN-compatible scanner attached to your system, all you need to do to scan an image is to click on the scan tool, at the left end of the toolbar, or select the Scan New option from the File menu. The scanner is activated, the image captured, and the result is displayed in the work area.

After an image is captured, you can add annotations to the image. This is done by displaying the Annotation Toolbox (by clicking on the tool with that name, just to the left of the Zoom drop-down list) or by choosing an annotation tool from the Annotation menu.

The Imaging accessory includes the following tools:

- **Selection Pointer.** This tool is used to select annotations that you previously added to your image. You can then move, copy, or cut the annotation by using the regular editing commands or tools.

- **Freehand Line.** This tool is used to draw lines. For instance, you may use the tool to draw a circle around a part of your image or to draw arrows pointing to information in the image.

- **Highlighter.** This tool is used to highlight portions of your image. Highlighting is always transparent and appears as a borderless rectangle. The highlighter color is yellow, but you can select any other color that you desire.

- **Straight Line.** This tool is used to draw straight lines.

- **Hollow Rectangle.** This tool is used to draw boxes on your image. The rectangle is considered hollow because it is not filled with a color.

- **Filled Rectangle.** This tool is the same as the Hollow Rectangle, except that it is filled with a color.

- **Typed Text.** This tool allows you to enter text as an annotation to your image.

- **Attach-a-Note.** This tool provides another way to add a text annotation, except it is presented differently. Instead of the text just appearing on the image, it is placed on a rectangle made to appear like a sticky-note.

- **Text From File.** This tool loads a text file and uses its contents as an annotation over the scanned image.

- **Rubber Stamps.** This tool allows you to stamp text messages on your image. These messages function in much the same way as a regular rubber stamp.

Each annotation tool allows you to define properties that control how the tool works. For instance, some tools may have properties that allow you to select a color, change a line width, or create a rubber stamp image. To access the properties for an annotation, right-click on the tool in the Annotation Toolbox.

Annotations are not made part of the actual captured image unless you choose the Make Annotations Permanent option from the Annotation menu. If you don't choose this option, the annotations that you make are gone if you later open the document.

When you are done annotating your scanned image, you can save it as a graphic file. You can save the image as either a TIF or BMP image. These images can then be used by other programs for further processing.

Note

If you later want to load your saved document in the Paint accessory, make sure that you save it in a BMP format. Paint does not understand the TIF format.

Using Multimedia Accessories

Windows NT Workstation provides a small contingent of multimedia-based accessories. Most systems that are sold today to run Windows NT Workstation also have the capability to run multimedia applications. Without going into the details of what a multimedia-compliant system is, you at least need to have a CD-ROM drive and a sound card.

In addition, make sure that you have all the proper drivers for your installed devices. Chapter 6 discusses what is necessary to install the proper drivers. Each of the following sections quickly reviews the various multimedia accessories.

Using the CD Player

You already know that many CD-ROM drives allow you to play audio CDs. Assuming that you have the proper hardware and connections to play audio CDs, you can start the CD Player in either of two ways. The first is to simply insert the audio CD into your drive.

The auto-run feature of Windows NT automatically detects the presence of the newly inserted disk and, if it is an audio disk, it launches the CD Player and begins playing.

If your system does not have the auto-run feature enabled (some people find it distracting), then you can manually start the CD Player accessory by following these steps:

STEPS

Starting the CD Player

Step 1. Choose the Programs option from the Start menu. This displays the Programs menu.

Step 2. Choose the Accessories option from the Programs menu. This displays the list of accessories that are installed on your system.

(continued)

STEPS *(continued)*

Starting the CD Player

Step 3. Choose the Multimedia option from the Accessories menu. This displays a list of multimedia accessories that are installed.

Step 4. Click on the CD Player option. Shortly you see the CD Player window, as shown in Figure 7-7.

Figure 7-7: The CD Player is used to play tracks from an audio CD.

If you use a CD player or a VCR at home, the CD Player accessory may look familiar. It mimics the "look and feel" of a real CD player. When you insert an audio CD into the CD-ROM drive, the control buttons to the right of the time display become active.

These buttons function the same as similar buttons on your home CD player. There are buttons that allow you to play, pause, stop, and skip individual tracks on the CD. There is even a button that allows you to eject the CD.

The Windows NT CD Player can do one thing that a normal CD player cannot. You can use it to keep track of your CD collection. If you look at the CD Player, you see three fields called Artist, Title, and Track. Notice that both the Artist and Track fields have drop-down lists.

If you have multiple CD-ROM drives on your system, you can use the Artist drop-down list to switch between the different drives. The Track field is used to switch between the tracks on the CD that is currently being played.

If the artist, title, and track information can be automatically derived from the audio CD, it is displayed in the corresponding fields. (Some audio CDs have this bibliographic information recorded on the CD; most do not.) If it cannot be derived, the CD Player checks a unique signature value, stored on the CD, to see if you have previously entered any information about the CD. If you have, then the information that you entered is displayed. If neither source of information is available, the CD Player displays the default information, as shown earlier in Figure 7-7.

Updating CD information

If you want to update the information about the CD, choose the Edit Play List option from the Disc menu. You then see the Disc Settings dialog box, as shown in Figure 7-8.

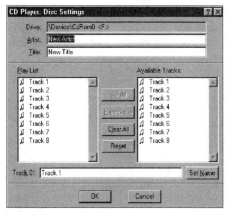

Figure 7-8: The CD Player allows you to save information about the discs that you play.

From this dialog box, you can change information about the CD artist, the title of the CD, and the names of any tracks. To change the artist name, simply click the Artist field and change the name. You can change the CD title in the same manner, using the Title field.

To change track names, follow these steps:

STEPS

Changing track titles

Step 1. In the Available Tracks list, highlight the track name that you want to change. The name of the track that you select also appears in the Track field at the bottom of the dialog box (to the left of the Set Name button).

Step 2. Highlight the current track name in the Track field. Replace it with the proper name for the track.

Step 3. Click on the Set Name button. The new name that you entered appears in the Available Tracks list, and the next track name is automatically selected for editing.

Step 4. Repeat steps 2 and 3 for each track on the CD.

When you are finished, click on the OK button. The CD Player saves the updated information about the CD; this information appears whenever you play the CD in the future.

Using the play list

The CD Player does not force you to listen to all of the tracks on a CD, nor do you need to listen to them in sequential order. You can completely customize the order in which you hear your music. You do this by creating a *play list,* which defines the order in which tracks should be played.

To edit the play list, choose the Edit Play List option from the Disc menu. You then see the Disc Settings dialog box, as shown earlier in Figure 7-8. You can then create a custom play list by following these steps:

STEPS

Creating a play list

Step 1.   Click on the Clear All button. This clears the information in the Play List area.

Step 2.   In the Available Tracks list, highlight the name of the track that you want to play.

Step 3.   Click the Add button to copy the track to the Play List area.

Step 4.   Repeat steps 2 and 3 until you have selected all the tracks that you want to hear, in the order you want to hear them. (You can even pick the same track multiple times.)

Step 5.   To remove a track from the Play List, select it and click the Remove button.

Step 6.   Click on the OK button to save your play list.

Play lists are remembered from one use of the CD to another. Thus, when you create a custom play list, you effectively create your own CD because what you hear is exactly what you want to hear.

Using the Volume Control

The Volume Control accessory is used to control the overall volume levels of your sound system components as well as other audio characteristics, such as balance.

The Volume Control accessory is accessed in the same way that you access all the other multimedia accessories. It provides a great deal of control over how your sound system is configured.

To access the primary Volume Control, follow these steps:

STEPS

Displaying the Volume Control

Step 1. Choose the Programs option from the Start menu. This displays the Programs menu.

Step 2. Choose the Accessories option from the Programs menu. This displays the list of accessories that are installed on your system.

Step 3. Choose the Multimedia option from the Accessories menu. This displays a list of multimedia accessories that are installed.

Step 4. Click on the Volume Control option. Shortly you see the Volume Control window, as shown in Figure 7-9.

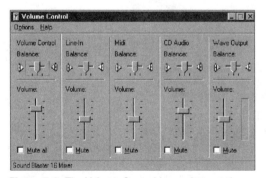

Figure 7-9: The Volume Control is used to set the volume levels for a variety of channels.

The exact appearance of the Volume Control window can vary depending on the capabilities of your sound device. For instance, your Volume Control could have an additional horizontal slider at the top of the dialog box. In general, however, there are three types of controls that you may see in the Volume Control window:

- **Horizontal slider.** This control appears at the top of the Volume Control window and represents the balance for the channel. Move the slider to the left, and the sound appears to come more from the left channel; move it to the right for the opposite effect.

- **Vertical slider.** This control appears in the middle of the Volume Control window and governs the volume for the channel. Move the slider up for more volume and down for less.

- **Check box.** There may be a check box at the bottom of a channel control; this is typically used to mute the sound from the channel.

You can also control what channels are displayed in the dialog box. This is done by selecting the Properties option from the Options menu, which displays the dialog box that is shown in Figure 7-10.

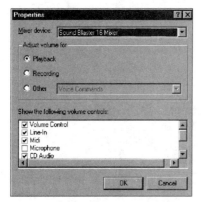

Figure 7-10: The Source Selection dialog box controls the channels that are displayed in the Volume Control window.

This Source Selection dialog box displays every audio channel that is supported by your audio card. To the left of each channel is a check box. If a check box is selected, then the corresponding channel appears in the Volume Control window. Using the Source Selection dialog box, you can customize how the Volume Control window appears.

After you set the volume levels that you want to use, close the Volume Control window. Windows NT remembers the levels until you explicitly change them at a later time.

Secret

You can also display the Volume Control by double-clicking on the speaker that appears at the right side of the Taskbar. If you never use the Taskbar Volume Control, you can remove it from the Taskbar. You do this by right-clicking on the Taskbar speaker, selecting Adjust Audio Properties, and then clearing the check box in the Playback section of the dialog box.

Using the Sound Recorder

Windows NT includes an accessory that allows you to quickly and easily record sounds from a microphone or other device. These sounds can be recorded in a variety of formats, depending on the capabilities of your audio card. The recordings are saved in the standard WAV audio format, which allows the sounds to be assigned as system sounds (described in Chapter 3) as well as to be used in a variety of other programs.

To start the Sound Recorder accessory, follow these steps:

STEPS

Starting the Sound Recorder

Step 1.   Choose the Programs option from the Start menu. This displays the Programs menu.

Step 2.   Choose the Accessories option from the Programs menu. This displays the list of accessories that are installed on your system.

Step 3.   Choose the Multimedia option from the Accessories menu. This displays a list of multimedia accessories that are installed.

Step 4.   Click on the Sound Recorder option. Shortly you see the Sound Recorder window, as shown in Figure 7-11.

Figure 7-11: The Sound Recorder accessory is used to record and edit audio files.

As with many other Windows NT multimedia accessories, the Sound Recorder provides a series of menu options as well as several control buttons. The most common menu options are accomplished through the use of the control buttons. These buttons, which appear similar to buttons on a CD or cassette tape player, perform the following tasks, from left to right:

- **Rewind.** This button moves the player to the beginning of the sound file. Click on this button before clicking on the Play button if you want to hear a sound file from the beginning. (The Tool Tips refer to this button as *Seek to Start.*)

- **Fast Forward.** This button moves the player to the end of the sound file. Click on this button if you want to record or add information at the end of the current sound file. (The Tool Tips refer to this button as *Seek to End.*)

- **Play.** This button begins playing a sound file from the current position within the file.

- **Stop.** This button stops whatever the Sound Recorder is playing. It does not rewind or fast-forward the sound file; you need to use the appropriate control buttons to do this.

- **Record.** This button starts recording at the current location within the sound file.

Recording an audio file

If your sound card allows you to use a microphone for input, you can use the Sound Recorder to capture your voice or any other sound desired. You do this by following these steps:

STEPS

Recording an audio file

Step 1.   Plug your microphone into the microphone connector of the sound card.

Step 2.   Start the Sound Recorder, as described in the previous section.

Step 3.   Choose the New option from the File menu. This instructs the Sound Recorder to eliminate any other sound file from memory.

Step 4. Choose the Properties option from the File menu. This displays the Properties for Sound dialog box, as shown in Figure 7-12.

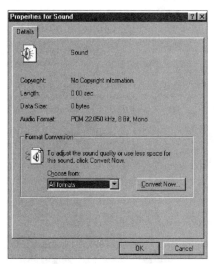

Figure 7-12: The Properties for Sound dialog box enables you to indicate how you want your sound recordings created.

Step 5. Click on the Convert Now button at the bottom of the dialog box. This displays the Sound Selection dialog box, as shown in Figure 7-13.

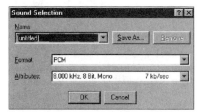

Figure 7-13: The Sound Selection dialog box is used to specify the type of recording quality you want used.

(continued)

STEPS *(continued)*

Recording an audio file

Step 6.   Using the Name pull-down list at the top of the dialog box, select the quality of recording you want to make. (The rest of the dialog box then reflects the specifics of your selection.)

Step 7.   Click on OK to close the Sound Selection dialog box.

Step 8.   Click on OK to close the Properties for Sound dialog box.

Step 9.   Click on the Record button (the right-most button, with the red dot). This starts the recording process.

Step 10.   Make the noises or sounds, or speak the words that you want the Sound Recorder to record.

Step 11.   Click on the Stop button to end your recording session.

Your sound recording is now complete. You can either play it back (by using the Rewind and Play buttons) or save it to disk by choosing Save from the File menu.

Editing an audio file

A number of different menu commands are available that allow you to edit any sound file that you have loaded (or recorded). The common editing tasks include the following items:

■ **Append.** Use the Fast Forward button to move to the end of the audio file, and then click on the Record button. Any sounds that the microphone can pick up are added to the end of the sound file.

■ **Insert.** Stops the sound file at the point where you want to insert another file, and then choose Insert File from the Edit menu. Enter the second file's name when prompted for it. The second audio file is then inserted in the current sound file.

■ **Erase.** Stops the sound file at the place where you want to erase. Use the Delete Before Current Position or Delete After Current Position command (both from the Edit menu) to erase everything before or after the point where you stopped.

- **Mix.** Mixing means that two sounds are combined over top of each other. Load the first audio file, and then choose Mix with File from the Edit menu. Enter the second file's name when prompted for it. Both files are then mixed in the Sound Recorder's buffer.

You can also use the Sound Recorder to add special effects to your file. This special type of editing is achieved by mathematically manipulating the digital information that is stored in the audio file. Each of the available special effects is initiated by selecting the appropriate choice from the Effects menu:

- **Volume adjustment.** You can adjust the amplitude (volume) of your audio file by choosing either of the first two options from the Effects menu. The Increase Volume (by 25%) option makes the sound louder, whereas the Decrease Volume option makes the sound softer.

- **Speed adjustment.** If you want to do an impersonation of a chipmunk, you can choose the Increase Speed (by 100%) option. This doubles the speed at which the sound recording is played back. Similarly, you can use the Decrease Speed option to slow the rate at which a sound file is played back.

- **Echo.** Use this option to simulate an echo by making a copy of the sound recording and then offsetting it from the original by a short time period. These offset copies are then mixed together. The result is the same as an echo.

- **Reverse.** This option reverses your audio file; it is similar to playing an album or tape in reverse. Choosing this option once reverses the sound recording; choosing it a second time reverses it again, which results in the original recording.

Secret

You can repeatedly use any of the Effects menu options for a cumulative effect on your audio file. For instance, if you wanted to increase the volume of an audio file more than 25 percent, you could select the Increase Volume (by 25%) option twice in a row. The effect is that the volume is increased by 56.25 percent, which is the result of 1.25×1.25. The other menu options operate in the same manner.

Using the Media Player

Earlier in this chapter, you learned about the capabilities of the Sound Recorder and the CD Player accessories. The Media Player combines many of the capabilities of these accessories but goes one step further. It also allows you to work with Video for Windows (AVI) files so that you can watch live-action video.

To start the Media Player, follow these steps:

STEPS

Starting the Media Player

Step 1. Choose the Programs option from the Start menu. This displays the Programs menu.

Step 2. Choose the Accessories option from the Programs menu. This displays the list of accessories that are installed on your system.

Step 3. Choose the Multimedia option from the Accessories menu. This displays a list of multimedia accessories that are installed.

Step 4. Click on the Media Player option. Shortly you see the Media Player window, as shown in Figure 7-14.

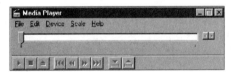

Figure 7-14: The Media Player is used to play any type of multimedia file that is supported by Windows NT.

Picking a media source

Using the Media Player, you can play files that are stored in a number of different formats and access audio CDs. The Media Player supports these popular multimedia files or devices:

- CD audio
- MIDI files
- WAV files
- AVI video files

To play an audio CD, simply choose the CD Audio option from the Device menu. To play any of the multimedia file types, you can either choose the appropriate option from the Device menu or simply load a file using the Open option from the File menu. After the file type or device type is set, the Media Player configures itself to best reflect the type of multimedia data that are being processed.

Understanding the controls

The controls that are displayed in the Media Player are consistent with those used in other accessories, such as the Sound Recorder and the CD Player. You can determine the purpose of each control button by using the Tool Tips feature of Windows NT. If you position the mouse pointer over a button and stop moving it for a moment, a tip box appears that indicates the purpose of the button.

Secret

After picking a media source, you can simplify the controls that are displayed by double-clicking the Media Player title bar. In most instances, this results in only the Play and Stop buttons being displayed. Double-click the title bar again to display the entire range of tools.

Two controls are unique to the Media Player. The Start Selection and End Selection buttons are used to mark the beginning and end of a portion of a media file or an audio CD. The work that you subsequently do with the file or device (playback, rewind, and so on) is done in relation to the selection. To change or remove a selection, you can also choose Selection from the Edit menu.

Setting a scale

If you drop down the Scale menu, you see that there are three choices. When you select a choice, the values shown in the Media Player slider control are changed. Three types of scales are used by Media Player:

- **Time.** This scale represents minutes and seconds of elapsed time.

- **Frames.** This scale represents the individual images in a video file. In normal live-action video, frames are displayed at a rate of 60 per second. In AVI video, frames are displayed at approximately 30 per second.

- **Tracks.** This scale represents the number of tracks on an audio CD.

The choices that are available at any given point depend on the type of file or device that you are working with. Table 7-3 shows the applicable scales for each type of file or device.

Table 7-3   Scales that are available for Media Player sources

Source	Scales
AVI	Time, frames
CD audio	Time, tracks
MIDI	Time
WAV	Time

Using the Notepad

The Notepad accessory has been around for a long time, providing you with the ability to view, edit, or print short text files. In previous versions of Windows, the Notepad would only support ASCII text, but the Windows NT Workstation 4.0 version supports files that are saved in the Unicode format. ASCII stores characters according to their 8-bit representation, while Unicode uses a 16-bit format.

The text editing capabilities of Notepad are rather rudimentary; in fact, they are downright minimal when compared with the WordPad accessory or a full-blown word processor. Such features were never the focus of Notepad, however. For quickly working with small text files, Notepad can't be beat.

To open the Notepad accessory, follow these steps:

STEPS

Starting the Notepad

Step 1. Choose the Programs option from the Start menu. This displays the Programs menu.

Step 2. Choose the Accessories option from the Programs menu. This displays the list of accessories that are installed on your system.

Step 3. Click on the Notepad option. Soon you see the Notepad window, as shown in Figure 7-15.

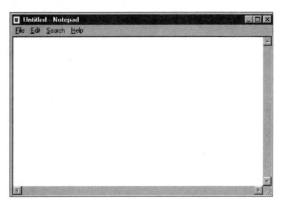

Figure 7-15: The Notepad accessory is used to edit small text files.

Tip

You can open the Notepad automatically by double-clicking on a file with a .TXT extension. If the file is too large for Notepad to load, Windows offers to open the file with WordPad.

The Notepad window consists of a display area, where you can view or edit a text file, and a simple menu bar. The different menus have the following purposes:

- **File.** This menu is used to open and save files, set the margins on a printed page, print the file that is displayed in Notepad, and exit the program.

- **Edit.** This menu allows you to edit text that is displayed in Notepad, control the wrapping of words at the side of the Notepad window, insert the time and date at the location of the cursor, and change the font that is used to display the text file.

- **Search.** This menu is used to search the text file. You can also replace occurrences of one string with another.

- **Help.** This option is used to access the Windows NT help system, as described in Chapter 1.

When you work with Notepad, you can only work with one file at a time. In addition, you cannot do any fancy character formatting — remember that you are working with text files, not word processing files. You can, however, change the font that is used to display the text file by choosing the Set Font option from the Edit menu.

Secret

The file handling that is done by Notepad requires that the entire text file be loaded into memory. Thus, some files may be too large to edit with Notepad. The actual file size limit depends on the resources that are available on your computer. This means that a system with lots of memory and few other applications on the Taskbar can open a larger text file than a system with less memory.

When you use the Save command from the File menu, the file that you are working on is saved under the same name and in the same format as it was originally. If you select the Save As command, you can save your file under a different name, and you can control whether it is saved in ASCII or Unicode format.

Using Paint

Windows NT Workstation 4.0 includes a drawing program that is similar to the old Paintbrush accessory that was included with previous versions of Windows. The new Paint accessory is more refined and capable, however. It allows you access to a different set of tools, and you can work on files that are stored in both BMP (Windows bitmap) and PCX (Paintbrush) formats.

You start the Paint accessory by following these steps:

STEPS

Starting Paint

Step 1.   Choose the Programs option from the Start menu. This displays the Programs menu.

Step 2.   Choose the Accessories option from the Programs menu. This displays the list of accessories that are installed on your system.

Step 3.   Click on the Paint option. Shortly you see the Paint window, as shown in Figure 7-16.

Figure 7-16: The Paint program is a useful graphics editor.

Understanding the interface

The Paint accessory has quite a few features. If you look at the program window as shown in Figure 7-16, you can see that the majority of the window is used for the workspace; this is where you draw your picture.

To the left of this area is the tool box, which is described in the next section. At the bottom of the program window is the color palette (which Paint refers to as the color box), along with an indicator of which color has been selected for the foreground and the background.

At the bottom of the program window (under the color palette) is the status bar. This area contains two important items. At the left side of the status bar is an indicator that shows which tool you are working with. To the right of this are two numbers that are separated by a comma. These numbers are visible whenever your tool is located in the workspace.

The numbers represent the coordinates at which the point of the tool is located. These coordinates are very helpful in determining where you should draw your objects or place your text.

Secret

If you move your mouse very fast — faster than the Paint accessory can keep up — you may be able to get your mouse pointer off the Paint screen with coordinates still showing in the status bar. In this case, simply move your mouse pointer back into the workspace. Paint updates the status bar to again show the correct coordinates.

At the top of the program window is a menu. This menu has the following six options:

- **File.** This menu allows you to open, save, configure, or print an image. If you are working with a BMP image, you can also allow Paint to configure Windows NT so that the image is used as your desktop wallpaper.

- **Edit.** This menu is used to edit different selections that you make within your image. The options include standard editing functions, such as clear, copy, cut, and paste.

- **View.** This menu is used to turn different parts of the display on or off. You can hide or display the tool box, the color box, and the status bar. In addition, you can use this menu to enlarge or shrink portions of the image.

- **Image.** This menu is used to apply special effects to a portion of your image or the entire image. You can also change the size of the image.

- **Options.** This menu is used to modify how colors are used by Paint.

- **Help.** This option is used to access the Windows NT help system, as described in Chapter 1.

Using the tools

You create or alter images in the workspace by using the different tools that are built in to Paint. These tools are collected in the tool box, normally displayed at the left side of your workspace.

Paint includes 16 different tools, and each affects your image in different ways. Though not as full-featured as many commercial drawing programs, Paint is very handy for quickly working with an image.

As you select different tools, notice that the area just beneath the tool box may change. This allows you to specify different ways in which the selected tool can be used. For instance, take a look at Figure 7-17.

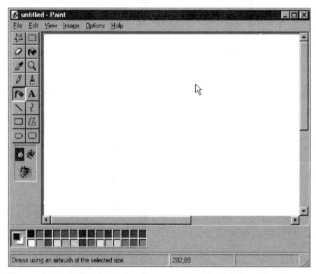

Figure 7-17: Different tools allow you to select different options on how they are used.

In this example, the spray-paint tool is selected. (Paint refers to this as an airbrush tool, but it looks more like a can of spray paint.) Beneath the tool box, there are three choices that you can make; each represents a different way in which the spray pattern from the spray-paint tool can appear. Other tools have similar options that allow you to affect their behavior.

The first two tools, at the top of the tool box, deserve some special attention. These tools are used to select different areas of your image, and they have images of dashed lines on them. The left one appears as an inverted star, and the right one shows up as a rectangle.

Both serve the same purpose, but the one on the left is used for selecting irregular areas, whereas the one on the right is used to select rectangular areas. Once an area is selected, you can use any of the Edit menu commands on it as well as several commands from the Image menu.

The best way to learn about different tools is to simply try them out. You can take some time to work with an empty image and then select each tool to see how it behaves. Make sure that you try out the different options that are available for each tool, as well. If you make a mistake, you can always use the Undo option from the Edit menu. This lets you backtrack to the last time that you changed a tool or saved the file.

Using colors

Paint enables you to work with a palette of up to 64 colors, chosen from over 16 million colors. This provides you with quite a bit of latitude on how you create your images. At the bottom of the program window is the color box, which is used to quickly select the colors that you want to work with.

At the left side of the color box are two small squares that overlap each other. These represent the foreground and background colors that you are using. The foreground color is used to do the actual drawing. For instance, if you draw or brush a line, the foreground color is used. The background color is used to fill areas when you have selected an option that uses two colors.

The bottom four tools provide "fill options." If you select an option that is filled in, the foreground color is used for the border of the shape and the background color is used for the inside of the shape.

To change the foreground and background colors, you have four options:

- Click on a color in the color box to change the foreground color.

- Right-click on a color in the color box to change the background color.

- Use the eye-dropper tool to "pick" a foreground color directly from your image. Simply move the tool over the color that you want, click once, and the foreground color is changed to match the color that you selected.

- Use the eye-dropper to change the background color by right-clicking on the color that you want to use.

In addition, you can alter the palette that is used by Paint. This is done by double-clicking on the color swatch (in the color box) that you want to change to a new color. When you do this, the Edit Colors dialog box is displayed, as shown in Figure 7-18.

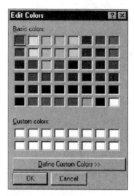

Figure 7-18: Paint allows you to create a palette of up to 64 different colors.

In the Edit Colors dialog box, you can see 48 different colors at the top of the dialog box; these are the basic colors that are defined for you by Paint. If you want to use one of these colors in your swatch in the color box, simply click on the color and then click on the OK button. The selected color is substituted for the color swatch.

If you look back at the Edit Colors dialog box, however, you can see that there are 16 blank color swatches at the bottom of the dialog box. These are used for custom colors, which you can define. To define a custom color, simply click on the Define Custom Colors button. (Seems natural, doesn't it?) This expands the Edit Colors dialog box so that it includes a color selector on the right side, as shown in Figure 7-19.

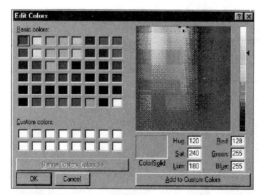

Figure 7-19: An expanded Edit Colors dialog box allows you to define your own custom colors.

To define a custom color, you have several options:

- You can click the mouse anywhere in the color selector, and it changes the color settings just below the selector.

- You can adjust the luminance bar at the right side of the color selector.

- You can enter numerical values for the hue, saturation, and luminance.

- You can enter numerical values for the red, green, and blue components of your color.

Using any of these methods affects the color that is displayed in the large color box below the color selector. When you are satisfied with your choice, click on the Add to Custom Colors button.

This adds your color to the next available color swatch in the Custom Colors area. You can then continue to create custom colors, if you desire.

When you are finished editing your color palette, click on the OK button to close the Edit Colors dialog box.

Printing your images

The Paint accessory can also be used to print graphic images. Printing is accomplished by performing two steps: setting up your page and then sending the image to the printer. Setting up the page is done the same as in many other programs that allow you to create printed output. To define your page setup in Paint, select the Page Setup option from the File menu. This displays the Page Setup dialog box, as shown in Figure 7-20.

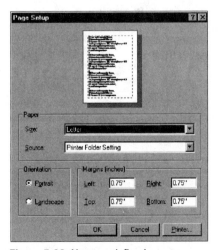

Figure 7-20: You can define how you want your printed output to look.

Using the control on this dialog box, you should pick the paper size and source, the orientation of your printout, and the margins that you want to use. These settings are only remembered for this session of using Paint; they are not stored with your image. When you are done setting up the page, click on the OK button to close the dialog box.

The next step is to send your output to the printer. This is done by selecting the Print option from the File menu. This displays the Print dialog box, as shown in Figure 7-21.

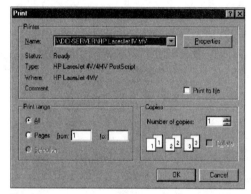

Figure 7-21: You can specify how many copies of your image you want to print.

The Print dialog box should look familiar; it is used in many other programs. Here you can specify the printer to which you want the output sent, which pages of your image you want to print, and how many copies to print. If you select the Print to File check box, your printer output is instead sent to a file, which you can specify.

When you are ready to print your image, click on the OK button. The image is sent to either the printer or to a file, according to your specifications. When done, you are returned to the Paint accessory window.

Using WordPad

WordPad is an accessory that was developed for Windows 95 but has now been included with Windows NT Workstation 4.0. This program is the most sophisticated of any of the built-in accessories. WordPad is a word processing program in its own right.

It allows you to read files in several different formats, edit them, format them, and print them. In fact, the features that are provided in WordPad would have been considered state-of-the art for a commercial word processing program just a few years ago.

If you are familiar with the Write accessory in older versions of Windows NT, WordPad will seem familiar in some respects. There are many new, robust tools and features, however, that let you produce and edit complex documents.

In fact, there are way too many features to delve into in this section; fully addressing all of the features could take an entire chapter by itself. After reading through the following sections, you will at least know the basics of how to use this valuable tool.

Starting WordPad

There are many different ways that you can start WordPad:

- Choose the WordPad option from the Accessories menu.

- Open a text file that is too large for Notepad to process. In this case, you are given the option of opening the file in WordPad.

- Open a different document type that is associated with WordPad.

This last method of starting may need a little explaining. WordPad understands several different file formats, and you can start the accessory by opening a document that has been stored in any of those formats.

WordPad understands the following formats:

- **Text.** WordPad can read text files, the same as Notepad. This includes text files that are saved in both ASCII and Unicode variations. Text files typically have a filename extension of .TXT.

- **Rich Text.** This format is created by many word processors. When you save a file in rich text format, it is written as an ASCII text file that contains tags to define how the text should be formatted. Rich text files typically have a filename extension of .RTF.

- **Word 6.** This format is created by Microsoft Word for Windows and Word for Macintosh. Word files typically have a filename extension of .DOC.

- **Write.** WordPad can read files that were created with the old Write accessory, which was included in earlier versions of Windows. Write document files typically have a filename extension of .WRI.

Because of the number of file formats understood by WordPad, it is much more versatile than previous accessories. The ability of WordPad to open these types of files by double-clicking on the document assumes, of course, that you have not installed another application that changed the associations to point to itself. For instance, if you have installed Microsoft Word for Windows, then it changes file associations so that .DOC files, when double-clicked, automatically start Word.

When you open WordPad, the program window appears, as shown in Figure 7-22. This example shows the accessory without a document loaded. If you opened WordPad by double-clicking on a document file, then it is automatically loaded into the program. If you later want to open a document, then you can choose the Open command from the File menu or click on the Open icon on the toolbar.

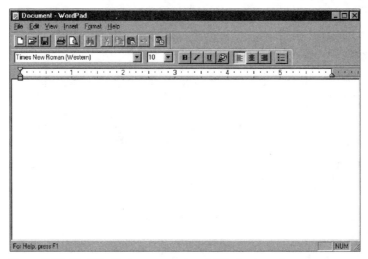

Figure 7-22: The WordPad accessory is a full-fledged word processing program.

Secret

There is no option in WordPad to open multiple documents. If you need to work on more than one document at a time, you can instead open different instances of WordPad. Thus, you can have two (or more) copies of WordPad running at the same time, each with a different document loaded.

The WordPad interface

If you look back at the WordPad window, you can see that it contains quite a few more items than the Notepad accessory which was discussed earlier in this chapter. Indeed, the interface that is used in WordPad is reminiscent of the interface used in Microsoft Word for Windows. At the top of the program window is the menu, followed by the toolbar, the format bar, and the ruler.

The menu contains the options that allow you to manage your documents and the WordPad accessory itself. The menu options include the following items:

■ **File.** This menu is used to open and save files, format the appearance of a printed page, print the document that is displayed in WordPad, and exit the program.

- **Edit.** This menu allows you to edit text that is displayed in WordPad, find and replace text in the document, and control embedded OLE objects. (*OLE* is an acronym for object linking and embedding. It refers to the ability to create objects in one program and place them in another program. For instance, you may create a spreadsheet and embed it as part of a WordPad document.)

- **View.** This menu is used to control how information is displayed in the WordPad window.

- **Insert.** This menu is used to insert either the date and time or an OLE object, as just described.

- **Format.** This menu is used to format characters and paragraphs in your documents.

- **Help.** This option is used to access the Windows NT help system, as described in Chapter 1.

The toolbar and format bar, which are displayed under the menu, are used to access shortcuts to many of the menu commands. For instance, if you click on the Find tool (it looks like a pair of binoculars), it is the same as choosing the Find command from the Edit menu.

Tip

If you want to discover what each button on the toolbar and format bar are used for, take advantage of the Tool Tips feature of Windows NT. Simply pause the mouse pointer above the button, and shortly you see a short description of what the button does.

Formatting a document

In addition to typing basic text, WordPad lets you apply special formatting to characters, words, and paragraphs. When you get the hang of it, you can really make your documents shine by applying a few formatting techniques. WordPad allows you to control the formatting of both characters and paragraphs.

Character formatting

You can format the appearance of individual characters in your documents. In fact, WordPad is versatile enough that you can format every character differently, if desired.

To format a character, follow the pattern of selecting what you want to format and then formatting it. For instance, you may be working with a document, and you want to format the word *especially;* you want to make it appear in italics. You would first select the word and then apply the italics.

To select a word, you have several options:

- You can use the mouse to click at the left of the first character of the word, hold the mouse button, and move the mouse until you have highlighted the entire word.

- You can use the mouse to double-click anywhere within the word.

- You can position the cursor to the left of the word and hold Shift as you use the right-arrow key to highlight the entire word.

Regardless of how you select the word, when it is selected, it is shown in reverse type, as you can see in Figure 7-23. With the word selected, you are ready to apply the character formatting that you want.

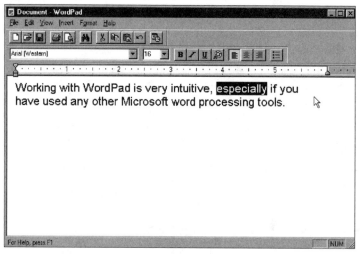

Figure 7-23: You need to select the text that you want to format before you apply the formatting.

You can apply several different types of character formatting:

- **Font.** This controls the general appearance of the characters that you have selected. Fonts are available for every occasion and for every purpose. You can use any font that you have installed on your system. The quickest way to select a font is to use the drop-down font list on the formatting bar. In Figure 7-23, the font is Arial (Western).

- **Type Size.** This controls how large the characters appear. Sizes are specified in points, which are equal to approximately $1/72$ of an inch. You can pick the font size by using the size drop-down list to the right of the font name. In Figure 7-23, the type size is 16 points.

- **Bold.** This makes the characters that you have selected look darker (like **this**). You can make your selection bold by clicking on the B button, to the right of the type size.

- **Italics.** This slants the characters that you have selected toward the right (like *this*). You can make your selected text italic by clicking on the I button, which is next to the bold tool.

- **Underline.** This adds a single line under the characters that you have selected (like <u>this</u>). You can make your selected text underlined by clicking on the U button, to the right of the italics tool.

- **Strikeout.** This adds a single line through the characters that you have selected, as if they have been marked through (like ~~this~~). You can only set this text attribute by using the menus, as described shortly.

- **Color.** This allows you to change the color of the selected text to any of 16 colors. You can set the color of your selection by clicking on the color palette tool, which is to the right of the underline tool.

Besides using the format bar to change the formatting of your characters, you can also use the menus. By selecting the text that you want to format and then choosing the Font option from the Format menu, you can access the Font dialog box, as shown in Figure 7-24.

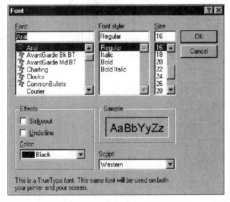

Figure 7-24: You can change all attributes of a text selection by using the Font dialog box.

Using the Font dialog box, you can change the same attributes that you change when using the format bar, plus some others. In addition, you can see an example of how a particular font looks. When you are satisfied with your settings, click on the OK button, and your changes are applied to the text.

Paragraph formatting

Besides applying formatting to individual characters, you can also format entire paragraphs. Formatting paragraphs does not format the way your characters look; it only affects the way the paragraph is indented and aligned. When you format a paragraph, you simply place the cursor anywhere within the paragraph and then use one of the formatting tools or commands:

- **Left alignment.** This causes each line of the paragraph to be positioned at the left margin. You can left-justify a paragraph (the default) by clicking on the align left tool, which is located next to the text color tool.

- **Center alignment.** This causes each line of the paragraph to be centered between the left and right margins. You can center a paragraph by clicking on the center tool, which is to the right of the align left tool.

- **Right alignment.** This causes each line of the paragraphs to be positioned at the right margin. You can right-justify a paragraph by clicking on the align right tool, which is located next to the center tool.

- **Left indent.** This causes each line of the paragraph to be indented from the left page margin a certain distance. You access this specification by using the menus, as described shortly.

- **Right indent.** This causes each line of the paragraph to be indented from the right page margin by a certain distance. You also access this specification by using the menus.

- **First line indent.** This causes the first line of the paragraph to be indented a certain amount, independent of the other lines in the paragraph. This specification, as well, is accessed through the menus.

- **Bullet style.** This causes the paragraph to be indented with a bullet character (a round dot) appearing to the left of the first line. You can use this feature by clicking on the bullet button, at the very right of the format bar.

To use the formatting menu, select the Paragraph option from the Format menu. This displays the Paragraph dialog box, as shown in Figure 7-25. This dialog box provides quite a bit more formatting capability than what is on the format bar alone.

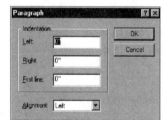

Figure 7-25: Paragraph formatting involves setting indents and alignment.

To use the Paragraph dialog box, simply enter values, representing inches, in each of the indent fields. You can also enter a negative amount in the first line indent, which allows you to create "hanging" paragraphs.

For instance, you could indent the left side of the paragraph by half an inch and then make the first line a negative half inch. This way, all lines except the first one are indented.

Printing a document

The quickest way to print your documents from WordPad is to click on the Print button, which is located on the toolbar. This button, which looks like a printer, instantly sends your document off to the printer. If you want to specify different parameters for your print job, then you must choose the Print option from the File menu. This displays the Print dialog box, as shown in Figure 7-26.

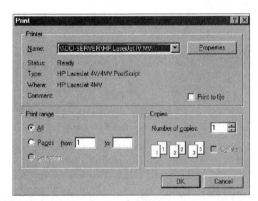

Figure 7-26: When you use the Print dialog box, you can specify how you want your job processed.

This dialog box is very similar to Print dialog boxes that are used in other applications. You can control which printer receives your document, which pages should be printed, and how many copies should be created. You can also indicate whether you want the print job sent to a disk file instead of the printer itself.

When you are ready to print your document, click on the OK button. The document is sent to either the printer or to a file, according to your specifications. When done, you are returned to the WordPad program window.

Summary

Windows NT includes quite a few accessories that you can use to accomplish your daily work. Although the accessories are not as full-featured as commercial software, many times you do not need a feature-rich program to accomplish a task.

In this chapter, you have had a quick introduction to the majority of the accessories that are provided with Windows NT. In particular, you have learned the following items:

▶ You can use the Calculator accessory in either of two views to meet your general or scientific calculating needs. Because the Calculator is used on-screen, you can cut and paste information between it and your other programs.

▶ The Character Map accessory can be used to access special font characters and insert them in your programs. You can also access all of the Unicode subsets that may be available in your fonts.

▶ When you open the Clipboard Viewer accessory, it really starts the ClipBook Viewer, which is a much broader, more powerful use of the Clipboard. Using ClipBooks, you can create a small database of objects that are selected from other programs and then make those objects available to other workstations on your network.

▶ The Clock accessory enables you to display either a digital or analog clock. Much of the reason for having the Clock has been removed with the addition of the time-of-day display on the Taskbar in Windows NT Workstation 4.0.

▶ With the Imaging accessory, you can scan images from a TWAIN-compliant scanner and make annotations to them. You can then save the files in common graphics formats so that you can use them with other programs.

▶ The CD Player accessory is great for listening to audio CDs while you work or play. You can also use it for categorizing and organizing your CDs.

▶ You can use the Volume Control accessory to adjust the volume and balance of each audio channel that is supported by your sound card.

▶ When you need to record or edit an audio file, you can use the Sound Recorder. It allows you to perform basic audio editing and to add special effects to your sounds.

▶ The Media Player accessory combines many functions of the CD Player and Sound Recorder accessories. Though it doesn't do everything that those accessories can do, it provides a way to play many of your favorite multimedia files, including video (AVI) files.

▶ The Notepad accessory is a tried-and-true method of editing simple text files. The version of Notepad that is provided with Windows NT Workstation 4.0 can be used to edit both ASCII and Unicode text files.

▶ The new Paint accessory is a replacement for the Paintbrush accessory that was included with older versions of Windows. The new features of the program allow for easier use and provide some additional capabilities.

▶ WordPad is a good entry-level word processor that can understand several types of common file formats. You can use the program to edit and format files. WordPad is great for creating short memos and reports.

Chapter 8

Controlling Your Software

In This Chapter

You use your computer system to run software. While this may sound like a simplistic statement, it is nonetheless true. If you could not run the software that you wanted or needed to, it is doubtful that you would use the computer system at all. With this in mind, Windows NT provides a number of ways in which you can gain control of your software. (Some of the features of version 4.0 make it easier than ever to control your software.)

In this chapter, you learn about the software environment (or environments) created by Windows NT and how you can take advantage of them. In particular, you learn the following items:

▶ How the Windows NT environment creates different software environments for different types of software

▶ The best ways to add software to your system

▶ How Windows NT lets you gain control of your DOS environment

▶ How you can remove software that was previously installed on your system

The Windows NT Environment

To understand how software is used within Windows NT, you need to understand a bit about the architecture of Windows NT. Since its earliest days, Window NT has been a modular operating system, which is something that cannot be said about other versions of Windows.

This modularity, as shown in Figure 8-1, means that Windows NT provides a base operating system, in which everything runs in kernel mode, and a series of interfaces that provide virtual environments (called *subsystems*) for various types of programs, which run in user mode.

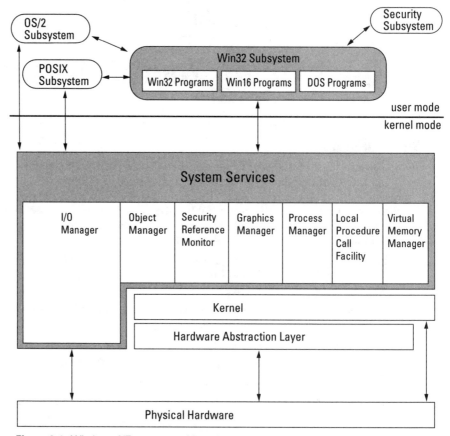

Figure 8-1: Windows NT system architecture.

While the modularity that is depicted in Figure 8-1 may appear confusing to some people, it allows the implementation of a robust, extensible, and powerful operating system. Because of this design, the user-mode subsystems can be replaced, as the needs of the operating system evolve, without requiring changes in the underlying kernel-mode services. The next several sections examine each part of the Windows NT architecture.

Kernel-mode operations

As far as the kernel mode is concerned, very little has changed since Windows NT was first released. The kernel mode consists of three primary parts: the system services, the Kernel itself, and the Hardware Abstraction Layer (HAL). It is easiest to start looking at these elements from the "ground up," so the following discussions start with the HAL.

The Hardware Abstraction Layer

The Hardware Abstraction Layer, or HAL, is provided in Windows NT as a shield to insulate the operating system from changes in underlying hardware. This layer makes it possible for the operating system to be easily ported to different hardware platforms.

The higher services of Windows NT access resources that are made available by the HAL, without regard for the type of chips or ports that are used by the actual computer.

The main purposes of the Hardware Abstraction Layer can be broken down as follows:

- Isolate the operating system from changes in the underlying hardware
- Provide a stable collection of common resources that can be accessed by the kernel and device drivers
- Implement symmetric multiprocessing for systems with multiple CPUs

The Kernel

The Kernel is the "central operations point" of Windows NT. It is responsible for scheduling tasks for the CPU to perform. In carrying out its responsibilities, the Kernel works closely with the HAL to access resources that are available on the computer.

Higher system services, such as the Process Manager and the Object Manager, use the Kernel extensively. Thus, the Kernel provides a platform on which higher components of the operating system can build; they don't need to bypass the Kernel and access lower portions of the operating system.

The biggest part of what the Kernel accomplishes is synchronization of lower activities. Whereas the HAL is responsible for implementing symmetric multiprocessing, the Kernel is responsible for optimizing the performance of the CPUs by synchronizing the work that they do.

The Kernel is also responsible for managing context switching; this means that it implements multitasking under Windows NT. The Kernel is the only portion of the operating system that cannot be context switched, meaning that it cannot be "turned off" for a short time while another process is being executed. There are two types of multitasking that are managed by the Kernel: cooperative and preemptive.

Cooperative multitasking

The first type of multitasking is known as *cooperative multitasking*. This is the type of multitasking that is used in Win16 programs, which are native to older versions of Windows. The Kernel must support this type of multitasking for compatibility reasons.

Cooperative multitasking relies on the different processes within the system to cooperate with each other. (Processes are described shortly, when discussing the Process Manager.) Under this model, the operating system basically trusts applications to periodically check a message queue to see what other tasks are waiting within the system.

If no tasks are waiting, then the application can continue using the system. If the operating system needs the application to relinquish control so that another process can use the CPU, then it places a message in the queue. The next time that the application checks the queue, it cooperates by relinquishing control to the operating system, which in turn passes control to the needy process waiting in the wings.

The problem with cooperative multitasking is that different programs check the queue at different times. For instance, one application may check it every few milliseconds.

Another application, however, may check it every five or 10 seconds. This results in inequitable use of the CPU by different applications. Under cooperative multitasking, it is not unusual for some programs to run slowly and others to run quickly, but all of them may run in a jerky, stop-and-start manner.

Even though Win16 programs use cooperative multitasking, Windows NT only implements this multitasking model within the context of preemptive multitasking, as discussed in the following section. This means that Win16 programs, running within the same address space, are cooperatively multitasked in relation to each other. In relation to other, non-Win16 processes on your system, the preemptive multitasking model applies.

Preemptive multitasking

A more equitable form of multitasking is known as *preemptive multitasking.* Under this model, the operating system acts as a traffic cop — it times each application and either takes control after a certain amount of time or grabs control if a higher-priority event needs to occur right away.

There are many benefits to preemptive multitasking, but perhaps the biggest benefits from a user standpoint are as follows:

- Applications don't need to check a queue; this means that there is less management code necessary within the application itself.

- A more even distribution of processing time to the various applications in your system means that your applications run more smoothly than under cooperative multitasking.

The system services

In some Windows NT documentation, the system services are referred to as the Windows NT Executive. The purpose of the Executive is to provide a collection of services that are accessible by other system components, including the subsystems in the user mode.

The services are managed by the seven components that make up the Executive:

- I/O Manager
- Object Manager
- Security Reference Monitor
- Graphics Manager
- Process Manager
- Local Procedure Call Facility
- Virtual Memory Manager

Remember that each component can contain multiple services; the purposes of the components are strictly coordination and management. Each of these components is discussed in the following sections.

I/O Manager

The I/O Manager component is one of the busiest parts of the Executive. This component is responsible for managing all input and output functions of the operating system. The I/O Manager does this by using a layered approach, which implements multiple abstraction layers to hide what is going on at lower or higher levels of the operating system (see Figure 8-2).

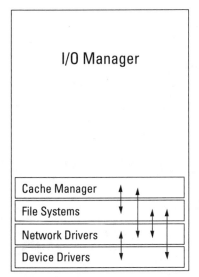

Figure 8-2: The I/O Manager uses a layered model to implement device access.

In Figure 8-2, the layers mentioned are for illustration purposes only; the actual number of layers depends on the devices that are installed in your system. Notice that each layer communicates only with the layer one or two levels above or below it.

Information that is transmitted between layers uses a data structure that is referred to as an *I/O request packet*. It is the responsibility of the I/O Manager to create and pass the packets between layers, where they are acted on by the appropriate functions in the appropriate layer.

Note

As you work with hardware devices (adding to and removing them from your system), as discussed in Chapter 6, you affect the way in which the I/O Manager does its job. Depending on the layer that you are affecting, you must sometimes restart your system for a device driver change to take effect.

Object Manager

Windows NT allows the creation and management of *objects*. These objects are similar in concept to objects that are used in an object-oriented programming language. Objects are created that refer to system resources or to processes and threads that are running in the operating system.

These objects include a system-defined data type, a collection of operations that can be performed on it (methods), and object attributes (properties). The Object Manager is responsible for creating, tracking, and managing the objects that are used in Windows NT.

Security Reference Monitor

The Security Reference Monitor is the portion of the Windows NT security system that operates in kernel mode. This component provides no user interface, but it does provide enforcement and implementation of the security measures that you have set up in your system.

For instance, it is the Security Reference Monitor that checks your user ID and password when you log in or try to access a protected resource. In addition, this component generates audit messages.

The security aspects of Windows NT are discussed in more depth in Chapter 16.

Graphics Manager

The Graphics Manager represents the biggest change in the kernel mode since the introduction of Windows NT. In Version 4.0, the core graphics routines were moved from the user mode to the kernel mode and became known as the Graphics Manager.

This change allowed faster response times during graphic operations, as the additional overhead imposed by intermodal calls was no longer necessary. The change was necessitated by more-demanding graphic applications being run in Windows NT.

Process Manager

A *process* is a task, or program, that is running on the computer. At any given time, you may have multiple processes running on your system. Each process has its own address space, a set of resources that it is using, and (optionally) a set of threads that it is executing.

Threads are portions of a process that operate concurrently. For instance, a spreadsheet program may be the process (program) that is being run on Windows NT, but the spreadsheet maintains individual threads that accomplish tasks such as waiting for user input, recalculating cells, updating a chart, or printing in the background.

In a nutshell, the Process Manager is responsible for the following items:

- Creating processes and threads.

- Providing system resources to the processes.

- Arbitrating between processes when they're competing for limited resources.

System resources are provided to processes as they're requested. If there is a conflict (such as two applications that need to use the same resource), then whenever possible, the resource is shared between the two processes. Some resources, such as memory or a disk drive, can be shared concurrently. Other resources, such as a printer, must be shared sequentially.

This means that the resource is used exclusively by a process for a time until it is no longer needed. Still other resources, such as a modem or an I/O port, cannot be shared; they are allocated exclusively for the use of a particular process. The Process Manager arbitrates the conflicts and makes sure that processes get access to the resources that they need, whenever possible.

Secret

In Chapter 2, you learned how you can end tasks. The Task Manager, which can show both processes and threads, allows you to glimpse the management that is done by the Process Manager.

Local Procedure Call Facility

When you run an application on your Windows NT system, it is implemented in an environment that is modeled, created, and managed by one of the subsystems. For instance, if you run a Windows 3.1 program, it is handled by the Win32 subsystem in a Win16 environment that is created and managed by that subsystem.

When the application needs something from the operating system, it typically calls an API (Application Programming Interface) function. The API then responds and fulfills the requested function for the application.

This all sounds fine from the perspective of the application. However, behind the scenes, there is much more going on. When the program calls the API function, a Local Procedure Call (LPC) is initiated. The Local Procedure Call Facility packages the information that is necessary for the API function into a message.

This message is then passed through the kernel mode and back to the user mode subsystem that can process the request. The message is then processed by the subsystem, passed back through the kernel mode, and then back to the user mode application that called the function in the first place.

The part of the Executive that takes care of packaging, passing, tracking, and unpackaging the message is the Local Procedure Call Facility. As far as the originating application is concerned, however, it simply called an API, which performed a function. This approach to calling and fulfilling functions through the Local Procedure Call Facility makes Windows NT security stronger and the operating system more modular.

Virtual Memory Manager

The Virtual Memory (VM) Manager is charged with controlling the memory resources that are available to your system, including both physical and virtual memory. The VM Manager does this through a process known as *memory paging*. This involves moving memory around in RAM and paging it to disk (and back) as necessary.

When the Process Manager creates a process, it requests the VM Manager to allocate an address space that the process can use. Depending on the type of process that is being created, different address space sizes and configurations are created. From the perspective of the VM Manager, however, one characteristic of the address space is that it is both flat and linear.

Flat and *linear* are characteristics of memory that mean it can be addressed with a single address register. This address register is 32 bits in size; this means that it can hold an address between 0 and 4,294,967,295. Thus, the largest address space that can be allocated is 4GB. The address space for a process (regardless of the size) is divided into blocks that are called *pages*.

Windows NT uses a technique called *demand paging*. This refers to a method by which code and data are moved in pages from physical memory to a temporary paging file on disk. The VM Manager takes care of this process of moving memory pages within RAM and to and from the disk, as indicated in Figure 8-3. As far as the process is concerned, however, the entire address space is available in RAM all the time.

The VM Manager also takes care of mapping virtual addresses from the process's address space to physical pages in the computer's memory. In doing so, it hides the physical organization of memory from the process. This ensures that the process can access its memory as needed but not the memory of other processes.

User-mode operations

On the user-mode side of the fence (refer to Figure 8-1), the majority of the activity takes place in the Win32 subsystem, which bears the lion's share of the subsystem responsibility. While at first it would appear that the OS/2 and POSIX subsystems are on an equal footing with the Win32 subsystem; this is not exactly true.

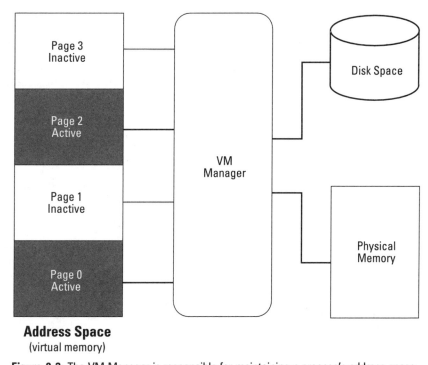

Address Space
(virtual memory)

Figure 8-3: The VM Manager is responsible for maintaining a process's address space.

Win32 provides many of the supporting routines that are necessary to implement both OS/2 and POSIX, such as keyboard and mouse input and video output. The Win32 subsystem is also responsible for creating the environments that are necessary to run Win32, Win16, and DOS programs. Each of these program environments is discussed in the following sections.

The Win32 environment

As you can see from Figure 8-1, the Win32 subsystem is used to implement the DOS, Win16, and native Win32 application environments. Thus, three general types of programs are managed by Win32:

- **Win32.** These are 32-bit Windows applications designed to take full advantage of the Windows NT environment. Many Windows 95 applications also fall into this category.

- **Win16.** These are traditional 16-bit Windows applications. They are carryovers from earlier versions of Windows but still operate satisfactorily in the Windows NT environment.

- **MS-DOS.** These are programs designed to run in DOS, not in Windows.

How Win32 handles the DOS and Win16 environments is covered in later sections of this chapter. When you run a Win32 program, the subsystem creates a separate address space for your application.

This address space provides the application with full access to all of the memory and resources that it needs, although resources may be limited by how you have defined the security aspects of accessing the resource.

If a Win32 application crashes for some reason, then the use of individual address spaces protects other processes (and the operating system) from being affected. If an application hangs, you can recover by pressing Ctrl+Alt+Del to access the Task Manager, or by right-clicking on the Taskbar and selecting the Task Manager option. From the Task Manager, you can end the offending process, as described in Chapter 2.

The DOS environment

When you run a DOS application on your Windows NT system, it is executed in what is called a Virtual DOS Machine (VDM). This VDM is created and maintained by the Win32 subsystem. You can think of the VDM as a logical computer within the physical computer.

It is possible to have multiple VDMs running within the same physical computer. From the perspective of your DOS program, it is running within its own computer. It believes it has full access to the resources of the entire system and that there are no other applications running within the system.

When the Win32 subsystem creates a VDM, it possesses its own address space. This means that your DOS program is secure, and other processes running on your system are secure from the DOS program.

This promotes greater system stability, because an error in the DOS program, or an outright program crash, does not affect other programs. In addition, it allows greater system security, because the DOS program cannot tamper with memory or resources that are allocated to other processes.

The Win16 environment

Win16 programs are those that were developed for non-NT versions of Windows prior to Windows 95. These programs are designed to effectively run in an environment that was originally crafted by DOS, so Windows NT runs Win16 programs in their own Virtual DOS Machine.

All of your Win16 programs run within a single address space, which is how these types of programs operated under the older versions of Windows. Win16 programs are the only ones that do this; all other programs operate in their own independent address spaces.

When you start a Win16 program, you can explicitly state that you want it to run in its own address space. Doing so, however, causes your system to run a bit slower, because this is equivalent to creating multiple VDMs for all of your open Win16 applications.

Caution

Because Win16 programs, by default, run in a single address space, a crash, bug, or error in one Win16 program can make all the other Win16 programs in the same address space unstable. In this case, you must close all of your Win16 programs and restart them.

The OS/2 environment

The OS/2 subsystem that is provided with Windows NT supports character-based OS/2 programs. In today's day and age, this means that Windows NT is not a great platform on which to run OS/2 programs. This is because most OS/2 programs now run on later versions of OS/2, on Presentation Manager, or on WARP. None of these program types can run under Windows NT.

Your OS/2 applications run in their own address space, separate from other processes. Function calls, data structures, and system I/O requests are translated between Windows NT expectations and OS/2 expectations by the OS/2 subsystem. The OS/2 environment relies on the Win32 subsystem for many support functions, such as screen I/O, keyboard input, and mouse input.

The POSIX environment

POSIX is a term meaning Portable Operating System Interface, as developed by the IEEE community to promote the portability of applications across a number of different UNIX implementations. In reality, there are over a dozen different POSIX standards; Windows NT has gained POSIX.1 compliance certification.

This means that you can run C programs, written to the POSIX.1 standard, on Windows NT — provided that you compile the program under Windows NT. This level of compliance is a source-code level, not a binary level. (You cannot run POSIX.1 programs that were compiled on a different system under Windows NT.)

POSIX programs run in their own address space, apart from other processes. To run POSIX programs on your system, make sure that you are using the NTFS filing system (see Chapter 4) on any drives that are to be accessed by the program. In addition, to ensure strict conformance with POSIX standards, you must disable the Bypass Traverse Checking right for those users running the POSIX programs. (For more information on user rights, refer to Chapter 16.)

Adding Software

Everyone needs to install software at some time. Some of you install quite a bit of software on your machines. The steps that you follow to install software don't necessarily change based on the type of software that you are installing. For instance, the procedure followed to install a Win16 program is typically the same as that for installing a DOS program.

There are two general ways that you can install software under Windows NT: with a Wizard or manually. There are pros and cons to both methods, but neither one is particularly difficult to do. In the following sections, you learn about both ways.

Note

Most DOS programs know little about Windows. Some do, it is true, but by and large, they assume that you'll be running the program outside of Windows. Because of the stability of the VDM that was created for a DOS application, you can generally install the application directly from within Windows.

Installing software with a Wizard

Windows NT includes a Wizard that you can use to add software to your system. This Wizard, located in the Control Panel, is the preferred method of adding software to Windows NT. As the Wizard installs the software, it updates the Registry with the information that is related to the program. (When you install DOS programs, the Registry is not affected.)

If the application that you're installing was created for Windows NT or for Windows 95, the program may also update the Registry with additional information. For instance, the Registry may contain information about the following items:

- The components that can be added to the software. For instance, you may have installed only a portion of the program, and the Registry contains information about what else can be installed.

- The parameters that are needed by the application to run properly.

- The files that can be deleted if the application is removed from the system.

To run the software installation wizard, follow these steps:

STEPS

Starting the Add/Remove Programs Wizard

Step 1. Choose the <u>S</u>ettings option from the Start menu. This displays the Settings menu.

Step 2. Choose the <u>C</u>ontrol Panel option from the Settings menu. The Control Panel shortly appears.

Step 3. Double-click on the Add/Remove Programs icon. This displays the Add/Remove Programs Properties dialog box, as shown in Figure 8-4.

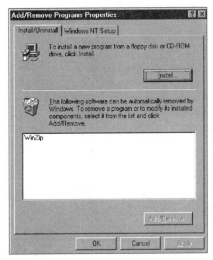

Figure 8-4: You can install programs using the Add/Remove Programs Wizard.

Step 4. Click on the Install button. This starts the Wizard, as shown in Figure 8-5.

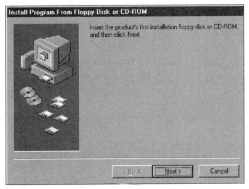

Figure 8-5: The first Wizard dialog box is informational in nature.

Step 5. Make sure that the installation floppy disk or CD-ROM is in the appropriate drive.

Step 6. Click on the Next button to proceed to the next step.

At this point, the Wizard looks through your disk drives and CD-ROM drives to find a setup program. It looks for program names, such as SETUP.EXE or INSTALL.EXE. When it finds a disk or CD-ROM that appears to contain setup files, a new dialog box (shown in Figure 8-6) is displayed, showing what was found.

Figure 8-6: The Wizard lets you know what setup programs it located.

The command-line field in the middle of the dialog box should reflect the command line that is necessary to install the software. You may want to check the software's documentation to make sure that the command line is correct. If necessary, you can click on the Browse button to locate a different program to install.

When you are satisfied that the command line is correct, click on the Finish button. This ends the Wizard and starts the setup program for your software (the program in the command line field of Figure 8-6).

The steps that you follow from this point depend on the software that you're installing. Remember — it is the software that is now running, not the Wizard. Different applications have different setup programs that require different user input.

Installing software manually

Microsoft does not suggest that you install your software manually; the company would prefer that you use the installation Wizard instead, as described in the previous section.

Manual installation means either of the following items:

■ Directly running the installation program that is supplied with the software

■ Copying the program files to a folder and running the program

In reality, there is little problem in doing this (regardless of what Microsoft says). After all, running the installation program is exactly what the Wizard does for you in the first place. There are a couple of instances when it is perfectly acceptable to run the installation program manually.

The most obvious is if you are installing Win32 software, which understands what to do with the Registry. The other is if you have a very small program that does not require an installation program. For instance, you may download a utility program from an on-line service or the Internet that does not require an installation program.

Note

If you have problems with the application after you install it manually, remove it from your system and contact the program vendor. They may have an update or a setup disk available that works properly with Windows NT.

In instances where you must install manually and you are installing a DOS program, it is a good idea to follow these general steps:

STEPS

Manually installing a DOS program

Step 1. Create a folder for the DOS program. Give it a name that is appropriate for the program.

Step 2. Using the desktop or the Explorer, copy the files from the DOS floppy disk to the new folder.

Step 3. Within the folder, right-click on an icon for an executable file. This displays a Context menu for the program.

Step 4. Choose Properties from the Context menu. This displays the Properties dialog box for the program.

Step 5. Set the memory, screen, and other properties that are particular to this program, as discussed later in this chapter. (You may need to refer to your program documentation for information about special needs of the program.)

Step 6. Click on the OK button to save your changes.

Step 7. Repeat Steps 3 through 6 for every executable file in the folder.

Controlling the DOS Environment

If you are running DOS programs under Windows NT, you need to be concerned with the environment in which that program operates. Earlier in this chapter, you learned that the Win32 subsystem creates a Virtual DOS Machine (VDM) to run your DOS programs. Fortunately, Windows NT allows you to control the properties that determine how this VDM is created.

In previous versions of Windows NT, you controlled the VDM by creating a PIF (program information file) that defined how the DOS environment should be established. To maintain the PIF, you used the PIF Editor program.

Windows NT Workstation 4.0 has done away with the PIF Editor; instead, you change the characteristics using a familiar Properties dialog box. You access this by right-clicking on the icon for a DOS program and then choosing Properties from the Context menu. Figure 8-7 shows an example of the Properties dialog box for a DOS program.

Figure 8-7: Windows NT allows you to control quite a few properties of the DOS program environment.

Notice that quite a few tabs are available in the dialog box. These tabs allow you to control different areas of the DOS environment that are necessary for a program.

In general, the tabs permit the following items:

- **General.** This tab, shown in Figure 8-7, provides general information about the DOS program and allows you to change the attributes of the file. (These attributes should be familiar to anyone who has used DOS files in the past.)

- **Security.** This tab allows you to change who has access to the file as well as how that access is recorded by the Windows NT security system. The use of this tab is no different than for other Windows NT files. Security is discussed in Chapter 16.

- **Program.** This tab allows you to control some aspects of how the program is started by Windows NT.

- **Font.** This tab controls the font that is used to display program information while the program is running.

- **Memory.** This tab is used to specify the memory requirements of the program.

- **Screen.** This tab controls how the DOS screen appears and how it behaves while the program is running.

- **Misc.** This tab is used to group various configuration options that don't quite fit on the other tabs.

How you use most of these tabs is discussed in the next several sections.

Program initialization

Many DOS programs require specific steps for a program to initialize properly. For instance, your program may require the presence of a particular environment variable or that a batch file be run to start the program. You can control the initialization of the DOS environment, and the subsequent running of your DOS program, quite effectively. The following sections describe how you can control several different initialization areas.

Setting environment variables

It is not uncommon for a DOS program to require the presence of specific environment variables to run properly. These variables are used by the program to control how it goes about its work.

One of the most common examples is the TEMP variable, which is typically used by a program to point to where temporary files should be stored. The easiest way to set environment variables is to create a batch file to run your DOS program.

As you create your batch file, it should contain the commands that are necessary to set your environment variables. The last line of the batch file should run the DOS program. For instance, if you needed to set the LIB environment variable to a specific directory, your batch file could appear as follows:

```
set LIB=c:\library\bin
e:\myprogram.exe
```

There are only two lines in this batch file. The first sets the required environment variable, and the second executes the DOS program. After it is created, you would run the batch file instead of running the actual DOS program.

You can set as many environment variables in this way as you want. Windows NT automatically adjusts the environment variable space to accommodate your changes.

Setting the path

Some DOS programs require certain directories to be included in the path. Windows NT allows you to set the path in two different ways: globally or temporarily. You would set the path *globally* if you need the default path changed, for all instances when you may use a DOS window. The default path, as originally set up by Windows NT, is as follows:

```
PATH=C:\WINNT\system32;C:\WINNT
```

You can modify this default path by following these steps:

STEPS

Changing the default path used by Windows NT

Step 1.   Right-click on the My Computer icon on your desktop. This displays a Context menu.

Step 2.   Choose the Properties option from the Context menu. This displays the System Properties dialog box.

Step 3.   Click on the Environment tab. The System Properties dialog box now looks like what is shown in Figure 8-8.

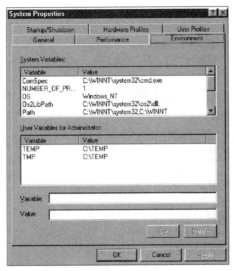

Figure 8-8: You can change the default path by modifying the system properties.

Step 4.   In the System Variables list, select the Path variable by clicking on it. This updates the information in the Variable and Value fields at the bottom of the dialog box.

Step 5.   Change the Value field to reflect how you want the default path to appear.

Step 6.   Click on the OK button to save your changes.

If you don't want to make global changes, you can change the path *temporarily* by using the batch file technique that was discussed in the previous section. Simply make sure that the batch file changes the path and that you end the batch file with the command to run your DOS program. When your program is done running and you close the DOS window, the temporary path is discarded by Windows NT.

Setting a working directory

At times it is helpful to start your DOS program using a specific directory as your working directory. Windows NT allows you to establish such a directory. For instance, you could start a editing program that used a specific folder as the source for its data files.

To change this setting, follow these steps:

STEPS

Specifying a working folder

Step 1. Right-click on the icon for your DOS program. This displays a Context menu.

Step 2. Choose the Properties option from the Context menu. This displays the Properties dialog box for the program, as shown earlier in Figure 8-7.

Step 3. Click on the Program tab. The Properties dialog box now looks like what is shown in Figure 8-9.

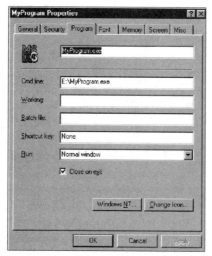

Figure 8-9: You can specify a working directory for your DOS program.

Step 4. In the Working field, enter the full path of the folder that you want to use for a data directory for the program.

Step 5. Click on the OK button to save your changes.

Secret

If your DOS program provides a way to set a working directory — within the program — then the value that you set there overrides the value that you set in the Properties dialog box.

The memory environment

If you have been around computers long enough, you probably remember the hocus-pocus that was used to configure DOS memory and the hodge-podge that area of computing became. Memory allocation and use in a DOS environment can be confusing, at best.

Even though it may seem that those days have been left behind, they are not necessarily gone if you are using DOS programs under Windows NT. This is because the DOS program that you are running may still expect certain types of memory to be available, in certain quantities.

When setting up the Virtual DOS Machine for your program, Windows NT does an admirable job responding to the memory needs of the program. In fact, for many programs, you may never need to concern yourself with your DOS memory settings. For some programs, however, it is an inescapable part of making the program work properly.

Fortunately, Windows NT allows you a great deal of control over how memory is configured for a DOS program. To change the majority of memory configuration settings, use the Memory tab of the Properties dialog box for the DOS program. This tab is shown in Figure 8-10.

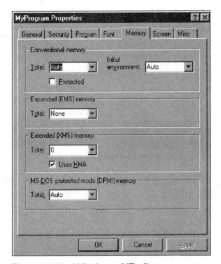

Figure 8-10: Windows NT allows you to configure memory settings for your DOS programs.

The following sections explain how to configure your program for each type of memory.

Conventional memory

Conventional memory is defined as that portion of memory below the 640K boundary that was historically imposed by DOS. This is the memory area where the majority of DOS programs actually execute. By using the Total field in the Conventional Memory area of the Memory tab, you can change the amount of conventional memory that Windows NT allocates for your DOS program.

You can set the conventional memory specification to any multiple of 40K, between 40 and 640K. You can also set the specification to Auto; this means that Windows NT makes the decision about what setting to use.

Expanded memory

Expanded memory (EMS) is a type of memory that is used by some older DOS programs for large blocks of data that cannot fit into conventional memory. Special functions were used to access and use this memory, and special drivers or memory managers were required.

You specify the amount of EMS memory required by using the Total field in the Expanded (EMS) Memory area of the Memory tab. You can configure Windows NT for any value between 1024 and 16,384K, in increments of 1024K. You can also set the value to None, which disables EMS memory, or to Auto, which allows Windows NT to determine the optimal setting.

Extended memory

Extended memory (XMS) is a memory specification that came into popularity about two years after EMS. Most modern DOS programs use XMS memory in preference to EMS memory. The XMS specification is more flexible in how it allows memory to be accessed and to what uses the memory can be put.

You can change the amount of XMS memory that is configured for your DOS program by changing the setting in the Total field of the Extended (XMS) Memory area of the Memory tab. You can pick any value between 1024 and 16,384K in 1024K increments. You can also set the value to None or Auto, which has the same effect that for the EMS setting.

Secret

If your DOS program seems to be having problems working with extended memory, change the XMS setting to a value such as 8192 or lower. Some programs have a hard time using more than 8MB of XMS.

At the bottom of the Extended (XMS) Memory area, you can also select the Uses HMA check box if your program uses the high memory area just under the 1MB memory boundary.

Secret

There are two settings on the Memory tab that have no bearing on running DOS programs under Windows NT. Regardless of what you set in the Initial Environment drop-down list or in the DPMI drop-down list, Windows NT ignores your settings. These settings are only used if you transfer the DOS program to a Windows 95 system.

Video memory

There is one area of memory usage that is not controlled on the Memory tab. Your video system uses memory to routinely display graphics, text, and other information in the DOS window. The way that your video system uses video memory for your DOS programs can be modified by displaying the Properties dialog box and then clicking on the Screen tab. The dialog box should then appear as shown in Figure 8-11.

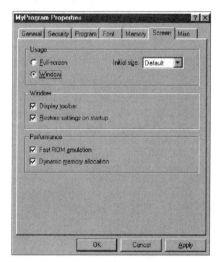

Figure 8-11: The Performance area of the Screen tab allows you to control how video memory is used in DOS programs.

At the bottom of the dialog box, in the Performance area, are two check boxes. These settings come into play when you are not running the DOS program in full-screen mode. The first setting, Fast ROM Emulation, causes Windows NT to move the ROM instructions into faster RAM. This uses a few more memory resources, but it also causes text and some graphics to be displayed faster in the DOS window.

The other setting, Dynamic Memory Allocation, controls how Windows allocates screen display memory for the DOS program. If this check box is selected, then Windows only uses the amount of memory necessary for the DOS program video area that is required by the current video mode of the program. If the check box is cleared, then Windows NT allocates the maximum amount of memory for video that could be used by the DOS program.

While selected, the check box provides better use of memory for all of your programs; clearing the check box can result in your DOS program running slightly faster, particularly if it does a lot of video mode switching.

The screen environment

Windows NT gives you a great deal of control over how your DOS program is displayed in its window. You can control items such as font characteristics, lines on the screen, and the size of the screen itself. Each of the following sections addresses these areas.

Setting the screen size

The new interface that is used for Windows NT gives you complete control over the size of your DOS windows. The first item that you need to determine is whether you want your DOS program to run as a full-screen application or only in window. If your program uses mostly text, then the windowed approach is more than adequate. If it uses lots of graphics, however, you should use full-screen.

If your program uses text, you can also indicate how many lines of text it should use. To specify how you want your screen to be used by the DOS program, follow these steps:

STEPS

Specifying screen usage

Step 1. Right-click on the icon for your DOS program. This displays a Context menu.

Step 2. Choose the Properties option from the Context menu. This displays the Properties dialog box for the program, as shown earlier in Figure 8-7.

Step 3. Click on the Screen tab. The dialog box now appears as shown earlier in Figure 8-11.

Step 4. In the Usage area, select the radio button that indicates how much of your screen you want the DOS program to use.

Step 5. Use the Initial Size drop-down list to pick the number of text lines to be displayed in the DOS screen.

Step 6. Click on OK to save your changes.

Secret

Many DOS programs explicitly set the number of screen lines within the program itself. If your DOS program does this, it doesn't matter how you set the Initial Size drop-down list; it is overridden by your program.

If you decide to use your DOS program in a window, you can change the program properties to specify an initial condition for the window. To set the initial window condition, display the Properties dialog box for the DOS program, and click on the Program tab. (This tab was shown earlier, in Figure 8-9.)

In the Run drop-down list, select how you want this DOS window to be opened. There are three choices:

■ **Normal window.** The window is simply another window on the desktop, neither minimized nor maximized.

■ **Minimized.** The window is minimized to a button on the Taskbar.

■ **Maximized.** The window occupies the entire screen.

Don't confuse the maximized condition with the full-screen setting for your DOS window; they are different. When maximized, there is still a title bar at the top of the screen and a Taskbar at the bottom. When you run your program in full-screen mode, there is nothing but the program — the other regular Windows items are nowhere to be found.

Setting the font

DOS windows, under Windows NT Workstation 4.0, are fully scaleable. This means that you can adjust the size of the window, and the font used within the window is automatically adjust to display the proper number of lines and columns in the available space.

Note, however, that there is a reciprocal relationship between the font and the window size. If you change the font size, then the window is resized automatically to reflect your change.

To change the initial font that is used by a DOS window, follow these steps:

STEPS

Choosing an initial screen font

Step 1.   Right-click on the icon for your DOS program. This displays a Context menu.

Step 2.   Choose the Properties option from the Context menu. This displays the Properties dialog box for the program, as shown earlier in Figure 8-7.

Step 3.   Click on the Font tab. The dialog box now appears, as shown in Figure 8-12.

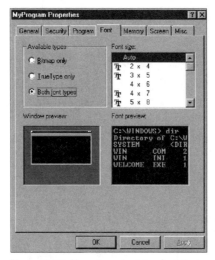

Figure 8-12: You can select the font that you want to use in the DOS window.

Step 4.   In the Available Types area, indicate the types of fonts from which you want to make your selection.

Step 5.   In the Font Size list, pick a font size to use in the window. The preview areas at the bottom of the dialog box are updated based on your selection.

Step 6.   Click on OK to save your changes.

Other environment considerations

There are a few other configuration settings that you can make for your DOS programs. Most of these are specified from the Misc tab of the Properties dialog box. This tab is shown in Figure 8-13.

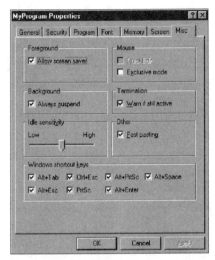

Figure 8-13: The Misc tab includes many items that affect your DOS environment.

The following sections examine the different ways that you can configure your DOS program using this tab.

Adjusting multitasking

Earlier in this chapter, you learned how multitasking works in the Windows NT environment. Your DOS windows are treated just like any other process when it comes to multitasking. Using some of the settings on the Misc tab, you can change how Windows multitasks a DOS window.

The first item that you should pay attention to is the Always Suspend check box. When this check box is cleared, it means that, when the DOS window is not in the foreground, it is treated like any other program window. If you select the check box, however, then when the DOS window is minimized or is in the background, the DOS program is suspended.

In other words, this check box is a way to pause your DOS program whenever its window is not active. Selecting the check box makes your other programs run faster, because Windows NT does not need to pay attention to the DOS window.

Another control that you should examine is the Idle Sensitivity slider bar. This control specifies how Windows NT treats the DOS program when the Win32 subsystem is waiting for keyboard input.

The lower the idle sensitivity, the longer the DOS program can run before Windows starts allocating resources to other tasks. Conversely, the higher the idle sensitivity, the shorter the time that is allowed before reallocation occurs.

You should only adjust the idle sensitivity if you feel your DOS program is not executing fast enough. When you move the slider toward the Low setting (meaning your DOS program holds on to resources longer when it is idle), your other Windows programs may run slower than otherwise.

The final setting that affects multitasking is the Fast Pasting check box. This check box controls how information is pasted into a DOS window from the Clipboard. If the check box is selected, information is pasted just as fast as in other program windows.

Most DOS programs can accept information at this rate, but some cannot. You should clear this check box if you try pasting something into the DOS window and it does not paste properly.

Choosing shortcut keys

Windows uses a standard group of shortcut keys for system operations. While you may not be aware of these shortcut keys (if you only use the mouse), they can cause conflicts with some DOS programs. Table 8-1 details the different shortcut keys and what they are used for.

Table 8-1   Windows shortcut keys

Shortcut	Meaning
Alt+Tab	Switch between tasks on the Taskbar
Alt+Esc	Cycle through tasks in the order that they were started
Ctrl+Esc	Display the Start menu
PrintScreen	Copy the contents of the screen to the Clipboard
Alt+PrintScreen	Copy the contents of the active window to the Clipboard
Alt+Enter	Switch between full-screen and window operation
Alt+Spacebar	Display the window's Control menu

If a DOS program expects to use one of these keystrokes, Windows NT normally pre-empts the key and captures it first. In most cases, the DOS program never knows that the shortcut was pressed.

You may want the shortcut to be ignored by Windows so that your DOS program can use it. If this is the case, follow these steps to make the change:

STEPS

Changing how shortcut keys are interpreted

Step 1. Right-click on the icon for your DOS program. This displays a Context menu.

Step 2. Choose the Properties option from the Context menu. This displays the Properties dialog box for the program, as shown earlier in Figure 8-7.

Step 3. Click on the Misc tab. The dialog box now appears as shown earlier in Figure 8-13.

Step 4. In the Windows Shortcut Keys area, make sure that only those shortcuts you want Windows to intercept are selected. If you want your DOS program to be able to use a shortcut, clear the check box.

Step 5. Click on OK to save your changes.

Controlling the mouse

The mouse is the main input device for Windows NT. Unfortunately, the mouse does not always work the same in a DOS window as in your other windows. If you find that your mouse does not work right, then you should set the mouse for exclusive mode. You can set exclusive mode for a DOS program; this means that when the program is running, the mouse only works in the DOS program window, not in any other window.

To turn on exclusive mode for the mouse, follow these steps:

STEPS

Setting exclusive mode for the mouse

Step 1. Right-click on the icon for your DOS program. This displays a Context menu.

Step 2. Choose the Properties option from the Context menu. This displays the Properties dialog box for the program, as shown earlier in Figure 8-7.

Step 3. Click on the Misc tab. The dialog box now appears as shown earlier in Figure 8-13.

Step 4. Make sure that the Exclusive Mode check box, near the upper-right corner of the dialog box, is selected.

Step 5. Click on OK to save your changes.

Notice that there is an option called QuickEdit on the Misc tab. This controls how the mouse can be used for editing within a DOS window. Unfortunately, this control is only available under Windows 95, not under Windows NT.

Removing Software

There may come a time when you want to remove software that you previously added to your system. Earlier in the chapter, you learned how to install software; removing it is sometimes more tricky.

The way you go about removing a program depends on the type of program that you are removing. The following sections discuss removing the three most common types of programs on an NT system: Win32, Win16, and DOS.

Removing a Win32 program

When you install a Win32 program on your system, you probably also installed an uninstall program at the same time. More 32-bit programs are including this type of facility, because the Registry makes it easy to track what software components belong to a particular software product.

When an uninstall program is present on your system, you can use the same Wizard that you used to install the software to remove it. If an uninstall feature was not added to your system, then you must remove the software according to the tried-and-somewhat-true methods of traditional Win16 software; this process is described in the next section.

To uninstall Win32 software that includes the uninstall information, start by following these steps:

STEPS

Removing software using the Wizard

Step 1. Make sure that the program you want to remove is not currently running.

Step 2. Choose the Settings option from the Start menu. This displays the Settings menu.

Step 3. Choose the Control Panel option from the Settings menu. The Control Panel shortly appears.

Step 4. Double-click on the Add/Remove Programs icon. This displays the Add/Remove Programs Properties dialog box, as shown in Figure 8-14.

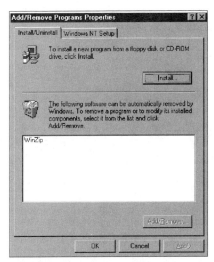

Figure 8-14: You can remove some software using the Add/Remove Programs Wizard.

Step 5. Examine the list at the bottom of the dialog box to see if the program that you want to remove is listed there. If it is not listed, you cannot remove it using the Wizard. Instead, you must remove the program manually as described in the next section.

Step 6. In the list of installed software, highlight the one that you want to remove by clicking on it.

Step 7. Click on the Add/Remove button at the bottom of the dialog box.

From this point, the software removal program for the application is running. Some programs include the removal as part of the setup program for the application, while others have a separate uninstall program. The steps that you follow vary based on how the setup or uninstall program was designed.

When the removal is complete, all elements of the application should have been removed. You may want to check to ensure that there are no shortcuts left over in places like the Startup folder or the Programs folder.

Removing a Win16 program

Earlier in this chapter, you learned that Win16 programs are those written for older versions of Windows. Removing these programs is not always easy, because the information about the program is not centralized in the Registry, as it is with Win32 programs. Instead, configuration information can be spread among several different system files, including your WIN.INI and SYSTEM.INI files.

To manually remove Win16 software, or any other software, follow these steps:

STEPS

Removing software manually

Step 1.   Delete the directories containing the program that you want to delete.

Step 2.   Remove any shortcuts or menu items that you had set up for the software.

Step 3.   Examine the INI files in the \winnt directory to determine whether any of them belonged to the application. If you can clearly make such a determination, delete the file. Better yet, copy it to a floppy disk in case you're mistaken and need to restore the file.

Step 4.   Examine the WIN.INI and SYSTEM.INI files to see if there are any entries in them that clearly belong to the application. If so, delete the entries.

Step 5.   Check the technical documentation for the program to see if it lists DLL files that are installed by the software. If so, you can remove the DLL files from either the \winnt or \winnt\system and \winnt\system32 directories.

This last step can be the trickiest. It is possible for more than one application to use the same DLL file. If you remove a DLL file that you believe was used only by the application that you are deleting but it was instead needed by another piece of software, then the other software can no longer function properly.

For this reason, you may not want to empty the Recycle Bin until you are sure that your system works fine without the deleted DLLs. If you find that it doesn't, then you must recover the DLLs from the Recycle Bin.

When these steps are complete, you have probably deleted the program. No absolute can be given, however, because different programs have different impacts on a traditional Win16 environment. There are, unfortunately, no absolutes with traditional Win16 software.

Note

There are many commercial "removal" programs on the market that profess to help clean up your Windows system. The success of these programs depends on many variables, such as how they are used, which software you are trying to remove, and how intimately you know your own system. Most of these programs were developed, however, for the Windows 3.1 (non-NT) market. If you want to use one of these programs, make sure you get one that is compatible with Window NT.

Removing a DOS program

Removing a DOS program is perhaps the simplest of all program removals. This is because DOS programs don't manipulate the Windows environment like Windows applications do. They don't add DLL files, change the Registry, modify system INI files, or clutter your directories with their own INI files.

To remove a DOS program, follow these steps:

STEPS

Removing DOS programs

Step 1. Delete the directories containing the DOS program that you want to delete.

Step 2. Remove any Windows shortcuts that you set up for your DOS programs.

Step 3. Check to see if any residual commands were left by the program in the CONFIG.SYS or AUTOEXEC.BAT files.

This last step can potentially be the most confusing. It assumes that you know what is in these files and how the commands got there. Your MS-DOS program, not knowing or caring about Windows NT, could have added lines to the files to run programs like SHARE, to set BUFFERS and FILES to a certain level, or to include the SETVER program. None of these is necessary under Windows NT, so they can safely be removed.

Summary

As you may imagine, creating a stable operating system that enables backward compatibility with a number of software environments is no easy task. Windows NT does just this, however, and comes through with shining colors. When you understand how software works under Windows NT, you can install the software that you want and then make sure that it operates as you expect.

In this chapter, you have learned about the software environment that is created by Windows NT. You have learned how to install, configure, and remove your software. In particular, you have learned the following items:

▶ The Windows NT architecture is modular, relying on a user mode and a kernel mode for the whole of the operating system.

▶ The kernel mode implements all of the basic features of the operating system in a secure environment. Different components work together to enable a secure, stable system regardless of the hardware platform on which it is running.

▶ The user mode provides different subsystems that implement a range of software environments. The workhorse of the subsystems, Win32, is relied on by all of the other subsystems for some of their functions.

▶ You can add software to your system by using a built-in Wizard or by manually running the installation program.

▶ The Windows software environment is automatically configured by the various hardware and subsystems that operate on your computer.

▶ Windows NT gives you intimate control over the software environment that is created for your DOS software. You can use the DOS program's Properties dialog box to configure a wide range of operational constraints.

▶ How you remove software on your system — and the difficulty of doing so — depends on the type of software that you want to remove.

Chapter 9

Using the Command Window

In This Chapter

Many people still think that DOS lurks somewhere behind Windows NT. While it is true that you can run DOS programs under Windows NT, the DOS that some people believe is there is really the command window. This window allows you to access a command line, where you can use traditional DOS commands. The commands that you can use, however, are in many ways a superset of old DOS commands. And the environment in which those commands is run is much more stable than the old DOS system.

While the graphical interface provided by Windows NT is great from a user's perspective, many times a command-line interface is preferable. For instance, you can create batch files that enable you to automate some of your tasks, or you can quickly get to the information that you need without using a menu. This chapter focuses on what you can do from the command window. In particular, you learn the following items:

▶ How to open and control a command window

▶ The different parts of a command and how you can recognize them

▶ What commands are different in Windows NT from those in DOS or Windows 95

▶ Which new commands have been added to Windows NT

Opening a Command Window

There are two ways in which a command window is opened under Windows NT. The first is when you execute a DOS program, for instance, if you double-click on the icon for a DOS program.

In this case, the command window is opened and the program is executed within that window. In Chapter 8, you learned quite a bit about the DOS environment that is created by Windows NT.

The other way in which to open a command window is quite easy. Just follow these two steps:

STEPS

Opening a Command Window

Step 1. Choose the Programs option from the Start menu. This displays the Programs menu.

Step 2. Choose the Command Prompt option from the Programs menu. Shortly you see a command window, as shown in Figure 9-1.

Figure 9-1: The command window looks very much like the traditional DOS environment.

If you have used a DOS window (another common name for the command window) under previous versions of Windows or if you are familiar with DOS, you should feel right at home using the command window. Notice that, when you first open a command window, it does not occupy the entire screen.

Depending on the size of your video monitor and the resolution of your video card, this may make the text in the window barely readable. You can increase the size of the window so it occupies the entire screen by pressing Alt+Enter. Pressing Alt+Enter again returns the full-screen command window to partial-screen status.

To close the command window, use the EXIT command at the command line. This closes the window and returns you to your Windows NT desktop. Another way of closing the command window is to click on the close icon in the upper-right corner of the DOS window.

Command-window properties

You can change the properties that are used in the command window by right-clicking on the command-window title bar and then choosing the Properties option. This displays the Properties dialog box, as shown in Figure 9-2.

Figure 9-2: The Properties dialog box is used to control how the command window appears.

The four tabs in the Properties dialog box each controls a different aspect of the command window appearance. The following sections address each of the tabs that you can use.

Window options

The Options tab, as displayed in Figure 9-2, enables you to define general characteristics of your command window. There are five general items that you can change on this tab:

- **Cursor Size.** This controls how large the cursor in the command window appears. You can select from three sizes, one of which should be just right for the program that you are running, the size and quality of your monitor, and your personal preferences.

- **Command History.** Windows NT keeps a command history of what you enter at the command prompt. You can access this history by using the up and down arrow keys on your keypad. This area of the tab allows you to specify how many commands are remembered by Windows NT.

Tip

■ **Display Options.** You already know that you can use the command window in either partial-screen or full-screen mode. This area allows you to control which mode you want to use.

Quite honestly, it is easier to simply press Alt+Enter to switch between the screen modes.

■ **QuickEdit Mode.** There are two ways that you can edit information in the command window. The first, which is the normal way, relies on the Edit menu, which is accessible when you right-click on the title bar.

Under this scheme, you select the Mar<u>k</u> option, pick the area of the command window that you want to copy, and then use the Cop<u>y</u> option to put the information in the Clipboard. You can then use the Paste option to place the Clipboard contents elsewhere.

The other way to edit is by using QuickEdit. When this check box is selected, you can use the mouse to make selections in the command window, and then use the Edit menu to copy and paste your selection.

■ **<u>I</u>nsert Mode.** With this check box selected, information that you enter at the cursor is inserted into the window; with it clear, information that you type replaces existing information.

Window fonts

The best way to control the appearance of your command window is to change the font that is used in the window. As you learned in Chapter 8, you can control the font that is used in a DOS window. If you click on the Font tab of the Properties dialog box, the dialog box appears, as shown in Figure 9-3.

Figure 9-3: The Font tab allows you to change how text is displayed in the command window.

If you examine the Font area of the dialog box, you can see that there are two fonts you can use in your command window. The first, Lucida Console, is a TrueType font, while the others, Raster Fonts, are bitmapped fonts. The bitmapped fonts display a little faster on most systems, but the Lucida Console can be more pleasing to the eye. You should pick the font that you like best. (You can see the results of your choice at the bottom of the dialog box.)

Once you pick a font, you can also pick a font size (in the Size area). When you pick different font sizes, Windows automatically adjusts the size of your command window so that the proper number of rows and columns can be displayed. You can see a sample of the window at the top of the dialog box and a sample of the font size at the bottom.

When you have made your selection, click on the OK button, and the command window is modified according to your specifications.

Window layout

When you click on the Layout tab, the Properties dialog box appears, as shown in Figure 9-4. The options in this tab are used to control the size and position of the command window, when the window does not occupy the entire screen.

Figure 9-4: The Layout tab allows you to change the size of the command window.

You can change three areas in this dialog box. The Screen Buffer Size area is where you specify the height and width of the window. Remember that this is the maximum height and width, in lines and characters, respectively.

A normal command window size is 80 characters wide by 25 lines high, but you can change to a different setting if you prefer. Remember that, if you are running a program in the command window, many times the height and width are dictated by the software that you are using.

Secret

If you work quite a bit with information that scrolls off the top of the screen, you can try to enlarge the screen buffer height. This causes NT to "remember" the scrolled lines (however many you specify) and allow you to review them.

In the Window Size area, you can specify how large the window itself should be. Normally, the width and height here are the same as in the Screen Buffer Size area. You cannot set the dimensions in this area larger than the Screen Buffer Size, but you can set them smaller. When they are smaller, Windows displays scroll bars, as appropriate, on your command window.

Finally, the Window Position area allows you to specify where you want the command window to be placed on your desktop. You indicate this by entering the position for the left border and the top edge, in pixels. As an alternative, you can allow Windows to decide the best place by selecting the appropriate check box.

Window colors

When working with a command window, you have quite a bit of latitude on the colors that are used to display your information. When you click on the Colors tab, the Properties dialog box appears, as shown in Figure 9-5. Using this tab, you can specify colors for four different items in the command window.

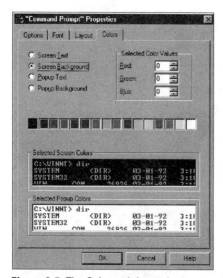

Figure 9-5: The Colors tab is used to choose the colors that display information in the command window.

Each of the four items can be set independently, and you can pick any of 16 standard colors. Using the Selected Color Values area, you can also create custom colors. As you modify the colors, the results of your selections are shown in the preview areas at the bottom of the dialog box.

Understanding the command line

If you have not used the command line before, you may be a bit intimidated by it. After all, there are no icons to help you and no buttons or messages to give you hints. Using a command line is quite simple, provided you remember that any command is composed of three parts:

- **Keywords.** This is the heart of the command; it tells the operating system what you want to do. There are scores of keywords that you can use at the command line.

- **Parameters.** Parameters are optional for some commands and mandatory for others. Sometimes there is a single parameter, and other times there are more than one. Parameters indicate what you want to use as the source or target of your command.

- **Switches.** These control the way in which the command is carried out. Switches always begin with a slash (/) and are followed by one or more letters that indicate the switch that you wish to use. Switches are always optional, because they dictate the way in which a command is executed.

In most instances, the bare minimum for a command is the keyword. Some keywords allow you to use parameters and switches; some *require* their use. When you use the three parts, they always follow each other on the command line, as in the following:

```
dir d: /s
```

In this case, the DIR command is used. This is a very simple command, but it illustrates the three parts of any command. In this case, the keyword is DIR, which tells the operating system that you want to view a directory.

The parameter, which is essentially the target of the keyword, is drive D. Thus, the operating system knows that you want a directory of drive D. Finally, a switch is used to modify how the keyword is carried out. In this case, the /s switch instructs the operating system to include all subdirectories in the output.

As you work at the command line, simply remember the three parts: keywords, parameters, and switches. As you read through the rest of this chapter, you can look for instances where all three parts are used.

Command-Line Commands

The vast majority of commands that you can use from the command prompt are the same as those that are available in MS-DOS. While including every possible command in this section is not practical, you can generally get a good DOS guide and use it as a basis for learning what you can do at the command prompt.

The information you learn in that way needs to be tempered with the information provided in the following sections. First, you learn about command differences between different operating systems. Then you learn which commands have been added to the Windows NT command line.

Windows 95 command differences

If you are coming to a Windows NT environment from Windows 95, you may be interested in knowing some of the differences between commands that you can use under Windows 95 and those that you can use under Windows NT.

If you were using DOS-based versions of Windows prior to Windows 95, you may know that various commands were dropped from the command prompt in Windows 95. Many of those commands that were dropped are still available in Windows NT.

The reason for this is the parallel development of Windows NT with mainstream Windows. The Windows 95 development team was, in a sense, taking the command line just a bit further than had been done under Windows NT.

In fact, you may find that some commands available under Windows NT don't make a whole lot of sense in the networked, multitasking environment that is created by the operating system. Table 9-1 shows the various commands that are not available in Windows 95 and how they are treated in Windows NT.

Table 9-1   Windows NT command differences

Command	DOS 6.22	Windows 95	Windows NT 4.0	Function
APPEND	Yes	No	Yes	Append subdirectories to the current directory.
ASSIGN	Yes	No	No	Attach an alias drive letter to an existing drive.
BACKUP	Yes	No	Yes	Back up files to floppy disk.
CHOICE	Yes	Yes	No	Used in batch files to get input from the user.

Command	DOS 6.22	Windows 95	Windows NT 4.0	Function
COMP	Yes	No	Yes	Compare two sets of disk files.
CTTY	Yes	Yes	No	Change the standard input and output devices.
DBLSPACE	Yes	Yes	No	Compress a disk drive.
DEFRAG	Yes	Yes	No	Defragment the files on a disk drive.
DELTREE	Yes	Yes	No	Delete a subdirectory and all its contents.
DOSSHELL	Yes	No	No	Full-screen graphical shell program for DOS.
DRVSPACE	Yes	Yes	No	Compress a disk drive.
EDLIN	Yes	No	Yes	Rudimentary command-line editor.
EMM386	Yes	Yes	No	Memory manager for expanded memory.
FASTHELP	Yes	No	No	Brief help for DOS commands.
FASTOPEN	Yes	No	Yes	Maintains directory information in memory so files can be quickly found and accessed.
FDISK	Yes	Yes	No	Change the partition information for a disk drive.
GRAFTABL	Yes	No	Yes	Load alternate character sets into memory for quick display.
GRAPHICS	Yes	No	Yes	Enables the Print Screen key to print the contents of a graphics screen on a graphics printer.
HELP	Yes	No	Yes	Display help information for commands.
INCLUDE	Yes	Yes	No	Used in the CONFIG.SYS file to include other configuration blocks in the commands of the current block.
INTERLNK	Yes	No	No	Connects the current computer to an external server, forming a simple network.
INTERSVR	Yes	No	No	Provides server services for an INTERLNK network.

(continued)

Table 9-1   *(continued)*

Command	DOS 6.22	Windows 95	Windows NT 4.0	Function
JOIN	Yes	No	No	Connects a drive to a subdirectory of another drive.
MEMMAKER	Yes	No	No	Configures the use of memory to optimize the availability of conventional memory.
MENUCOLOR	Yes	Yes	No	Changes the color used in a startup menu.
MENUDEFAULT	Yes	Yes	No	Specifies the default choice in a startup menu.
MENUITEM	Yes	Yes	No	Adds an item to a startup menu.
MIRROR	Yes	No	No	Saves FAT and root directory information for subsequent use by the UNFORMAT command.
MSAV	Yes	No	No	The Microsoft Anti-Virus utility.
MSBACKUP	Yes	No	No	Back up your hard drive to floppy drive.
MSCDEX	Yes	Yes	No	Enable access of CD-ROM drives.
MSD	Yes	No	No	The Microsoft Diagnostics utility.
MWAV	Yes	No	No	The Microsoft Anti-Virus utility for Windows.
MWAVTSR	Yes	No	No	Provides full-time anti-virus protection in Windows.
MWBACKUP	Yes	No	No	Backup program for Windows.
MWUNDEL	Yes	No	No	Undelete program for Windows.
NUMLOCK	Yes	Yes	No	Controls the state of the NumLock key when starting your system.
POWER	Yes	No	No	Support for Advanced Power Management (APM) in laptop computers.
PRINT	Yes	No	Yes	Print spooling and management capabilities.
QBASIC	Yes	No	Yes	Full-screen, interactive programming environment for BASIC.

Command	DOS 6.22	Windows 95	Windows NT 4.0	Function
RECOVER	Yes	No	Yes	Used to rebuild the file allocation table from a damaged disk.
REPLACE	Yes	No	Yes	Selectively updates files on a target disk from the primary disk.
RESTORE	Yes	No	Yes	Restores information backed up with the BACKUP command.
SCANDISK	Yes	Yes	No	Drive analysis utility.
SHARE	Yes	No	No	Enables support for file and record locking.
SMARTDRV	Yes	Yes	No	Disk-caching utility for DOS.
SMARTMON	Yes	No	No	Monitor and adjust the performance of SMARTDRV.
SUBMENU	Yes	Yes	No	Create menu blocks within the CONFIG.SYS file.
SYS	Yes	Yes	No	Transfer system files to a disk.
TREE	Yes	No	Yes	Display the directory structure of a drive.
UNDELETE	Yes	No	No	Undeletes previously deleted files.
UNFORMAT	Yes	No	No	Unformats a disk.
VSAFE	Yes	No	No	Memory-resident program to monitor disk access by suspicious programs.

Table 9-1 does not list every possible command that you can use at the command prompt. Instead, it lists only those commands whose inclusion is different under the operating systems that you may have used.

New commands

If you are familiar with using commands under the DOS environment, you are likely to be confident in using the command line of Windows NT. You should know, however, that NT has quite a few additional commands that are not available in DOS. In addition, many of the commands are also not available from the Windows 95 command line.

The new commands that you may encounter can be divided into three categories: network commands, TCP/IP commands, and other commands. The following sections address each of these areas.

Network commands

Windows NT is, if nothing else, a network operating system. With this in mind, there are quite a few command-line commands that you can use to control your network. Many of these commands were available in previous versions of NT, and many are in Windows 95. None of these commands were available in Windows 3.1 or in DOS, however. The vast majority of the network commands consist of at least two keywords, where the first keyword is always NET.

The following are the basic network commands that you can use:

- IPXROUTE
- NBTSTAT
- NET ACCOUNTS
- NET COMPUTER
- NET CONFIG
- NET CONTINUE
- NET FILE
- NET GROUP
- NET HELP
- NET HELPMSG
- NET LOCALGROUP
- NET NAME
- NET PAUSE
- NET PRINT
- NET SEND
- NET SESSION
- NET SHARE
- NET START
- NET STATISTICS
- NET STOP
- NET TIME
- NET USE
- NET USER
- NET VIEW

Each of these commands is covered in the following sections.

IPXROUTE

The IPXROUTE command allows you to display and change the information that is stored in the IPX routing tables. To use this command, you must have the IPX protocol installed and bound to an adapter.

This command can take three forms, as follows:

- **IPXROUTE SERVERS.** Displays the SAP table for your servers, sorted by server name.

- **IPXROUTE STATS.** Displays or clears the statistics for the IPX router.

- **IPXROUTE TABLE.** Displays the IPX routing table, sorted by network number, or allows you to make changes in the table information.

The IPX routing tables are normally set up by Windows NT automatically as you make changes in your network properties.

NBTSTAT

The NBTSTAT command displays a table showing information about your network. The information is derived by using NBT (NetBIOS over TCP/IP) instead of TCP/IP protocols alone. This command is diagnostic and can be used to resolve some network difficulties.

Because it is a diagnostic tool, it is much more likely to be used by network administrators than by workstation users. This command is only available if you have the TCP/IP protocols installed.

The NBTSTAT command uses a number of command-line switches to control what information is returned. Table 9-2 indicates the various switches that you can use.

Table 9-2   NBTSTAT command-line switches

Switch	Meaning
-a *host*	Uses the name table from the specified *host* computer.
-A *address*	Uses the name table at the specified IP *address*.
-c	Lists the contents of the NetBIOS name cache, providing the IP address for each name in the cache.
-n	Lists local NetBIOS names.
-R	Purges the NetBIOS name cache and reloads the LMHOSTS file.
-r	Lists name resolution information for Windows networking.
-S	Displays both client and server sessions, using IP addresses for remote hosts.
-s	Displays both client and server sessions, using host names (from the HOSTS file) for remote hosts wherever possible.

(continued)

Table 9-2 *(continued)*

Switch	Meaning
interval	Indicates the refresh interval, in seconds, for the information that is displayed by NBTSTAT. Using this parameter places NBTSTAT in a continuous updating mode that is halted by pressing Ctrl+C.

NET ACCOUNTS

The NET ACCOUNTS command allows you to set account policies from the command line. You can set the following information using this command:

- Minimum password length

- Maximum password age

- Minimum password age

- Password history count

In addition, you can force all user accounts to be disconnected, and you can force your domain controllers to synchronize with your PDC (primary domain controller — the computer that manages the accounts on your network). If you want to set additional account policies, you must do so with the User Manager, as described in Chapter 12.

To use NET ACCOUNTS, you must have Administrator privileges. You signify what you want to do by using any of the switches that are shown in Table 9-3.

Table 9-3   NET ACCOUNTS command-line switches

Switch	Meaning
/domain	When the NET ACCOUNTS command is used from a workstation, the only computer typically affected is the local computer. If you use this switch, then the changes affect the primary domain controller for the network.
/forcelogoff:no	Indicates that you no longer want accounts to be forced off. This can be used to counteract the effects of the /forcelogoff:*xx* switch.
/forcelogoff:*xx*	Indicates that all user accounts should be automatically logged off after *xx* minutes. A message is broadcast immediately, indicating that the account will be logged off in *xx* minutes. When two minutes remain, another message is broadcast indicating that the account must log off immediately. You typically use this form of NET ACCOUNTS when you need to bring the server down and you need to get everyone off of it.

Switch	Meaning
/maxpwage:*days*	Used to specify the maximum age, in *days,* that a password can exist. After a password reaches the specified age, the user must change it. Valid values are from 1 to 49,710 days.
/maxpwage:unlimited	Used to specify that passwords never expire.
/minpwage:*days*	Used to specify the minimum age, in days, that a password can exist. This prohibits users from changing their passwords before the specified duration is reached. Valid values are from 0 to 49,710 days.
/minpwlen:*xx*	Used to specify the minimum length for a password, as *xx* characters. You can specify any length between 0 and 14. (Zero indicates that blank passwords are acceptable.)
/sync	Forces the backup domain controllers in your network to synchronize with the primary domain controller.
/uniquepw:*xx*	Specifies the number of unique passwords that must be used before a password can be reused. Valid values are from 0 to 8 passwords.

If you use NET ACCOUNTS without parameters, you can see the current account policies. For instance, Figure 9-6 shows what the output from NET ACCOUNTS looks like.

Figure 9-6: The NET ACCOUNTS command can display your current account policies.

NET COMPUTER

If you are connected to a Windows NT Server network, you can use the NET COMPUTER command to add computers to the database on the primary domain controller. The syntax is as follows:

```
net computer UNC
```

The UNC parameter is the name of the computer, in UNC notation. Thus, if the computer name is MySystem, then the UNC would be \\MySystem. In addition, you must include a switch at the end of the command line that indicates whether you want to add or delete the computer from the domain.

For example, if you wanted to add the computer, you would use the following:

```
net computer \\MySystem /add
```

Likewise, if you wanted to delete the computer, you would use the following:

```
net computer \\MySystem /del
```

NET CONFIG

The NET CONFIG command displays and allows you to change information about either your server or workstation. If you use the NET CONFIG command without additional parameters, then it indicates whether you can display or modify information about the workstation or server.

For instance, Figure 9-7 shows the information that is returned if you use NET CONFIG WORKSTATION as your command.

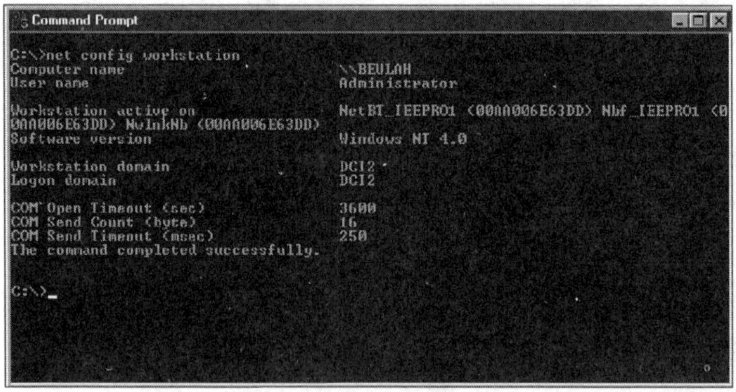

Figure 9-7: The NET CONFIG command displays information about your system.

If you decide that you want to change any of the parameters that are shown in the information, you can do so by using the various switches that are designed for this command. Table 9-4 lists the switches that you can use with NET CONFIG.

Table 9-4   NET CONFIG command-line switches

Switch	Type	Meaning
/autodisconnect:*xx*	server	Indicates the number of minutes (*xx*) after which an inactive user session can be inactive before it is disconnected. Valid values range from –1 (never disconnect) to 65,535 minutes.
/charcount:*bytes*	workstation	Specifies the number of characters (*bytes*) that NT should buffer before transmitting them. Valid values range from 0 to 65,535 characters.
/chartime:*xx*	workstation	Indicates the amount of time (*xx*, in milliseconds) that NT should pause between transmitting batches of information. Values range from 0 to 65,535,000 milliseconds (18 hours, 12 minutes, 15 seconds).
/charwait:*xx*	workstation	Specifies the amount of time (*xx*, in seconds) that NT waits for a communications channel to be available. Valid values range from 0 to 65,535 seconds.
/hidden:no	server	Indicates that the server's name should not be hidden in server listings (the name appears in the listings).
/hidden:yes	server	Indicates that the server's name should be hidden in server listings (the name does not appear in the listings).
/srvcomment "*message*"	server	Specifies a comment that should be displayed, for the server, when using the NET VIEW command. The *message* can be up to 48 characters long and must be enclosed in quotation marks.

Secret

The NET CONFIG command is not necessarily the best way to change server or workstation parameters. You have much more control over what is changed by editing the Registry directly. (Editing the Registry is discussed in Chapter 10.)

NET CONTINUE

The NET CONTINUE command is the opposite of the NET PAUSE command. It is used to restart a network service that was previously suspended. On Windows NT Workstation, the following services can be continued:

- ftp publishing service
- lpdsvc
- net logon
- network dde
- network dde dsdm
- net lm security support provider
- remote access server
- schedule
- server
- simple TCP/IP services
- workstation

To use the NET CONTINUE command, simply issue the command followed by the name of the service (from the foregoing list) that you want to continue.

Tip

You can use the NET START command, with no parameters or switches, to view the services that are currently started on your system.

NET FILE

Windows NT allows you to share directories and files over the network. When you share your files, you are acting as a server, even though you are technically running Windows NT Workstation. If you discover any files that have been left open by mistake, you can use the NET FILE command to close them.

If you use NET FILE without any parameters, you see a list of the different files that are open on your system. These files are listed with a file number, the filename, the user name, and whether the file is locked. When you then want to close a file, you enter the following:

```
net file num /close
```

Make sure that you replace the *num* parameter with the file number that was returned when you listed the open files on your system.

NET GROUP

Essentially, the NET GROUP command is used to do many of the same tasks that are normally associated with the User Manager program. You can use the command to manage global groups and to manage the users within those groups.

If you use the NET GROUP command without any parameters, then the groups that are defined on your local computer or your domain are listed. If you then add a group name to the command line, you can see the users belonging to that group. Other uses of the NET GROUP command are shown in Table 9-5.

Table 9-5 NET GROUP command line uses

Usage	Meaning
net group *groupname* /add	Adds the specified *groupname*.
net group *groupname* /comment:"*comment*"	Adds the specified *comment* to the information that is stored for the specified *groupname*. Comments can be from 0 to 48 characters long.
net group *groupname* /delete	Removes the specified *groupname*.
net group *groupname* *username* /add	Adds the specified *username* to the existing *groupname*.
net group *groupname* *username* /delete	Removes an existing *username* from the specified *groupname*.

For information on how to make changes in local groups, see the NET LOCALGROUP command.

Tip Normally, the NET GROUP command works only on your local computer. If you have administrator rights, you can instead modify the information that is maintained by your PDC by using the /domain switch at the end of any NET GROUP command line.

NET HELP

The NET HELP command displays a short amount of help information for the different network commands that are supported by Windows NT. As an example, Figure 9-8 shows an example of how such a help screen looks.

Figure 9-8: The NET HELP command is used to display the syntax and a short description of different network commands.

Notice that the NET HELP command, to be complete, must be followed by the name of the command on which you want help. In this case, you don't need to include the second iteration of NET, but including it doesn't hurt either.

For instance, you can use NET HELP NAME, and it is translated the same as NET HELP NET NAME. You can also get help on a network command by entering the command as you normally would and then using either the /? switch or the /help switch after the command.

It is possible for a help screen to occupy more than a single window. To see information a single screen at a time, use the syntax NET HELP NAME | MORE.

Secret

NET HELPMSG

The NET HELPMSG command is similar to the NET HELP command, except that it is used to display the meaning of various error messages; it is not used for help with individual commands. You issue the command by immediately following NET HELP with the four-digit error number that you want to check out.

For instance, Figure 9-9 shows the output of NET HELPMSG.

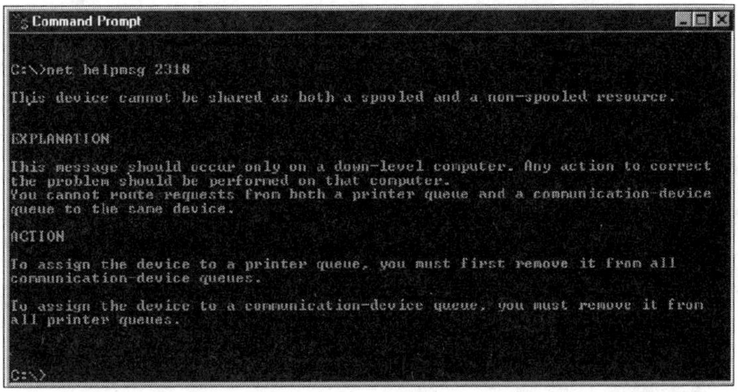

Figure 9-9: The NET HELPMSG command provides information about the meaning of an error code.

You do not need to use NET HELPMSG immediately after receiving an error message, although that is when it may be the most helpful. The amount of information that is returned by the command is spotty, at best. For some error codes, the information can be very terse (as few as four words), while for others, it can be quite helpful, providing workarounds and alternative actions.

Secret

If you use the NET HELPMSG command and find that the information scrolls off the top of the screen, add the MORE command, as in NET HELPMSG 2318 | MORE.

NET LOCALGROUP

The NET LOCALGROUP command has the same effect on local user groups and users as NET GROUP has on global groups and users. In fact, the syntax and usage are exactly the same as NET GROUP, so you should refer to that command for more information.

NET NAME

When you install Windows NT, it installs a special service called the Messenger service. This service is used to transfer message packets between named resources on your system. From a user's perspective, the resources are typically groups, users, computers, and so on.

Using the NET NAME command, you can add or delete names with which the Messenger service can communicate. You can then use the NET SEND command to broadcast messages to the names that you have created.

If you use NET NAME with no parameters, it indicates the names that have been defined on your system. Three types of names can be displayed:

- Computer names, which are added when the Workstation service starts

- User names, which are added when the user logs on

- Names that are created with the NET NAME command

You can use NET NAME to add names by simply following the command with the name that you want to add and the /add switch. Names can range from 1 to 15 characters long. For instance, if you wanted to add *george* as a message name, you would use the following command:

```
net name george /add
```

The next time that you used the NET NAME command to list users, you would see output similar to Figure 9-10, indicating that GEORGE is now a name in your system. (Notice that names are converted to uppercase automatically.)

```
Command Prompt                                          _ □ ×

C:\>net name

Name

BEULAH
ADMINISTRATOR
The command completed successfully.

C:\>net name george /add
The message name GEORGE was added successfully.

C:\>net name

Name

BEULAH
ADMINISTRATOR
GEORGE
The command completed successfully.

C:\>
```

Figure 9-10: The NET NAME command allows you to create messaging names under NT.

If you later want to eliminate a name that you have created, use the same command that you used to create the name, except the last switch becomes /delete. Note that you can only delete names that you have created; you cannot delete user names or machine names.

Secret

Microsoft documentation indicates that the NET NAME switch to remove a name is /delete. You can also shorten this to /del — the result is the same.

NET PAUSE

The NET PAUSE command is the opposite of the NET CONTINUE command. It is used to suspend a network service that is currently running on your system. On Windows NT Workstation, you can pause the following services:

- ftp publishing service
- lpdsvc
- net logon
- network dde
- network dde dsdm
- net lm security support provider
- remote access server
- schedule
- server
- simple TCP/IP services
- workstation

To use the NET PAUSE command, simply issue the command followed by the name of the service (from the foregoing list) that you want to pause.

NET PRINT

In effect, NET PRINT provides a way to control a printer queue from the command line rather than using the Printers folder. Available options enable you to view the queue as well as to pause, resume, and delete individual jobs.

The normal way that you use the command is to first view the queue. This is done using the following command:

```
net print UNC
```

The only parameter that you need is the UNC path for the computer or for the specific printer on the computer. Thus, if you wanted to view the queues for the printers on your computer and your computer's name was MySystem, then you would use the following command:

```
net print \\mysystem
```

If you had more than one printer queue on your computer, then you could use a UNC that included the share name for the printer that you want to view, as in the following command:

```
net print \\mysystem\epson
```

Using the NET PRINT command in this way returns a list of the print jobs that are currently in the queue along with the associated job number. This number can then be used in a NET PRINT command that affects the individual job. For instance, if you want to delete print job 31 on your system, you would use the following command:

```
net print \\mysystem\epson 31 /delete
```

NET PRINT recognizes two other switches as well — /pause and /resume. You can use these switches on the command line in the same way that you used /delete.

NET SEND

The NET SEND command is used to transmit a message to a named system, user, or messaging channel. (Messaging channels are created with the NET NAME command.) There are five ways that you can use the NET SEND command; they are listed as follows:

Usage	*Effect*
net send name message	Sends the message to the defined name in your workgroup
net send * message	Sends the message to all names in your workgroup
net send /domain message	Sends the message to all names in your domain
net send /domain: name message	Sends the message to a specific name in your domain, but outside your workgroup
net send /users message	Sends the message to all users connected to the server

NET SESSION

The NET SESSION command is used to determine who is connected to your system, how long they have been connected, and what resources they are using. If you use the NET SESSION command with no parameters, you are shown a list of computer names connected to your system, the name of the user who is logged on at that computer, what type of operating system he or she is running (such as NT or Windows 95), how many resources on your system the user has open, and how long the user has been idle.

You can display the details for a specific computer by using the computer name along with NET SESSION. For instance, if you discover, by using NET SESSION alone, that the user named Martha is connected to your system using the computer \\RESEARCH12, then you can use the following command to see exactly what that user is accessing:

```
net session \\research12
```

If you subsequently decide to terminate that user's session with your system, you can enter the following command:

```
net session \\research12 /delete
```

Secret

Instead of using only the formal NET SESSION command, you can use the alternates of NET SESSIONS or NET SESS.

NET SHARE

If you want to manage your shared resources, you use the NET SHARE command. Used by itself, without any parameters, NET SHARE displays all of the resources that you currently have shared on your system. (See Figure 9-11.)

Figure 9-11: The NET SHARE command can be used to display the resources that you are sharing on your system.

You can also follow the NET SHARE command by the name of a shared resource, which displays information specific to that resource. For instance, supplying the name of a shared folder indicates the share name, the path on your system, the number of maximum users, and the names of users that are currently using that resource.

Other uses of NET SHARE allow you to define shared folders, control the number of users of that resource, set comments for it, and remove the shared resource. Table 9-6 lists the various switches and parameters that you can use with the NET SHARE command.

Table 9-6 NET SHARE command-line parameters and switches

Parameter or Switch	Meaning
sharename	Indicates the resource that you want to view (when used alone), change (when used with most other switches), or remove (when used with /delete).
sharename=drive:path	Specifies a new share name and the *drive* and *path* to be shared.
drive:path	Specifies a *drive* and *path* for a share that is being removed. Used with the /delete switch.
/users:*xx*	Indicates that only *xx* users can concurrently use the shared resource.
/unlimited	Specifies that there is no limit on the number of concurrent users that can use the resource.
/remark:"*comment*"	Sets a *comment* for the specified share name.
/delete	Removes the specified share or drive and path.

NET START

The NET START command is used to start various network services. To start a service, simply follow the NET START command with the name of the service that you want to start. If the service name contains spaces, then you must enclose the service name in quotation marks.

Table 9-7 lists the different services that you can specify on the command line. (Those services that are noted for workstations also work on servers; those that are noted for servers only work on servers.) Most services must have been installed on your network prior to using them with the NET START command.

Table 9-7 NET START services

Service	System Type	Meaning
alerter	workstation	Service is used to alert users to problems or errors that are encountered by the system.
client service for netware	workstation	Service is used to connect Windows NT to a Novell network and operate as a client to that network.

Service	System Type	Meaning
clipbook server	workstation	Service is used for sharing information over the network, as described in Chapter 7.
computer browser	workstation	Service enables you to browse other computers and for them to browse your system.
dhcp client	workstation	When using TCP/IP, enables you to obtain an IP address for a DHCP server.
directory replicator	workstation	Service enables you to use file replication between computers on your network.
eventlog	workstation	Enables the use of the event log on your system.
file server for macintosh	server	Allows you to share files with Macintosh computers.
ftp publishing service	workstation	If the Internet Information Server has been installed, this enables the FTP server.
gateway service for netware	server	Allows your system to act as a gateway to Novell NetWare file and print services.
lpdsvc	workstation	Enables UNIX computers to print to a printer on your system, using TCP/IP.
messenger	workstation	Service allows you to use the NET NAME and NET SEND commands.
microsoft dhcp server	server	If you are using the TCP/IP protocol, this controls the DHCP server.
net logon	workstation	Allows users to log on to the computer and the network.
network dde dsdm	workstation	Manages shared DDE conversations over the network.
network dde	workstation	Provides a secure implementation of DDE services over the network.
network monitor agent	workstation	Service enables the remote monitoring of network communications.
nt lm security support provider	workstation	Provides NT security services to remote procedure calls that do not use named pipes.
ole	workstation	Service enables use of object linking and embedding (OLE) on the system.
printserver for macintosh	server	Allows your server to accept print jobs from Macintosh computers.

(continued)

Table 9-7 *(continued)*

Service	System Type	Meaning
remote access connection manager	workstation	If RAS has been installed on the system, this enables the use of the connection manager.
remote access isnsap service	workstation	Provides ISNSAP services for use over RAS links.
remote access server	workstation	Starts the RAS service on your system.
remote procedure call (rpc) locator	workstation	Enables the locator portion of the RPC service. This service permits the use of distributed applications over the network.
remote procedure call (rpc) service	workstation	Enables the service portion of the RPC service. This portion allows RPC applications to use dynamic endpoint mapping.
remoteboot	server	Allows remote booting of the server over a network.
schedule	workstation	Allows you to schedule the execution of programs using the At command.
server	workstation	Allows you to share resources that are on your system with other network users.
simple tcp/ip services	workstation	If you have the TCP/IP protocol installed, this enables the use of elemental TCP/IP services.
snmp	workstation	If you have the TCP/IP protocol installed, this allows your system to report its status to an SNMP management system over the network.
spooler	workstation	Enables the print spooler service.
tcp/ip netbios helper	workstation	If you have the TCP/IP protocol installed, this allows you to use NBT (NetBIOS over TCP/IP).
ups	workstation	Allows you to interface NT with an uninterruptible power supply.
windows internet name service	server	If you have the TCP/IP protocol installed, this enables the WINS server.
workstation	workstation	Allows you to access and use resources on other computers in your network.

NET STATISTICS

The NET STATISTICS command allows you to view detailed statistics on either a server or a workstation. If you use the command without any parameters, then you can see which systems (server or workstation) you can use with the command.

Figure 9-12 shows an example of information that is provided when the NET STATISTICS WORKSTATION command is used.

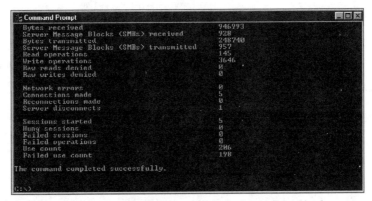

Figure 9-12: The NET STATISTICS command displays quite a bit of information about your system.

NET STOP

The NET STOP command is the opposite of the NET START command; it is used to halt network services. To use the NET STOP command, you simply append the name of the service that you want to stop. You can use the same service names that were detailed under the NET START command.

NET TIME

The NET TIME command is used to view the time on another computer in your domain. This remote computer is called a *time server*. You can also use the command to synchronize the time on your workstation with the time on the remote system. You can use any of the following versions of this command:

Command	Meaning
net time	Displays the time for the default time server in your workgroup
net time *UNC*	Displays the time on the computer that is specified by the UNC path name

(continued)

Command	Meaning
net time /domain	Displays the time on the default time server in your domain
net time /domain:*name*	Displays the time on the time server in the specified domain

In addition, if you append the /set switch to any of the NET TIME commands, then you can set the time on your workstation to the time on the selected system.

NET USE

The NET USE command allows you to manage your network connections with remote resources such as disks or printers. This command is similar in purpose to the network mapping functions of Windows NT.

You can also use NET USE to display information about existing connections. You can see the network connections that you currently have defined by using NET USE without any parameters.

To connect to a remote resource, simply provide the name of the local device to which you want the resource mapped and then provide the path to the network resource. For instance, if you wanted to map the printer at //research/dyesub to the LPT2 port on your system, you would use the following command:

```
net use lpt2: //research/dyesub einstein
```

This example assumes that the password for the printer (if necessary) is *einstein.* After this command is successfully completed, anything that you print to LPT2 is automatically sent to the research department's printer.

Likewise, you can map a local drive letter to a directory that is available on the network by using the same type of command line (here the password is *fluff*):

```
net use g: //marketing/campaign/newyear fluff
```

Secret

If you use an asterisk (*) instead of a drive letter when mapping a network drive, the next available drive letter is automatically used. Likewise, using an asterisk in place of a printer port indicates that the next available printer port should be used.

You can also indicate whether you want your associations to be persistent by using the /persistent:yes or /persistent:no switches. *Persistence* is defined as the ability to retain a connection over several sessions. Thus, if you turn on persistence, then your connection is established every time that you log on to Windows NT.

To later disconnect the mapped resource, simply provide the local name that you used for the mapping and then use the /delete switch. For instance, if you wanted to delete the association between LPT2 and the printer, you would use the following command line:

```
net use lpt2: /delete
```

NET USER

The NET USER command provides a way for you to manage users on your system. The command provides many of the same capabilities of the User Manager, in relation to users. (If you want to work with groups, use the NET GROUP or NET LOCALGROUP command.)

If you use NET USER with no parameters, then you are shown a list of the users that are defined for your local system, or if you use the /domain switch for the domain of which you are a part. For instance, Figure 9-13 shows what the output of such a command would appear.

Figure 9-13: The NET USER command can display a list of your domain user accounts.

Notice that all users are listed, not only those logged in to the system. If you want to add an account to the system, you can do so by entering the user's name, entering his or her password (if you are assigning one), and using the /add switch. For instance, if you were adding an account named Tiffany, and his password was *yellow,* then you would use the following:

```
net user tiffany yellow /add /domain
```

This is the simplest way to add accounts; however, you can also specify options that affect different parameters of the account. These parameters are added as additional switches on the command line. The options that you can use are listed in Table 9-8.

Table 9-8   NET USER account option switches

Switch	Meaning
/active:yes	Enables the account.
/active:no	Disables the account.
/comment:"*text*"	Sets the comment filed for the account. The *text* can have as many as 48 characters and must be enclosed in quotation marks.
/countrycode:*nnn*	Specifies the country code (*nnn*) that is to be used for help and error messages for the user.
/expires:*date*	Indicates that the user's account expires when *date* is reached. Dates can be specified as mm/dd/yy or by any other setting that is dictated by the /countrycode option.
/expires:never	Indicates that the user's account never expires.
/fullname:"*name*"	Sets the contents of the user's full name field in the account. The *name* must be enclosed in quotation marks.
/homedir:path	Sets a path for the user's home directory.
/homedirreq:yes	Indicates that a home directory is required.
/homedirreq:no	Indicates that a home directory is not required.
/passwordchg:yes	Indicates that the user can change his password.
/passwordchg:no	Indicates that the user cannot change his password.
/passwordreq:yes	Indicates that the account must have a password.
/passwordreq:no	Indicates that the account is not required to have a password.
/profilepath:*path*	Sets a path for the user's log-in profile.
/scriptpath:*path*	Sets a path for the user's log-in path. The *path* cannot be absolute; it must be relative to the c:\winnt\system32\repl\import\scripts directory.
/times:all	Indicates that there are no restrictions on when the user can log in.
/times:*times*	Indicates the days and hours when the user can log in. The *times* parameter consists of a day indicator followed by an hour indicator. The days can be spelled out or abbreviated as M, T, W, Th, F, Sa, and Su. Days can also be a range, as in M-F. The day is separated from the hour by a comma, and the hour must be a value between 0 and 24 or 12AM and 11PM. You can separate day/time pairs by a semicolon, as in M-F,8AM-6PM;Sa,9PM-2AM.

Switch	Meaning
/usercomment: "comment"	Sets the user comment field for the account to the *comment*, which must be surrounded by quotation marks.
/workstations:*	Indicates that the user can log in to all workstations.
/workstations: *names*	Indicates that the user can only log in to the listed workstations. The *names* parameter consists of up to eight UNC paths for the workstations where log in is allowed, separated by commas.

If you decide to delete a user account, you can do so by using NET USER, followed by the user's name and the /delete switch. For instance, if you want to delete an account named Jerome, you would use the following command line:

```
net use jerome /delete
```

NET VIEW

The NET VIEW command is used to determine which computers are available in a domain or which resources are being shared by a specific computer on the network. To see a list of the computers that are in your domain, use the NET VIEW command without any parameters.

To see a list of computers that are in a specific domain, simply include the name of the domain, using the /domain switch. For instance, if you wanted to see the information for the production department's domain, you would use the following command:

```
net view /domain:production
```

You can also use the NET VIEW command to see a list of the resources that are used by a specific workstation. You do this by including the UNC path to the workstation on the command line. For instance, if you wanted to see the resources that are on the research department's system, you would enter the following command:

```
net view \\research
```

TCP/IP commands

TCP/IP is an acronym for transport control protocol/Internet protocol. As you may already know, this is the protocol that is used on the Internet. Windows NT includes several commands that are made available only when you have the TCP/IP protocol installed on your system.

These include the following commands:

- arp
- finger
- ftp

- hostname
- ipconfig
- lpq
- lpr
- netstat
- nslookup
- ping
- rcp
- rexec
- route
- rsh
- telnet
- tftp
- tracert

These commands are descendants from similar utilities on UNIX systems, which is where the TCP/IP protocol started. Their UNIX ancestry is also the reason why the command names are in lowercase letters. This is traditional for UNIX systems, whereas most DOS commands are shown in uppercase characters.

Many of the TCP/IP commands are typically used over the Internet. For this reason, several of the commands are best described in Chapter 14. The balance of the TCP/IP commands are described in the following sections. You can only use these commands if you have the TCP/IP protocol installed on your network.

arp

ARP is an acronym for *address resolution protocol.* This command enables you to modify the IP-to-Ethernet or Token Ring address translation tables that are used by the network services. You use the arp command from the command line in an MS-DOS window.

The switches that you can use with arp are as follows:

Switch	Meaning
-a *address*	Displays information from the arp table. If *address* is provided, then only information on that IP address is returned.
-N *netaddr*	Displays information from the arp table. The *netaddr* parameter indicates the server from which the arp table information should be used.

Switch	Meaning
-d *address*	Deletes the arp table entry specified by the IP *address*.
-d *address netaddr*	Deletes the arp table entry that is specified by the IP *address* on the server at *netaddr*.
-s *address physical*	Adds an arp table entry, associating the IP *address* with the *physical* Ethernet address.
-s *address physical netaddr*	Adds an arp table entry, associating the IP *address* with the *physical* Ethernet address, using the arp table on the server specified by *netaddr*.

hostname

This simple command quickly returns the name of the host (workstation) on which it is executed.

ipconfig

This command allows you to see the TCP/IP configuration settings for the system on which you execute it. If you use ipconfig without any parameters, then you get a quick display of the IP address, subnet mask, and default gateway values for the workstation. If you use it with the /all switch, then you get much more information, as shown in Figure 9-14.

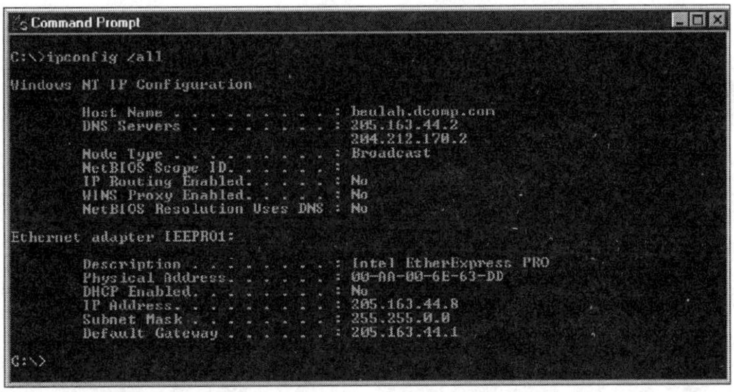

Figure 9-14: The ipconfig command can display quite a bit of information about your workstation.

If you are using DHCP on your network, then the ipconfig command can be particularly helpful in determining which IP address you have been assigned by the DHCP server. You can also use the /renew and /release switches to control what DHCP does.

If you use the /renew command with an optional adapter name, you cause DHCP to renew all of its IP address leases. (You would include the adapter name if your system has multiple adapter cards using TCP/IP.)

As an example, you may want to renew the DHCP leases for the adapter shown in Figure 9-14. In this case, you would use the following command line:

```
ipconfig /renew ieeepro1
```

Likewise, you can use the /release command (with an optional adapter name) to clear the DHCP configuration and disable TCP/IP on your network.

lpq

The lpq utility is used if you are running a mixed NT and UNIX network, and you are running an LPD server that allows information to be printed from the UNIX workstations to a printer on the NT side of the fence. The lpq utility displays the status of one or more print queues on your network.

The following three switches can be used with the command:

Switch	Meaning
-S server	Used to specify the name of the server that contains the printers whose queues you want to display
-P printer	Used to specify the printer whose queue you want to display
-l	Indicates that a detailed status report should be displayed

lpr

The lpr utility is used if you are running a mixed NT and UNIX network, and you are running an LPD server that allows information to be printed from the UNIX workstations to a printer on the NT side of the fence. The lpr utility sends a file to the printer, allowing you to indicate job parameters that are associated with the file.

You can use the following switches with the command:

Switch	Meaning
-S server	Used to specify the name of the server that contains the printers whose queues you want to display.
-P printer	Used to specify the printer whose queue you want to display.

Switch	Meaning
-C *class*	Indicates the information (*class*) to be printed on the print job banner that is produced at the beginning of the job.
-J jobname	The name by which you want this print job to be known.
-01	Indicates the type of file that is being printed. You don't need to use this for text files, but if the file is a binary representation that is understood by the printer, you should use this switch.

netstat

The netstat command displays information and statistics about your current TCP/IP network connections. Information that is displayed by netstat includes the IP address and port number of a network connection, the IP address of your local system, the protocol that is used by a connection, and the status of a connection.

The format and exact content of the information that is displayed by netstat can be modified by using the switches listed in Table 9-9.

Table 9-9   Netstat command-line switches

Switch	Meaning
-a	Shows all network connections.
-e	Shows only Ethernet statistics.
-n	Displays information in numerical form as opposed to doing DNS lookups for names.
-s	Displays statistics by protocol.
-p *protocol*	Indicates the protocols for which statistics should be displayed. Valid values for *protocol* without using the -p switch are tcp and udp. If you use the -p switch in conjunction with the -s switch, valid values for *protocol* are tcp, udp, icmp, or ip.
-r	Shows the contents of the network routing table.
interval	Indicates the interval, in seconds, at which the requested statistics should be updated and redisplayed. Using this parameter places netstat in a continuous updating mode; you can break the cycle by pressing Ctrl+C.

rcp

The rcp command is used to transfer files from your NT system to a UNIX system that is running rshd or vice versa. The rshd (remote shell daemon) is a server program that some UNIX systems use for file transfer.

The command is very easy to use and is similar to the COPY command that you may already be familiar with. For instance, you may want to copy a file named MyFile.doc from your system to a UNIX system (on your network) named *research*.

In this case, you would use the following command line:

```
rcp MyFile.doc research:
```

Notice the use of the colon on the UNIX system name. This indicates to rcp that you are copying to a computer. The default directory and user are used on the UNIX system. If you wanted to copy the same file to another system on the Internet, you need to know a user name on the remote system. (This way the remote system knows where to store the file that it is receiving.)

In this case, you would use the following command:

```
rcp MyFile.doc truckee.eden.ucal.edu:fred
```

You can modify the command even further to include a filename for the remote system. The following example copies your file to a file named upload.doc at the remote site:

```
rcp MyFile.doc truckee.eden.ucal.edu:fred/pub/toyou/upload.doc
```

Notice that the example also included a full path for the remote filename. Copying files from the UNIX system to your system would be just as easy; you simply need to switch the two sides of the command line (the *from* and *to* sides). You can also change the behavior of rcp by using one of several switches that are available:

Switch	Meaning
-a	Indicates that you are transferring an ASCII file. This transfer mode processes the files that are being transferred so that your files always end up with a carriage return/linefeed combination (for paragraph termination), and the UNIX system always ends up with just a linefeed character.
-b	Indicates that you are transferring a binary file. No translation is performed on the files that are being transferred.
-h	Includes hidden files in the transfer from your system.
-r	Indicates that you want to recursively process subdirectories, similar to the capabilities of the XCOPY command.

rexec

Some UNIX systems use a service called rexec. This service allows users at remote terminals to execute commands on the system. The rexec command under Windows NT allows you to send commands, for execution, to a remote UNIX system. You use the command in the following manner:

```
rexec computer command
```

Notice that only two parameters are mandatory: the name of the computer on which you want to run the command and the command itself. Some systems may require you to include a password to receive execute privileges on the system.

In this case, you can use the -l switch, followed by the password, on your command line:

```
rexec computer -l password command
```

For more information on how rexec is implemented on specific hosts, discuss the program with your system administrator for the UNIX system.

Note

The implementation of the rexec command under Windows NT is very similar to the implementation of the rsh command. Both do the same thing, but each one uses a different protocol to accomplish its work.

route

The route command is actually four commands in one. When used as the initial part of the command, it enables you to manage the routing table that is used by your network. The different forms of the command are as follows:

- **Route add.** Adds an entry to the routing table.
- **Route change.** Changes an existing entry in the routing table.
- **Route print.** Prints the routing table.
- **Route delete.** Deletes an existing entry from the routing table.

To add a gateway entry to the routing table, follow the command by the host name, the mask name, and the gateway to use, as in the following:

```
route add host mask mask gateway
```

In this example, *host, mask,* and *gateway* should be replaced with their respective IP addresses. The syntax is the same if you are changing, printing, or deleting — the only change in the command is the second word.

You can also use the route command, with only the -f switch, to clear the entire routing table. You would enter this command as follows:

```
route -f
```

Secret

If you use the -f switch in a command line with any other route command, the clearing takes place before the other portion of the command line (add, change, print, or delete) is completed.

rsh

The rsh command is used to send commands, for execution, to a remote UNIX system that is using the rsh service. The command is operationally the same as the rexec command, even to the point of using the same syntax and switches. Refer to the rexec command for more information.

tftp

If you are communicating with a UNIX system over a network, you can use the tftp command to transfer files between your system and the remote system. The tftp is a very simplified version of the ftp program that is described in Chapter 14.

The basic syntax of the tftp command is as follows:

```
tftp host command source destination
```

In this example, *host* is replaced with the name of the remote computer. The *command* is either put or get, depending on whether you are sending the file (put) or receiving the file (get). Both *source* and *destination* are filenames that are recognized by your system and the remote system.

Normally, tftp assumes that the files being transferred are ASCII files. This means that limited processing is done by tftp on the files being transferred.

If you are transferring from your system to the remote system, then all carriage return/linefeed combinations are replaced with only linefeeds. If you are transferring to your system, then a reverse translation takes place. If you don't want any translation to occur, use the -i switch to indicate that you are transferring an image (binary) file.

Other commands

Besides network-related commands, Windows NT also introduces a few new commands that can be helpful in a variety of situations. These new commands are as follows:

- ACLCONV
- AT
- CACLS
- CONVERT
- DISKPERF
- DOSONLY
- ECHOCONFIG
- ENDLOCAL

- FINDSTR

- FORCEDOS

- FTYPE

- NTBOOKS

- NTCMDPROMPT

- PENTNT

- POPD

- PORTUAS

- PUSHD

- SETLOCAL

- START

- TITLE

Some of these commands have already been discussed in other areas of this book. For instances, the CONVERT command was covered in Chapter 4. The commands that have not been covered elsewhere are discussed in the following sections.

AT

The AT command is used to schedule tasks to be run at certain times on your system. It is used in conjunction with the Schedule service, which must be running before the AT command can be used. The AT command can be used to schedule tasks on your local system or on another computer to which you have access through the network.

The simplest way to use AT is by itself, in which case it lists all of the tasks that are currently scheduled. If you want to schedule a task, use the following format:

```
AT time "command"
```

In this instance, *command* is replaced with the command that you want to have executed; the quotation marks are mandatory. The *time* refers to the time of day at which you want the task to be executed. The *time* is specified in a 24-hour format, as in 14:32.

With this usage, the task is executed a single time. You can, however, schedule a task to be run on a regular basis. Simply include one of the command switches before the actual command but after the time specification. You can use the following three switches:

Switch	Meaning
/every:*date*	Indicates that the task should be run on a certain day of the week or a specific day of the month. For days of the week, you can use the abbreviations M, T, W, Th, F, S, and Su. If you indicate a number, then it is taken to be a day of every month. You can specify multiple dates with commas, as in /every:1,16.
/next:*date*	Indicates that the task should be run on the next occurrence of a day of the week or day of the month. For *date,* you can use the same nomenclature as for the /every switch.
/interactive	Allows the task to interact with whoever is using the computer at the time that it is executed.

You learn more about the AT command in Chapter 17.

DISKPERF

In Chapter 18, you learn how you can use the Performance Monitor to analyze how your system is doing during daily operation. Windows NT allows you to maintain disk-performance monitoring statistics, which can subsequently be used by the Performance Monitor.

The maintenance of these statistics does not occur automatically. Instead, you must start the counters and then restart your system. The following command starts the counters:

```
diskperf -y
```

You can add the UNC path for a computer name at the end of the command, which causes the performance counters to start on a specific computer other than your local system. If you are using a stripe set on your disk, you can use the following command to enable extended counters that are specific to the stripe set:

```
diskperf -ye
```

After the startup command is issued, you must restart your computer for the change to take effect. If you later want to turn off the counters, you can issue the following command:

```
diskperf -n
```

FINDSTR

The FINDSTR command is used to locate strings, within files, that meet the criteria that you specify. It is a powerful command that can help you quickly locate the files that you need.

The simplest use of the command is to use it with the keywords that you want to find and the files in which you want to search. For instance, if you wanted to search for the word *graphic* only in your text files, you would use the following:

```
findstr "graphic" *.txt
```

The information that is returned by the FINDSTR command shows the name of the file in which it located the word along with the text surrounding the keyword that you wanted. If you inserted additional words into the search, then any occurrence of those words, individually, would result in a match.

For example, consider the following command:

```
findstr "graphic program" *.txt
```

In this instance, you may be tempted to believe that FINDSTR will now search for a phrase, but it doesn't. Instead, it finds any occurrence of *graphic* or *program*. If you want to instead search for a phrase, you must use one of the many switches that FINDSTR understands. These switches are detailed in Table 9-10.

Table 9-10 FINDSTR command-line switches

Switch	Meaning
/b	Matches a pattern at the beginning of a line.
/e	Matches a pattern at the end of a line.
/l	Treats the search string as a literal; turns off pattern matching.
/c:*string*	Treats *string* as a literal search string.
/r	Turns on pattern matching; treats the search string as a regular expression.
/s	Includes all subdirectories in the search.
/i	Makes the search insensitive to character case.
/x	Displays lines that match exactly.
/v	Displays lines that do not contain a match.

(continued)

Table 9-10 *(continued)*

Switch	Meaning
/n	Displays the line number of matching lines.
/m	Displays only the filename of files containing a match.
/o	Displays the character offset before matching lines.
/g:*file*	Retrieves search strings from the specified *file.*
/f:*file*	Retrieves the file list (to be searched) from the specified *file.*

Using the information in Table 9-10, you can determine how to search for a specific phrase. Using the previous example as a starting point, you can look for a phrase by using the /c switch, as follows:

```
findstr /c:"graphic program" *.txt
```

Besides searching for characters that exactly match your specifications, you can probably tell from Table 9-10 that FINDSTR understands regular expressions. This means that you can indicate patterns for which FINDSTR should look.

The patterns use a mixture of literal characters and metacharacters. The literal characters include all letters and numbers and most symbols.

A few symbols have special meaning as metacharacters, however. These symbols provide the guidelines that FINDSTR uses as a pattern for searching. Table 9-11 indicates the different metacharacters that you can use in your search strings.

Table 9-11   Metacharacters that are used for regular expression patterns in FINDSTR

Character	Meaning
.	Match any single character.
*	Repeat occurrences of the previous character or class. (Do not confuse this with a DOS wildcard character.)
^	Beginning of line.
$	End of line.
[*class*]	Any character in the set *class.*

Character	Meaning
[^ *class*]	Any character not in the set *class*.
[*beg-end*]	Any characters in the range defined by *beg* and *end*.
\	The following character is to be treated as a literal, not as a metacharacter.
word	Beginning of *word*.
word\\>	End of *word*.

The pattern-matching capabilities of FINDSTR make it very powerful. You can mix metacharacters to literally search for anything that you desire. For example, you may want to search for every occurrence of the word *license*, but you aren't quite sure how to spell it, nor are you sure if the author of the documents that you are searching knew how to spell it.

You could use the following as your command line:

```
findstr /s "li[cs]en[cs]e" *.doc
```

This searches for all occurrences of the words *license, lisense, licence,* and *lisence* in any document file in the current directory and all subdirectories. You can use pattern matching is similar ways to create the types of searches that you want to use.

FORCEDOS

The FORCEDOS command is used to execute a program in the DOS subsystem. Normally, Windows NT can automatically recognize which environment a program needs to properly execute. For instance, it can tell when you are running a 16-bit Windows program, a DOS program, or a 32-bit Windows program.

There may be rare instances, however, when Windows NT cannot recognize the type of program that is being executed. By including the FORCEDOS command at the beginning of your command line, you force Windows NT to create a DOS environment for your program.

As an example, if you need to run a program called MyProgram, you would normally do it as follows:

```
myprogram param1 param2 /s1 /s2 /s3
```

In this case, MyProgram uses two parameters and three switches. If MyProgram is a DOS program, but instead Windows NT tries to run it under Windows, then you can substitute the following command line:

```
forcedos myprogram param1 param2 /s1 /s2 /s3
```

FTYPE

You can use the FTYPE command to view or modify the list of file associations that are used in Windows NT. If you use the command alone, with no parameters, then all of your current associations are listed. If you want to set an association, then you use a command similar to the following one:

```
ftype txt=c:\winnt\system32\notepad.exe %1
```

This instructs Windows NT to open the Notepad accessory, with the file-name as a parameter, whenever a file with the TXT extension is encountered. You can use the following characters in your command line, to the right of the equal sign:

Characters	Meaning
%0	Filename triggering the association
%1	Filename triggering the association
%3	First parameter used
%4	Second parameter used
%*	All parameters used

Note

The meaning of the characters used in the FTYPE command may look odd, but that is the way the parameters have been designated by Microsoft.

NTBOOKS

The NTBOOKS command is a method by which you can access the Windows NT help system. Specifically, the command is used to access the on-line version of either the workstation or server manuals. Information is presented using the familiar help-system interface. When used by itself, NTBOOKS accesses the on-line manuals in the location where you last used them.

Several switches that are provided for NTBOOKS allow you to modify its behavior:

Switch	Meaning
/s	Look for on-line server documentation
/w	Look for on-line workstation documentation
/n:*path*	Look for the documentation using the noted *path*

PENTNT

A couple of years ago, there was a much-publicized incident in which the Pentium chip was determined to have an error that caused incorrect results in some math calculations. Intel eventually replaced tens of thousands of the popular CPUs, but only after much embarrassment and the associated field day in the press. The PENTNT command determines if your Pentium CPU has the mentioned flaw.

If it does, the command modifies Windows NT to work around the problem. You can use three possible switches with the command:

Switch	Meaning
-c	Enable software workaround only if the Pentium error is detected
-f	Force software workaround even if the Pentium error is not detected
-o	Turn off software workaround if the Pentium error is not present

Regardless of which switch you use, you must restart Windows NT for the changes to take place.

POPD

The POPD command is used to return to a directory that is stored by the PUSHD command. See the PUSHD command for more information.

PUSHD

The PUSHD command is a two-phase command. First, it saves (in memory) the current directory. This directory can later be restored with the POPD command. Then PUSHD switches to the directory that you have specified on the command line.

For instance, you may want to create a batch file that would switch to the TEMP directory, delete all of the temporary files there, and then return to the original directory. You could use the following as such a batch file:

```
@echo off
pushd \temp
del *.tmp
del *.bak
del *.old
echo Files deleted!
popd
echo All done!
```

In the second line of the program, the directory from which the batch file was executed was stored, and \temp was made the current directory. The files were then deleted, and the POPD command fetched the saved directory and used it to set the current directory.

START

The START command provides a new way to execute a program. Normally, all you need to do to run a program is to simply enter the program name at the command line; Windows NT takes care of the rest.

For instance, to run your favorite game you may enter a command such as PLAY at the command line. This would search for a file, such as PLAY.COM, PLAY.EXE, or PLAY.BAT, and then execute that file, running it in the current window.

If you preface the program name with the START command, the program is run in a new window. For instance, if you wanted to run your favorite game, you may enter the START PLAY command. Windows NT then opens a new window for the program and executes the PLAY program within that window.

When you exit the PLAY program, the window that is opened for it is automatically closed. All the while, your original window (the one in which you executed the START command) is still available for other purposes.

TITLE

The TITLE command is used predominantly in batch files. It allows you to set the text that appears in the title bar of the current window. After you use the TITLE command, you can only use the TITLE command to make any subsequent changes in the title bar.

Thus, if your batch file runs a program that normally would have changed the title bar, it remains set to the text that you explicitly used with TITLE, regardless of what the program tries to do.

To use the TITLE command, just follow it by the text that you want to use, as in the following example:

```
@echo off
title Delete Temporary Files
pushd \temp
del *.tmp
del *.bak
del *.old
echo Files deleted!
popd
echo All done!
```

In this case, the title bar displays the words *Delete Temporary Files.*

Summary

Many people are familiar with the user interface and environment that were traditionally available with DOS. Windows NT does a marvelous job of re-creating the same environment, but within the context of a Windows system. When you work in the command window, you have access to a number of commands that are not available in regular DOS.

In this chapter, you have learned what commands are available as well as how those commands can be used. In particular, you have learned the following items:

▶ Command windows are opened by running a DOS program or by choosing the Command Prompt option from the Programs menu.

▶ You can change the size, location, color, and various other attributes of a command window.

▶ You can switch between a full-screen and partial-screen command window by using the Alt+Enter shortcut.

▶ Commands are composed of three parts: keywords, parameters, and switches. The keywords are mandatory, and some parameters may be optional (depending on the keyword). Switches are typically optional and affect the way that a command is executed.

▶ Many commands are available in NT that are not available in Windows 95 or in DOS. In addition, some commands have been dropped in Windows NT because they do not make sense in the NT environment.

▶ There are many new commands in Windows NT that control the networking capabilities of the operating system. Many of these commands provide the same functions that you can find from within the Windows interface.

▶ If you have the TCP/IP protocol installed on your system, there are a handful of commands that allow you to use common TCP/IP utilities.

▶ Some new commands are unique to Windows NT and provide a greater degree of flexibility. Some other commands allow you to take advantage of features that are new to Windows NT.

Moving Beyond the Basics

PA**R**T

◆　◆　◆　◆

◆　◆　◆　◆

Chapter 10

Understanding the Registry

The Registry Structure

The Registry is a hierarchical database that is maintained by the operating system as a repository of configuration information. The concept behind the Registry may seem confusing at first, but once understood, its organization is very logical.

The Registry consists of four distinct parts, which are as follows:

- **Trees.** These are the major divisions of the Registry.
- **Hives.** These are the major divisions of the Registry trees.
- **Keys.** These are groups of related settings within a hive.
- **Values.** These are the data that are stored within a key.

As you make changes to system settings (typically using elements of the Control Panel), the new changes are stored in the Registry. Information is stored in the form of values, which are placed in keys that are determined by the nature of the program doing the placing.

Thus, if you use the Control Panel to change the display settings for your system, then your information is stored in either the keys that control the appearance of the desktop or the keys that are used to control your video hardware.

Registry trees

The Registry consists of five major trees. These trees comprise all aspects of the Windows NT operating system:

- **HKEY_CLASSES_ROOT.** OLE-related information, including shortcuts. Also includes information on file associations.
- **HKEY_CURRENT_USER.** Specific profile settings for the user that is currently logged on to the system.
- **HKEY_LOCAL_MACHINE.** Machine-related specifics, such as installed hardware, swap file settings, startup settings, and so on.
- **HKEY_USERS**. User-specific settings for all user profiles that are defined for the system.
- **HKEY_CURRENT_CONFIG.** Configuration information about the current hardware settings, such as notebooks that plug into a docking station.

Even though five trees are in the Registry, this can be deceiving. Windows NT uses pointers for several of the keys. For instance, the HKEY_CLASSES_ROOT is nothing but a pointer to the HKEY_LOCAL_MACHINE\SOFTWARE\CLASSES subkey.

Likewise, HKEY_CURRENT_USER is a pointer to a subkey within the HKEY_USERS key. Thus, of the five trees, only three (HKEY_LOCAL_MACHINE, HKEY_CURRENT_CONFIG, and HKEY_USERS) actually represent information that is stored on disk.

Registry hives

The first major division under each of the Registry trees is known as *hives.* These were named as such because of their resemblance to beehives; these are where your Registry information is stored on disk. According to Microsoft information, a hive is a discrete body of keys, subkeys, and values that is rooted at the top of the Registry hierarchy.

For instance, the HKEY_LOCAL_MACHINE tree contains the following hives:

- HARDWARE
- SAM
- SECURITY
- SOFTWARE
- SYSTEM

Hives are the part of the Registry either stored on disk or constructed in memory. Of the five hives here, only the first (HARDWARE) is constructed in memory when your system is first started. The other four hives represent at least two separate disk files on your system.

The first file is the Registry file, which uses the same name as the hive name. The second file is a log file, which uses the same name as the hive, with a filename extension of LOG. Most of the hive files are stored in the c:\winnt\system32\config directory, but they don't need to be there.

Table 10-1 shows the different hives that are used in the Registry along with the files that are used to store those hives. (If there is no file listed for a hive, then the hive is created in memory every time that you use Windows NT.)

Table 10-1   Windows NT Registry hives

Tree	Hive	Registry File	Log File
HKEY_LOCAL_MACHINE	HARDWARE		
HKEY_LOCAL_MACHINE	SAM	Sam	Sam.log
HKEY_LOCAL_MACHINE	SECURITY	Security	Security.log
HKEY_LOCAL_MACHINE	SOFTWARE	Software	Software.log
HKEY_LOCAL_MACHINE	SYSTEM	System	System.log
HKEY_CURRENT_CONFIG	SOFTWARE		
HKEY_CURRENT_CONFIG	SYSTEM		
HKEY_USERS	.DEFAULT	Default	Default.log
HKEY_USERS	Varies	Varies	Varies

Registry keys

Registry hives are broken down into *keys*. These keys are organizational units for Registry information. They are analogous to folders on your hard drive in that they are designed to contain information.

In fact, the Registry Editor, presented later in this chapter, presents keys using a file-folder symbol, just like the symbol used in the Explorer for disk-drive folders.

Each key within the Registry can contain values and subkeys. In turn, the subkeys can contain additional values and subkeys. Just as disk-drive folders can contain files and additional folders, the keys under each hive can contain values and subkeys.

This is the basis of the hierarchical organization of information in the Registry and means that information within the Registry can be presented in a tree fashion — again, very similar to how information is represented in the Explorer.

Registry values

Values within a key (or subkey) contain data. These data consist of the current setting for the value. For instance, a value may contain the starting position for a window or the amount of memory in your system.

Data can be of five basic types:

- **REG_BINARY.** This is numeric information that can be of any length.
- **REG_DWORD.** This is numeric information that is limited to a length of 32 bits.
- **REG_EXPAND_SZ.** This is string information that can be any length and whose length can change over time. Normally, this data type is used for system and program variables.
- **REG_MULTI_SZ.** This is a series of string values, each separated by a NULL character. This data type is typically used for information lists, such as those displayed in drop-down lists.
- **REG_SZ.** This is a string value that can be of any length but is static; its value does not change.

In addition, applications can define their own special types of data. The exact type of data maintained for a value is determined by the purpose for which the value is used.

Editing the Registry

The Registry is perhaps the most dynamic area of Windows NT. Because it contains all of the system settings and configuration information for your system, it makes sense that the Registry would be busy. In some cases, the Registry is updated automatically by Windows NT.

For instance, you may add a new hardware device that Windows automatically detects. In such a case, the drivers are loaded automatically, and settings are changed. The information about these drivers, the device, and any settings is stored automatically in the Registry.

Other Registry changes require some interaction on your part. Typically, you change the Registry by using the various applets in the Control Panel. As you make changes to your system settings, the changes are saved in the Registry. Other changes are introduced by using system tools, such as the User Manager or the Disk Administrator.

Windows NT also allows you to make changes directly to the Registry. While this is not as easy as making changes using the Control Panel (or other tools), the effect is the same. This is because you are changing system settings, and those are used to control how Windows NT functions.

Caution

If you decide to manually make changes in the Registry, you do so at your own risk. Whereas the Control Panel (and other system tools) includes many safeguards to protect you from making changes that don't make sense — or that may be hazardous to your system health — manually editing the Registry provides no such safeguards. Make sure that you know what you are changing before you make the change.

To change the Registry manually, you use the Registry Editor. This program is not available from any of the regular Windows NT menus. (This is probably due to the potential adverse consequences of misusing the Registry Editor.) Instead, you need to start the program either from the Run option on the Start menu or from the command line.

The problem with describing the Registry Editor is that Windows NT typically installs two different registry editors on your system out of a possible three choices:

- Windows NT Registry Editor
- Windows 3.*x* Registry Editor
- Windows 95 Registry Editor

Which Registry Editor should you use?

The Registry Editor that you use is largely up to your personal preferences. Each has its own strong and weak points, and each allows you to accomplish roughly the same work (albeit in slightly different ways).

My personal favorite is the Windows 95 Registry Editor. The user interface is less cluttered, and the various hives of the Registry are easier to work with. In addition, the search capabilities are more useful for finding information that is buried within the Registry.

These Registry Editor names do not refer to the actual Registries which they edit; instead they refer to the interface that is used in the Registry Editor. All three Registry Editors make changes to the Windows NT Registry.

The Windows NT Registry Editor is installed on all Windows NT systems. The other Registry Editor that is installed depends on how your system was configured when you installed NT.

If either of the following conditions are met, then the Setup program installs the Windows 3.*x* version of the editor:

- You install Windows NT in a directory that already contains Windows 3.*x*.

- You are upgrading an earlier version of Windows NT, and that earlier version was originally an upgrade to Windows 3.*x*.

Thus, the only way to make sure that the Windows 95 Registry Editor is installed is to upgrade your Windows 95 system to Windows NT, or make sure that you are starting with a fresh install of the operating system (not an upgrade).

Because each of the Registry Editors is fundamentally different, they are discussed individually in the following sections. You may want to read through the information and decide which Registry Editor you want to use; each has its strengths and weaknesses.

The Windows NT Registry Editor

The Windows NT Registry Editor is installed on all systems; this is one Registry Editor that you can count on being available. This Registry Editor is patterned after the program that has been available since Windows NT was first released. This editor is provided for those users with a Windows NT background who may be comfortable with the interface.

To run the Windows NT Registry Editor, follow these steps:

STEPS

Running the Windows NT Registry Editor

Step 1. Choose the Run option from the Start menu. This displays the Run dialog box.

Step 2. In the Open field, type **regedt32**. (This is the name of the Registry Editor program.)

Step 3. Click on the OK button. Shortly you see the Registry Editor, as shown in Figure 10-1.

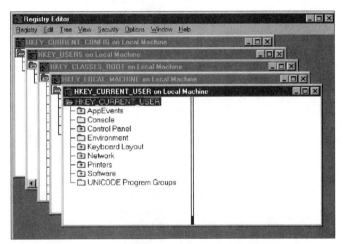

Figure 10-1: The Registry Editor displays the different Registry trees in different windows.

The interface that is used in the Registry Editor is similar to other Windows NT tools, although it does not take full advantage of the slick Windows NT 4.0 interface. The program window contains five other windows, one for each of the Registry trees.

Within a tree window, the display is divided. At the left side of the window, you can see the keys of the Registry tree. In the right side, you can see the data (if any) that are stored in a key.

Secret

If your tree windows are not divided in half, you should select the Tree and Data option from the View menu.

Finding information

The sheer size of the Registry and the amount of information that it contains makes it mandatory that you know what you want to edit before you begin poking around. With many Windows NT configuration items, you can browse through the different parts of the Control Panel and decide what you want to change as you find it.

It is not unusual to find a new capability, have it catch your imagination, and then make some changes based on your discovery. Not so with the Registry; while you can snoop through the Registry, the chances of intuitively finding things to change is remote. Thus, you must know what you want to do *before* you start your editing trek.

This is particularly true in the Windows NT Registry Editor. Despite the amount of information that is in the Registry, the program does not have a good find feature. While you can search for information, you can only do so at a key level; you cannot search the contents of the keys.

To search for something, choose the Find Key option from the View menu. This displays the Find dialog box, as shown in Figure 10-2.

Figure 10-2: The Windows NT Registry Editor allows you to search the Registry for keys.

In the Find what field, you can enter exactly what you want to find. At the bottom of the dialog box, you can specify whether the Find command should be case sensitive and whether whole words should be the only matches that are returned.

You can also search forward or backward through the current tree. When you click on the Find Next button, the Registry Editor attempts to find a key matching the string that you entered. If a match is found, it is highlighted in the tree windows.

Editing values

You change Registry settings by changing the contents of a value. There are two ways that you can edit a value:

- Double-click on the value name in the right side of the tree window
- Click on the value name and press Enter

Either method produces the same results; you are shown a dialog box that allows you to edit the information in the value. The type of dialog box that you see depends on the type of data that are contained in the value that you are editing. (You learned about data types earlier in this chapter.)

As an example, if you are editing a value that contains multi-string data, the editing dialog box appears as shown in Figure 10-3.

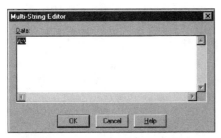

Figure 10-3: As you edit Registry values, the way that you edit depends on the data type of the value that you are editing.

When you are finished making changes in the value, click on the OK button. The information is immediately saved, and you can edit additional values.

Secret

Even though your Registry changes are saved immediately, many times your changes do not take effect until you restart your system. Whenever you are done editing the Registry, it is always a good idea to restart your system.

Creating keys or values

The dynamic nature of the Registry means that the information it contains is always changing depending on the needs of the operating system, programs, or you. Therefore, it is possible to add new values to the Registry or to even add new keys. (You cannot add new hives; these are set in stone by the operating system.) The Registry Editor allows you to quickly and easily add values or keys.

Why would you want to add keys or values? Quite honestly, it doesn't do you much good to add either item unless you know that it is going to be used by an application or by the operating system itself.

To add a key, select the existing hive or key under which the new key should appear. You should select the hive or key in the left side of a tree window. (This is the same concept that you use when using the Explorer to add a new folder.)

As an example, consider adding a new key to the HKEY_LOCAL_MACHINE\ SOFTWARE hive. Just follow these steps:

STEPS

Adding a new key

Step 1. Make sure that the HKEY_LOCAL_MACHINE tree window is selected.

Step 2. Click on the SOFTWARE hive. This selects the hive.

Step 3. Choose the Add Key option from the Edit menu. This displays the Add Key dialog box, as shown in Figure 10-4.

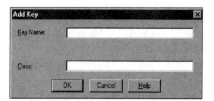

Figure 10-4: The Add Key dialog box is used to define the name of a new key for the Registry.

Step 4. In the Key Name field, enter the name for your new key. (You can ignore the Class field; it is not really used in the Windows NT Registry Editor.)

Step 5. Click on the OK button. The new key is added under the SOFT-WARE hive.

At this point, you have created a new key. You can then add values to the new key, following much the same process (only you select the Add Value option from the Edit menu). The information that you add to the Registry remains there until it is either changed by you or by a program that you may be using.

Deleting Registry items

Deleting keys or values is quite easy. Select the item that you want to remove, and then press Delete. Windows checks to make sure that you really want to delete the item, as shown in Figure 10-5. If you click on the Yes button, the item is deleted.

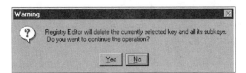

Figure 10-5: The Registry Editor allows you to confirm any deletions that you want to make.

Caution

The Registry Editor is very obedient on deleting items. You need to make very sure that you want to delete something before you do so. If you delete a critical key or value by mistake, you are simply out of luck. (If you delete the wrong thing, you can cripple your software or disable your entire system.)

In such a circumstance, you have only a couple of options available, which are as follows:

- Manually re-create the deleted keys and values.
- Reload the Registry keys, if you previously exported them.
- Reinstall Windows NT.

It should go without saying that none of these are particularly attractive options. Since, in this case, an ounce of prevention really is worth a pound of cure, take extra care when you are working with the Registry.

Printing the Registry

The Windows NT Registry Editor allows you to print all or a portion of any Registry hive. The printed copy is a great boon if you are planning on making changes to the Registry and you want a record of the condition of the Registry before your changes.

You can print by following these steps:

STEPS

Printing the Registry

Step 1. Choose the Printer Setup option from the Registry menu. This displays the Print Setup dialog box. (This dialog box is very similar to the corresponding dialog box in other programs.)

Step 2. Modify the printer setup options as desired for your printout. When you are done, click on the OK button.

Step 3. In the tree window, click on the key (or hive) where you want to start printing.

Step 4. Choose the Print Subtree option from the Registry menu.

At this point, your printout begins. When done, you can continue to work with the Registry or select a different area of the Registry to print.

Tip

Be careful what you choose to print. If you print a key (and its subkeys), then your printout may be quite manageable. Printing an entire hive can be very lengthy, however. For example, printing the HKEY_LOCAL_MACHINE hive takes a bit over 1,900 pages!

Remote Registry editing

If you have the proper permission level, you are not limited to only editing your local Registry — you can also edit the Registry on other computers to which you are connected. (You need to be part of the Administrator group to edit remote Registries.) Editing someone else's Registry allows troubleshooting or checking to occur without having to be in front of the remote machine.

To access the Registry on a remote system, follow these steps:

STEPS

Editing a remote Registry

Step 1. Minimize all of the tree windows in the Registry Editor. This helps you keep the editor window less cluttered when you open the remote Registry.)

Step 2. Choose the Select Computer option from the Registry menu. This displays the Select Computer dialog box, as shown in Figure 10-6.

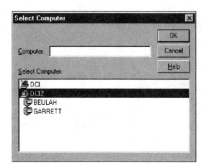

Figure 10-6: You can edit the Registry of any computer that is on your network.

Step 3. In the browser section at the bottom of the dialog box, select the computer whose Registry you want to edit. As an alternative, enter the remote computer's UNC in the Computer field.

Step 4. Click on the OK button.

At this point, two tree windows appear, as shown in Figure 10-7. Notice that only the HKEY_LOCAL_MACHINE and HKEY_USERS tree windows appear. This makes sense if you remember the discussion from earlier in the chapter.

Figure 10-7: You can edit two trees of a remote Registry.

These trees are two of only three real trees in a system. The other tree is created in memory when you first start the system, so it doesn't make sense to edit that tree remotely.

You can make changes in the remote computer's Registry as desired. When you are done, make sure that you select either of the remote tree windows and then choose Close from the Registry menu.

The Windows 95 Registry Editor

There is a good chance that the Windows 95 Registry Editor is installed on your system. If not (if the Windows 3.x Registry Editor was instead installed), you can install this version by copying the following files from your Windows NT Workstation 4.0 CD-ROM:

- REGEDIT.EXE
- REGEDIT.HLP
- REGEDIT.CNT

You can install these files to any directory that you want. However, if the Windows 3.x Registry Editor is installed on your system, Microsoft recommends that you do not copy the Windows 95 Registry Editor to your system directory (typically c:\winnt).

The reason is that you may overwrite the Windows 3.x Registry Editor. This may not present a problem except for those people running a dual-boot system for Windows 3.x and Windows NT.

When you are ready to run the Windows 95 Registry Editor, follow these steps:

STEPS

Running the Windows 95 Registry Editor

Step 1. Choose the Run option from the Start menu. This displays the Run dialog box.

Step 2. In the Open field, type **regedit**. (This is the name of the Windows 95 Registry Editor program.)

Step 3.   Click on the OK button. Shortly you see the Registry Editor, as shown in Figure 10-8.

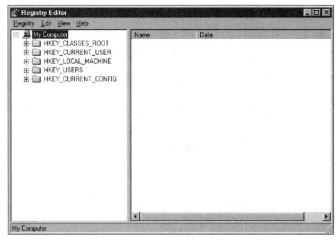

Figure 10-8: The Registry Editor displays the different Registry trees in different windows.

The interface used in the Windows 95 Registry Editor is much simpler than the interface of the Windows NT Registry Editor. There are two parts to the Registry Editor window. The left part displays the different trees, hives, and keys of the Registry, while the right part displays the values.

Finding information

As you learned earlier in the chapter, to edit the Registry effectively you must know exactly what you want to edit. Many times you can determine what you should edit by reviewing the documentation for an application or by talking to the technicians for a program. Unfortunately, there is no comprehensive guide to possible Registry entries, and anyone who claims that he has a comprehensive guide is fooling you.

While base information can be documented, the Registry is used by programs from so many different sources that there is no way to keep up with it all. This means that you must almost become a detective to figure out what the settings in the Registry mean.

The biggest help in your detective work is the search command of the Registry Editor. You can start this command by choosing Find from the Edit menu. When you do this, the Find dialog box appears, as shown in Figure 10-9.

Figure 10-9: The Windows 95 Registry Editor allows you to search every nook and cranny of your Registry.

In the Find What field, you can enter exactly what you want to find. At the bottom of the dialog box, you can specify where the Registry Editor should look for the information: Keys, Values, or Data.

When you click on the Find Next button, the Registry Editor attempts to find the string that you entered. If a match is found, it is highlighted in one of the editor windows, depending on where the information was found.

For instance, if the match was found in a key name, then the information is displayed in the left portion of the editor window. Conversely, if the match was found in a value, the information is displayed in the right portion.

Editing values

You may remember from the discussion earlier in the chapter that values are essentially placeholders for information in the Registry. When you change a Registry setting, you change the contents of a value. Your first task in editing a value is to locate the item that you want to edit. This is done by using the Find function, as described in the previous section.

Once you locate a value that you think you want to change, you need to carefully examine it in the context of what you understand about the Registry structure and then make an educated guess as to whether it is the value that you want.

The problem, however, is that when you are poking about on your own, you are never really sure unless you "try things out." Thus, in many respects, working with the Registry Editor is a trial-and-error proposition unless you are given a detailed reference or specific guidance.

Most editing tasks take place in the values that are shown in the right por-tion of the editor window. To edit a value, either double-click on the value name (in the right side of the editor window) or highlight the value and press Enter.

You then see a dialog box that prompts you to change the contents of the value. The exact dialog box that you see depends on the data type of the value.

For instance, if you are changing a value that contains binary data, you see a dialog box similar to the one shown in Figure 10-10.

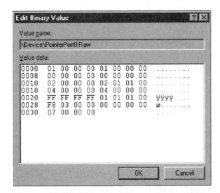

Figure 10-10: When editing values, different dialog boxes are displayed, depending on the type of data being edited.

When you are done making changes, click on OK, and the Registry value is changed.

Adding keys or values

The Windows 95 Registry Editor allows you to quickly and easily add new keys or values to the Registry. Why would you want to do this? Quite honestly, it doesn't do you much good to add either item unless you know that it is going to be used by an application or by the operating system itself.

To add a key, select the existing hive or key under which the new key should appear. You should select the hive or key that is in the left side of the editor window.

Then choose the New option from the Edit menu, and select the Key option. The new key is added, and you can change its name as desired.

If you want to add a value to an existing key, you can do so in much the same manner. To add a value, follow these steps:

STEPS

Adding a new value

Step 1. Click on the plus signs at the left of the hive or keys that lead to where you want the new value. This expands the Registry tree to show the path to the key in which you want the value placed.

Step 2. Choose the New option from the Edit menu. This displays a submenu of items that you can create.

Step 3. Click on the choice that represents the type of value that you want to create.

These three steps add a new value to the key and allow you to change the name of the value in the right side of the editor window (see Figure 10-11). Remember that this creates the value only; it does not store anything in the value. To store something in the value, you need to edit the newly created value, as described in the previous section.

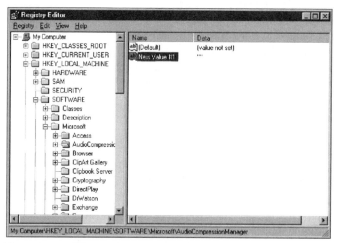

Figure 10-11: When adding a new value, you need to supply a name and subsequently the contents for the value.

Deleting Registry items

Deleting keys or values is quite easy. Select the item that you want to remove, and then press Delete. Windows checks to make sure that you really want to delete the item, as shown in Figure 10-12. If you click on the Yes button, the item is immediately and permanently deleted from the Registry.

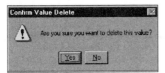

Figure 10-12: You are always asked to confirm your action when deleting a Registry item.

Importing and exporting the Registry

The Windows 95 Registry Editor has a feature that allows you to export the Registry to a text file and later import the text file back into a Registry. If used properly, this feature can save you some time and provides a great way to back up your Registry.

The time savings are realized if you have quite a few machines that all need to be configured in the same way. If the systems all have the same hardware, software, and drivers, you can save a great deal of time by simply exporting the Registry from one system and then importing it into each of the other systems. This saves you from using the Control Panel on each system to go through detailed configuration steps.

To export the Registry, choose Export Registry File from the Registry menu. This displays the dialog box that is shown in Figure 10-13. This file specification dialog box should look familiar; it is used in many different Windows applications.

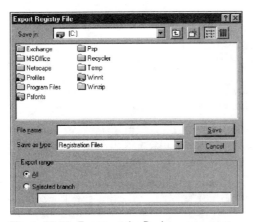

Figure 10-13: To export the Registry, you must provide the name of the text file to be created.

You then provide the name of the text file that you want used to save the Registry. You can also specify whether you want to save all or a particular branch of the Registry. When you click on the Save button, the text file is created and the Registry saved.

Secret

Unless you explicitly provide a filename extension, the Windows 95 Registry Editor uses an extension of .REG. This is a registered filename extension, and Windows recognizes the file as a Registry export file.

When you later decide to import the Registry file, you can do so by choosing Import Registry File from the Registry menu. Again you see a dialog box that allows you to select a file. When you specify a filename, it is imported to the current Registry.

Information in the import file automatically overwrites any settings with the same value and key names. Conversely, if there are any Registry items with names that don't exist in the import file, then these items remain in the new, modified Registry.

Importing a Registry does not take long. When the import is successfully completed, you see a notification, as shown in Figure 10-14.

Figure 10-14: The Registry Editor notifies you of a successful Registry import.

Printing the Registry

The Windows 95 Registry Editor allows you to print all or a portion of the Registry. A printed copy can be very helpful if you are planning to make changes to the Registry and you want a record of the condition of the various values before your changes.

To print all or part of the Registry, choose the Print option from the Registry menu. This displays the Print dialog box, as shown in Figure 10-15.

The Print dialog box is similar to the Print dialog boxes in other programs, except for the Print range area at the bottom of the dialog box. Here you can specify to either print all of the Registry or a print specific branch. (If you had selected a hive or key before choosing the Print option, then the Selected Branch field would have been filled in.)

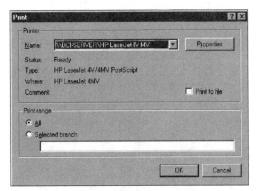

Figure 10-15: The Print dialog box is similar to corresponding dialog boxes in other programs.

When you are satisfied with your choices, click on the OK button. At this point, your printout begins. Depending on what you chose to print, your printout could be quite long. When done, you can continue to work with the Registry or select a different area of the Registry to print.

Remote Registry editing

If you are a network administrator, you can edit other the Registries in other computers on your network without leaving your desk. Editing someone else's Registry allows troubleshooting or checking to occur without having to be in front of the remote machine. (This can be a real time saver for larger networks.)

To access the Registry on a remote system, follow these steps:

STEPS

Editing a remote Registry

Step 1.   Choose the Connect Network Registry option from the Registry menu. This displays the dialog box that is shown in Figure 10-16.

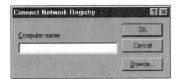

Figure 10-16: You can edit the Registry of any computer that is on your network.

(continued)

STEPS *(continued)*

Editing a remote Registry

Step 2.   In the <u>C</u>omputer Name field, enter the name of the computer whose Registry you want to enter. (You can also click on the <u>B</u>rowse button to find the computer.)

Step 3.   Click on the OK button.

At this point, the remote computer is contacted, the Registry information transferred, and the Registry Editor window updated. With a remote Registry open, you can work with the Registries of multiple machines, as shown in Figure 10-17.

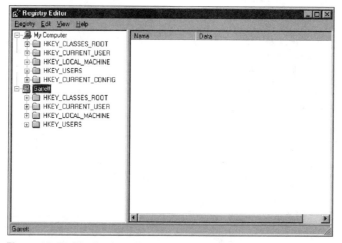

Figure 10-17: The Registry Editor allows you to view the Registries of multiple machines.

After the remote Registry is loaded, you can make changes in it the same as you would for your local machine. When you are done with the remote Registry, select <u>D</u>isconnect Network Registry from the <u>E</u>dit menu to break the link between you and the remote Registry.

The Windows 3.x Registry Editor

In reality, the Windows 3.x Registry Editor does not deserve to be called such. Those who have been using Windows for a while understand that the Registry, as we know it, began with Windows NT and then was adopted by Windows 95. Windows 3.x never had a real Registry.

The Windows 3.x Registry Editor is really a Registration Info Editor. This tool is used to help modify the Windows 3.x database of registered file types and indicate how they should be handled by the system.

This facility was the forerunner of the full-featured file association that is used in Windows NT Workstation 4.0. (For more information on file associations, refer to Chapter 4.)

If you enter **regedit** at the Run option or at a command line, the Registration Info Editor is opened, as shown in Figure 10-18.

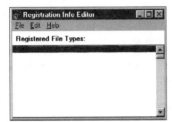

Figure 10-18: The Registration Info Editor is used to create advanced file associations for Windows 3.x programs.

Because the Registration Info Editor is not really germane to a discussion of the Windows NT Registry database, it is not discussed in this chapter.

Unless you plan on installing 16-bit Windows 3.x programs on your system, you can safely delete the c:\winnt\regedit.exe program.

Recovering the Registry

By this point, you should be very aware that everything in Windows NT revolves around the Registry. The Registry is so powerful in its control of the system that I cannot stress strongly enough that you should not make Registry changes without being sure of exactly what you are changing. There is no "undo" feature, and changes are essentially written to the Registry immediately.

If the Registry becomes corrupted for some reason, you have trouble with a capital T. There are a couple things that you can do, however, to try to recover your system.

The first thing that you should do is to restart your system. Whenever you restart your system, Windows NT displays a message instructing you to press the spacebar for the Last Known Good Menu.

If you don't press the spacebar, Windows NT copies the last-used Registry to a backup copy of the Registry. If you press the spacebar (which you should if you have corrupted the Registry), then the backup copy of the Registry is not made.

Instead, the backup copy is used to start the system. You may lose all of the Registry changes that you made since your last startup, but that can be a good thing if your Registry is corrupted.

After you have started Windows NT, there are a couple of things that you can do or should check out:

- If you have a copy of the Registry that you recently exported to a text file, start the Windows 95 Registry Editor and import the copy. This overwrites the current Registry settings and restores your system to its latest condition.

- If you installed programs during your last Windows NT session, you must reinstall them.

- Even though the program files are on disk, the configuration information that was written to the Registry was lost when you tossed out the last version of the Registry.

- If you deleted programs during your last Windows NT session, you must delete them again. This may sound strange, because the programs are no longer on your hard drive.

- Because you restored an earlier version of the Registry, however, Windows NT still thinks that the programs are installed. Deleting them again causes the Registry to be updated.

- If you made changes in your desktop configuration during your last session, you need to make the changes again.

Summary

The Registry is the heart, soul, memory, and conscience of Windows NT. It is the single repository for all information that is necessary for starting, configuring, and working with Windows NT.

In this chapter, you have learned the ins and outs of the Registry, including how you can change it. In particular, you have learned the following items:

▶ The Windows NT Registry is a hierarchical database made up of trees, hives, keys, and values.

▶ You have complete control over the contents of the values and the organizational composition of the Registry.

▶ Information at the hive level is stored in files on the disk. These files comprise the actual Windows NT Registry. You can only change these files if you have administrator-level permissions on the system.

▶ Windows NT includes three different Registry Editors that you can use according to your personal preference or based on the type of task that you need to accomplish.

▶ Editing the Registry directly has the potential for catastrophic problems if you delete or change the wrong information.

▶ The Windows NT Registry Editor uses an interface that is reminiscent of older Windows NT programs. Using the editor, you can change, manage, print, and otherwise manipulate the entire Registry.

▶ The Windows 95 Registry Editor uses a newer interface and displays information in a simpler manner than the Windows NT Registry Editor. This version of the Registry Editor may not be installed on all systems but can be copied from the Windows NT CD-ROM.

▶ Both the Windows NT and Windows 95 versions of the Registry Editor allow you to manage Registries across a network.

▶ The Windows 3.*x* Registry Editor, installed on some systems, is really the Registration Info Editor. It allows you to make changes in the advanced file association database for Win16 programs.

▶ If your Registry becomes corrupted or if you experience other problems, you can recover by modifying the startup sequence that is used by Windows NT.

Chapter 11

Advanced Disk Topics and Tools

In This Chapter

By historical standards, Windows NT is definitely considered an advanced operating system. It provides many tools and features that are designed to help you manage your data efficiently and wisely. This chapter focuses on some of the more advanced features of the operating system. Here you learn what you can do to seriously protect the data on your hard drives. In particular, you learn the following items:

▶ What fault tolerance means, particularly in relation to disk systems

▶ How fault tolerance is implemented in the Windows NT environment

▶ How you can use disk compression on NTFS volumes

▶ How to scan your disks for errors

▶ How to back up the information on your system

Understanding Fault Tolerance

One of the high-powered features of Windows NT is the support of fault-tolerant systems. The term *fault tolerance* means just what it says — that the system is tolerant of any faults that may occur during regular operations. A whole section of the computer industry is designed around the idea of implementing fault tolerance in critical systems. This is understandable, particularly because so many PC networks are beginning to be used for mission-critical data.

The term *mission critical* means that the system being used is critical to the success of the mission of the organization. For instance, consider a company that implements its customer database on a Windows NT network. As the company grows, there are more people that come to rely on the customer database. The number of network users grows, and eventually there may be 20 people (or more) accessing the database to accomplish their work.

If the database is not available for some reason, the people cannot accomplish their work. Imagine how critical that network is to the mission of the company — if it goes down, then the company essentially stops operating.

This scenario is not as far-fetched as it once may have sounded. As applications, like the database, are implemented on PC networks, people need to be concerned with the integrity of their data, even under extraordinary circumstances, such as the failure of a piece of hardware. This is why fault tolerance becomes a matter of concern for companies of all sizes.

What does this have to do with you, as a Windows NT Workstation user? Two things:

■ First, you may need to understand how fault tolerance is implemented in your network.

■ Second, fault tolerance is not just implemented at a server level.

Indeed, if you are working on critical information and storing it on your local workstation, you may want to implement fault tolerance to protect your data.

As an example, you may be doing financial work for your company. The spreadsheets, budgets, and forecasts that you prepare are kept on your local hard drive rather than on the company server. Is this information critical to the success of your company? Of course it is — you are a prime candidate for a fault-tolerant system.

There are two approaches to fault tolerance: hardware and software. For some devices, the hardware solution is the only way to approach the problem. For instance, you can get power supplies that are fault tolerant. Essentially, there are two (or more) power supplies in one; if one power supply goes down, the next one kicks in automatically and immediately. The result is that there is no downtime for your system.

Another hardware solution is redundant CPUs. Many systems now come with multiple CPUs, and if one goes out, the operating system can automatically adjust to work with only the remaining CPUs. (Windows NT does this automatically, because it supports symmetric multiprocessing.)

Finally, the other big area is disk drives. These items tend to be used quite a bit in mission-critical applications, and the data on the disk drives are very important. Thus, many fault-tolerant schemes center on disk drives.

If you use hardware-based fault tolerance, you can get a RAID array that provides the protection you need. (RAID is an acronym for redundant array of inexpensive drives. It is discussed fully later in this chapter.)

The advantages of a hardware-based RAID array are as follows:

■ **Less memory overhead.** When you use software-based RAID support, additional memory overhead is required for the routines that control the array.

■ **Better I/O optimization.** This means that you generally get faster performance from a hardware solution because the firmware, in the hardware cabinet and on the controller board, has been optimized for the type of RAID that is being implemented.

- **Drives are hot-swappable.** This means that you can remove a damaged drive and replace it without taking your network down.

On the other hand, such solutions can be quite expensive, especially for small companies. To overcome this, you can implement a software-based solution to RAID. This is where Windows NT comes into play. If you add multiple hard drives to your system, you can use the Disk Administrator to implement different RAID strategies at an operating system level. Later in this chapter, you learn how to do this with Windows NT.

Understanding RAID

RAID is an acronym for redundant array of inexpensive drives. The concept was developed in 1988 by David A. Patterson, Garth Gibson, and Randy H. Katz of the University of California at Berkeley. The trio published a paper that described five ways in which drives could be combined into arrays to protect data.

Since that time, many different vendors have produced RAID solutions that have led to some confusion in the marketplace. This is because there was no standardization on what constituted the different RAID levels — there was only the loose definitions as originally published.

To promote standardization and education in the field of RAID technology, a group of vendors formed the RAID Advisory Board (RAB) in 1992. As of this writing, there are more than 50 board members, and there are six widely accepted levels of RAID (levels 0 through 5).

The RAB also offers a certification program for RAID vendors, which hopefully brings a bit of order to the chaos in the marketplace. Those vendors that comply with the RAB definitions can use the RAB compliance logos on their products; the logos indicate which of the RAID levels the product fits into. The following sections describe the six generally accepted RAID levels.

RAID 0

This level of RAID is generally viewed as a method of improving drive performance, not as a method of implementing fault tolerance. RAID 0 is often referred to as *disk striping,* which means that information is divided into portions, and each portion is written on different disks.

For example, you may have four drives designated as a stripe set. Any information written to disk is automatically broken down into four parts, and each part is written in identically sized partitions on each of the four disk drives, as illustrated in Figure 11-1.

Windows NT supports disk striping, using anywhere from 2 to 32 disk drives. Stripes are written in 64K portions, meaning that each stripe is 64K in size. Thus, disk striping only becomes advantageous if you are writing relatively large files.

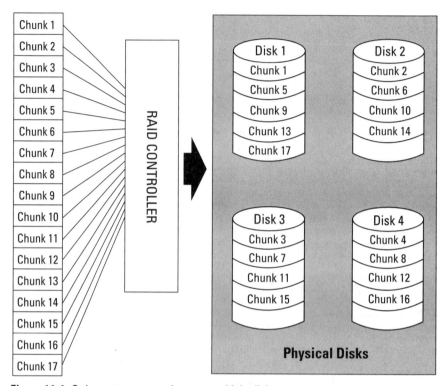

Figure 11-1: Stripe sets are spread across multiple disks.

For instance, your stripe set may have 10 disks. Because the stripe size is 64K, then any file less than 640K in size is wasting space on the stripe set. If you write a file that contains 32K, it still consumes 640K of disk space.

In and of itself, disk striping is not fault tolerant. This means that if one of the disk drives in the stripe set becomes damaged, the information on the entire stripe set is lost.

One drawback to stripe sets is the fact that the reliability of your stripe set is lower than it would be for a single drive. One specification that hard drive manufacturers provide for their hard drives is known as the MTBF — mean time between failure. This is a theoretical time frame after which you can expect drive failure.

For instance, the MTBF for a drive may be 1 million hours. This means that your drives will fail once in 1 million hours. If you have eight drives in your stripe set and they are identical, then your drives will fail eight times in that same 1 million hours.

Thus, your MTBF becomes 125,000 hours instead of 1 million. If you were using the Windows NT maximum of 32 drives in your stripe set, then your

MTBF for the same drives becomes 31,250 hours, or roughly 3.5 years. With no fault tolerance, this can be a big drawback for some sites.

With these drawbacks — increased cost and decreased reliability — why would anyone implement a stripe set? The reason is performance. Remember that information to be written to a disk drive is divided into portions, and each portion is written to its respective disk.

Thus, each write (or read) takes only a fraction of the time that it would on a single drive. For instance, if you are writing a 1MB file to a stripe set composed of 10 drives, then each drive receives 10 percent of the file. Because modern controllers can write to the disks in parallel (at the same time), you can write or read information 10 times faster than if you were using a single drive.

RAID 1

By definition, RAID 1 is disk mirroring. *Disk mirroring* is a technology that is used in secure systems or with critical data. When implemented, partitions on two separate drives are used to store identical information. The information that is written to the partition on the primary disk is also written to the mirror partition on the other disk, as shown in Figure 11-2.

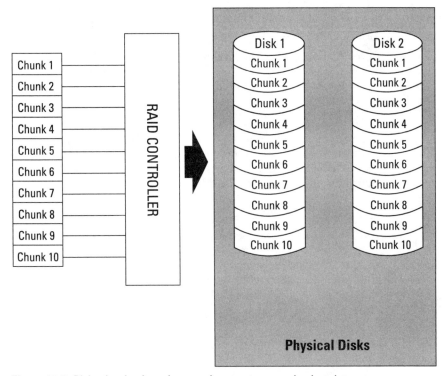

Figure 11-2: Disk mirroring is an inexpensive way to use redundant data.

If one disk fails, the system is able to use the data from the other disk. Disk mirroring is typically done as a software solution, not in hardware. Windows NT supports disk mirroring as a way of implementing low-cost fault tolerance. Although the RAID 1 specification allows for more than two disks to be used in a mirrored configuration, Windows NT only supports a two-disk configuration: a primary disk and the shadow disk (the mirror disk).

With disk mirroring implemented, there is no operational difference in Windows NT. Thus, disk mirroring is transparent to all programs and users. When you set up a disk mirror, the two partitions that are used must reside on physically different disk drives, not just two partitions of the same disk drive.

When implementing disk mirroring, you can either use a single drive controller or multiple controllers. If you use a single controller, your drive performance suffers.

This is because, for every write, you must send twice as much information through the controller. For instance, if you are writing a 1MB file, it must be written to the primary drive and then to the mirrored drive: a total of 2MB.

If you use two controllers, you regain your performance. Because each controller can write to its disks in parallel, there is no increase in how long it takes to write information.

Another advantage of using multiple controllers is that it provides your system with additional redundancy. Because you have two controllers, your system is still operational if one controller goes bad.

Note   Some operating systems and documentation use the term *disk mirroring* when you use a single controller for two drives and *disk duplexing* when you use two controllers for two drives. Windows NT makes no semantic distinction between the two.

RAID 1 is a fault-tolerant level. This means that if one of your drives is damaged, you can still retrieve your data from the other drive. If a drive goes bad and you replace it, then the operating system (or controller, if implemented in hardware) can rebuild the replaced drive by automatically mirroring the information from the other drive.

RAID 2

RAID 2 uses an error detection and correction technology commonly referred to as the Hamming code. This is the same technology that is often used in RAM chips to detect and correct errors. When implemented, the bits from each portion of your data are written across the disks in the array so that the bits are interleaved. The Hamming code is written to one or more disks at the end of the array. Figure 11-3 illustrates how RAID 2 works.

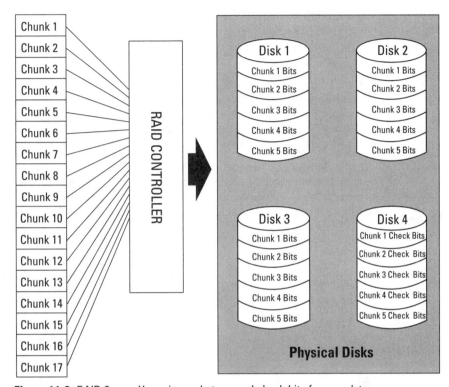

Figure 11-3: RAID 2 uses Hamming code to record check bits for your data.

If one of the drives should fail in a RAID 3 array, the controller is able to automatically rebuild the data based on the information that is in the other drives and the parity drive. This error detection and recovery is transparent to the user, except that the system administrator is typically notified that a drive failed. When the bad drive is replaced, its contents can automatically be regenerated from the contents of the other drives.

Figure 11-3 uses a simplistic approach to illustration. In reality, RAID 2 requires many data disks and several check disks. Typically, RAID 2 is implemented through a hardware solution and then only for larger computer installations. RAID 2 is seldom used in a PC environment and is not supported by Windows NT.

RAID 3

RAID 3 is essentially the same as RAID 1, but with the addition of a single check disk to record parity information that is based on the data written to the other drives. (For this reason, the check disk is sometimes called a *parity disk.*)

The information that is written to the check disk is the XORed values of the stripes that it represents, as shown in Figure 11-4. Thus, the first stripe on the check disk contains the parity values for the first stripes on all of the other disks in the set.

The RAID 3 definition requires tight synchronization between the rotation of the platters on all drives in the set. This is because information is designed to be written to each drive in parallel. In addition, all I/O requests under RAID 3 result in all disks within the set being read or written.

Because of the internal design and technology of RAID 3 arrays, they are particularly valuable for large files or for recording streaming data. Conversely, these arrays are not that efficient when it comes to small files or transactional processing, where small records are read or written at random from a larger database. Windows NT does not support RAID 3, but you may be able to get a RAID 3 hardware option about which Windows NT does not need to know.

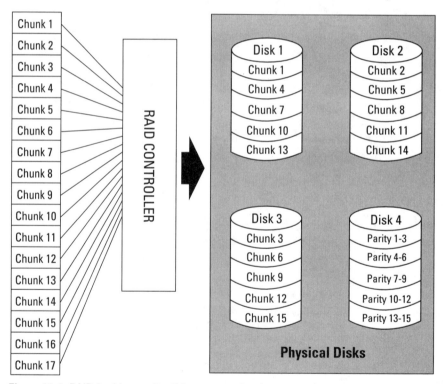

Figure 11-4: RAID 3 adds a parity disk to a normal stripe set.

RAID 4

RAID 4 uses the same disk layout as that used in RAID 3 (see Figure 11-4). The difference is the way in which I/O requests are handled under RAID 4. In this scheme, the disks operate independently, so that not all disks in the set need to be accessed when the information can be written or retrieved from just one disk in the set.

The result is an implementation that is better suited to small files and transactional processing than is RAID 3. Windows NT, however, does not support RAID 4 at an operating system level. The reason for this is that, even though it would be somewhat easier to implement than RAID 3, doing so would still introduce quite a bit of overhead into the disk I/O routines that are used in Windows NT.

If you lose a disk drive under RAID 4, it can either be a data disk or the parity disk. If you lose a data disk, the controller is still able to reconstruct the missing data based on the contents of the other drives and the parity disk.

If you lose the parity disk, then the original data are still intact. If you operate the array without the parity disk, however, you have no fault tolerance; the loss of another drive would mean the loss of the data on all drives in the set, because there is no way to recover the data at that point.

RAID 5

RAID 5 is similar in concept to RAID 4 (and thus, RAID 3), but there is not a single check disk in the disk set. Instead, the equivalent of a single check disk is used, but the parity information is spread among all drives in the set. Figure 11-5 illustrates this concept.

Notice that there is no dedicated check disk. Instead, the parity information is stepped from one disk to another. In Figure 11-5, the first stripe's parity information is on Disk 4, the second's is on Disk 3, the third's on Disk 2, and so on.

In addition, the design of RAID 5 allows for asynchronous disk I/O, as in RAID 4 (and unlike RAID 3). You experience higher disk performance under RAID 5, however, because there is no "bottleneck drive" (the single parity drive) on which all I/O requests must wait.

Just like under RAID 3 and RAID 4, if you have a disk failure under RAID 5, the controller can correct for the loss of a single disk drive. Unlike the lower levels, however, there is no single parity disk to risk losing, so a loss of any drive does not completely remove the fault-tolerant characteristics of your array.

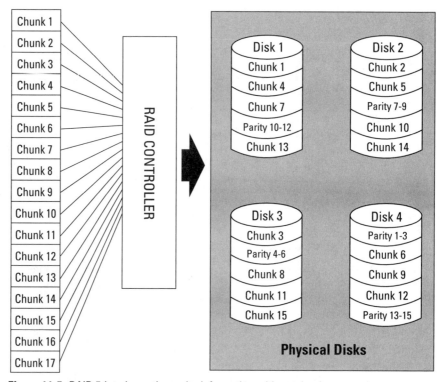

Figure 11-5: RAID 5 interlaces the parity information with regular data.

Windows NT supports RAID 5, referring to it as *stripe set with parity.* When using this level, you can use from 3 to 32 disk drives in the set. If you need fault tolerance, Microsoft recommends that you choose RAID 5. Implementing RAID 5 at an operating system level, however, results in higher I/O system overhead, as the routines take more memory to implement.

Thus, you need to make sure that you increase the amount of RAM in your system whenever you use RAID 5. In addition, you cannot include the boot partition or the system files as part of your stripe set; they must reside on their own partition, separate from the set.

Workstation versus server

When comparing the capabilities of Windows NT Workstation with Windows NT Server, there is bad news and good news. The bad news is that both versions of the operating system do not implement the same fault-tolerant features. The good news is that you can always use hardware-based solutions, regardless of which version you are using. Table 11-1 shows the different RAID levels and how they are supported by Windows NT.

Table 11-1	RAID support under Windows NT		
RAID Level	**Windows NT Name**	**Workstation**	**Server**
RAID 0	Disk Striping	X	X
RAID 1	Disk Mirroring		X
RAID 2			
RAID 3			
RAID 4			
RAID 5	Disk Striping with Parity		X

Remember that the information in Table 11-1 indicates which RAID levels are supported at an operating system level by Windows NT. (In other words, they are supported as part of the software.) You can purchase hardware subsystems for most of the RAID levels, and they work just fine with Windows NT.

Implementing Fault Tolerance

As you learned in the previous section, Windows NT Workstation does not support software fault tolerance on local drives. If your network uses fault tolerance on a Windows NT server, then accessing those drives is transparent to your workstation. If you need fault tolerance on your local system, then you are left with only two options: upgrade to Windows NT Server or install a RAID hardware solution.

Hardware solutions

Because hardware solutions are implemented at a lower level then the operating system, you can use a hardware RAID array with Windows NT without needing to configure the operating system. The operation of the array is transparent to the operation of the computer.

For instance, if you have a hardware array that uses eight drives in a single controller cabinet, as far as Windows NT is concerned, you are using a single disk drive. All redundancy, mirroring, or mapping is taken care of by the hardware.

Drive striping

Although not technically a fault-tolerant technology, drive striping is often considered in the same arena because it uses much of the same technology that is used in other RAID levels. Windows NT Workstation allows you to use drive striping on your system.

To use disk striping, the following conditions need to be met:

- The partitions that are used in the stripe set must be on physically separate disk drives.

- Your stripe set can be composed of disk space on from 2 to 32 disk drives.

- You cannot include the boot partition in your stripe set.

- Stripe sets must be created from unused disk space; you cannot include partitions that are currently mapped as disk drives.

If your workstation meets these requirements, you can implement disk striping by following these steps:

STEPS

Creating a stripe set

Step 1. Choose the Programs option from the Start menu. This displays the Programs menu.

Step 2. Choose the Administrative Tools (Common) option from the Programs menu. This displays a list of administrative tools from which you can select.

Step 3. Click on the Disk Administrator option. In short order, this displays the Disk Administrator, as shown in Figure 11-6.

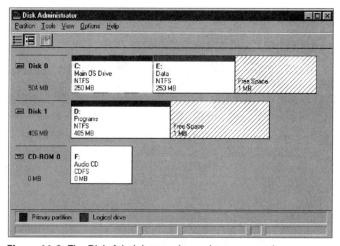

Figure 11-6: The Disk Administrator is used to create stripe sets.

Step 4. Click on the unused disk space on one of your disk drives.

Step 5. Hold Ctrl as you click on the unused disk space on another drive. (Repeat this step for every drive that you want to be included in the stripe set.)

Step 6. Choose the Create Stripe Set option from the Partition menu. This displays the Create Stripe Set dialog box, as shown in Figure 11-7.

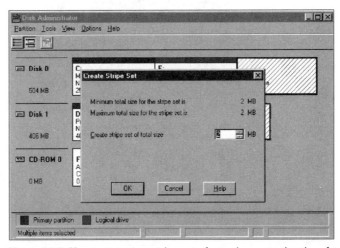

Figure 11-7: You can create a stripe set of any size, up to the size of the smallest unused disk area that you have chosen.

Step 7. In the field provided, specify the size of the stripe set that you want to create. You can pick a size up to the size of the smallest unused disk area that you selected in Steps 4 and 5.

Step 8. Click on the OK button. This returns you to the Disk Administrator.

Step 9. Choose Commit Changes Now from the Partition menu. You are asked to confirm your changes.

Step 10. Click on the Yes button to save your changes. You are then walked through restarting your system.

Step 11. Once your system is restarted, repeat Steps 1 through 3. You should see the Disk Administrator displayed.

Step 12. Right-click on one of the partitions in the new stripe set. This displays a Context menu.

(continued)

STEPS *(continued)*

Creating a stripe set

Step 13.   Choose the Format option from the Context menu. This displays the Format Drive dialog box, as shown in Figure 11-8.

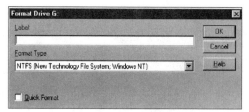

Figure 11-8: You need to format a new stripe set before you can use it.

Step 14.   From the Format Type drop-down list, select the type of filing system that you want to use when formatting the stripe set.

Step 15.   Click on the OK button to format the stripe set.

Step 16.   Close the Disk Administrator.

Disk striping suggestions

When implementing disk striping on your system, keep the following guidelines in mind:

- The stripe set that you create on your system cannot be used on another system. This means that you cannot remove the drives from your system and hope to install them in another NT system. When NT creates a stripe set, it adds special values at the beginning of the stripe set that make it recognizable only to the system that created it.

You can, however, transfer the drive configuration information (through the Disk Administrator) to the other NT system and have the stripe set recognized.

- You get better system performance if your swap file is stored on a nonstriped disk.

- Stripe sets are file-system independent. They can be formatted with any filing system that is supported by Windows NT.

After you are done creating your stripe set, you can use it just like you would any other disk drive. From a user's perspective, there is no operational difference between a regular drive and a stripe set.

Using your disk configuration files

The Disk Administrator does its work by maintaining special disk configuration files. (Actually, these files are saved in the Windows NT Registry, not in separate files.) The Disk Administrator allows you to export these files to a floppy disk so that you can use them on another system.

Although this may not seem like a valuable idea, it can prove immensely important when you are using a stripe set. Perhaps an example can clear up this area. You may have four disk drives in your system. You decide to use the first disk drive for your system files. You decide to use the other three disks as a stripe set.

Everything is going along fine, until one day the disk that you are using as your system disk crashes. This means that you need to install a new hard drive and then install the Windows NT operating system files on the disk. All is fine until you decide to try accessing your stripe set.

When a stripe set is created, Windows NT encodes a special value at the beginning of each partition in the stripe set. This value, stored in the Registry by the Disk Administrator, is used in later accessing the stripe set. Because your old Registry is now gone (remember, you had to reinstall Windows NT), so is the special value. If you previously exported your disk configuration information, however, you can now import it into your new version of NT and restart your system, and your stripe set is again accessible.

To export your disk configuration to a floppy disk, follow these steps:

STEPS

Exporting disk configurations

Step 1. Make sure that you have a blank, formatted, high-density floppy disk on which to save your configuration information.

Step 2. Choose the <u>P</u>rograms option from the Start menu. This displays the Programs menu.

(continued)

STEPS *(continued)*

Exporting disk configurations

Step 3. Choose the Administrative Tools (Common) option from the Programs menu. This displays a list of administrative tools from which you can select.

Step 4. Click on the Disk Administrator option. In short order, this displays the Disk Administrator.

Step 5. Choose the Configuration option from the Partition menu. This displays a submenu with three choices.

Step 6. Choose the Save option from the submenu. This displays the Insert Disk dialog box, as shown in Figure 11-9.

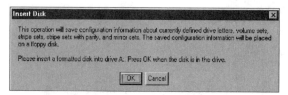

Figure 11-9: When saving your disk configuration, you are prompted to insert a diskette in the drive.

Step 7. Insert your floppy disk in the drive, and click on the OK button. The configuration information is saved to the disk. When the saving is done, you are notified and returned to the Disk Administrator.

Tip

You should update your disk configuration floppy every time you change your configuration information.

To later import your disk configuration information, follow these steps:

STEPS

Restoring a disk configuration

Step 1. Choose the Programs option from the Start menu. This displays the Programs menu.

Step 2. Choose the Administrative Tools (Common) option from the Programs menu. This displays a list of administrative tools from which you can select.

Step 3. Click on the Disk Administrator option. This starts the Disk Administrator. Don't be surprised that your drive configuration in the Disk Administrator does not look like you think it should; this is natural (and the reason that you are restoring your configuration).

Step 4. Choose the Configuration option from the Partition menu. This displays a submenu with three choices.

Step 5. Choose the Restore option from the submenu. This displays a warning dialog box, as shown in Figure 11-10.

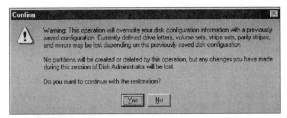

Figure 11-10: You must confirm your action before restoring a disk configuration.

Step 6. Click on the Yes button to start the restoration. You are prompted to insert the configuration disk in your floppy drive.

Step 7. Insert your floppy disk, and click on the OK button to proceed. The information from the floppy disk is copied to the Registry. When done, you are informed that you need to restart your system.

Step 8. Click on the OK button to restart your system.

Once restarted, your system should function just as before. This means that you should be able to access all of your partitions and stripe sets as expected.

Removing a stripe set

There may come a time when you need to remove a stripe set from your system. This may occur because you are planning on using the computer for a different purpose, you are removing the drives for use in other systems, or you just need to reconfigure.

To remove an existing stripe set, first make sure that you have backed up the information that is on the stripe set (as described later in this chapter) or that you no longer need the data. Then you can follow these steps:

STEPS

Removing a stripe set

Step 1.   Choose the Programs option from the Start menu. This displays the Programs menu.

Step 2.   Choose the Administrative Tools (Common) option from the Programs menu. This displays a list of administrative tools from which you can select.

Step 3.   Click on the Disk Administrator option. This starts the Disk Administrator.

Step 4.   Right-click on one of the partitions in the stripe set. This displays a Context menu.

Step 5.   Choose the Delete option from the Context menu. You are asked to confirm your action.

Step 6.   Click on the Yes button to remove the stripe set. The stripe set is deleted and returned to free space.

Step 7.   Exit the Disk Administrator.

Disk Compression

If you have used other versions of Windows, you may be familiar with the concept of disk compression. For instance, Windows 95 supports Double-Space, which is Microsoft's disk compression feature that was introduced several years ago. Windows NT, however, does not support DoubleSpace drives, nor does it support any other disk compression techniques that were previously used in the DOS or Windows worlds.

If you are using any NTFS drives in your system, then you have a compression feature that is built into Windows NT. While it is not compatible with other disk compression approaches, the NTFS compression allows you to compress files, folders, or entire disks. This could not be done under the DoubleSpace scheme, which only allows entire disk drives to be compressed.

The compression scheme that is used by Windows NT is very similar in purpose and function to the scheme that is used by DoubleSpace. The result is that the compression ratios achieved by the Windows NT compression are comparable with those gained by DoubleSpace.

Compression is treated as an attribute that you can apply to files, folders, or entire disks. Once a folder or disk is marked as compressed, anything that is copied to that folder or disk also inherits the compressed attribute.

Secret

When you copy a compressed file, even to another compressed disk or folder, the file is uncompressed, copied, and recompressed. This means that if your target drive is short of disk space, it still must have enough disk space to temporarily hold the uncompressed file. If it does not, then the file cannot be copied, even if the compressed file would have fit on the drive.

To change the compression attribute on a disk, folder, or file on an NTFS drive, simply right click on the icon for the object, and then choose Properties from the Context menu. Figure 11-11 shows an example of the Properties dialog box for a folder.

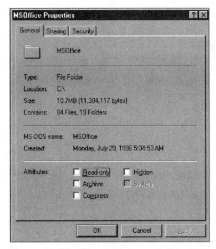

Figure 11-11: Files, folders, and disks
under NTFS have a compression attribute.

At the bottom of the dialog box (regardless of the object it is for) is a check box for compression. If you select this check box, the object is compressed when you close the dialog box. If you are changing the properties of a folder or disk drive, then you are also asked if you want to compress all of the files and folders that are contained within that object.

Secret

You cannot compress the swap files that are used by Windows NT. Dynamic compression means that files are compressed and decompressed on the fly, which results in them being moved about on the disk. Because swap files cannot be moved, Windows NT simply refuses to compress such a file.

After an object is compressed, there is nothing special about it; you simply use it as you normally would. If you select the compressed object in a window folder or in the Explorer, the status bar always indicates the uncompressed size of the item.

The only time that you can see a difference in the item is when you view the Properties dialog box (where the compression check box is selected and a compressed size is indicated) or when viewing details in the Explorer or a folder window. In this instance, the Attributes column for the file has a C in it, indicating that the object is compressed.

Tip

If you find not being able to tell a compressed object from an uncompressed object to be confusing, you can force Windows to display compressed objects in a different color than noncompressed objects. You do this by choosing Options from the View menu in either the Explorer or in a folder window. This displays the Options dialog box, as shown in Figure 11-12.

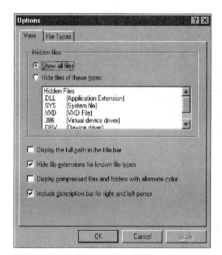

Figure 11-12: You can force Windows NT to display compressed objects in a different color than regular objects.

Select the second check box from the bottom. After it is selected and applied, your compressed files, folders, and drives are indicated in blue. (Icon colors are not changed, only the text appearing beneath the icon.)

Tip

Because compressed files are displayed in light blue when the check box is selected, make sure that you don't change your background color to blue. Doing so renders the filename (and associated information) invisible.

Scanning for Errors

Windows NT provides two different tools that you can use to check your disk drives for errors. These tools are similar to the ScanDisk utility that is used in other versions of Windows. The two tools are accessible through the Disk Administrator or from the desktop.

Checking from the Disk Administrator

Earlier in this chapter, you learned how to use the Disk Administrator to access some advanced capabilities of Windows NT. The Disk Administrator is also a logical place to check your disk for errors. With the Disk Administrator running, just right-click on a disk drive and then choose the Check for Errors option from the Context menu. This displays the Check for Errors dialog box, as shown in Figure 11-13.

Figure 11-13: You can quickly check a drive for errors from the Disk Administrator.

There are three options on the Check for Errors dialog box. These options affect the checking in the following ways:

- **Do not fix errors.** This option simply checks for errors, calling them to your attention as they are found. You have the opportunity, on an error-by-error basis, to correct any errors that are detected.

- **Fix file system errors.** This option, which is selected by default, causes the checking program to fix any errors that it detects in the system areas that are used by the filing system. This type of check is generally very quick to perform.

- **Scan for bad sectors.** If this option is selected, then errors are corrected as they are detected, and a full surface scan is performed on the drive. Using this option can greatly increase the time that is required to check your disk drive.

You can only select one of the three options. When you have made your choice, click on the OK button to begin the checking. When the check is complete, you are shown an on-screen report that indicates the findings. Such a report is shown in Figure 11-14.

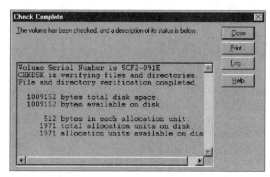

Figure 11-14: The scanning program always reports a summary of its findings.

When you close the report dialog box, you are returned to the Disk Administrator.

Checking from the desktop

Another convenient way to scan a disk for errors is directly from the desktop. This method of checking is essentially the same as what you access from the Disk Administrator, except that the interface is different.

To check your disk from the desktop, follow these steps:

STEPS

Checking a disk for errors

Step 1. Double-click on the My Computer icon on your desktop.

Step 2. Right-click on one of your local disk drives. This displays a Context menu.

Step 3. Choose the Properties option from the Context menu. This displays the Properties dialog box for the disk drive.

Step 4.   Click on the Tools tab. (This tab is not available on a CD-ROM drive or a mapped network drive.) The Properties dialog box now appears as shown in Figure 11-15.

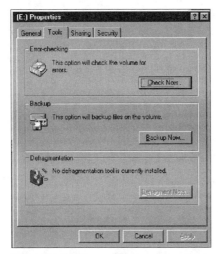

Figure 11-15: You can access a couple of tools from the Tools tab.

Secret

Even though a defragmentation option is available on the Tools tab, no defragmenter is provided with Windows NT. The reasoning for this is unclear, although it appears that Microsoft was not able to get one written (or licensed) in time for the release of Windows NT 4.0.

Step 5.   Click on the Check Now button at the top of the dialog box. This displays the Check Disk dialog box, as shown in Figure 11-16.

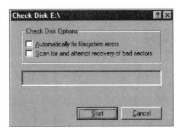

Figure 11-16: The Check Disk dialog box allows you to check the integrity of your disk drive.

The two check boxes on the Check Disk dialog box have the same purpose as the three radio buttons that were described in the previous section.

There are four conditions that you can have on this dialog box:

- **Both check boxes cleared.** This causes Windows NT to do a quick check of the filing system areas of the disk, reporting any errors that it finds. As an error is detected, you have the opportunity to repair it.

- **First check box selected.** This results in a quick check of the filing system areas, with any detected errors being fixed automatically.

- **Second check box selected.** This results in a full check of your system, including a surface scan of the disk. This results in the longest time being taken for the check.

- **Both check boxes selected.** This results in both the system area being checked and the disk surface being scanned.

When you are finished making your selections, click on the Start button. The scanning is conducted as you specified, and when it is done, you are informed of the results. When completed, the Properties dialog box is still visible.

Backing Up Your System

Backing up your data is an essential part of making sure that you protect the investment you have made in your system. Windows NT includes two ways that you can back up your system:

- From the Windows interface

- From the command prompt

Which one should you use? If at all possible, use the regular backup program from the Windows interface; it is much friendlier. Both programs do not perform the same functions, however, so you may be forced to use both of them from time to time.

The biggest difference is the media that the programs can accept. The regular backup program is used to transfer your data to a tape, while the command-line version is used to send your backups to floppy disk. Both of these methods are covered in the following sections.

The backup program

The Windows NT backup tool allows you to perform quick and painless backups of your data. You can easily select folders, drives, or groups of information and back them up with the click of a button.

In addition, if you are connected to a network, you can back up any of the data that you choose from other computers — all from your desktop. The backup tool gives you numerous ways to back up your data in the least painful way.

Before you can use the backup program, make sure that you have the proper drivers installed for your tape drive. If you already have your tape drive drivers installed, then you can skip the next section and proceed directly to the succeeding one.

Installing your tape device driver

When you add a tape drive to your system, make sure that Windows NT is configured properly to use the device. If you install the drive and then start your system, there is a good chance that Windows NT may have detected it. If so, then you were probably prompted for the proper drivers at that time.

If you added your tape drive with your system turned on (which is possible with an external tape drive connecting through an existing SCSI port), then you need to explicitly instruct Windows NT to install the drivers.

You do this by following these steps:

STEPS

Installing tape drive drivers

Step 1.   Double-click on the My Computer icon on your desktop. This displays a folder window showing the resources that are on your system.

Step 2.   Double-click on the Control Panel icon. Shortly you see the Control Panel window.

Step 3.   Double-click on the Tape Devices icon in the Control Panel. This displays the Tape Devices dialog box, as shown in Figure 11-17.

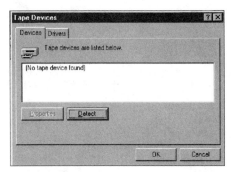

Figure 11-17: The Tape Devices dialog box lists which drivers are loaded for tape drives on your system.

(continued)

STEPS *(continued)*

Installing tape drive drivers

Step 4. If your tape drive is listed in the Tape Devices dialog box, you are done and you can click on the OK button.

Step 5. Make sure that your tape drive is connected properly and turned on.

Step 6. Click on the Detect button. Windows NT attempts to detect your tape drive. If one is located, you are informed of what was discovered, as shown in Figure 11-18.

Figure 11-18: Windows NT informs you of which tape device it located.

Step 7. Click on the OK button to install the driver for the tape drive. (You may be prompted to insert your Windows NT CD-ROM so that the driver can be loaded.) After this is done, the new driver appears in the Tape Devices window.

Step 8. Click on the OK button to close the Tape Devices window.

Step 9. Close the Control Panel.

Backing up your files

With your tape device connected and configured, you are ready to use the backup program. There are two easy ways that you can start the backup program:

- Select the Programs option from the Start menu, choose Administrative Tools (Common), and then select Backup.

- Right-click on a drive icon in the My Computer window, and then select Properties. In the Properties dialog box, click on the Tools tab, and then click on Backup Now.

Regardless of the way you choose, the Backup program window appears as shown in Figure 11-19.

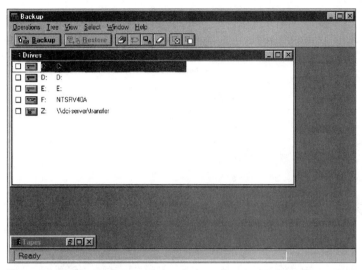

Figure 11-19: The Backup program window allows you to see the contents of your drives and your tapes.

A backup is easy to create. Essentially, you just specify the files, folders, or drives that you want to back up. This is done visually as you view the layout of your system in the Backup program window. To choose the drives, folders, or files that you want to back up, click on the square to the left of the desired object.

Click on a drive or folder, and everything in that object is automatically selected. If you double-click on an object, then the object is opened to reveal the detail that it contains. You can then continue selecting objects to back up.

When you are finished selecting objects to back up, click the Backup button at the top of the Backup window. This displays an information dialog box, as shown in Figure 11-20. (The dialog box may already contain information, if the tape was previously used. This is the case in Figure 11-20.)

You can fill in the information on the tape as desired for your backup needs. Of particular importance is the Verify After Backup check box. If this check box is selected, then Windows NT automatically rewinds the backup tape and checks to make sure that the backup was done correctly. When you are ready to proceed, click on the OK button to start the backup.

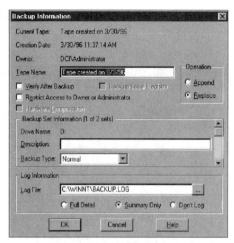

Figure 11-20: You can specify how you want the backup done and what information should be stored with the backup.

You are informed of the progress of the backup as it proceeds. When the backup is completed, click on the OK button to close the Status window. You can then close the Backup program window and put your backup tape away in a safe place. (You never know when you may need it.)

Restoring from a backup

The Windows NT backup program also allows you to restore the information that you previously backed up. You do this by first inserting the backup tape in the tape drive and then starting the backup program as described in the previous section. The Backup program window should appear as shown in Figure 11-19.

In looking at the figure, notice that the Drives window is open, and the Tapes window is minimized at the bottom of the Backup program window. You need to double-click on the Tapes window. When open, the Backup program window looks similar to Figure 11-21.

You use the Tapes window in the same way that you used the Drives window in the previous section. You navigate through the contents of the tape, selecting the files and folders that you want to restore.

After you have selected the files, simply click on the Restore button at the top of the Backup program window. This displays the Restore Information dialog box, as shown in Figure 11-22.

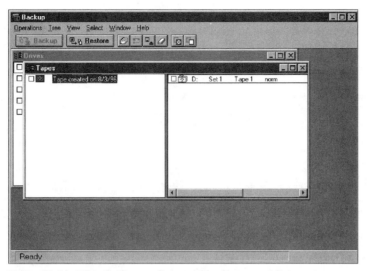

Figure 11-21: With the Tapes window open, you are ready to restore your files.

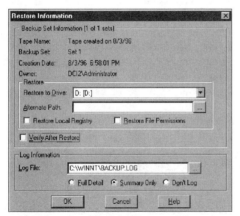

Figure 11-22: The Restore Information dialog box is used to indicate how your files should be restored.

Using this dialog box, you can specify exactly how you want the files to be restored. For instance, you can use the Alternate Path field to indicate where the files should be restored. If you want them to be restored in the same location from which they were backed up, just click on the OK button to proceed.

At this point, the files that you specified are located on the backup tape and restored to the indicated location on your hard drive. Again, Windows NT displays a status dialog box to show how the restoration is proceeding. When completed, click on the OK button to close the dialog box, and exit the backup program.

Backing up from the command line

Secret

If you want to back up data to floppy drives, you are forced to do this from the command line. Windows NT includes a command-line backup program that is very similar to the old backup program included with DOS. This inclusion is not well publicized with Windows NT — in fact, you can't find it anywhere in the documentation. Nonetheless, it exists, and you can make backups on floppies.

As an example of how to use the program, consider backing up the contents of your D drive to floppy disks in the A drive. In this case, you would type the following at the command line:

```
backup d:\*.* a: /s
```

This example shows the general format of the backup command. You issue the command (backup) followed by the source (d:*.*, in this case), the destination (a:), and any switches that you want to use with the command (/s). The switches that you can use are shown when you use the backup command with the /? switch to get help, as shown in Figure 11-23.

```
Command Prompt                                          _ □ ×
Microsoft(R) Windows NT(TM)
(C) Copyright 1985-1996 Microsoft Corp.

C:\>backup /?
Backs up one or more files from one disk to another.

BACKUP source destination-drive: [/S] [/M] [/A] [/F[:size]]
        [/D:date[/T:time]] [/L[:[drive:][path]logfile]]

  source           Specifies the file(s), drive, or directory to back up.
  destination-drive: Specifies the drive to save backup copies onto.
  /S               Backs up contents of subdirectories.
  /M               Backs up only files that have changed since the last
                   backup.
  /A               Adds backup files to an existing backup disk.
  /F:[size]        Specifies the size of the disk to be formatted.
  /D:date          Backs up only files changed on or after the specified
                   date.
  /T:time          Backs up only files changed at or after the specified
                   time.
  /L:[drive:][path]logfile]
                   Creates a log file and entry to record the backup
                   operation.

C:\>
```

Figure 11-23: The backup command can use several different switches.

As your backup proceeds, you are informed of what is going on. Information that previously existed on the floppy disks is erased, and the information that is stored on the diskettes is compressed automatically.

Even so, it is not unusual (unless you are backing up only a couple of files) to need multiple disks to perform the entire backup. You are prompted when to change disks, and you may need to do so several times before the backup is complete.

Tip

Make sure that you label and number your backup disks sequentially. You will need them, in the proper order, when you later restore your information.

If you want to restore files that you have placed on floppies, you can use the restore command from the command line. The syntax of this command is very similar to that of the backup command: you issue the command (restore) followed by the source, the destination, and any switches.

For example, if you wanted to restore your previous backup, but this time to a directory on the E drive, you would issue the following command:

```
restore a: e:\temp /s
```

Just as with the backup command, you can review all of the possible ways to use restore by using the command followed by the /? switch at the command line.

Summary

When you use Windows NT on your computer system, you are using one of the most powerful operating systems in the world. As such, Windows NT has many capabilities that are considered to be advanced.

In this chapter, you have learned about some of those capabilities in relation to your disk system. Windows NT supports many types of disks and a multitude of configurations. You can set up your system to take advantage of everything from easy backing up of your data to complete fault tolerance.

In particular, you have learned the following items:

▶ There are six different RAID levels that define different configurations of disk systems.

▶ Windows NT Server supports three RAID levels (0, 1, and 5), whereas Windows NT Workstation allows you to implement only level 0.

▶ RAID 0 (disk striping) is technically not a fault-tolerant disk implementation, but it can be used to increase the performance of your disk system.

▶ You can purchase hardware solutions for RAID that can be implemented transparently with Windows NT Workstation.

▶ If you are using NTFS on a drive, you can automatically compress files, folders, and entire disks. Compression is treated as simply another property of these objects.

▶ There are two ways that you can scan your disks for errors under Windows NT. Although both methods accomplish the same thing, they use different interfaces to accomplish their work.

▶ Windows NT includes a full-featured backup program that you use for saving information on tape drives and later restoring it.

▶ If you want to back up information to floppy drives, you can use the BACKUP command from the command line. Later, restoring the information is done using the RESTORE command.

Chapter 12

Effective Networking

In This Chapter

You are well aware that Windows NT is a networking operating system. In fact, even though Windows NT Workstation provides a stable environment on a standalone computer, you cannot take full advantage of the operating system until you are connected to a network. Then you can reach out and connect to resources and make your resources available to others.

For Windows NT networking to function properly, you must understand a few basics. In many chapters of this book so far, you have learned how you can put the networking features of Windows NT to work for you. The fundamentals that are behind that networking, however, need to be understood so that you can control the basis on which your networking features are made available. This chapter teaches those fundamentals.

Here you learn what makes your Windows NT network tick, and how you can assemble the building blocks that are necessary to create or access a network. In particular, you learn the following items:

▶ What network models are available and how Windows NT Workstation works in those models

▶ How network components are used by Windows NT to build network connectivity

▶ How to add, configure, and manage your network components

▶ How to use the Find tool to locate computers on your network

Understanding Network Basics

The basics of networking baffle many people. Otherwise, sane and intelligent computer users are often confused and frustrated when it comes to figuring out how a network is put together. Windows NT does a great job of simplifying your network as much as possible. The following sections describe the various network models that you can adopt as well as the components that make those models a reality.

Network models

When examining networks at a high level, you quickly discover that there are two types of networks that you can implement:

■ client/server

■ peer-to-peer

Windows NT Workstation can participate in both types of networks. In the following sections, you learn what identifies each type of network.

Client/server networks

If your workstation belongs to a large network, it probably uses the *client/server* model. In the client/server environment, the network is composed of one or more specialized servers and a number of different clients, as shown in Figure 12-1.

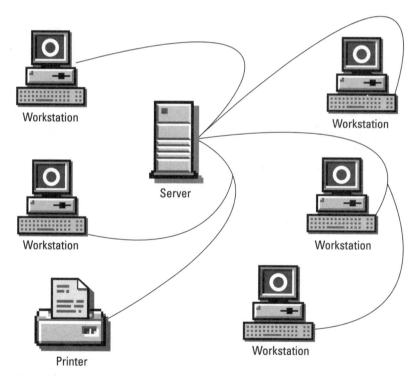

Figure 12-1: The client/server model relies on workstations and other devices that are attached to a centralized server.

The servers are designed to provide centralized services, and the clients are the individual users' PCs that are connected to the network. In a client/server environment, the PCs that are connected to the network may be called clients, nodes, or workstations; from a user's standpoint, there is little technical difference between the three terms.

There are many types of servers that can be used in a client/server network. Because servers are used to provide dedicated services to the network as a whole, servers are typically added to a network as it grows and the individual needs of the network dictate.

Specialized hardware servers include the following common types:

- **File server.** A computer that is dedicated to providing centralized file storage and management.

- **Print server.** A computer or device that is dedicated to providing centralized print services.

- **Communications server.** A computer that is dedicated to providing dedicated modem, fax, and electronic mail services.

- **Database server.** A computer that is dedicated to running a centralized database program.

It is possible to mix and match servers in a network, or the network can have more than one particular server type. For instance, your network may have multiple print servers or file servers. At a minimum, a client/server network has one file server, with other types of servers being added as the needs of the organization grow and develop.

Because the servers provide centralized services for the entire network, you can view the client/server model as a top-down approach to networking. Although the client/server model is very powerful, it does have drawbacks.

Perhaps the biggest drawback is that, if a server goes down (for whatever reason), the entire network is down in relation to the resources that are provided by the server. For example, if a print server becomes unavailable, there is no way to print through the network until the server is again available.

Because keeping the network running is such a critical issue, most environments using the client/server model rely on a single person (or an entire department) to run the network. This person, or the head of the department, is known as the *network administrator*.

The network administrator requires a high degree of networking proficiency and an understanding of how all of the network pieces fit together. The network administrator, as well as the costs of an organization supporting such a person, is the reason why the client/server networking model is typically used only in larger networks.

Windows NT Workstation easily takes advantage of the client/server networking model. If you are connected to a Windows NT Server network, then you belong to a client/server network. The computer on which Windows NT Server is installed is typically the file server.

In addition, this server provides centralized domain information for security purposes and to control access to the resources of the network. Your computer, running Windows NT Workstation, is one of the clients on the network.

Peer-to-peer networks

Under the *peer-to-peer network* model, there are no centralized servers. Instead, every node on the network provides services that can be accessed by other nodes on the network. For instance, one node may have a printer that can be used by other nodes, whereas a different node may have data files that are made available to other network users. Figure 12-2 shows an example of peer-to-peer networking.

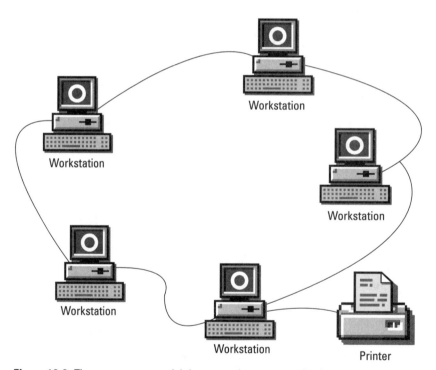

Figure 12-2: The peer-to-peer model does not rely on a centralized server.

Peer-to-peer networking is traditionally used for smaller networks or work-groups. This model eliminates several of the disadvantages inherent in the client/server approach. For instance, if one of the computers on the network goes down, the entire network is not disabled.

Granted, the resources that are shared by that system are no longer available, but alternate services can be used through other computers on the network. In addition, a network administrator is typically not necessary, because each person using the network generally supports his own machine and manages his shared resources.

Windows NT Workstation can be used in a peer-to-peer network. Other computers on the network may include systems that are also running Windows NT Workstation, or they may be running Windows 95 or Windows for Workgroups.

Understanding network components

Regardless of the type of network model that you use in your environment, Windows NT Workstation uses the concept of *network components* to implement the network. These components can be viewed as building blocks for your network.

When you combine the building blocks in the proper order, then you are able to connect to your network and communicate with other computers. Three types of network components are used in Windows NT Workstation:

- Adapters
- Protocols
- Services

Each of these components is discussed, from a conceptual standpoint, in the following sections. Later in this chapter, you learn how to change and configure the components that are used in your Windows NT Workstation.

Adapters

An *adapter* is the physical computer card that is used to connect your computer to the network. If you take a look at the back of your computer case, you should be able to locate the network cable.

The point at which this cable connects to your computer is the network adapter. (Another name for the network adapter is the network interface card, or NIC.) The adapter takes care of translating the communications signals used within your computer to a format that can be understood by the network itself.

Literally hundreds of different NICs are on the market, and Windows NT Workstation directly supports (by name) over 120 different models. Normally you have a single NIC installed in your system, but it is possible to install several NICs to enable communication with different networks.

Secret

Although using different NICs is possible, it is not typically done. Depending on the protocol, you may only be able to load the protocol on one network card (as is the case with the IPX protocol, for instance). Trying to load a protocol on more than one card in effect turns your system into a router, which NT was never really designed or optimized to do.

Protocols

Protocols are simply a set of rules that are used to ensure reliable communication. Without the rules being followed, no communication can occur. In the world of human communication, a protocol can be compared to the languages that we use to communicate with each other.

In network terminology, the protocol determines the format of the information that is transmitted over the network. Just as two people must speak the same language to communicate effectively, two hardware devices on your network must understand the same protocols to exchange information reliably.

In the Windows NT world, the protocol networking component is made up of three distinct parts. The relationship of these parts is illustrated in Figure 12-3.

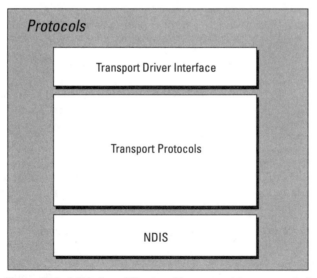

Figure 12-3: A Windows NT networking protocol is composed of three parts.

At the lowest layer, closest to the NIC, is the *NDIS interface*. NDIS is an acronym for Network Device Interface Specification. Windows NT adheres to NDIS 3.0, which is an industry-supported definition of how transport protocols and NICs should talk to each other.

NDIS can be compared to a communication layer that is adhered to by both the NIC and the Windows NT transport protocols; it is the translator that allows proper interfacing between the protocol and the NIC.

The next higher level is the *transport protocol layer*. Transport protocols are the "packagers" that determine how information is communicated across the network. The following are common transport protocols:

- AppleTalk (Macintosh networks)
- DLC (IBM and HP networks)
- IPX/SPX (Novell networks)
- NBF (Windows NT networks)
- NetBEUI (Windows networks)
- TCP/IP (UNIX and the Internet)

Windows NT Workstation 4.0 understands all of these common protocols and allows you to easily implement them in your network.

At the highest level is the *transport driver interface* (TDI), which is used to provide an isolation layer between the transport protocol and the redirector. (The *redirector* is used by Windows NT as a communications point between the operating system and the protocol that you have selected.) In effect, the TDI provides the same function in relation to the transport protocols and the operating system as NDIS does in relation to the transport protocols and the NIC.

Services

Services are the networking components that allow you to accomplish specific network operations. For example, a service may allow browsing through another system's shared files or it may print to a shared network printer. The services that you install use both the protocol and adapter components to accomplish their work.

Windows NT Workstation 4.0 supports a wide variety of network services. The following services are available:

- **Client Service for NetWare.** This service provides a way for Windows NT Workstation to connect to Novell NetWare 3.x and 4.x servers, as well as resources that are provided through a NetWare network.

- **Microsoft Peer Web Services.** This service can be used to implement a limited Web server on your system. Peer Web services are discussed in more depth in Chapter 14.

- **Microsoft TCP/IP Printing.** This service allows you to use the TCP/IP protocol for printing information to network printers.

- **NetBIOS Interface.** This service allows Windows NT to access information using the IPX/SPX protocol. Some programs may require the use of this service, if they were written to NetBIOS specifications. (NetBIOS programs are not as prevalent as they once were.)

- **Network Monitor Agent.** This service is used to enable real-time network traffic monitoring. The service is used by some NT tools and by some third-party administrative tools.

- **Remote Access Service.** This service allows others to dial into your system and be connected over a phone line. They can then access network resources as if they were connected with a regular NIC.

- **RPC Configuration.** This service allows distributed applications, including Windows NT, to use the remote procedure calls (RPC) naming conventions. This service is used in conjunction with the Server and Workstation services.

- **RPC Support for Banyan.** This service provides the proper remote procedure calls drivers for use with Banyan VINES networking.

- **SAP Agent.** The Service Advertising Protocol (SAP) is used by NetWare clients to perform name resolution on NetWare networks. NetWare servers advertise their services through periodic SAP broadcasts, and IPX routers (including NetWare servers) store the server name and IPX internetwork address in tables. You need the SAP Agent if you are connecting with a Novell network.

- **Server.** This service is used in conjunction with the RPC Configuration service to provide file and print sharing. It also provides support for named pipe sharing.

- **Simple TCP/IP Services.** Installs a collection of common TCP/IP services originally rooted in the UNIX environment. You should install this service any time you install TCP/IP as a protocol on your network.

- **SNMP Service.** This service, used in conjunction with the TCP/IP services, allows reporting of server status to a Simple Network Management Protocol (SNMP) management system over a TCP/IP network.

- **Workstation.** This service, which is mandatory for use with Windows NT Workstation, provides support for network connections and inter-machine communications.

Understanding bindings

In Windows NT, *bindings* are the links that exist between network adapters and network protocols. The bindings inform the operating system which protocols should be used with which network adapters.

If your workstation is simple, then you may only have a single network adapter and one or two protocols. In this case, both protocols are bound to your network adapter. The binding effectively establishes a communication channel from the protocol to the adapter.

If you are connected to a more complex network, then the bindings may be more complex as well. For instance, you may be connected to three different networks with your workstation. For the three, you have three separate adapter cards. To make matters worse, all three networks use different protocols.

The first uses TCP/IP, the second IPX, and the third NetBEUI. Normally, Windows NT takes care of picking your bindings for you. In this case, however, Windows NT doesn't have a clue as to which protocol should be routed to which adapter. To cover all bases, Windows automatically binds every protocol to every adapter.

While this may work, it wastes resources and decreases your network efficiency. Instead, you need to optimize your system by adjusting the bindings so that the proper protocol is paired with the proper adapter. (You learn how to change bindings later in this chapter.)

Managing Network Components

Windows NT makes it easy to add (and later remove) your network components. These actions are taken by using the Network dialog box. There are two ways that you can access this dialog box:

- Right-click on the Network Neighborhood icon on your desktop. This displays a Context menu, from which you should select the Properties option.

- Open the Control Panel, and then double-click on the Network icon.

Regardless of which method you use, you shortly see the Network dialog box, as shown in Figure 12-4.

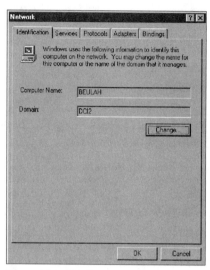

Figure 12-4: The Network dialog box is used to add and remove network components.

Notice that the Network dialog box includes five tabs. Each tab is used to control the various components of your network along with additional networking information. The following sections describe how to use the various tabs to configure your network components.

Adding adapters

To add a network adapter to your system, click on the Adapters tab after the Network dialog box is displayed. The dialog box then appears as shown in Figure 12-5.

The Adapters tab, when selected, should list every physical network adapter that is installed in your system. If it does not, then you need to add the drivers for that adapter. To add an adapter, click on the Add button. This displays the Select Network Adapter dialog box, as shown in Figure 12-6.

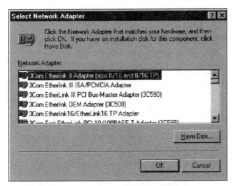

Figure 12-5: The Adapters tab displays information on the NICs that are installed in your system.

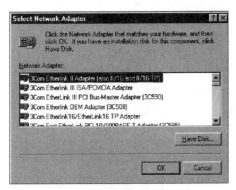

Figure 12-6: Windows NT Workstation supports a large number of network adapters.

At this point, you simply need to select the adapter that you want to add and then click on the OK button. This displays the Network dialog box again, but this time, the new adapter is listed in the Adapters tab. You can continue adding adapters, as necessary, until the list in the Adapters tab matches what you have physically installed in your system.

If your adapter is not listed in the Select Network Adapter dialog box, you need to contact your vendor to get a Windows NT driver. Make sure that you get a driver that works with Windows NT 4.0, however, as older NT drivers do not work properly. When you have the driver on a disk, you can click on the Have Disk button to load the driver from the disk.

Adding protocols

Adding a protocol to your network configuration is just as easy as adding an adapter. To add a protocol, click on the Protocols tab, after which the Network dialog box appears, as shown in Figure 12-7.

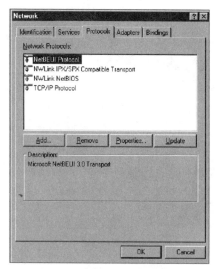

Figure 12-7: You can load multiple protocols for your network configuration.

The protocols that are listed in the Protocols tab should match those that are selected in other computers on your network. For instance, if you are part of a Windows NT Server network, then the Protocols tab should list the same protocols as those listed in the server's comparable dialog box. If you are connected to more than one network, then the list should contain all of the protocols that are used on all your networks.

At times, your workstation may need additional protocols that are not specifically used by other computers on your network. A good example is when you need to communicate with a device (such as a printer) that uses a particular protocol, and other computers don't need to communicate with that device. In this case, add the appropriate protocols that you need.

As with other tabs in the Network dialog box, you can add protocols by clicking on the Add button. This displays the Select Network Protocol dialog box, as shown in Figure 12-8.

Six protocols are listed in the Select Network Protocol dialog box. You should highlight the protocol that you want to add and then click on the OK button. This adds the protocol to the Protocols tab of the Network dialog box. If you need to add other protocols, you can continue doing so in this manner.

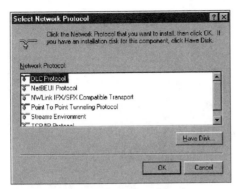

Figure 12-8: Windows NT supports a number of different protocols.

If you look at the Select Network Protocol dialog box, notice that it also has a Have Disk button. This is provided in case your network vendor provides a new protocol that is not natively supported by Windows NT. The probability of using this button is pretty slim in the protocol arena, however.

Adding services

Windows NT Workstation enables you to add services to your system in much the same way that you add other network components. To start, click on the Services tab on the Network dialog box. The dialog box then appears as shown in Figure 12-9.

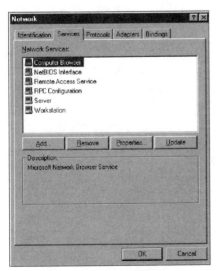

Figure 12-9: Windows NT services are used to provide network functionality.

In total, there are 13 different services that you can use with NT Workstation. If you want to add services to your workstation, click on the Add button. This displays the Select Network Service dialog box, as shown in Figure 12-10.

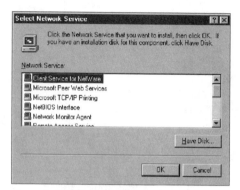

Figure 12-10: A wide range of network services can be installed in Windows NT.

To add a service, simply select it from the list of available services and then click on the OK button. The service name then appears in the Services tab of the Network dialog box.

Secret

You should only add the services you need. Adding additional services consumes resources on your system — resources that may be better used on other programs.

Microsoft provides a way for third-party developers to create network services that you can add to your system. Thus, you may run across a third-party program that needs to be installed as a service.

If this is the case, the installation instructions for the program may tell you to use the Have Disk button on the Select Network Service dialog box to add their special service. If this is the case, the new service then appears in the Services tab, the same as any other network service.

Configuring network components

When you first add a network component, you may need to change the configuration of the component itself, without affecting your other network components. In addition, you may need to change configurations as you make changes in the way that your network is laid out. The following sections detail how to change and configure your network components.

Changing adapter properties

To change the properties of an adapter that you have installed in your system, follow these steps:

STEPS

Changing adapter properties

Step 1. Open the Network dialog box, as described earlier in this chapter.

Step 2. Click on the Adapters tab. The dialog box now appears, as shown earlier in Figure 12-5.

Step 3. In the adapter list, at the top of the dialog box, select the adapter that you want to configure.

Step 4. Click on the Properties button. This displays a dialog box similar to that shown in Figure 12-11.

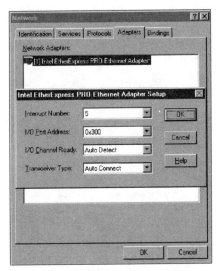

Figure 12-11: Different adapters possess different properties that you can change.

Step 5. Change the properties of the adapter, as desired.

Step 6. Click on the OK button to save your changes.

The appearance of the properties dialog box for your adapter is probably different from what is shown in Figure 12-11. This is because different adapters have different configuration options that you can set.

Changing protocol properties

You can also change the properties of the various protocols that are installed in your system. In fact, some protocols must be configured before they can work properly (most notably, TCP/IP). To configure a protocol, follow these steps:

STEPS

Changing protocol properties

Step 1.   Open the Network dialog box, as described earlier in this chapter.

Step 2.   Click on the Protocols tab. The dialog box now appears, as shown earlier in Figure 12-7.

Step 3.   In the protocol list, at the top of the dialog box, select the protocol that you want to configure.

Step 4.   Click on the Properties button. This displays a properties dialog box for the protocol.

Step 5.   Change the properties of the protocol, as desired.

Step 6.   Click on the OK button to save your changes.

The appearance of the dialog box that is used for the protocol properties can differ, depending on the protocol that is being configured. Some protocols may not even have configuration options, in which case a properties dialog box is not displayed.

As an example of how configuration should occur, however, Figure 12-12 shows an example of the properties dialog box for the TCP/IP protocol.

The TCP/IP protocol is perhaps the most complex protocol to configure, but it is not overly complex. The configuration options that are available for TCP/IP are just more diverse than those offered for other protocols. Regardless of the protocol, however, you simply need to make sure that the configuration matches or is complementary to the settings that you made in other workstations on your network.

Note

You learn more about configuring TCP/IP in Chapter 14.

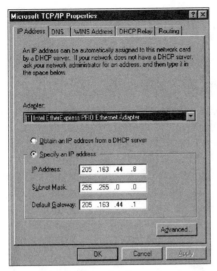

Figure 12-12: Properties for protocols can vary, based on the protocol that is being configured.

Changing service properties

You can also change the configuration of your installed services. This is not often required but is sometimes necessary to adjust how a service functions under Windows NT.

To change the properties of a service, follow these steps:

STEPS

Changing service properties

Step 1. Open the Network dialog box, as described earlier in this chapter.

Step 2. Click on the Services tab. The dialog box now appears, as shown earlier in Figure 12-9.

Step 3. In the Services list, select the service that you want to configure.

Step 4. Click on the Properties button. This displays a properties dialog box for the service.

Step 5. Change the properties of the service, as desired.

Step 6. Click on the OK button to save your changes.

As with other network components, the configuration options that are presented in the Properties dialog box may differ based on the service that you are configuring.

Adjusting bindings

Earlier in the chapter, you learned what bindings are; now you can learn how to change the bindings. Normally, Windows NT creates bindings that are all-inclusive. This means that every protocol you use is bound to every network adapter in your system. If you have multiple adapters, then you probably don't want every protocol bound to every adapter.

If you click on the Bindings tab of the Network dialog box, you can see which bindings Windows NT Workstation has established, as shown in Figure 12-13.

Figure 12-13: The Bindings tab displays information in a hierarchical tree.

The information in the Bindings tab is presented in a tree fashion. This simply means that you can select different network components (services, protocols, or adapters) from the drop-down list and then see the different bindings in the body of the dialog box. When you click on one of the plus signs to the left of a component name, then the bindings for that component are displayed.

Notice that, at the bottom of the dialog box, there are four buttons that control how the binding is treated by Windows NT Workstation. To change a binding, simply highlight it and then click on one of the four buttons:

- **Enable.** This is the default condition of a binding. If you previously disabled the binding, you can later click on this button to make the binding available again.

- **Disable.** Clicking on this button eliminates a binding.

- **Move Up.** Clicking on this button makes a particular binding a higher priority. (The priority of a binding is indicated by its position in the bindings list.)

- **Move Down.** Clicking on this button makes a particular binding a lower priority.

Tip

To improve your system's performance, disable the binding between the protocol and a component that you know never uses that protocol. This frees resources and makes your networking run slightly faster.

Identifying yourself

For your workstation to be visible and addressable on the network, you must identify it. This process is quite easy and only needs to be done once.

To change your identification information, follow these steps:

STEPS

Identifying your workstation

Step 1. Open the Network dialog box, as described earlier in this chapter. The Identification tab should be selected, as shown in Figure 12-4.

(continued)

STEPS *(continued)*

Identifying your workstation

Step 2. Click on the Change button. This displays the Identification Changes dialog box, as shown in Figure 12-14.

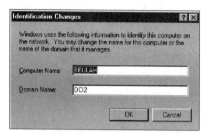

Figure 12-14: You can easily change the identification information for your workstation.

Step 3. In the Computer Name field, enter the name by which you want your workstation to be known to others on the network.

Step 4. In the Domain Name field, indicate the domain to which this workstation belongs. The domain name must be spelled correctly and exactly the same as is done in the other computers in the domain.

Step 5. Click on the OK button to save your changes.

When entering information in the Computer Name or Domain Name fields, you can enter up to 15 characters. The names you enter, however, cannot contain any of the characters that are listed in Table 12-1.

Table 12-1   Illegal characters for computer and domain names

Character	Name
!	Exclamation point
#	Pound sign
$	Dollar sign
%	Percent sign
&	Ampersand

Character	Name
'	Apostrophe
( )	Parentheses
–	Minus sign/dash
.	Period
@	At sign
^	Caret
_	Underscore
{ }	Braces
~	Tilde
	Space

Tip

If your workstation belongs to a well-established network, your company may already have some sort of identification system set up for computers on the network. Check with your network administrator to see if there are guidelines that you need to follow in naming your computer.

Searching for Computers

In Chapter 4, you learned how you can use the Windows NT Find tool to locate elusive files on your disk drives. That tool can also be used to help locate computers in your network.

The Find tool is most helpful in this type of search when you are part of a network that is comprised of multiple domains. For example, if you belong to a network that has 12 domains, each with an average of 40 computers, you could spend quite a while looking for an individual computer. Using the Find tool, you can locate the same computer in short order.

To use the Find tool to search for a computer, follow these steps:

STEPS

Finding a computer

Step 1. Choose the Find option from the Start button. This displays a submenu with two options.

(continued)

STEPS *(continued)*

Finding a computer

Step 2.   Choose the Computer option from the submenu. This displays the Find Computer dialog box, as shown in Figure 12-15.

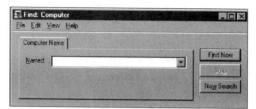

Figure 12-15: Windows NT allows you to search for computers that are on your network.

Step 3.   In the Named field, enter the name of the computer that you want to find. You must enter the whole name; there are no wildcards that you can use.

Step 4.   Click on the Find Now button.

Each domain in your network is quickly searched to locate the computer that you specified. If the computer is found, it is displayed in the bottom of the Find Computer dialog box (see Figure 12-16). If you want to change your search, click on the New Search button.

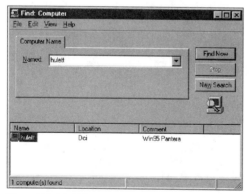

Figure 12-16: When located, computers are listed showing their name and location (domain).

Tip

You can redo a previous search by using the drop-down list that is built in to the Named field.

The information at the bottom of the Find Computer dialog box indicates the name of the computer that was found (which you already know, because you entered it to start the search) as well as the location of the computer. This location is the domain to which the computer belongs.

To access any computer that is listed, simply double-click on the computer name, and you can see a folder window that shows the resources available on that computer.

Summary

Today, it seems that for most places where two or more computers are located, they are often networked. Networks allow the easy sharing of information and thereby can help increase productivity. Understanding how networking is configured and managed in the Windows NT environment is helpful to making the most of your computing experience.

This chapter has covered the basics of networking, providing the information that you need to build a firm understanding of how Windows NT networks operate. In particular, you have learned the following items:

▶ Two network models define the relationship between computers on the network: the client/server model and the peer-to-peer model. Windows NT Workstation can take advantage of both models.

▶ When configuring your network, Windows NT enables you to work with adapters, protocols, and services. Each component enables you to communicate over the network, access resources, and make resources available to others.

▶ You can add and remove network components by using the various tabs in the Network dialog box.

▶ You may need to configure your network components before they can be used. Configuring is done by using the Properties button within the appropriate tab of the Network dialog box.

▶ Bindings define the relationship between network components. The bindings are used by Windows NT to determine how the components should be used with each other.

▶ The Find tool, which is typically used to locate misplaced files, can also be used to locate specific computers on complex networks.

Chapter 13

Controlling Communications

In This Chapter

To many people, using their computers to communicate with others is a natural extension of their daily work; it's just one more thing that they can do with their computers. To other people, connecting their computer to a phone line and actually communicating with another computer is a black art — one in which they don't want to participate. It seems that no matter what your background and experience are, the subject of data communications evokes either feelings of anticipation or fear and loathing.

This chapter introduces you to the communications capabilities of Windows NT Workstation. Here you learn the ins and outs of using your modem to communicate with others. In fact, the information in this chapter essentially lays the groundwork for information that is also presented in the following two chapters. When you understand the information in this chapter, hopefully you will have more anticipation and less fear and loathing.

In particular, this chapter teaches you the following items:

▶ How modems work to enable data communications over ordinary phone lines

▶ How Windows NT implements computer telephony

▶ How to set up and configure your modem correctly

▶ What you can accomplish through Dial-Up Networking

▶ How to configure your system as an RAS Server

Serial Communications: The Short Course

A good part of this book has been spent teaching you how to communicate with others over a network. In many ways, communicating with others over a phone line is very similar. Just as it helped to understand the technology and terminology behind networking, it also helps to understand the same in relation to data communications.

Unfortunately, data communications is one of those computer industry specialties that tends to sound very arcane and esoteric. In fact, entire books have been written about small parts of the data communications field.

Before you can fully understand how to effectively use Windows NT to communicate, you need to understand at least a small part about communications in general. The following sections introduce you to the basics of the topic.

Why we need modems

In your computer, information is transmitted from one part to another in a *parallel* fashion. This simply means that the bits making up the information that is being transmitted travel their own separate communications paths.

For instance, if a communications path exists between the motherboard in your computer and an adapter card, it is probably a 16-bit data path. This simply means that 16 bits of information can travel over the data path at the same time, one bit on each of 16 wires. This is parallel communication.

For the most part, data communication is handled in a *serial* manner. This is a different way of transmitting information, where each bit does not travel at the same time as the other bits. Instead, the bits are transmitted sequentially, one after the other, on a single wire. Data communications relies on serial communications.

The reason for this is your phone line. In most homes and businesses, your phone line consists of two wires, referred to as a pair or a twisted pair. This made it a natural for serial communications, simply because there are not enough wires in the physical connection to allow for parallel communication.

When you speak into the phone, the sound waves of your voice are converted into an analog format that is easily transmitted over the phone wires. The characteristics of this signal can vary, based on the pitch (frequency) and volume (amplitude) of your voice.

Any time that a signal directly varies according to external changes, the format of the signal is said to be *analog*. Computers, however, communicate with *digital* signals. Everything is represented by a series of 0s and 1s, which correspond to information bits.

This basic and fundamental difference in the way that information is transmitted represented a problem. It meant that some device had to serve as the intermediary, to translate from one format to another.

This is where the modem comes in. The term *modem* is short for modulate-demodulate. A modem is used to convert digital information to an analog format. The process of conversion is called *modulation*.

Understanding ISDN

In some areas of the country (typically in larger cities), Integrated Services Digital Networks (ISDNs) are available. These specialized networks are slowly replacing the traditional analog phone lines, and they should be available in most places by the first part of the next century.

As the name implies, ISDN is digital in nature. It can be used to simultaneously carry voice, data, and image transmissions.

Because ISDN is digital, you don't need a traditional modem to use it. This makes sense, as the purpose of the modem was to convert between digital and analog signals. Unfortunately, you cannot plug your computer directly into an ISDN line.

Instead, you need a specialized converter between your computer and the ISDN line. Sometimes referred to as an ISDN modem, this device is technically known as an ISDN Terminal Adapter. Regardless of the name, the device simply converts between the simple digital signal used in your computer and the more complex messaging signal used on the ISDN line.

At this point, ISDN modems are still rather expensive, but their prices are coming down. Over the next couple of years, the price should drop to the point where they are price-competitive with traditional modems.

Conversely, at the opposite end of a modem connection, the modem changes information from analog format to digital, which the receiving computer can understand. This reverse transformation is known as *demodulation*.

Although the basic purpose of a modem is to modulate and demodulate the digital signal from your computer, not all modems are the same. The biggest difference between modems is the speed at which they can transmit data.

When modems first became available for PCs, they transmitted information at a rate of 300 bps (bits per second). This meant that you could send or receive about 30 characters per second, based on using 10 bits to represent a single character.

Although this may seem fast, it is not. The reason is that we typically send huge amounts of information over the phone lines. For instance, if you send a graphic file that contains 50K of data, it can take just under 30 minutes to transfer the file at 300 bps.

Over the years, modem speeds have improved dramatically. The fastest modems on the market today can transmit information at 28,800 bps, or roughly 96 times the speed of the early modems. This means that the same 50K file can now be transferred in just under 20 seconds!

Modulation standards

For two modems to communicate reliably, they must share the same communication characteristics. For instance, both modems must be able to communicate at the same speed. Modem speed is not the only attribute that must be the same, however. Collectively, the shared attributes are referred to as *modulation standards.*

When modems for the PC were first available, they conformed to the Bell 103 modulation standard. This standard uses a modulation technique known as frequency shift keying (FSK), which allowed 300 bps to be transmitted over the connection. In later years, there were a number of different standards introduced, each enabling faster communication.

The latest modulation standard is known as V.34, which enables transmission speeds of 28,800 bps. Table 13-1 lists the various modulation standards that have been introduced over the years.

Table 13-1   Modulation standards used in modems

Standard	Comments
Bell 103	300-bps transmission using frequency shift keying (FSK)
Bell 212A	1200-bps transmissions using differential phase shift keying (DPSK)
V.22bis	2400-bps transmissions using quadrature amplitude modulation (QAM)
V.32	9600-bps transmissions using trellis-coded quadrature amplitude modulation (TCQAM)
V.32bis	14,400-bps transmissions, also using TCQAM
V.34	28,800-bps transmissions

Automatic error control

Communicating with a modem is of little use unless the communication can occur with few, if any, errors. Unfortunately, the analog telephone system is subject to all sorts of noise and disruption during a normal connection. (You may have noticed static, echo, or fadeouts as you were talking with someone on the phone.)

Although your phone line does not have to be perfectly clear to establish a data communications link, most modems include some sort of error-control mechanism to compensate for those times when conditions are below average.

The error control that is built into modems consists of two basic parts: error detection and error correction. Over the years, these two parts have been codified into a set of standards that define the protocols to be used. For error control to be effective, the modems at both ends of a connection must understand and use the same error-control protocol.

There are several different error-control protocols in use:

- **LAPM.** This is an acronym meaning link-access procedure mechanism for modems, a standard developed by Hayes Microcomputer Products.

- **MNP.** This is an acronym meaning Microcom networking protocol, a series of standards developed by Microcom, Inc. There are four classes (1 through 4) of MNP error-control protocols, none of which are compatible with LAPM.

- **V.42.** This is an error-control standard that incorporates both LAPM and MNP. The standard first attempts to use LAPM and then falls back to MNP standards.

Data compression

Many of today's modern modems provide not only error control but also data compression. This means that mathematical formulas are applied to the data, as it is sent, to remove redundancy or to otherwise code the data. The modem at the other end applies the same formulas, in reverse, to restore the original data.

Data compression means that you can effectively transmit more data in less time. The amount of compression that is attainable depends on the characteristics of the data that you are transmitting, but it is not unusual to compress data as much as 50 percent. This means that your effective transfer rates are increased by 100 percent, because you can transmit twice the data in the same amount of time.

The first modem data compression algorithms were popularized by Hayes Microcomputer Products, with a competing algorithm being developed by Microcom and released as MNP Class 5. The V.42bis standard supersedes both of these earlier standards, however. This standard is an extension of the V.42 error-correction protocol.

Understanding Telephony

The use of telephones, together with computers, has spawned a new branch of technology known as *telephony.* The term has been very broad in its application, essentially covering anything that even remotely involves the use of telephone lines and your computer.

For instance, connecting computers with modems, sending a fax with your computer, dialing the phone with your computer, and answering the phone line with a computerized phone switch — all of these fall into the area of telephony.

With so many standards and variables in modem technology (and the burgeoning field of telephony), you may be starting to agree with those people that believe data communications is a black art. Apparently the people at Microsoft also thought that data communications was too complicated, so they came up with a new standard known as *TAPI*.

TAPI is an acronym for Telephony Application Programmers Interface. It is an interface that allows programmers to develop software that takes advantage of a consistent, device-independent, and stable communications environment.

Technically, TAPI consists of two interfaces:

- **Applications programming interface (API).** This interface is used by programmers as a consistent way to access communications functions.

- **Service provider interface (SPI).** This interface is used to establish a connection with a specific telephone network. This can be as simple as a single phone line or as broad as a dedicated PBX or phone switch.

In many respects, the TAPI model is very similar to the one that is implemented by printer drivers. Programs send information to the printer driver, which then writes information to the print spooler on the back end.

In the case of TAPI, the communications program is writing to a TAPI interface, just as programs can write to a printer driver. TAPI has been integrated into the Windows NT operating system, so it is available at all times.

For the user, TAPI means you can take advantage of applications that intelligently use the modems on your system. The biggest benefit of TAPI is the ability for multiple programs to share a common modem line. Although two programs cannot place or receive calls at the same time, sharing is much more friendly than it was during pre-TAPI days.

As an example, if you use software that also understands TAPI, then you can run a program that awaits an incoming call (such as RAS, described later in this chapter) and use the same modem to send an outgoing fax. Before the days of TAPI, you would have been required to end the RAS program before the modem line would be freed for use by another program.

Another big advantage is a logical outgrowth of the printer driver analogy. When you use a Windows NT program, you no longer have to worry about your printer. A few readers may remember the days of DOS when you needed to provide printer drivers or specialized printer configurations for every program that was installed on your system.

Windows, by centralizing the printing system, did away with the hodgepodge of drivers that was previously necessary. TAPI has enabled this same approach in modem configuration.

Because TAPI is integrated into the Windows NT operating system, and all of the communications accessories included with Windows NT take advantage of TAPI, you now only need to set up your modem once.

Just like setting up your printer once, you now define your modem and configure it a single time. The programs that take advantage of TAPI then access that information to make their use of the modem easier and more consistent.

Setting Up Your Modem

To use any of the communications utilities that are included with Windows NT, you must define and configure your modem. This is an easy process that is done, in most instances, by simply selecting your modem from a list, just as you do when setting up your printer.

To add a modem to your system, open the Control Panel and then double-click on the Modems icon. The dialog box that you see depends on whether you have defined any other modems for your system. If you have no other modems defined, then a Wizard is started that allows you to step through the process of adding a modem.

Adding a modem

The first screen of the Install New Modem Wizard is shown in Figure 13-1. From this screen, you can indicate how you want the Wizard to locate your modem.

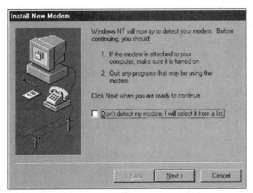

Figure 13-1: A Wizard leads you through adding a modem to your system.

By default, the Wizard attempts to automatically determine the type of modem that is in your system. If you select the check box, Windows NT allows you to select your modem from a list.

If you allow the Wizard to search for your modem, it searches all of your serial ports to see if any devices are attached. If it detects a device, the Wizard sends modem commands to the serial port. If the device responds, then the Wizard can determine what type of modem is connected to the port.

Secret

The automatic detection feature does not work well on specialty modems, such as those that you connect to a parallel port. Also, it is not good at detecting multiple modems in your system; the Wizard stops at the first modem that it finds. If you have modems that fall into these categories, you should specify the modem manually instead of allowing the Wizard to detect it.

When you have made your decision on this step of the Wizard, click on the Next button to continue. The steps that you follow from this point depend on how you responded to the first step.

Automatic modem detection

If you specified that the Wizard should search, then it begins looking for a modem that is connected to your system. During the checking process, you are informed of the progress of the search. If the Wizard locates a modem, you are shown a dialog box similar to what is shown in Figure 13-2.

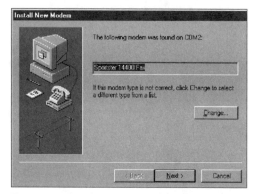

Figure 13-2: The Wizard informs you of the modem that it located in your system.

Note

If the Wizard cannot find a modem after examining your system, it automatically kicks you into manual mode. Skip to the next section to learn how to add your modem manually.

If the modem type is incorrect, you can click on the Change button. This allows you to select the modem manually, as described in the next section. If the modem shown is correct, clicking on the Next button installs the modem information. Installation then proceeds as discussed later in "Finishing the installation."

Manually adding the modem

If you specified that you wanted to select a modem manually, then the Wizard displays the dialog box that is shown in Figure 13-3.

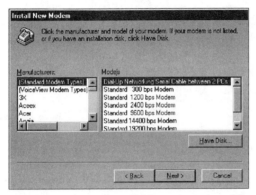

Figure 13-3: You can specify the make and model of the modem in your system.

This dialog box is similar to ones that you have used in adding other devices to your system. From the list of manufacturers, select the maker of your modem. Then, in the list of models, choose the model of modem that you have. Windows NT literally supplies hundreds of different makes and models.

If your modem is new, it may not be listed in the Wizard. In this case, look through the materials that are provided with your modem; a Windows NT modem driver was probably provided. If not, click on the Cancel button (to exit the Wizard) and contact the vendor for the proper drivers.

Without the drivers, Windows NT cannot take advantage of your modem. If you are able to get a set of device drivers from your modem vendor, clicking on the Have Disk button allows you to install the new drivers.

When you are ready to proceed, click on the <u>N</u>ext button. This takes you to the next installation step, as shown in Figure 13-4.

Figure 13-4: Windows NT needs to know where your modem is connected.

At this dialog box, you can pick how the modem is connected to your system. In the list of available ports, click on the port to which the modem is connected. This activates the <u>N</u>ext button, which you should then select.

Finishing the installation

The final steps in installing a modem involve specifying where your modem is located. At this time, refer to the dialog box that is shown in Figure 13-5.

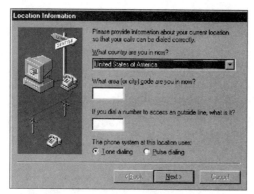

Figure 13-5: As part of the modem setup, you can specify location information.

As part of the TAPI enhancements, Windows NT requires that you specify a location of your system. This information is then used so that the drivers can make intelligent decisions about how a phone call should be dialed. (Later in this chapter, you learn how you can specify multiple locations for your system.)

This dialog box requires you to make four distinct settings:

- **Country.** First, you need to specify the country in which you are located. The default is the United States of America, although you can select a couple hundred other countries if you use the drop-down list.

- **Area or city code.** Second, you must indicate the area code (or city code) in which you are located. As an example, if your system is located in Denver, then you would enter 303 as the area code.

- **Access number.** Next, indicate if you need to dial a special number to access an outside line. For instance, you may need to dial 9 (or some other code) to get an outside line at your company.

- **Dialing type.** Finally, you need to specify if your phone line uses pulse or tone dialing. You can figure out your dialing type by listening to the sounds that your phone makes as you dial a number.

  If you hear a single beep for each number that you dial, then you use tones. If you hear a series of clicks for each number that you dial, then you use pulses.

When you have completed entering your information, click on the Next button. You then see the dialog box that is shown in Figure 13-6.

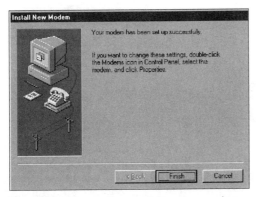

Figure 13-6: You are done installing your modem.

At this point, your modem installation is complete, and you can click on the Finish button.

Configuring your modem

After you have installed your modem, you can modify the modem properties at any time. To do this, simply open the Control Panel and then double-click on the Modems icon. This displays the Modems Properties dialog box, as shown in Figure 13-7.

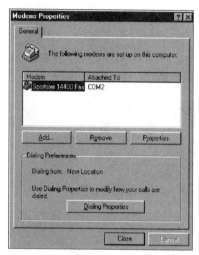

Figure 13-7: The Modems Properties dialog box is used to control your modem definitions.

Note

Note that Microsoft decided to use a dialog box to display your modems, rather than a window as they did with the printers. After all, both the Modems Properties dialog box and the Printers folder allow you to do essentially the same thing.

On your system, the Modems Properties dialog box may show more than one modem installed. If this is the case, select the modem that you want to configure. When you click on the Properties button, you see the dialog box that is shown in Figure 13-8.

As with many other devices, modems come in all sizes, shapes, and capabilities. Because of this variation, the appearance of the Properties dialog box for your modem may differ from what is shown here. At a minimum, however, you should have both a General tab and a Connection tab.

Figure 13-8: Individual modems can be easily configured in Windows NT.

The General tab

The General tab, which is displayed when you first open the Properties dialog box for a modem, allows you to specify only a couple of different options for the modem. In the Port drop-down list, at the top of the tab, you can indicate the port to which this modem is connected.

You first specified this when you added the modem to your system. The only time that you should need to change this option is if you physically moved your modem to a different communications port.

In the middle of the tab, you can specify the volume of your modem's speaker. Not all modems have speakers, but speakers are quite common with external models. If you are able to adjust the volume, you can use the slider control to set it to any of four levels, including off.

At the bottom of the tab is another drop-down list. This control allows you to specify the speed at which your modem connection should be established. This speed is specified in bps (bits per second), as discussed earlier in the chapter.

Secret

With most modern modems, you can specify a modem speed that is higher than what the modem is rated for. (Remember — this is a maximum speed, not an absolute speed.) For instance, if you are using a 14,400-bps modem, you can set the speed to 19,200 or 38,400 bps. This enables Windows NT to send information to the modem as quickly as possible. You should only set a slower speed or lock in a specific speed, if you have tested your modem and know it does not work with the higher speed.

The Connection tab

The Connection tab is where you specify the default communications parameters for your modem. Figure 13-9 shows an example of the Properties dialog box with the Connection tab selected.

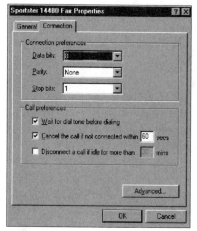

Figure 13-9: The Connection tab is used to modify default communications parameters.

In the Connection preferences area at the top of the dialog box, you can set three different elements of your communication protocol:

■ **Data Bits.** Information that is sent over a serial data connection is sent in packets, which contain a certain number of data bits. These data bits actually represent the information that is being transmitted.

■ **Parity.** Some services that you connect with require a parity bit in the information packets. This bit provides rudimentary error detection.

Possible settings are Even (parity is based on whether there are an even number of data bits set to 1), Odd (opposite of Even), None (parity is not used), Mark (parity bit is always set to 1), or Space (parity bit is always set to 0).

■ **Stop Bits.** An information packet also contains stop bits that mark the end of the packet. You can select from 1, 1.5, or 2 stop bits.

When setting the connection preferences, you should use the requirements of the service that you connect with as a guideline. Also, remember that these are default values, meaning they can be overridden the communication software that you're using.

The next area of the dialog box allows you to indicate, in general, how a call should be handled. You can indicate whether the modem should wait for a dial tone before dialing (typically a good idea) and how long the modem should wait (in seconds) before giving up on making a connection.

Also, you can select the option at the bottom of the tab that disconnects a call after a certain period of time. If you do quite a bit of unattended modem work, you may want to select this option and choose an inactivity time in minutes.

Secret

If you are using the modem definition to establish a connection with a network, then setting the disconnect option may do no good. Network protocols typically send information across a connection every few seconds, whether or not you are actively communicating. These polling values can fool Windows NT into thinking that a connection is active, when in fact it isn't.

Advanced connection settings

At the bottom of the Connection tab there is a button labeled Advanced. If you click on this, the dialog box that is shown in Figure 13-10 appears.

Figure 13-10: The Advanced Connection Settings dialog box controls how Windows NT controls the modem behind the scenes.

Like so many other dialog boxes in Windows NT, the exact controls that appear (or are available) in your version of the Advanced Connection Settings dialog box may vary, based on the capabilities of your modem. In general, however, you can use the settings on this dialog box to control how the modem controls a communication session.

At the upper-left corner of the dialog box, you can indicate if you want to use error-control protocols in your connection. If you select this dialog box, there are three check boxes in the same area that become active:

- **Required to connect.** If you want to make sure that error control is in place in your connection, then you should select this check box. If you then try to connect with a modem that does not support error correction that is compatible with yours, Windows NT breaks the connection.

- **Compress data.** From the discussion earlier in the chapter, you may remember that data compression is an extension of the error-correction protocols that are used in modems. If you select this check box, then data compression is used, as long as it is supported by the modem at the other end of the connection.

- **Use cellular protocol.** Some modems are designed to work from cellular phones. These portable modems have additional error-correction capabilities built into them. These capabilities are required because, as you travel with a cellular connection, you can automatically be handed from one phone cell to another by the phone company.

  When you are talking on a cellular phone, this may sound like a momentary dropout or a bit of static. When computers are talking, such events can be fatal to the connection. If you are using a cellular modem, you definitely should choose this option.

Secret

Even though cellular protocols are helpful when you are on the move, they can be detrimental if you are staying in one place. If you aren't going to move during the communication session, you may want to disable the cellular feature. Without the option selected, you can get connected faster and achieve higher data speeds.

In the upper-right corner of the dialog box, you can indicate how you want to handle the flow of data between your computer and your modem. Flow control is used to govern the rate at which data are transferred.

There are three possible ways that you can set this area:

- If you turn off the Use Flow Control check box, flow control is not done, and data are sent or received without regulation. If you select this check box, then you can further specify which type of flow control you want to use.

- Hardware (RTS/CTS) is the most common choice. If possible, you should select hardware flow control, as it is the most efficient and reliable. Most modern modems, whether they are internal or external, can use hardware flow control.

- Software (XON/XOFF) works best when you are connecting your computer to dumb text-based systems by modem, typically at lower speeds.

In the middle of the dialog box is the Modulation Type drop-down list. Here you indicate how you want the modem to communicate when working at 300- and 1200-bps connections. This is typically not an issue; most modem connections are handled at rates of 9600 bps or greater.

Next you see a field called Extra Settings. This field is used to send special initialization strings to the modem after the initialization information from Windows NT has been sent. Normally this isn't necessary, but if it is, you should refer to the manual that was provided with your modem. It describes the various initialization commands that are understood by your modem.

Finally, there is a check box in the bottom-left corner labeled Record a Log File. If this check box is selected, Windows NT maintains a record of all modem commands and responses.

This is helpful if you are trying to troubleshoot a modem. The log file (MODEMLOG.TXT) is stored in your Windows NT system directory. When you are done troubleshooting your modem, don't forget to turn the log file off, as it can quickly become very large.

Setting dialing properties

In Windows NT jargon, *dialing properties* are the attributes that control how a phone call is made with a modem. These properties include location, prefixes, and calling card information.

You set some of this information when you installed your first modem. Windows NT allows you to continue working with dialing properties, however, so that they reflect your actual use of the modem.

Dialing preferences affect all of your modems. To modify dialing preferences, start at the Modems Properties dialog box, as shown earlier in Figure 13-7. At the bottom of the dialog box is a button labeled Dialing Properties. When you click on this button, the Dialing Properties dialog box is displayed, as shown in Figure 13-11.

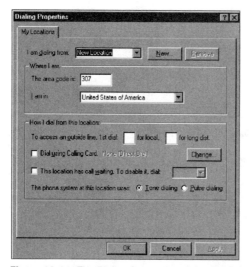

Figure 13-11: The Dialing Properties dialog box allows you to specify how your outgoing calls should be placed.

The Dialing Properties dialog box is divided into two general areas, but there are three items in relation to this dialog box that need to be explained. Each of the following sections addresses these areas.

Dialing locations

At the top of the Dialing Properties dialog box, you can specify where you make calls from with this computer. These locations are nothing but saved configurations that you can select in the drop-down list at the top of the dialog box.

In Figure 13-11, the name of the location is New Location. This location was saved when you first installed your modem. You may want to define different dialing locations, however, if either of the following conditions are met:

- You move your computer to different locations, as is often the case with a portable computer.

- You use your computer under different dialing conditions. For instance, you make business and personal calls from the same computer, and you need different dialing parameters for each type of call.

To add a new location, simply click on the New button to the right of the location drop-down list. You are asked what you want the location called, after which the name is added to the location list.

The first item that you need to specify for any location profile is where you are calling from. You do this by entering both the area code (or city code) and country of origin in the appropriate fields. You can then modify the other dialing properties, as discussed in the next two sections.

If you have defined multiple locations for your system, at some time you may want to remove a location profile. This is done by choosing the location name in the drop-down list and then clicking on the Remove button.

You are asked to confirm your action, after which the profile is erased. The one restriction to this, however, is that you cannot remove the New Location profile.

Secret

Even though you cannot remove the New Location profile (which can be viewed as a default profile for your system), you can rename it. Simply change the name in the drop-down list, and then close the Dialing Properties dialog box. The name retains your change, as evidenced when you next enter the Dialing Properties dialog box.

How to dial

At the bottom of the Dialing Properties dialog box, you can specify how the call, made using this dialing location profile, is to be made. The first two fields are used to indicate prefix numbers that you may need to dial to get an outside line for both local and long distance calls.

You may find that you frequently need to use a prefix number to gain access to lines. For instance, in many offices, you may need to dial 9 to get an outside dial tone. If you are using your computer on the road, many hotels require you to dial 9 for a local call and 8 to access a long-distance line.

Secret

Computers can dial the phone very quickly. On some phone systems, this is acceptable, whereas on others it can cause problems. One potential problem area is when gaining an outside line. Most PBX (private branch exchange) systems used in businesses and hotels have a little delay between when you dial the access number and when you get the outside line. For this reason, it is a good idea to include a comma in the number that you dial for the outside lines. For example, the prefix number would be 9, rather than just 9. The comma forces your modem to pause two seconds. This pause should accommodate any delays introduced by the office or hotel switching system.

The next check box on the Dialing Properties dialog box allows you to specify if a calling card should be used. Windows NT does a great job of supporting calling cards, as you discover in the following section. Suffice it to say, for right now, that if you want calls dialed using this location profile to use the calling card information, you should select the check box.

The next check box allows you to specify what Windows NT should do about call waiting. We all know about call waiting — the feature that allows you to receive multiple calls on a single line. Usually it is a click or a tone on the line that signals that you have the other call.

This click or tone can play havoc with a data communications call. In fact, 99 percent of the time, it disconnects your call. If you select the check box in the call waiting area, you can indicate the proper numbers to use to disable it.

Windows NT includes three different disable codes in the drop-down list: *70, 70#, and 1170. You can also define custom sequences (up to five characters) that disable call waiting; simply type them into the field. The exact sequence that is used to disable call waiting can vary among phone systems.

Check with the local phone company for the location that you are defining to determine the proper sequence to use. (Many phone companies provide this information in the front of the local phone book.)

Finally, at the bottom of the dialog box, you need to specify if your phone line uses tone or pulse dialing. As discussed earlier in this chapter, you can figure out your dialing type by listening to the sounds that your phone makes as you dial a number.

Listen to the phone as you push a button. If you hear a single beep when you push a button, then your phone uses tones. On some phones, however, you may hear a series of clicks whenever you push a button.

For example, if you push the number 4, you would hear four clicks. Likewise, pushing 7 would generate seven clicks. This indicates that you are using pulse dialing.

If your phone system uses pulse dialing, it cannot understand the tones that your modem can generate. Conversely, if it uses tone dialing, it can typically understand both tones and pulses. If your phone system uses tones, you should use tones, however. Doing so can save you quite a bit of time in dialing a number.

Using calling cards

It seems that every time you change your long distance carrier, one of the benefits offered you is a calling card for your account. These cards have the same size, look, and feel of credit cards, but you use them to access the phone system when you are on the road. Windows NT supports the use of calling cards when placing a modem call.

In the Dialing Properties dialog box, you signify that you want to use a calling card in your call by clicking on the Dial Using Calling Card check box in the middle of the dialog box. Selecting this check box enables the rest of the line on which the check box appears.

To specify a particular calling card to use, simply click on the Change button. This displays the Change Calling Card dialog box, as shown in Figure 13-12.

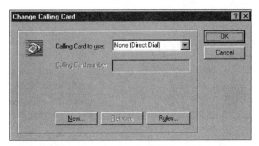

Figure 13-12: The Change Calling Card dialog box is used to define how your calling card is used.

At the top of the dialog box, you can specify which calling card you want to use. Windows NT includes definitions for 22 of the most common calling cards:

- AT&T Direct Dial via 10ATT1

- AT&T via 10ATT0

- AT&T via 1-800-321-0280

- British Telecom (UK)

- Calling Card via 0

- Carte France Telecom

- CLEAR Communications (New Zealand)

- Global Card (Taiwan to USA)

- MCI Direct Dial via 102221

- MCI via 102220

- MCI via 1-800-674-0700

- MCI via 1-800-674-7000

- MCI via 1-800-888-8000

- Mercury (UK)

- Optus (Australia) via 008551812

- Optus (Australia) via 1812

- Telecom Australia via 1818 (fax)

- Telecom Australia via 1818 (voice)

- Telecom New Zealand

- US Sprint Direct Dial via 103331

- US Sprint via 103330

- US Sprint via 1-800-877-8000

To use one of these predefined cards, simply select the card, enter the calling card number in the Calling Card Number field, and then click on OK. There may be a specialized calling card that you want to use, however. After all, it seems like there are new phone companies springing up all the time.

If you want to define your own calling card, click on the New button at the bottom of the dialog box. You are asked for the name of the calling card, which you should provide.

Windows NT then notifies you that you must define the rules by which this card is used. When you click on the OK button to clear the notification, the Dialing Rules dialog box appears, as shown in Figure 13-13.

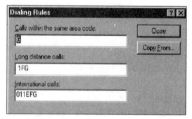

Figure 13-13: The Dialing Rules dialog box is used to specify how a calling card is used.

The information that is currently contained in the dialog box is not important; it reflects the rules that are used for the calling card that you had selected when you clicked on the New button.

The Dialing Rules dialog box contains three fields, each of which can contain a dialing rule:

- **Local.** The first field is used to define the code that is used to dial calls in the same area code or city code.

- **Long distance.** The second field is for domestic long-distance calls.

- **International.** The third field is for international long-distance calls.

You use these fields by entering in each a series of characters that define how the calling card is used. Table 13-2 shows the characters that you can include in a dialing rule, along with what they mean.

Table 13-2   Characters used in calling-card dialing rules

Character	Meaning
!	Generate hook-flash
$	Wait for calling card prompt tone
*,#	Disable digits (tone dialing only)
,	Pause for two seconds
?	Pause for user input during dialing sequence
@	Wait for ringback followed by five seconds of silence
0-9	The digit is dialed
E	Country code
F	Area or city code
G	Local number
H	Calling card number
P	Switch to pulse dialing
T	Switch to tone dialing
W	Wait for second dial tone

Dialing rules are quite flexible. Indeed, they need to be, because every phone company has its own sequence that you need to follow. As an example, one of the rules that are defined for dialing long-distance calls via MCI is 102220FG$TH. (This rule is saved in the predefined *MCI via 102220* calling card.)

When encountering this rule, Windows NT initiates the following dialing steps:

1. Dial 102220.

2. Dial the area or city code.

3. Dial the phone number.

4. Wait for the calling card prompt tone.

5. Switch to tone dialing (in case pulse dialing was used so far).

6. Dial the calling card number.

When you are done defining your dialing rules, click on the Close button to save the rules and close the Dialing Rules dialog box. You can then click on the OK button to close the Change Calling Card dialog box. This returns you to the Dialing Properties dialog box, where you can see your calling card of choice listed on the calling card line.

Using Dial-Up Networking

In previous versions of Windows NT, the operating system included a feature called *RAS,* or Remote Access Server. In this version of NT Workstation, RAS has two facets: a client and a server.

The client portion of the program is known as *Dial-Up Networking* (DUN), whereas the server portion is still known as RAS. DUN is described in this section, while RAS is described later in this chapter.

Dial-Up Networking is a client program that allows you to connect to a remote system (which must be running RAS or its equivalent) and then function as if you were physically connected to that system's network. Thus, if you are at a remote location or out on the road, you can use your modem to connect to the system back at the office and conduct your regular network business.

You should not confuse Dial-Up Networking with general-purpose communications software. DUN is simply a client program that enables you to establish a network connection with a remote system.

The only requirement is that both your system and the remote server must be running one of the following connection protocols:

- Point-to-point protocol (PPP)
- Serial line Internet protocol (SLIP)
- Windows NT RAS
- Windows for Workgroups RAS
- Novell NetWare Connect

One of the big uses of Dial-Up Networking is to connect to the Internet using a dial-up account. Using Dial-Up Networking to specifically connect to the Internet is outside the focus of this book, although you may find it helpful to understand how DUN functions.

The same connection procedures apply whether you are connecting to your office's network or to the network that is established by an Internet service provider. (How you can use the various Window NT Internet tools is covered in Chapter 14.)

Setting up Dial-Up Networking

The easiest way to start Dial-Up Networking is to double-click on the My Computer icon on your desktop and then double-click on the Dial-Up Networking icon. If this is the first time that you have used Dial-Up Networking, you are informed that DUN is currently uninstalled; you are also asked if you want to install it. To continue, click on the Install button on the dialog box.

At this point, you are prompted for the location from which Dial-Up Networking can be installed. The location you enter should be the install directory on your Windows NT Workstation CD-ROM. When the files are finished being copied, you are shown the dialog box in Figure 13-14.

Figure 13-14: Because Dial-Up Networking uses modems, you need to specify which modem to use.

Here you need to pick a modem or other device to use for your dial-up connection. You can use the drop-down list to select a device you already have installed, or you can click on one of the Install buttons to add another device. (You learned how to install modems earlier in this chapter.)

When you have selected a device, click on the OK button to continue. This displays the Remote Access Setup dialog box, as shown in Figure 13-15.

Figure 13-15: You can specify multiple devices to use for Dial-Up Networking.

At the Remote Access Setup dialog box, you can specify additional devices to be used for DUN. You do this by using the Add button at the bottom of the dialog box. When you are done, click on the Continue button in the upper-right corner.

This causes the setup program to finish installing the network components that are necessary for Dial-Up Networking. When done, you are prompted to restart your system. When you click on the Restart button, your Windows NT session is ended and your system is restarted.

Even though your system has restarted, you are still not quite done setting up Dial-Up Networking. To finish, open the My Computer window again and then double-click on the Dial-Up Networking icon.

This displays a dialog box indicating that your phone book is empty and prompting you to press OK to add an entry. When you click on OK, a Wizard is started that helps you set up your first phone book entry, as shown in Figure 13-16.

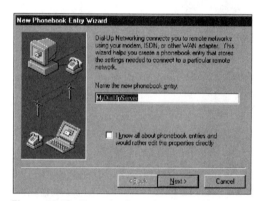

Figure 13-16: Phone book entries are used to define who you can call using Dial-Up Networking.

In this first dialog box, enter the name to use for this connection. This can be a descriptive name, such as the name of the company or server you plan to contact with the connection.

Then click on the Next button to continue. This displays the Server dialog box, shown in Figure 13-17.

This dialog box provides three check boxes that are used to specify the type of connection you are establishing. These check boxes provide general guidance to the Dial-Up Networking service, so it knows what to expect when establishing the connection. You can click as many of the check boxes as apply to your connection.

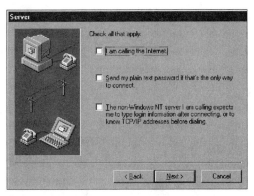

Figure 13-17: You need to indicate what type of connection you are making with this phone book entry.

Note

As you can tell from Figure 13-17, establishing a Dial-Up Networking connection presupposes that you know exactly what type of connection you are establishing. In most cases, it is helpful to talk to the network administrator of the network to which you are connecting.

For instance, if you are creating a phone book entry for your home office, then you should talk with the network administrator responsible for the server to which you are connecting. Likewise, if you are connecting to an Internet provider, you should talk with the support personnel at that company. Either way, the individual that you speak with should be able to provide guidance on what his or her RAS server expects when connecting with a Windows NT system.

When you are done making your selections, click on the Next button to continue. This displays the Phone Number dialog box, as shown in Figure 13-18.

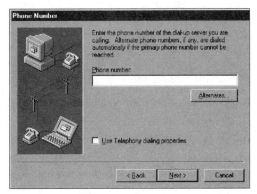

Figure 13-18: To make a call, you must supply a phone number.

Here you can enter the area code and phone number of the server that you are calling. You can also click on the check box at the bottom of the dialog box. This displays the information in the dialog box in accordance with the telephony features that you learned about earlier in this chapter.

When you click on the Next button, you see a dialog box indicating that you are done defining your phone book entry. When you click on the Finish button, your information is saved to disk, and you can see the Dial-Up Networking dialog box, as shown in Figure 13-19.

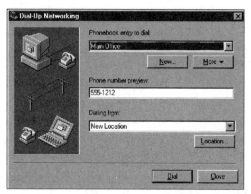

Figure 13-19: The Dial-Up Networking dialog box is where you specify who you want to call.

The Dial-Up Networking interface

Under Windows NT Workstation 4.0, Dial-Up Networking functions by defining phone book entries, which are then used to define how a call and connection should be made. In the previous section, you created your first phone book entry, and in Figure 13-19 you saw the Dial-Up Networking dialog box. This is the same dialog box that you should see from now on whenever you start Dial-Up Networking.

The Dial-Up Networking dialog box is fairly easy to use, but its interface is slightly different than other Windows NT dialog boxes. At the top of the dialog box, in the drop-down list, you can specify which phone book entry you want dialed.

Selecting a different entry here changes the information in the phone number field in the middle of the dialog box. Finally, at the bottom of the dialog box, you can specify where you are calling from. These are the same locations that you defined when setting up your modem, as described earlier in this chapter.

Dial-Up Networking preferences

If you click on the <u>M</u>ore button, Dial-Up Networking displays quite a few options that you can use. Many of these options deal with managing the selected phone book entry and are described elsewhere in the surrounding sections. At the bottom of the menu, however, are two selections that allow you to configure Dial-Up Networking according to your preferences. (Both choices, User Pre<u>f</u>erences and Lo<u>g</u>on Preferences, display essentially the same dialog box.)

If you choose the User Preferences option, the User Preferences dialog box is displayed, as shown in Figure 13-20.

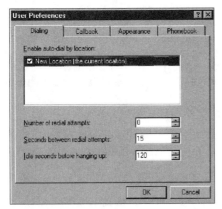

Figure 13-20: You can set many preferences for how you want Dial-Up Networking to function.

Four tabs available are in the User Preferences dialog box. You can use the controls on these tabs to specify exactly how you want Dial-Up Networking to function. The purposes of the different tabs are as follows:

- **Dialing.** These options are used to control how dialing is done by DUN. At the top of the tab, you can specify if you want a DUN connection auto-matically associated with a modem location.

  If you select the check box next to a location, then every time that the phone number of the phone book entry is referenced, it is dialed using the selected location. At the bottom of the tab, you can specify how you want automatic redialing handled.

- **Callback.** These options control automatic callback by the server that you are connecting with. Many servers support or require callback; this means that, before a permanent communications connection is estab-lished, the server calls you back at a location it already knows. One of the biggest reasons for callback is to increase the security of any dial-in service that is maintained by the server.

- **Appearance.** These options control what DUN does while it is initiating a call, while the connection is being established, and immediately after the connection is completed.

- **Phonebook.** These options control which phone book is used by DUN. You can use either the system phone book, your personal phone book, or an alternate phone book. The system and personal phone books are stored automatically in the system file directory of Windows NT, whereas an alternate phone book can be accessed in a different directory.

When you are done configuring the user preferences, click on the OK button. This returns you to the Dial-Up Networking dialog box.

Creating a new phone book entry

To create a new phone book entry, just click on the New button in the Dial-Up Networking dialog box. This displays the same Wizard that you used earlier in the chapter to define your first phone book entry. When you are finished defining the phone book entry, it appears in the drop-down list in the Dial-Up Networking dialog box, and you can use it to establish a connection.

Configuring a phone book entry

You did not need to provide many specifications when you defined your phone book entry. Windows NT allows you to specify many other properties, however, if you choose the Edit Entry and Modem Properties option from the More button of the Dial-Up Networking dialog box.

Doing so displays the dialog box that is shown in Figure 13-21.

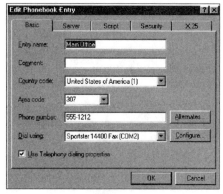

Figure 13-21: The Edit Phone Book Entry dialog box is used to configure a Dial-Up Networking entry.

The Edit Phone Book Entry dialog box allows you to configure how a connection should be established with the remote site. There are five tabs in the dialog box, and each is discussed in the following sections.

The Basic tab

The Basic tab is the first tab displayed when you enter the dialog box; it is shown in Figure 13-21. The options on this tab are used to control the name, modem, and phone number that are used to establish the connection.

The Server tab

The Server tab, shown in Figure 13-22, is used to define the protocols that are used to establish the connection. The protocols that you specify in this tab must match those used by the service with which you are connecting.

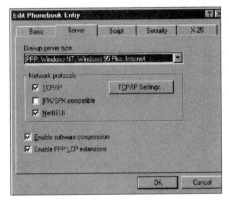

Figure 13-22: The Server tab is used to specify protocols.

At the top of the tab is a drop-down list that you use to define the connection protocol that is to be used by the server to which you are connecting. The default value is PPP, but you can change it to any of the following items:

- PPP: Windows NT, Windows 95 Plus, Internet

- SLIP: Internet

- Windows NT 3.1, Windows for Workgroups 3.11

Select the connection protocol that is required by either the remote server or (if you are connecting to the Internet) by your Internet provider. Changing your protocol also modifies the other options that are available in the Server Types dialog box.

This is because different protocols support different capabilities. By definition, PPP supports all of the options in the dialog box. Other options provide only subsets of these options. You should select the protocols and options that define both the communication protocol you plan to use and the options for the connection protocol.

The Script tab

The Script tab is used to define what you want Windows NT to do immediately upon connecting to the remote server. When you click on this tab, the dialog box that is shown in Figure 13-23 appears.

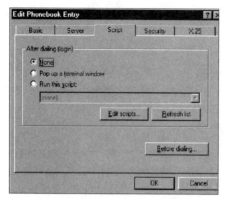

Figure 13-23: The Script tab is used to specify what happens when a connection is established.

There are three options on this tab, and each defines what Windows NT should do upon connecting.

■ The default, <u>N</u>one, means that nothing is done; you are simply left connected to the remote server. This choice is appropriate if the remote server immediately connects you in a PPP or SLIP environment.

If, however, the remote system requires you to manually log in (which is not unusual for many UNIX systems used by Internet providers), then you should choose one of the other two options.

■ If you click on the second option, a terminal window is displayed whenever you connect to the remote system. This terminal window allows you to manually log in to the remote system before the connection protocol is enabled.

You can use the terminal window to exchange information with the remote system as required. For instance, you may need to enter a user ID and a password, and then choose a menu selection that initiates the connection protocol that you are using.

■ The third option is similar to the second, except that input is not received from the keyboard (what you enter) but from a disk file, which you created. The script file can be used to automate the log-in process on many servers.

Secret

You can create a log-in script by clicking on the Edit Scripts button. This starts the Notepad accessory and loads a file called SWITCH.INF. Reading this file provides instructions for creating your own log file.

If you click on the Before Dialing button at the bottom of the dialog box, you can specify the same three choices (none, terminal window, or script) to occur before dialing the connection phone number.

The Security tab

The Security tab, shown in Figure 13-24, is used to specify how authentications (passwords) are to be exchanged with the remote system.

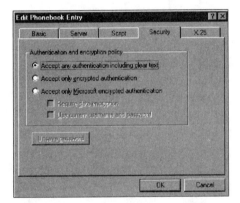

Figure 13-24: The Security tab controls how passwords are sent over your connection.

There are several accepted standards for exchanging password information while negotiating a connection. Most services allow you to send clear text, meaning that the password is sent in ASCII format, unencrypted.

Windows NT actually supports multiple formats that can be used to enhance the security of your remote connection. You should check with your network administrator or Internet service provider to determine which way that person prefers the information to be transmitted.

The X.25 tab

If your connection is to be established with an X.25 network provider, then you need to fill in the information on the X.25 tab. These types of connections are specialized networking connections, typically established over ISDN lines. The X.25 tab is shown in Figure 13-25.

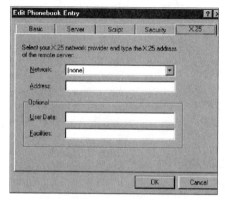

Figure 13-25: When establishing an X.25 connection, you must supply additional connection information.

If you are not using an X.25 connection, then you can leave all of the information in this tab blank. If you are establishing this type of connection, then your network administrator or service provider can give you the information that you need to complete the X.25 fields properly.

Establishing a connection

After you have your phone book entry created and configured properly, you can use Dial-Up Networking to connect with the remote server. You can do this by following these steps:

STEPS

Connecting through Dial-Up Networking

Step 1. Double-click on the My Computer icon on your desktop. This opens the My Computer window.

Step 2. Double-click on the Dial-Up Networking icon. This displays the Dial-Up Networking dialog box.

Step 3. In the drop-down list at the top of the dialog box, select the phone book entry that you want to use for your connection.

Secret

If, after selecting the phone book entry and dialing location, the phone number in the middle of the dialog box does not represent the entire phone number to be dialed (including any prefixes), you must make some changes. If the phone number is incorrect, you need to edit the phone book entry, as described earlier. If the prefix is missing or incorrect, you need to change the dialing preferences of the modem. If this is the case, you must exit Dial-Up Networking completely, make the changes, and then start Dial-Up Networking again.

Step 4. Change the dialing location at the bottom of the dialog box, if desired.

Step 5. Click on the Dial button. This displays the Connect dialog box, as shown in Figure 13-26.

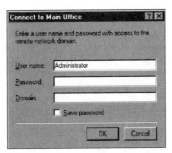

Figure 13-26: You need to supply a user ID and password for a remote connection.

Step 6. Make sure that the user name, password, and domain match what they should be for this server and connection.

Step 7. Click on the OK button to continue. DUN attempts to establish the connection.

Step 8. If prompted, supply any additional user IDs, passwords, or other log-in information that is required.

When connected to the remote server, you see a message indicating that you have successfully made a connection (as in Figure 13-27). At this point, click on the OK button, and you can use the network through the modem as if you were connected directly to the network. This means that you can effectively do anything from a dial-up connection that you would normally do from a connection via a regular LAN cable.

Figure 13-27: You have successfully made a connection with the remote system.

Secret

If you hear strange, high-pitched sounds when you are connected to the remote system, these are due to the sound capabilities of DUN. If you find this distracting (which it easily can be), you can change it using the Dial-Up Monitor, as described in the following section.

Using the Dial-Up Monitor

Whenever you connect to a remote service, Windows NT runs a special program called the Dial-Up Monitor. This program is normally hidden from view, but you can see it under two circumstances:

■ If you are not connected via a DUN link, you can double-click on the Dial-Up Monitor applet in the Control Panel.

■ If you are connected via a DUN link, you can double-click on the Dial-Up Monitor icon that is next to the system time on the right side of the Taskbar.

The Dial-Up Monitor is designed to keep you informed of how your connection is progressing. If you display the Dial-Up Monitor, it appears as shown in Figure 13-28.

You see three tabs, which are as follows:

■ The Status tab, which is shown in Figure 13-28, allows you to see statistics of your connection. You can see how much information you have both sent and received over the link, along with a report of any errors that were detected. At the bottom of the dialog box, you can click on the Hang Up button to break the connection.

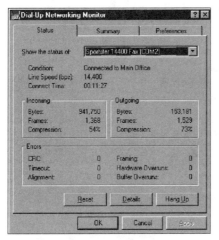

Figure 13-28: The Dial-Up Monitor is used to display the status of a DUN connection.

- The Summary tab is useful only if you have multiple connection points on your workstation. Windows NT allows you to establish multiple concurrent connections to the same remote server through different devices on your system.

  For instance, if you had two modems and two phone lines, you could connect to the same server through both of them simultaneously. In this case, the Summary tab shows connection information for both of your connection points.

- The Preferences tab is useful when you want to configure the Dial-Up Monitor program. For instance, you can cause Dial-Up Monitor to play sounds when different events occur, or you can indicate that you want to see the Dial-Up Monitor on the Taskbar itself. The preferences that you set are remembered from one session to the next.

Breaking your connection

When you are done working on the remote system, it is a good idea to break your connection. If you are dialing long distance, it saves money either for you or for the company to whose server you are connected. In addition, it frees the communications port on the other end of the connection for someone else to use.

One way to break your connection, as you learned in the previous section, is to use the Hang Up button on the Dial-Up Monitor. There is another way, however, that is very fast if you don't already have the Dial-Up Monitor displayed.

You can disconnect by right-clicking on the Dial-Up Monitor icon on the right side of the Taskbar. This, of course, displays a Context menu. On the menu is a choice named Hang Up Connection.

When you move the mouse over this choice, the name of your current connection appears in a submenu. When you click on the name of the connection, you are asked if you really want to break the connection. When you click on the Yes button, the connection is broken, and you are no longer able to use the remote network services.

Using RAS

RAS, or *Remote Access Server*, is the flip side of Dial-Up Networking. Whereas DUN is the client program, RAS is the server with which the client does its work. Normally, RAS is run on a Windows NT Server system, but you can also run it on Windows NT Workstation 4.0.

When you installed Dial-Up Networking, you unknowingly also installed RAS. In fact, Dial-Up Networking used to go by the name of RAS (client and server) in previous versions of Windows NT. If you look back at some of the setup screens that were used for Dial-Up Networking, you may have noticed that the term Remote Access Server was used in some of the title bars and in other places.

With Dial-Up Networking installed, you simply enable RAS. You do this by following these steps:

STEPS

Configuring your system as a RAS Server

Step 1.   Choose the Settings option from the Start menu. This displays the Settings menu.

Step 2.   Choose the Control Panel option from the Settings menu. This opens the Control Panel.

Step 3.   Double-click on the Network icon in the Control Panel. This displays the Network dialog box.

Step 4. Click on the Services tab of the Network dialog box. This displays the network services that are installed on your system.

Step 5. In the services list, click on the Remote Access Service item.

Step 6. Click on the Properties button. This displays the Remote Access Setup dialog box, as shown in Figure 13-29.

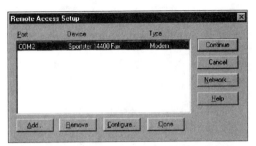

Figure 13-29: The Remote Access Setup dialog box is used to configure your RAS service.

Step 7. If you have multiple RAS ports defined, select the one on which you want to receive calls.

Step 8. Click on the Configure button. This displays the Configure Port Usage dialog box, as shown in Figure 13-30.

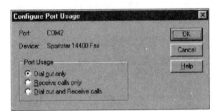

Figure 13-30: You can configure an RAS port for both incoming and outgoing calls.

Step 9. In the Port Usage area, click on the radio buttons to indicate how you want the RAS port to be used: to dial out, to receive calls, or both. (If you want to use RAS as opposed to DUN, you must choose something other than dial-out only.)

Step 10. Click on the OK button to close the Configure Port Usage dialog box.

(continued)

STEPS *(continued)*

Configuring your system as a RAS Server

Step 11. Click on the Network button. This displays the Network Configuration dialog box for the RAS port, as shown in Figure 13-31.

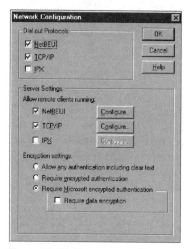

Figure 13-31: You can specify protocols for both incoming and outgoing calls.

Step 12. Make sure that the information in the Server Settings area reflects the same settings that you want used by those people connecting with your RAS Server.

Step 13. For each of the server protocols you plan to use, click on the Configure button to set up the parameters for the service. (See information on protocol configuration in the following sections.)

Step 14. Click on the OK button to close the Network Configuration dialog box.

Step 15. Click on the Continue button to close the Remote Access Setup dialog box.

Step 16. Click on the Close button to save your new network settings.

When you are done enabling RAS Server for your system, you are prompted to restart your system. This is required because the binding information for your network components has changed based on your RAS configuration. When prompted, click on the Yes button to restart.

Configuring RAS Server protocols

When you are setting up RAS Server on your system, you need to specify which network protocols are used for incoming calls. The way in which you configure those protocols depends on which protocols they are.

The following three sections detail how to set up the protocols that are most often used on RAS Servers.

Configuring for the NetBEUI protocol

NetBEUI is a native protocol to Windows, and configuring your RAS Server to use NetBEUI is easy. When you are working on Step 13 of setting up your RAS Server and you click on the Configure button, the dialog box shown in Figure 13-32 is displayed.

Figure 13-32: Configuring RAS Server for NetBEUI is easy.

In this dialog box, simply specify whether you want someone calling in to have access to only your workstation or to the entire network. For security reasons, you may want to limit the person to your single workstation.

When you are finished making changes, click on the OK button to save your selection.

Configuring for the TCP/IP protocol

If you have TCP/IP installed on your network, you can configure RAS to recognize the protocol. Typically you would do this if you want your caller to have access to non-Windows machines on your network, to have access to an intranet, or to have access to the Internet through your network. When you are working on Step 13 of setting up your RAS Server and you click on the Configure button, you can see the dialog box shown in Figure 13-33.

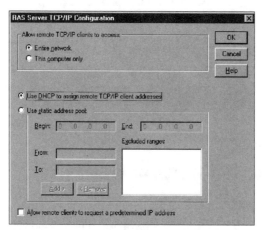

Figure 13-33: Configuring TCP/IP requires some knowledge of your IP address setup.

When you are configuring RAS Server to use TCP/IP, you need to know a little bit about IP addressing. You learned about TCP/IP programming in Chapter 14. The majority of this dialog box is used to specify how the client, calling your system, is to be assigned an IP address.

Before you start assigning IP addresses left and right, you should discuss the matter with your network administrator. He or she may have some technical guidance on this matter. Besides, you need his input if you are going to start assigning IP address for which he is ultimately responsible.

Notice, as well, that at the top of the dialog box, you can again specify how much of your network you want the client to have access to. When you are done configuring for TCP/IP, click on the OK button to close the dialog box.

Configuring for the IPX protocol

The IPX protocol is used many times for NetWare networks. When you are working on Step 13 of setting up your RAS Server and you click on the Configure button, you can specify settings as shown in Figure 13-34.

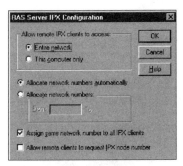

Figure 13-34: Configuring IPX settings requires knowledge of how your network assigns network numbers to IPX workstations.

Here you can again specify how much of the network you want the user to have access to. You can also specify how you want network numbers (addresses for IPX machines) to be assigned to the calling client. This, again, is another technical issue for your network administrator.

When you are done setting the configuration information, click on the OK button to close the dialog box.

Starting the RAS Server service

After you have configured your RAS Server and then restarted your system, you are ready to start the service. This is done by following these steps:

STEPS

Starting the RAS Server service

Step 1. Choose the Settings option from the Start menu. This displays the Settings menu.

Step 2. Choose the Control Panel option from the Settings menu. This opens the Control Panel.

Step 3. Double-click on the Services icon in the Control Panel. This displays the Services dialog box.

(continued)

STEPS *(continued)*

Starting the RAS Server service

Step 4. Scroll through the list of services until you can select the service entitled Remote Access Server. The Services dialog box should now appear as shown in Figure 13-35.

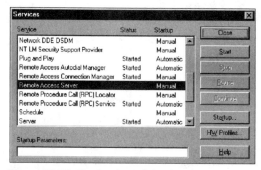

Figure 13-35: The Services dialog box is used to configure how different network services are started.

Step 5. Notice that, in the Startup column, there is an indication of how the service is designed to be started. If set to Manual, then you must manually start RAS Server each time you want it used. If set to Automatic, then it starts for you every time that you start your system. If you want to always start the service manually, skip to step 9.

Step 6. Click on the Startup button. This displays the Service dialog box, as shown in Figure 13-36.

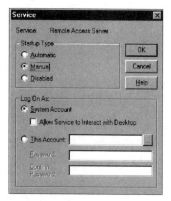

Figure 13-36: The Service dialog box allows you to specify the startup method used for a service.

Step 7. In the Startup Type area, click a radio button to select a method by which you want the RAS Server service to begin.

Step 8. Click on the OK button to close the Service dialog box.

Step 9. Click on the Start button. This starts the RAS Server service, and you should see the Status column change to *Started*.

Step 10. Click on the Close button to close the Services dialog box.

With the RAS Server service started, you are now ready to receive client's calls.

Secret

If you later decide to disable the RAS Server service (so you cannot receive any more calls), simply repeat all these steps, but in Step 7, choose the startup type Disabled.

Receiving a client's call

Once you have RAS Server up and running, it is a simple matter to receive a call from a client system. You need to make sure that your modem is connected and turned on.

Besides this, there are only a few guidelines that you (and the client) must remember:

- To receive a phone call from a client system, the client must be running Dial-Up Networking either on a Windows NT system or on Windows 95.
- The client must have its protocols set the same as in your RAS Server, as specified earlier in Figure 13-31.
- The client must have a user ID and password that are defined on your system. (This is covered in Chapter 16.)

Other than this, the client uses the same procedures in dialing in to your system that you followed earlier in the chapter when you connected to a different RAS Server.

Summary

Using your computer to communicate with others has been practiced for many years. Windows NT Workstation makes communicating easy with powerful features that extend the power of your system through a modem link. By using Dial-Up Networking and RAS, you can connect your system to another system and then communicate using the regular networking features of Windows NT.

In this chapter, you have learned the basics of serial communication, how to configure your modem, how to set up and use Dial-Up Networking, and how you can put RAS to work. In particular, you have learned the following items:

▶ Modems work by converting the digital signals that are used by computers to the analog signals that are used by telephone equipment, and vice versa.

▶ Windows NT enables you to easily add modems to your system and configure them.

▶ The dialing properties in Windows NT allow you to define how calls should be made from your system.

▶ The telephony features of Windows NT allow you to set your modem configuration and dialing parameters one time and then have those settings used by all of your communications programs.

▶ Using Dial-Up Networking, you can connect your system to a Remote Access Server and then communicate with that system as if you were connected to it via a network.

▶ Windows NT Workstation includes the capability to configure your system as a Remote Access Server, thereby allowing remote clients to establish a Dial-Up Networking connection with your system.

Chapter 14

Using Tools for the Internet

In This Chapter

The Internet is the hottest area of computing right now, with millions of PC users connecting to the Internet every day. Windows NT Workstation 4.0 includes several tools that make it a great client on the Internet. Many of these tools have migrated from the UNIX environment, where the roots of the Internet lie. Other tools have definitely come from Windows roots, which are so evident in other parts of NT.

In this chapter, you learn how to use the tools that can make the Internet more useful. These are the tools that are supplied directly with Windows NT Workstation 4.0. In particular, you learn the following items:

▶ How Internet addressing works, including domain and IP addressing

▶ How to configure your system for TCP/IP, which is the protocol used on the Internet

▶ Using the ping command to reach out to another computer on the Internet

▶ Using nslookup to reveal information that is stored in DNS servers

▶ Using tracert to find the route that is followed when communicating with a distant host

▶ Putting ftp to work to transfer files to and from remote sites

▶ Using telnet to act as a terminal to another system

▶ Starting to use the Internet Explorer to browse the World Wide Web

▶ Adding Peer Web Services to your workstation

Understanding Internet Addressing

To do anything on the Internet, you need to work with addresses; this is an inescapable fact of life. These addresses can be one of two types — DNS addresses or IP addresses. Of the two, DNS addresses are the most under-standable by humans, but IP addresses are the ones that really make things happen on the Internet.

Although discussing addresses may not, at first, seem that important to using Windows NT, understanding Internet addressing is essential to effectively using the Internet tools that are provided by Windows NT. The following two sections discuss the DNS and IP addressing basics that you need to know.

DNS addressing

DNS is an acronym for *domain naming system,* and it refers to a type of addressing that is readable by humans. In noncomputer areas, addressing has been used for centuries as a way of identifying people, places, or information. We all use addresses every day to accomplish our routine work.

Consider the following address, in a form with which we are all familiar:

Allen L. Wyatt
Discovery Computing Inc.
PO Box 738
Sundance, WY 82729

This address consists of a name, company, street address, city, state, and zip code. Without all of these elements, the address is considered incomplete. All of the elements are necessary to avoid confusion on who the intended recipient is.

For instance, if you omit the name, then the package could be intended for any person at Discovery Computing. Likewise, if you leave off any part of the city, state, or zip code, the carrier does not know where to send the item.

The purpose of using full addressing is to avoid ambiguity. The DNS addressing system is no different; by using a full DNS address, you avoid ambiguity concerning the intended recipient. The following is an example of a valid DNS address:

awyatt@dcomp.com

In this example, the address is divided into two parts, separated by an @ sign. The portion to the left of the @ sign (awyatt) identifies an individual person, while the following portion identifies a particular computer. Thus, the address is read as "awyatt at dcomp.com." This implies (and rightly so) that awyatt is a user at the computer named dcomp.com.

In any DNS address, the portion of the address before the @ sign identifies a user ID at a particular network system that is connected to the Internet. The portion to the right of the @ sign is referred to as the domain or host; it identifies the organization or network to which the user belongs.

The domain name portion of the address can be long or short. Longer domain names typically consist of additional levels, as in the following hypothetical address:

> jdavis@mail.beulah.sundance.edu

In this example, the domain name is quite a bit longer. Each portion of the domain name is separated by periods. Each period represents an additional refinement, or layer, of the division to the right of the period.

For those familiar with the hierarchical filing system used in Windows NT, the periods are like the backslashes that are used in directory names. Thus, sundance identifies a division of edu, whereas beulah is a further division of sundance, and finally mail is a subdivision of beulah.

Just like directory names are up to the discretion of the person creating them, domain names are handled by the person or organization that is responsible for them. The right-most portion of a domain name (edu, in the previous example) is simply referred to as "the domain."

These domains can either be organizational or geographical in nature, and they are quite limited. Both of these types of domains are discussed in the following sections.

The next level down (sundance.edu, in the previous example) is referred to as a "top-level domain." These names must be globally unique, meaning that only one organization in the world can have this top-level domain.

The name is registered with a responsible organization, and that organization depends on who everyone agrees has responsibility for the organizational or geographic domain. (The responsible organizations are also discussed in the following sections.)

Below the top-level domain, the organization and meaning of the domain name are up to the organization that registered the domain name. Thus, the domain name for Discovery Computing, Inc. is dcomp.com.

Within this domain, the further breakdown of the domain or the addition of more levels depends on our organizational needs. As our organization grows and we add additional computers, we assign those computers names that can be used in a domain name.

Organizational domains

An *organizational domain* is a three-letter abbreviation that indicates the type of organizations that belong to that domain. Organizational domains are used predominantly in the United States, where there are seven different designations (see Table 14-1).

Table 14-1	Organizational domains and their meanings
Domain	**Meaning**
com	For-profit commercial entities
edu	Educational facilities
gov	Nonmilitary government organizations
int	International (NATO) institutions
mil	Military installations
net	Network resources
org	Nonprofit groups

If you ever see an organizational domain as part of an address, you can be almost certain that the address belongs to a company that is located in the United States. Companies or individuals wishing to register a name in one of the organizational domains do so by working with an organization known as InterNIC.

The name registration services that are provided by InterNIC are used by thousands of people every day. (You can contact InterNIC at http://www.internic.net.)

Geographic domains

A *geographic domain* is a two-letter designation of the country in which the organizations that belong to the domain reside. Geographic domains are used in most parts of the world and are administered by a registering organization within the country to which the code has been assigned.

For instance, the two-letter geographic domain for the United States is US; this particular domain is also administered by InterNIC. In other countries, different organizations are responsible for registering all top-level domains within the geographic domain. (Like most other addresses on the Internet, geographic domains are typically lowercase characters. They are shown as uppercase in this section for clarity during the discussion.)

Geographic domains are based on the two-letter country codes that are specified in ISO 3166, which is a document of the International Standards Organization. As you may imagine, there are literally dozens of geographic domains, and they periodically change as political boundaries change around the world. Table 14-2 shows several of the common geographic domains in use as of this writing.

Table 14-2 A selection of geographic domains and their countries

Domain	Country
AR	Argentina
AU	Australia
BR	Brazil
CA	Canada
CO	Colombia
CR	Costa Rica
CU	Cuba
DE	Germany
DK	Denmark
EG	Egypt
FI	Finland
FR	France
GR	Greece
GL	Greenland
HK	Hong Kong
IS	Iceland
IN	India
IE	Ireland
IL	Israel
IT	Italy
JP	Japan
MX	Mexico
NL	Netherlands
NZ	New Zealand
NI	Nicaragua
NO	Norway
PA	Panama

(continued)

Table 14-2 *(continued)*	
Domain	*Country*
PE	Peru
PH	Philippines
PL	Poland
PT	Portugal
PR	Puerto Rico
SA	Saudi Arabia
SG	Singapore
ZA	South Africa
ES	Spain
SE	Sweden
CH	Switzerland
TH	Thailand
TR	Turkey
GB	United Kingdom
US	United States
VN	Vietnam

IP addressing

DNS addresses are very understandable. Although the different levels that are used within a domain name may sometimes look odd, a DNS name is still quite understandable. And although DNS addresses are great for people, they are not great for computers.

Computers understand only numbers. This is where IP (Internet protocol) addresses come in. These addresses consist entirely of numbers, so they are readily understood by computers. All addressing on the Internet must be converted to IP addresses so that the computers doing the work can know what to do with the address.

An IP address is a unique 32-bit address that defines a single location on the network. For human usage, IP addresses are written as a series of four numbers separated by periods. For instance, the following is a hypothetical example of an IP address:

205.44.163.29

Don't confuse the purpose of the periods that are used in an IP address with the purpose of the periods in a DNS address. The periods here are simply used to separate the four 8-bit values (called *octets*) that make up the entire 32-bit IP address.

Thus, each of the four numbers in this address (205, 44, 163, and 29) represent an 8-bit number. The notation that is used to express IP addresses is sometimes referred to as *dotted-decimal* or *dotted-quad notation*.

Because each octet of an IP address represents an 8-bit value, the range of any given octet is 0 to 255. This means that the lowest possible IP address is 0.0.0.0, and the highest is 255.255.255.255.

You shouldn't assume, however, that every possible address within this range is available for use; some addresses are used for overhead purposes by the network itself. Every computer that is connected to the Internet must have a unique IP address.

How IP addresses are assigned

The Internet, as you may know, is a network of computer networks; it is a way for those networks to communicate with each other quickly and effectively. IP addresses are assigned to networks based on the size of the network. There are three classifications of networks: A, B, and C. Class A addresses are assigned to very large networks, Class B go to smaller networks, and Class C are for the smallest networks.

The purpose of the different octets in an IP address depends on the class of the network that is under discussion. For instance, in a Class A network, the first octet refers to the network itself, while the remaining three octets refer to hosts within that network.

Conversely, for a Class C network, the first three octets identify the network, and the final octet represents the host. Table 14-3 shows how the octets are used in the different classes of networks.

Table 14-3   How network size corresponds to IP address usage

Network Class	Range of First Octet	Net ID Octets	Workstation ID Octets	Nets in Class	Workstations per Net
Class A	1–126	1	2–4	126	16,777,214
Class B	128–191	1–2	3–4	16,384	65,534
Class C	191–223	1–3	4	2,097,151	254

Address resolution

The process of converting a DNS address to an IP address is known as *resolution*. Even though you can use either a DNS or an IP address on the Internet, most people use the DNS address simply because it is easier for humans to read and understand.

The resolution of DNS addresses to IP addresses is handled automatically by software known as a DNS server. DNS servers operate all over the Internet to perform the resolution of the billions of addresses that are used daily.

Because name resolution occurs behind the scenes, you generally don't need to be concerned with it. There may be times, however, when you need the full IP address for a host.

For instance, if you supply a domain name that the DNS server cannot resolve for some reason, you are notified that your action cannot be completed. In such a case, you can use the IP address instead of the domain name.

Configuring TCP/IP

The Internet relies on the TCP/IP network protocol; it is the way in which all Internet computers communicate with each other. This means that if you want to use the Windows NT Internet tools, you must have the TCP/IP protocols installed in your system as a networking component. Before proceeding with this section, and indeed this chapter, make sure that you have the TCP/IP protocols installed, using the information that was provided in Chapter 12.

For your Windows NT Workstation to function properly within a TCP/IP environment that is the Internet, several addresses must be assigned to your computer. These addresses can either be supplied by your Internet provider (if you are connecting to the Internet using Dial-Up Networking) or by your system administrator (if you are connecting through your local-area network).

The necessary addresses include the following items:

■ An IP address for your workstation

■ A subnet mask for your network

■ A default gateway address for your network

As you learned earlier, your IP address is a unique identifier for your workstation. The second component, the subnet mask, allows your workstation to identify the network of which it is a part.

It is called a mask because it is used to mask out the parts of the IP address that are not necessary for the type of network to which you belong. For instance, if your IP address is for a Class C network, then within your local network, the first three octets of the address are of no importance; only the last octet defines the various workstations that are in your network. Thus, a subnet mask of 255.255.255.0 can be used to "wipe out" the first three octets in an IP address.

The third required component is the default gateway address. This is an IP address of the system to which your workstation should route information that is not destined for workstations on the local network. The default gateway address is used in conjunction with the subnet mask.

Remember that the subnet mask is used to identify information that is destined for a workstation on the local network. The information that is filtered out by the subnet mask (which is not destined for a local workstation) is then routed to the gateway, which in turn sends it on to its ultimate destination.

When you have the required three addresses, you are ready to configure your TCP/IP properties. You can change the properties by displaying the Properties dialog box as follows:

STEPS

Changing TCP/IP properties

Step 1. Choose the <u>S</u>ettings option from the Start menu. This displays the Settings menu.

Step 2. Choose the <u>C</u>ontrol Panel option from the Settings menu. This displays the Control Panel.

Step 3. In the Control Panel, double-click on the Network icon. This displays the Network dialog box.

Step 4. Click on the Protocols tab.

(continued)

STEPS *(continued)*

Changing TCP/IP properties

Step 5.   In the list of installed protocols, click on the TCP/IP protocol and then click on the Properties button. This displays the Properties dialog box that is shown in Figure 14-1.

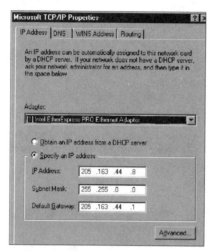

Figure 14-1: You can set many properties for TCP/IP.

The TCP/IP Properties dialog box used by Windows NT Workstation contains four different tabs. The options on each of the tabs define how your system uses the TCP/IP protocol and, in turn, interacts with the Internet.

Each of the tabs is discussed in the following sections.

The IP Address tab

The IP Address tab is the one that is first selected when you open the TCP/IP Properties dialog box. Here you need to enter some of the addresses that you received from your Internet provider.

Notice that there are two radio buttons in the dialog box. The first button instructs your workstation to obtain an IP address from a DHCP (dynamic host configuration protocol) server. You should check with your network administrator or your Internet provider to see if they are using a DHCP server. If they are, then you don't need to worry about entering the IP addresses for your system; your computer takes care of it automatically.

Note

A DHCP server is used in some Windows NT networks that support the TCP/IP networking protocol. This server, which is provided with Windows NT Server, is used to dynamically assign an IP address to a workstation whenever it logs on to the network.

The value of such a server is particularly evident in larger networks, where manually configuring every workstation with an IP address would be quite tedious. For more information on DHCP servers, check a good book about Windows NT Server, or discuss the matter with your network administrator.

If you are not using a DHCP server, then you should select the second radio button. This enables you to enter the three IP addresses that are discussed in the previous section. Enter each address in the space provided.

The DNS tab

Earlier in this chapter, you learned about Internet addressing. You learned that all domain names must be converted to IP addresses to route information over the Internet. The DNS tab is used to specify how DNS resolution should occur. When you click on the tab, the TCP/IP Properties dialog box appears, as shown in Figure 14-2.

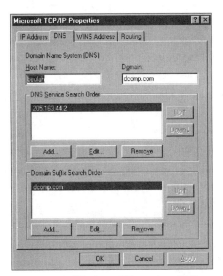

Figure 14-2: Windows NT requires DNS information to use TCP/IP properly.

At the top of the DNS tab, you can specify the host name and domain for your workstation. This information is typically provided by your network administrator, but it is not difficult to discern yourself. The Host Name field should contain the name of your computer; this is the name by which your computer is known on the Internet. The Domain field is used to specify the Internet domain of which you are a part.

In Figure 14-2, the example computer has a host name of beulah and a domain of dcomp.com. Thus, the entire domain name for this system is beulah.dcomp.com.

In the middle of the DNS tab, you can specify the addresses of your DNS servers. You should have access to at least two DNS servers — a primary server and a secondary server.

You need to know the IP addresses for both of these, and your primary server should be listed first. You manipulate the addresses in the list by using the three buttons below the list and the two to the right.

- **Add.** This button is used to add a new item to the end of the list.

- **Edit.** This button is used to make changes to a selected list item.

- **Remove.** This button is used to delete a selected list item.

- **Up.** This button is used to move a selected list item toward the top of the list.

- **Down.** This button is used to move a selected list item toward the bottom of the list.

At the bottom of the DNS tab is an area where you can specify the order in which domains are searched in the DNS servers. This information is optional, but it doesn't hurt to add your own domain and perhaps any domains of related networks. You can enter up to six domains in this area, using the same type of buttons that you used to manipulate the DNS server IP address list.

The WINS Address tab

WINS is an acronym for Windows Internet Naming Service. Because the Internet and your local Microsoft network both use different naming conventions, Microsoft came up with the WINS concept to provide an all-inclusive addressing scheme. In some networks, a WINS server is used instead of a

DNS server. This server is used to convert IP addresses to symbolic Microsoft network names.

If your network uses a WINS server, you need to fill out the information on the WINS Address tab. When you click on this tab, the TCP/IP Properties dialog box appears, as shown in Figure 14-3.

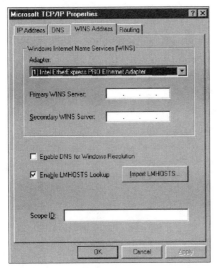

Figure 14-3: Some networks may require you to provide WINS information.

At the top of the WINS Address tab, you can specify the primary and secondary IP addresses for your WINS servers. At the bottom of the dialog box, you can use the check boxes to indicate, first of all, if your DNS server should be used to resolve Windows host names, rather than using WINS. You can also specify if you want the LMHOSTS file to be used to look up host names.

Note

The LMHOSTS file is another way in which Windows NT enables you to map host names to specific computer information. A discussion of LMHOSTS is beyond the scope of this book, but you can use this option if your network administrator lets you know that it is applicable to your network.

The Routing tab

The Routing tab, shown in Figure 14-4, contains only a single check box.

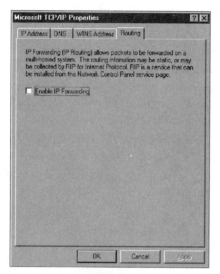

Figure 14-4: The Routing tab is used to control routing between interface cards in your system.

In most instances, you don't need to use this tab. You should select the check box only if these strict criteria are met:

- Your workstation contains multiple network adapters
- You have different IP addresses assigned to each card
- You are using static routing between cards

Check with your network administrator to see if you meet these requirements.

Using Ping

The simplest Internet command that is provided with Windows NT is the ping command. This command originated with the UNIX operating system and was converted to Windows NT when it started providing TCP/IP support. The command is designed to determine if a remote host can be reached from your computer system through a TCP/IP network, such as the Internet.

The ping command is used from the command prompt. You simply enter the command, followed by the address that you want to check. For instance, if you wanted to check out the Discovery Computing host, you would use the following command:

```
ping dcomp.com
```

Windows NT then sends an IP packet to the remote system. The remote system hopefully answers, and NT can display the response time. In the form used here, there are four packets sent. A sample of how the ping command's output appears is shown in Figure 14-5.

```
Command Prompt                                                    _ □ X
Microsoft(R) Windows NT(TM)
(C) Copyright 1985-1996 Microsoft Corp.

C:\>ping dcomp.com

Pinging dcomp.com [205.163.44.2] with 32 bytes of data:

Reply from 205.163.44.2: bytes=32 time<10ms TTL=32
Reply from 205.163.44.2: bytes=32 time<10ms TTL=32
Reply from 205.163.44.2: bytes=32 time<10ms TTL=32
Reply from 205.163.44.2: bytes=32 time<10ms TTL=32

C:\>
```

Figure 14-5: The ping command displays a response time for each IP packet that it sends.

Secret

Like most other Internet commands, you can use an IP address instead of a DNS address. If you use the DNS address and there is no response, try the IP address. If there is a response with the IP address, then there is a problem with either your DNS server or the DNS server for the remote system.

Because the ping command is used to determine if a remote system is accessible, it is considered to be diagnostic. Nevertheless, it is fun to use periodically to see how long it takes to reach far-away locations. There are a number of command-line switches that you can also use with ping, as shown in Table 14-4.

Table 14-4   Command-line switches for ping

Switch	Meaning
-a	Disables host IP address resolution. Shows network addresses as IP addresses instead of as host names.
-f	Causes packets sent to the remote system to be unfragmented by intermediate gateways.
-i *ttl*	Indicates the value to use for the *Time To Live* field in the IP packets. Effectively limits the number of intermediate gateways through which the packets can travel.
-j *hosts*	Specifies a group of hosts that you want included on the route to the destination, where *hosts* is a series of host names (up to nine addresses separated by spaces). The route may include additional hosts besides those in your list.
-k *hosts*	Same as the -j switch, except that only those hosts listed in the command can be used on the route; no additional hosts can be added.
-l *length*	Indicates the amount of data (in bytes) to be included in each packet that is transmitted. The default *length* is 64, but you can specify any value between 1 and 8192.
-n *count*	Indicates how many packets to send in each ping. If omitted, the default *count* of four packets is used.
-r *count*	Indicates how many hosts should be recorded during the round trip taken by the packets. You may specify a *count* between 1 and 9.
-s *x*	Indicates the time stamp (*x*) to be used for each leg of the route when you use the -r switch.
-t	Continuously pings the specified host until interrupted by pressing Ctrl+C.
-v *tos*	Indicates the value to use for the *Type of Service* field in the IP packets.
-w *timeout*	Indicates the *timeout* interval, in milliseconds.

Secret

You can combine command-line switches for ping as long as the switch does not require a value. For instance, the following is a legal combination of the -a and -f switches:

```
ping -af
```

Using Nslookup

The nslookup command is used to query and troubleshoot a DNS server. This diagnostic tool is a descendent from tools of the same name in the UNIX environment. The actual usage of nslookup is quite complex, and entire sections of books have been written on how to use the tool. The information provided here will get you started, but you may want to refer to a book on UNIX for more detailed information.

Starting nslookup

Windows NT provides a command-line version of nslookup that enables you to connect to DNS servers that are running on remote systems. The easiest way to start nslookup is to type the following at the command prompt:

```
nslookup
```

After you press Enter, you see a bit of information displayed, and then a prompt:

```
Default Server:  dci-server.dcomp.com
Address:  205.163.44.2

>
```

At this point you are no longer working at the Windows NT command line. Instead, the nslookup program is running. The information displayed indicates which DNS server the program is currently using. If you had started the program by using the address of a different server, then that server would have been used.

Using nslookup commands

Once the nslookup command prompt is displayed, you can no longer use regular Windows NT command-prompt commands. Instead, you use commands that are understood by nslookup. You enter the commands directly at the prompt, using the proper parameters or switches that are required by the command. The various nslookup commands are listed in Table 14-5.

Table 14-5   Commands used at the nslookup command prompt

Command	Meaning
?	Displays a short command summary. Same as the help command.
exit	Exit the nslookup utility, returning to the Windows NT command prompt.

(continued)

Table 14-5 *(continued)*

Command	Meaning
finger *user*	Displays finger information associated with the optional *user* name.
help	Displays a short command summary. Same as the ? command.
ls *options domain*	Lists the various names maintained by the specified domain. Valid options are -a (list cannonical names and aliases), -d (list all records), and -t *type* (list records of the given *type*).
lserver *name*	Changes the default server to *name,* using the information in the initial default server to locate the new server.
name server	Displays information about a particular host or domain, as specified by *name.* Information is derived from the specified *server.*
name	Displays information about a particular host or domain, as specified by *name.* Information is derived from the default server.
root	Sets the current default server to the root server.
server *name*	Changes the default server to *name,* using the information in the current default server to locate the new server.
set all	Displays all the current option settings used by nslookup.
set class=*type*	Specifies the query classification to use. The default classification is IN (Internet).
set d2	Displays extensive debugging information.
set debug	Displays simple debugging information.
set defname	Appends the domain name to each query you enter. This is a default option setting.
set domain= *name*	Specifies the default domain *name* to be used when domain names are appended to queries. Initially set to your current domain.
set nod2	Turns off the display of extensive debugging information. This is a default option setting.
set nodebug	Turns off the display of simple debugging information. This is a default option setting.
set nodefname	Domain names are not appended to the queries you enter.
set norecurse	Turns off recursive query answering.
set nosearch	Turns off use of the domain search list.

Command	Meaning
set novc	Turns off use of virtual circuits. This is a default option setting.
set querytype= *type*	Specifies the *type* of queries to perform. The default query type is A. Same as the set type command.
set recurse	Queries are answered recursively, where appropriate. This is a default option setting.
set retry=*num*	Sets the retry count to *num*. The default value is 3.
set root=*server*	Specifies the *server* to use as the root server. The default root server is ns.nic.ddn.mil.
set search	Use the domain search list. This is a default option setting.
set srchlist= *name1 ... name6*	Specifies the domain names (name1 through name6) to be used as a search list. The domain you specify as name1 is also set as the default domain name.
set timeout=*num*	Sets the timeout duration to *num* seconds. The default value is 2.
set type=type	Specifies the type of queries to perform. The default query type is A. Same as the set querytype command.
set vc	Turns on use of virtual circuits.
view *file*	Display the contents of *file*.

As you can tell from examining the various nslookup commands, the nature of the program is for diagnostics work. Nslookup is typically used by system administrators to debug and troubleshoot DNS servers for which they are responsible.

Using Tracert

The tracert command (short for trace route) is closely related to the ping command. You can use tracert to discover the route that your packets take between you and a remote site.

For instance, you may have the address for the server at the Congreso Nacional de Chile (National Congress of Chile), which is congreso.cl, and you want to know the route from your site to theirs. You can discover this by entering the following at the command prompt:

```
tracert congreso.cl
```

When you press Enter, a series of "steps" appear on your screen. These steps represent different gateways (hosts) through which your message passes. The route that is followed can be different from one day to the next, or even from one moment to the next.

This is because information on the Internet is constantly being rerouted to avoid trouble spots and to get your message through in the shortest possible time. The result of tracing the route to Chile is shown in Figure 14-6.

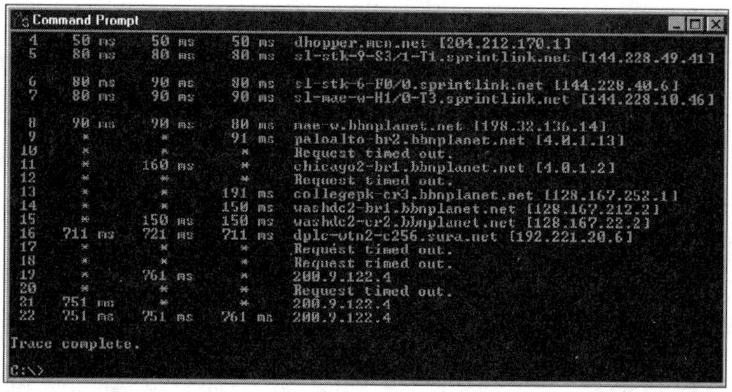

Figure 14-6: The tracert command shows how your messages travel from you to a remote site.

You can see from the feedback of the tracert command that it tries each leg of the trip three times. If it cannot get reliable feedback within those three attempts, it indicates that the request timed out.

The message goes on, however, and you are informed of how long the next leg of the trip took. Any usage of the tracert command only lists up to 30 hops (links) before it stops displaying information. You can modify this by using the command-line switches for tracert; these are shown in Table 14-6.

Table 14-6 Command-line switches for tracert

Switch	Meaning
-d	Disables host IP address resolution. Shows network addresses as IP addresses instead of as host names.
-h *steps*	Indicates the number of *steps* that tracert should use before giving up. The default (if -h is not used) is 30 steps.
-j *hosts*	Specifies a group of hosts that you want to have included on the route to the destination, where *hosts* is a series of host names (up to nine addresses separated by spaces). The route may include additional hosts besides those in your list.
-w *timeout*	Indicates the *timeout* interval, in milliseconds.

Using ftp

The ftp utility was developed in the UNIX environment as a way of transferring files across a TCP/IP network. The term *ftp* is an acronym for *file transfer protocol*. As you can tell from the first two sentences of this paragraph, ftp is both a utility and a protocol. (The utility was named after the protocol, which it relies upon.)

Similar to many other network utilities, ftp is implemented using a client/server model. This means that you use the ftp client program to connect with an ftp server that is running somewhere in the world. Many ftp servers are used as file archive sites, and you can easily access them to download information.

Starting ftp

Windows NT provides a command-line version of ftp that allows you to connect to ftp servers that are running on remote systems. The easiest way to start ftp is to type the following at the command prompt:

```
ftp
```

After you press Enter, you see the ftp command prompt:

```
ftp>
```

This command prompt means that ftp is running and awaiting your command. In the next section, you learn the different types of commands that you can use at the ftp prompt.

Although ftp is very easy to start, it includes some switches that you can use on the command line. Table 14-7 lists the various command-line switches for ftp.

Table 14-7	Command-line switches for ftp
Switch	*Meaning*
-d	Turns on debug mode, meaning that all commands passed between the ftp client and server are displayed.
-g	Turns off the capability to use wildcard characters in filename specifications.
-i	Turns off interactive prompting while transferring multiple files.
-n	Turns off autologon when initially connected to the server.
-s: *filename*	Specifies a script file named *filename*. This file contains ftp commands that run when the ftp command first starts.
-v	Turns off the display of ftp server responses.

In addition to starting the ftp utility either alone or with one of the switches, you can include a host name on the command line. Doing so attempts to log you in to the remote system. An example would be the following:

```
ftp dcomp.com
```

This attempts to connect you with the ftp server at the host dcomp.com. (You can accomplish the same thing from the ftp command prompt by using the open command, as introduced in the next section.)

When a connection is established, you see a greeting from the remote ftp server, as shown in Figure 14-7. Different systems use different greetings; this one is quite basic.

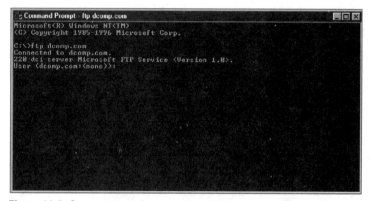

Figure 14-7: Once connected to a remote system, the remote server displays a message.

The ftp server is now waiting for you to log in to its system. If you have a user account on the remote system, enter your user ID. Most people who use ftp, however, use something called *anonymous ftp*.

This simply means that you log in to the remote system as a guest and browse through the files which that system permits you to see. To start an anonymous ftp session, enter the word *anonymous* as your user ID.

After you enter your user ID and press Enter, the remote server typically asks you to enter your password. (Some servers, when using anonymous ftp, don't require passwords.) If you have an account on the remote system, enter your password. If you are using anonymous ftp, then enter your e-mail address as your password.

Although you are not denied access if you enter someone else's e-mail address, common Internet courtesy dictates that you use your own. As you enter your password, what you type is not displayed on the screen; this is done for security reasons.

Once you have entered your user ID and password correctly, you are fully connected to the remote ftp server, and you should see the ftp prompt. Your screen now appears similar to what is shown in Figure 14-8. (Again, what you initially see depends on the system to which you are connecting.)

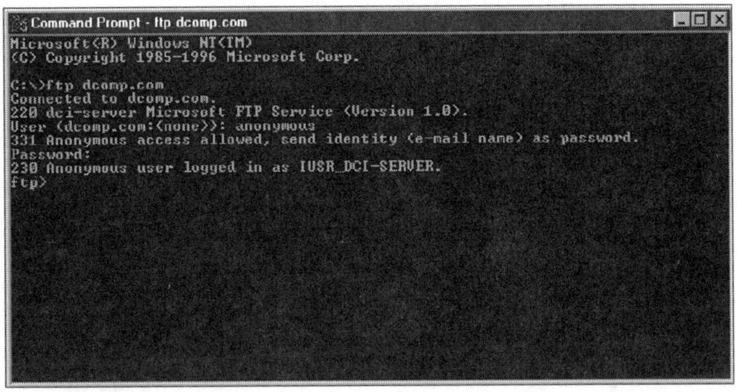

Figure 14-8: It takes both a user ID and password to fully connect with an ftp server.

Using ftp commands

Once the ftp command prompt is displayed, you can no longer use regular Windows NT command-prompt commands. Instead, you use commands that are understood by the ftp client program.

You enter the commands directly at the prompt, using the proper parameters or switches that are required by the command. The various ftp commands are listed in Table 14-8.

Table 14-8   Commands used at the ftp prompt

Command	Meaning
! command	Runs the specified command on the local computer.
?	Displays descriptions for ftp commands. This is identical to the help command.
append	Appends a local file to a file on the remote computer, using the current file type setting.
ascii	Sets the file transfer type to ASCII (the default).
bell	Toggles the bell setting. If the bell is on, a bell rings after each file transfer is completed; if it is off (the default), no bell is used.

(continued)

Table 14-8 *(continued)*

Command	Meaning
binary	Sets the file transfer type to binary.
bye	Breaks the connection with the ftp server and exits the ftp program. This is the same as the quit command.
cd *directory*	Changes to the specified *directory* on the remote computer.
close	Breaks the connection with the ftp server and returns to the ftp command prompt. This is the same as the disconnect command.
debug	Toggles the debug setting. If on, the messages between the client and server are displayed; if off (the default), these messages are suppressed. This command is the same as the -d command-line switch.
delete *filename*	Deletes the specified file (or files, if using wildcards) on the ftp server.
dir	Displays a directory on the ftp server.
disconnect	Breaks the connection with the ftp server and returns to the ftp command prompt. This is the same as the close command.
get *filename*	Copies *filename* from the ftp server to your system using the current file transfer type. This is the same as the recv command.
glob	Toggles the filename globbing setting. If on (the default), wildcard characters can be used in filename specifications; if off, wildcard characters cannot be used. This command is the same as the -g command-line switch.
hash	Toggles hash-mark setting. If on, a pound sign (#) is displayed for every 2K of data transferred with get or put; if off (the default), hash marks are not displayed.
help	Displays descriptions for ftp commands. This is identical to the question mark (?) command.
lcd *directory*	Changes to the specified *directory* on the local computer.
ls	Displays an abbreviated directory on the ftp server.
mdelete *filelist*	Deletes multiple files on the ftp server.
mdir *filelist*	This command is the same as the dir command but allows you to specify multiple files or directories.
mget *filelist*	Copies the files in *filelist* from the ftp server to your system using the current file transfer type.
mkdir *directory*	Creates a *directory* on the ftp server.
mls *filelist*	This command is the same as the ls command but allows you to specify multiple files or directories.

Command	Meaning
mput *filelist*	Copies the files in *filelist* from your system to the ftp server using the current file transfer type.
open *host*	Establishes a connection with the ftp server whose host name or IP address is specified by *host*. This is the same as using a host name on the ftp command line.
prompt	Toggles the prompting setting. If on (the default), it prompts you during multiple file transfers before transferring each file; if off, then no prompting occurs. This is the same as the -i command-line switch.
put *filename*	Copies *filename* from your system to the ftp server using the current file transfer type. This command is the same as the send command.
pwd	Displays the name of the current directory on the ftp server.
quit	Breaks the connection with the ftp server and exits the ftp program. This command is the same as the bye command.
recv *filename*	Copies *filename* from the ftp server to your system using the current file transfer type. This command is the same as the get command.
rename *file1 file2*	On the ftp server, this command renames *file1* to *file2*.
rmdir *directory*	Deletes a *directory* on the ftp server.
send *filename*	Copies *filename* from your system to the ftp server using the current file transfer type. This is the same as the put command.
status	Displays the current status of the ftp connection and any toggles.
trace	Toggles the packet tracing setting. If on, it displays the route (between the client and server) of each data packet; if off (the default), then routing is not displayed.
type *xfertype*	Sets or displays the file transfer type. Type *binary* is the same as the binary command; type *ascii* is the same as the ascii command. Without the *xfertype* parameter, the current transfer type is displayed.
verbose	Toggles the verbose setting. If on (the default), it displays all ftp responses; if off, no responses are displayed. This is identical to the -v command-line switch.

Although the list of commands that you can use at the ftp prompt looks rather long, you will probably only use a couple of them. For instance, the most common commands are get (which transfers a file to your system) and bye (which disconnects you from the remote system).

You may also have noticed that many of the commands are simply synonyms for other commands. For instance, the get and recv commands do the same thing, as do the bye and quit commands. If the synonyms were removed, there would be approximately one-third fewer ftp commands.

Some of the actions that are performed by ftp commands affect the ftp server (the remote system), whereas others are intended for use only on your local system (the client). You use many of the ftp commands as you work through the next several sections.

Moving about

After you are connected with a remote system, you can use various navigation commands to look around. Navigation on most ftp sites is done using many of the same commands that you are already familiar with.

For instance, you can use the dir command to display a directory and the cd command to change the current directory. Remember, however, that these commands are performed on the remote system, not on your local system. (If you want to perform the command on your local system, use a bang — an exclamation mark — followed by the command, as in ! cd.)

Many of the systems with which you connect use either UNIX or Windows NT directories. Both operating systems can include long filenames and directory names, including names that have embedded spaces.

In those instances when you need to reference a file or directory that contains a space, make sure that you include quotation marks around the name. For example, the following correctly changes the directory to the long directory name:

```
cd "These are really neat files
```

Notice that you don't need to include the trailing quotation mark, just the one at the beginning.

Transferring files

Transferring files is at the heart of ftp; it is why people use the utility in the first place. Using ftp to transfer files is actually a two-step process. First, you must make sure that you are using the proper transfer type, and then you issue a transfer command to copy the remote file to your system.

The ftp utility recognizes two types of file transfers: ascii or binary. The ascii transfer type should be used when transferring text files; all other files should use the binary transfer type. The default transfer type used by ftp is ascii, but you can change to the binary transfer type by using the following at the ftp command prompt:

```
binary
```

After you change the transfer type, it stays changed (during your current ftp session) until you explicitly change it again. If you later need to switch the transfer type back, use the ascii command.

After you have specified your transfer type, you are ready to transfer files to your system. There are three commands that you can use, but two of them are synonyms.

The get and recv commands are identical, allowing you to transfer a single file from the ftp server to your system. The mget command is used to transfer multiple files, but again it *can* be identical to get and recv when you can use wildcard characters with those commands. (The mget command is typically used when you have turned off wildcard characters or when the remote system does not understand wildcards.)

Tip

Before transferring a large file, it is helpful to use the hash command. This causes hash marks (#) to be displayed while the file transfer is in progress. Without the hash marks, you may be tempted to believe that your system has "crashed" or that the transfer is not happening satisfactorily.

After locating the file that you want to transfer, you can issue the get command, followed by the filename, to transfer the file to your system. The example in Figure 14-9 shows how your screen looks after transferring a small file.

```
 Command Prompt - ftp dcomp.com                                   _ □ ×
02-12-96   04:52PM                   315  GreenRule.gif
02-12-96   03:21AM                   349  log.gif
02-12-96   03:21AM                   244  mrange.gif
02-14-96   03:44PM                   836  mrn-bar.gif
01-30-96   03:57PM                  2560  netres.gif
02-12-96   03:32PM                  1160  PurpleRule.gif
02-12-95   08:58PM                  1969  RainbowRule 1.gif
02-21-96   07:03AM                  2530  RainbowRule 2.gif
02-21-96   03:12PM                  1130  StoneRule.gif
02-21-96   08:23PM                  2759  WoodgrainRule.gif
02-20-96   09:05PM                   130  YellowRule.gif
226 Transfer complete.
1354 bytes received in 0.09 seconds (15.04 Kbytes/sec)
ftp> hash
Hash mark printing On (2048 bytes/hash mark).
ftp> bin
200 Type set to I.
ftp> get "Construction Rule 3.gif
200 PORT command successful.
150 Opening BINARY mode data connection for Construction Rule 3.gif(19770 bytes)
########
226 Transfer complete.
19770 bytes received in 0.08 seconds (247.13 Kbytes/sec)
ftp>
```

Figure 14-9: Transferring a file with ftp is quick and easy.

The time that it takes to transfer a file depends on four things:

- The size of the file

- The workload at the remote site

- The condition of the connection between you and the remote site

- The speed of the connection that you are using

If you get tired of waiting for a file to download, you can always press Ctrl+C to terminate the transmission. Doing so, however, stops the ftp program and returns you to the command prompt. If you still want to transfer files, you must use the ftp command again to restart the program.

Secret

When you transfer a file to your system, it is placed in your current directory. If you want the file in a different directory, then you must either move it after you are done with the ftp program or use the lcd command to change to a different directory on your local system.

Breaking the connection

When you are done transferring files, you can end your ftp session with the remote computer in two ways. If you are done with ftp completely, simply enter the following at the ftp prompt:

```
bye
```

This command logs you off the remote system and quits the ftp program. (The quit command can also be used for the same purpose.) If you want to remain within the ftp program (perhaps you want to contact a different ftp server), then you use the following command:

```
disconnect
```

The close command is the same as the disconnect command, so it can also be used. Either way, the connection with the remote server is broken, and you are left at the ftp prompt, where you can continue your work.

Using Telnet

You may want to connect to a remote system, over the Internet, as if you were a terminal to that system. The telnet command is designed just for this purpose. After you are connected, you are simply another user at another terminal, as far as the remote system is concerned.

While you are connected, everything that you type is sent to the remote computer, and everything that is sent to you by the remote computer is displayed on your system. Thus, telnet enables you to conduct real-time, two-way communication with the remote host.

You can use telnet to connect to any system around the world, provided that you have the proper credentials to use the system to which you are connecting. Most systems on the Internet require at least user IDs and passwords to gain full access, although there are a few limited utilities that you can access freely with telnet.

Starting telnet

Unlike many of the other Internet accessories, the Windows NT implementation of telnet uses the Windows interface — not the command line. To start the program, follow these steps:

STEPS

Starting the telnet utility

Step 1. Choose the Programs option from the Start menu. This displays the Programs menu.

Step 2. Choose the Accessories option from the Programs menu. This displays a list of accessories that are installed on your system.

Step 3. Click on the Telnet option. This starts the program, displaying the window that is shown in Figure 14-10.

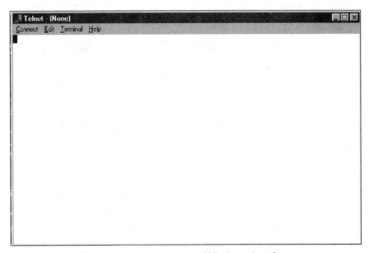

Figure 14-10: The telnet program uses a Windows interface.

At the top of the telnet window are four menu choices. Because there is no toolbar for the program, the menu choices are what you use to control your communications session.

The purpose of the options that are available under each menu are as follows:

- **Connect.** This menu contains options that you use to initiate a session, end a session, and exit the program. Also included is a list of the sites that you have most recently visited.

- **Edit.** This menu contains the same options that are available on most other Edit menus in any other Windows program. Using these options, you can copy, paste, and select text in the telnet window.

- **Terminal.** This menu contains choices that allow you to change the attributes of your telnet window or telnet session.

- **Help.** This menu is used to access the Windows NT help system.

Setting terminal preferences

As with many other Windows programs, telnet allows you to specify your preferences regarding how the program should look and behave. To change the preferences, just select the Preferences option from the Terminal menu. This displays the Terminal Preferences dialog box, as shown in Figure 14-11.

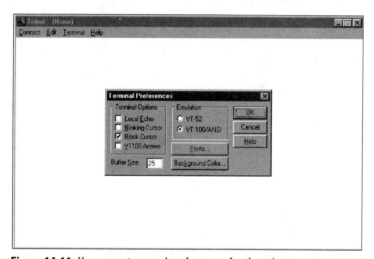

Figure 14-11: You can set several preferences for the telnet program.

The Terminal Preferences dialog box crams many controls into a small area. The radio buttons in the Emulation section (top-center of the dialog box) are perhaps the most important in terms of any connection that you may make. The two choices here control what type of terminal telnet emulates.

The choice that you make determines how telnet reacts when it receives control codes over your Internet connection. For most cases, you can leave the emulation set to the VT-100/ANSI terminal type. If have deciphering the screen after you are connected to a remote site, you can always switch to the VT-52 terminal emulation at any time.

Note

Most telnet sessions you use work just fine with VT-100 emulation; it is very common. There are some systems that you connect to, however, that don't use either type of terminal that is supported by telnet. In that case, you may need to forget connecting to the site or get a different version of telnet, many of which are available on the Internet at no charge.

At the left side of the Terminal Preferences dialog box is the Terminal Options section. The check boxes in this area allow you to control how telnet looks to you, as you are using it.

The purpose of the four check boxes is as follows:

- **Local Echo.** Some remote systems do not echo your characters as you type them. If, as you are typing, you cannot see the characters that you are entering, select this option. If you see two of every character that you type, turn this option off.

- **Blinking Cursor.** This option controls whether the cursor blinks. Sometimes a blinking cursor helps you locate its position on the screen; other times it is distracting. Set the option according to your personal preferences.

- **Block Cursor.** The telnet cursor can either be a block (full height of your letters) or an underline. This check box controls which way the cursor appears.

- **VT100 Arrows.** This option indicates what character sequence telnet should transmit when you press the arrow keys on your system. If you know the system to which you are connected can use the cursor-control keys to control the cursor, then select the option.

The Buffer Size setting (just below the Terminal Options section) indicates how large a buffer you want designated for received information. The value represents lines of text, and you can set it to any value up to 399 lines.

Secret

You should choose a buffer size larger than 25 lines. Many remote services send information in bursts, meaning that you may get 40 or 50 lines of information at a time. Unless your buffer is large enough, you can't scroll through the information that is received.

The two buttons in the bottom-center of the Terminal Preferences dialog box allow you to specify the Fonts that are used to display information and the Background Color that is used by the telnet window. Clicking on either of these options presents dialog boxes that are very similar to dialog boxes that you have used in other Windows accessories. (Going over them again at this point would probably be redundant.)

When you have specified your preferences, click on the OK button. Telnet remembers your choices and saves them from one session to the next.

Connecting to a site

With the telnet program window open, you are ready to connect to a remote site. Connecting is easy; simply select the Remote System option from the Connect menu.

This displays the Connect dialog box, as shown in Figure 14-12.

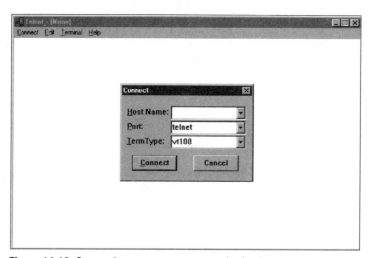

Figure 14-12: Connecting to a remote system is simple.

There are three fields in the Connect dialog box, as follows:

- **Host Name.** This field is where you enter the address of the system with which you want a connection. If you click on the drop-down arrow at the right of the field, you can select from recent connections that you have made.

- **Port.** This field is used to specify the IP port that should be used for the connection. Unless you have a good reason to change it (perhaps you know that the remote system uses a different port), you should leave it alone.

- **TermType.** This field is used to pick the type of terminal that telnet emulates when it is connecting to the remote system; it is not the same as the options in the Terminal Options dialog box. For most connections on the Internet, the default setting is appropriate.

For example, you may want to connect with the Wyoming State Ferret system. (This is a computer network that is operated by the State of Wyoming.) You can do this by entering the address ferret.state.wy.us in the Host Name field.

When you click on the Connect button, you are connected to the remote system. Figure 14-13 shows what you should see when connected to this system.

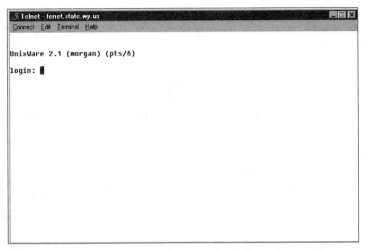

Figure 14-13: Many systems require you to log in for a telnet session.

The Wyoming State Ferret is a public, free-access system. The only thing that you need to know is the connection ID for the system. (This is not unusual for many systems.) In this case, the ID is **ferret**; type this, and you are connected to the system, as shown in Figure 14-14.

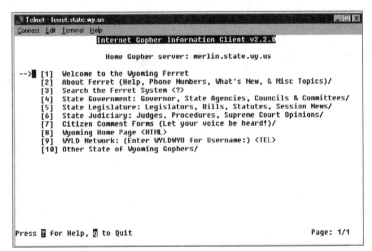

Figure 14-14: Telnet displays information from the remote system in the terminal window.

Note

If a system you want to access requires a connection ID, then you will need to determine that ID either from printed sources, on-line information, through e-mail, or by talking to someone who knows the ID.

Now that you are completely logged in to the system, you can use it to gather the information that is offered by the service or to access resources for which you have the proper permission.

Breaking the connection

When you are done working on the remote site, there are three ways that you can break your connection, which are as follows:

- The most abrupt way is to simply exit the telnet program. This breaks the connection and closes your telnet window. Although this may be quick, sometimes the remote system may not "appreciate" the sudden loss of the connection. It is possible that this could disrupt the remote service or tie up the connection port for an inordinately long period.

- Perhaps the best way to disconnect is to simply end the program that you are working with at the remote site. Different systems use different commands to do this, or you may need to enter a phrase such as quit or exit.

  When you end a session in this manner, the remote site breaks the link, and telnet informs you that it has lost the connection.

- The third way to end your session is to choose the <u>D</u>isconnect option from the <u>C</u>onnection menu. When you choose this option, the connection is closed, the telnet window is cleared, and you are ready to establish another connection, if you desire.

Using the Internet Explorer

Internet Explorer is Microsoft's Web browser. It enables you to take advantage of the World Wide Web, which is the multimedia portion of the Internet.

Millions of resources are available on the Web, and the Internet Explorer allows you to access them all. To start the Internet Explorer, just double click on the Internet Explorer icon on your desktop.

This displays the program window that is shown in Figure 14-15.

There are several items of the Internet Explorer that you need to understand to use it effectively. These items are intimately involved with the user interface, so each part of the interface is explored in detail in the following sections.

There is no way that I can cover every aspect of the Internet Explorer in this chapter; in fact, entire books have been written about this feature-rich tool.

The information that is provided here, however, can help you get started
using the Internet Explorer.

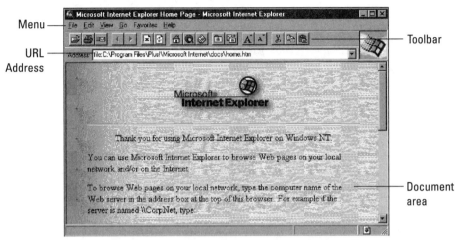

Figure 14-15: The Internet Explorer allows you to connect to the
resources on the World Wide Web.

Using the Internet Explorer is very intuitive. Don't be afraid to jump right in
and start using the program.

The menu

At the top of the Internet Explorer window is the menu. This menu enables
you to access the commands that are necessary to fully use the Internet
Explorer.

The six items on the menu have the following meanings:

- **File.** This menu allows you to open files or windows, save information,
  print a document, view document properties, and exit the program.

- **Edit.** This is the same as a basic Edit menu in most programs. The
  choices allow you to cut, copy, paste, and find information.

- **View.** The choices on this menu control what is displayed in the window
  and which fonts are used, and allow you to look at the source code for a
  document.

- **Go.** The choices in this menu allow you to navigate the Web.

- **Favorites.** These choices represent areas of the Web whose addresses you
  have saved. You can chose the options here to revisit those favorite sites.

- **Help.** This menu allows you to access the Windows help system.

The toolbar

Many of the choices that are available from the menus can also be accessed by using the toolbar. There are 17 tools, divided into 7 groups, which are as follows:

- The first group on the left consists of three tools. These tools allow you to open a file, print a document, and send an e-mail message.

- The second group of tools consists of a left-pointing and right-pointing arrow. The left-pointing arrow is used for moving back to the previous Web page that you viewed. After you have used this tool, you can use the right-pointing arrow to move forward a page.

- The next set of two tools is used to stop a download from a remote Web server and to reload the current page from the Web server.

- The fourth group of tools, which consists of three tools, starts with one that has a picture of a house on it. When you click on this button, you return to what is often referred to as your *home page*. This is the startup page that you first see when you start using the Internet Explorer. The next tool is used to search the Internet (through the Microsoft Network). The final tool in the group is used to access a newsreader utility.

Secret

You can change your home page designation by choosing Options from the View menu and then changing the information on the Start and Search Pages tab.

- The next group of tools controls the information that is in your favorites list. If you click on the first tool (the file folder with a star burst on it), you can see a list of the favorite addresses that you have saved. The next tool toward the right is used to add the address of the current document to your list of favorites.

- The next group has two tools with the letter A on them. The first one increases the size of the font that is used in the document window, and the next decreases the font size.

- The final group of three tools allows you to access the same options as are on the Edit menu. Most readers should be familiar with the common tools in this group.

The URL address

Sandwiched between the toolbar and the document window is the URL address field. This is where the address of the current page that you are viewing is indicated. In addition, you can enter an address here to visit a different location.

Documents, or pages, on the Web are stored in files that are maintained by Web servers. The address of these Web servers, when combined with the path to a specific document on that server, comprises what is known as the *URL,* or universal resource locator. The URL is the address to a unique piece of information on the Web; it is the way in which information is identified and located.

In many ways, you can think of a URL as an expanded domain address, as discussed earlier in this chapter. The difference is that a URL also includes an indicator of the type of resource at a particular location, and it may contain directory name and filename information as well.

Consider the following URL:

> http://www.dcomp.com

This URL contains an indicator of what is located at the address (the http: part) as well as a domain name for the server containing the information (www.dcomp.com). The resource type and the domain name are separated by two slashes.

Secret

If you use a URL with only a single slash after the resource type, Internet Explorer generates an error; two slashes are required for proper syntax. You can, however, omit the http:// prefix under Internet Explorer; it then adds that information automatically.

When you enter a URL in the address field of Internet Explorer, the server at the specified address is contacted, and it sends a default document to the browser. The server returns the default file because the URL that you entered does not contain a filename.

Take a look at another URL:

> http://www.dcomp.com/aladdin

This URL is very similar to the first, except that a directory name has been appended. In any URL, the first element is the resource type (http), the second is the server address (www.dcomp.com), and anything after that is considered a directory path. In this case, the URL points to a directory named *aladdin.*

When the server is contacted, it looks for the aladdin directory and then returns the default file from that directory. Again, the default file is returned, because no filename is specified in the URL.

The following URL is slightly different:

> http://www.dcomp.com/dci/authoring.htm

Here a full specification is provided, including a filename. In this case, the server returns the specified file (authoring.htm) to the browser. If you understand these basics of how a URL works, you can feel a lot more confident about using them as you work with the Internet Explorer.

The document area

When you enter a URL into the address field, a document is retrieved from the location that you specify. The time that is required to download the document from the remote site can vary, depending on many factors.

This depends on how busy the other site is, how much traffic exists between here and there, how large the document is, and the type of modem connection that you have. While the document is being downloaded, however, the Microsoft Windows flag, to the right of the address field, continues to wave. When the waving stops, the downloading is complete.

Tip

You can stop a document during a download by clicking on either the Stop tool (first tool in the third group) or by clicking on the waving Microsoft Windows flag.

As documents are transferred to your system, they are displayed in the document area. Normally, the document area displays formatted text and graphics, as the author of the document intended.

Documents are created using a language known as *HTML* (hypertext markup language). The HTML documents are simply text files that contain the codes necessary to control how a page is viewed.

You can view the HTML source code for a document by choosing the Source option from the View menu. This displays the document's source HTML code in a Notepad window, as shown in Figure 14-16. (When you are done viewing the source code, simply close the Notepad window.)

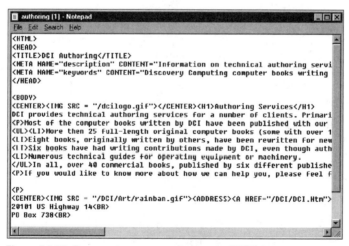

Figure 14-16: Documents are created using the HTML language.

If the document that you are viewing is large enough, the document area contains scroll bars below and to the right of the document. You can scroll through the entire document by using these scroll bars, much as you would in any other program.

Understanding links

The most fascinating thing about the World Wide Web is that it is interconnected. This means that you can be reading a document, click on a link, and suddenly be viewing a different document from another place around the world. In the Internet Explorer, document links are shown as blue, underlined text.

This effect is illustrated in Figure 14-17.

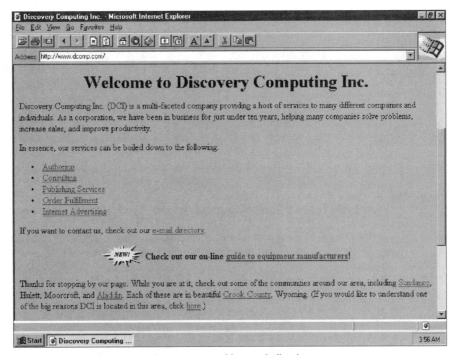

Figure 14-17: Links between documents are blue, underlined text.

Secret

You can change the appearance of links by choosing Options from the View menu and then changing the Shortcuts information on the Appearance tab.

If you think that the information at the linked site may be interesting, you can click on the link. Immediately the document at the linked location is loaded to your browser, and you can view that document. You can also follow other links from that point to other locations, or you can click on the Back button (on the toolbar) to return to your previous page.

Using Peer Web Services

As you can tell from the contents of this chapter, Microsoft is making a strong push in the area of Internet utilities, connectivity, and services. One facet of that push has been in the area of servers.

These are the programs that provide services to other people on the Internet. With Windows NT Workstation 4.0, Microsoft includes a product called *Peer Web Services*.

The Peer Web Services are more than what their name implies. Indeed, they provide not only a Web server but also a Gopher server and an ftp server.

Tip

The Peer Web Services are basically a subset of the Internet Information Server, which Microsoft has been supplying for some time. By Microsoft's own admission, the Peer Web Services are not meant to provide full-strength Internet services.

Instead, they can be used for a small intranet within your own company. If you are interested in getting a server for larger use, such as on the Internet as a whole, you should investigate a more full-featured product, such as Internet Information Server (from Microsoft) or any of the Netscape servers.

Installing the Services

The Peer Web Services are not installed during a normal installation. Instead, you need to explicitly request that they be installed.

To install the Peer Web Services, follow these steps:

STEPS

Installing the Peer Web Services

Step 1.   Choose the <u>S</u>ettings option from the Start menu. This displays the Settings menu.

Step 2.   Click on the <u>C</u>ontrol Panel option on the Settings menu. This opens the Control Panel.

Step 3.   Double-click on the Network icon. This displays the Network dialog box.

Step 4.   Click on the Services tab.

Step 5. Click on the <u>A</u>dd button. This displays the Select Network Service dialog box, as shown in Figure 14-18.

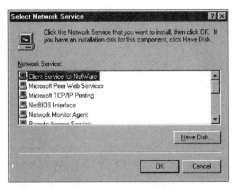

Figure 14-18: You need to install Peer Web Services as a network service.

Step 6. Click on the OK button to begin the installation.

Step 7. Insert your Windows NT CD-ROM as prompted. Some programs are copied from the CD-ROM to your hard drive, and a dialog box appears informing you that you should close all other programs during installation.

Step 8. Click on the OK button to continue. The Setup dialog box appears as shown in Figure 14-19.

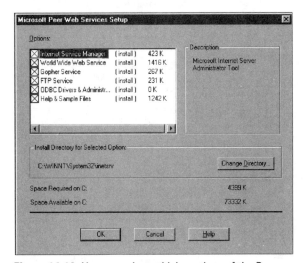

Figure 14-19: You can select which portions of the Peer Web Services you want to install.

(continued)

STEPS *(continued)*

Installing the Peer Web Services

Step 9.   Select the options that you want to install for your site. You can select or unselect an item by clicking on the check box to the left of the item name.

Step 10.   Change the directory in which the programs will be installed, if desired.

Step 11.   Click on the OK button to continue. This displays the Publishing Directories dialog box, as shown in Figure 14-20.

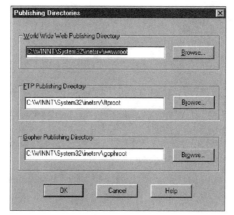

Figure 14-20: You need to specify where the information that is published by each of your services is to be stored.

Step 12.   To publish information with your servers, you need to specify a directory where the source documents are to be stored. Change the directory information, as desired.

Step 13.   Click on the OK button to continue.

At this point, the Peer Web Services files are copied from the CD-ROM to the proper location on your hard drive. When completed, a dialog box informs you that installation is done. You can then click on the OK button to clear the dialog box.

Using the Services

As you have already learned, the Peer Web Services provided by Microsoft are actually several products in one. As you may imagine, the proper configuration and use of those products can be quite involved. In fact, entire books have been written about how to use the various Microsoft servers that are embodied in the Peer Web Services.

In a nutshell, you configure the Peer Web Services by using the Internet Service Manager, which is installed when you follow the installation instructions in the previous section.

You start the program by following these steps:

STEPS

Starting the Internet Service Manager

Step 1.   Choose the Programs option from the Start menu. This displays the Programs menu.

Step 2.   Choose the Microsoft Peer Web Services (Common) option from the Programs menu. This displays a list of the available service options.

Step 3.   Click on the Internet Service Manager (ISM). This starts the ISM, and shortly you see the window that is shown in Figure 14-21.

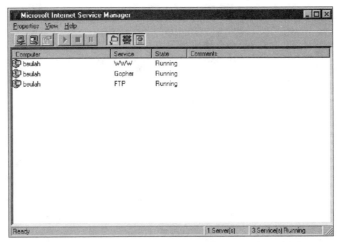

Figure 14-21: Your Peer Web Services are managed from the Internet Service Manager.

The Internet Service Manager lists each of the Internet services that you have running on your computer. You can change the configuration of any of the services by double-clicking on the icon at the left side of the line containing the service name.

Thus, if you wanted to configure your Web services, you would double-click on the icon at the left side of the WWW service line. When you are done with the Internet Service Manager, you simply close the program window.

The Internet Service Manager is one of those rare products for which Microsoft includes rather complete documentation. Because fully exploiting the Peer Web Services is beyond the scope of this book, you may want to refer to the documentation that is provided.

Follow these steps:

STEPS

Viewing Product Documentation

Step 1. Choose the Programs option from the Start menu. This displays the Programs menu.

Step 2. Choose the Microsoft Peer Web Services (Common) option from the Programs menu. This displays a list of the available service options.

Step 3. Click on the Product Documentation option. This starts the Internet Explorer (or another browser, if you have it installed) and displays the beginning page for the documentation.

Step 4. Click on the Installation and Administration Guide link on the first Web page. This displays the beginning of the product documentation, as shown in Figure 14-22.

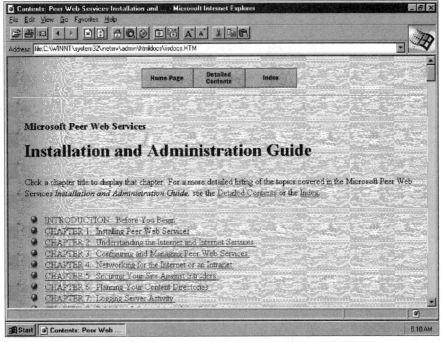

Figure 14-22: The Peer Web Services include a complete on-line book.

Tip

If you want a printed copy of the documentation, simply load each chapter of the book into the browser, in turn, and then click on the Print button on the toolbar.

Summary

The Internet is a busy place, and it seems to keep getting busier every day. As a dynamic portion of the computer world, the Internet provides the premier opportunity for computers to communicate and share information.

As a reflection of how critical the Internet is to computers, Windows NT Workstation includes many different tools that you can use to exploit the Internet. This chapter has focused on the tools that you have available with Windows NT Workstation.

In particular, you have learned the following items:

▶ The Internet uses two types of addresses: domain addressing and IP addressing. Domain addresses are used for human understanding, whereas IP addresses are used by computers.

▶ Domain addresses consist of an organizational or geographic domain, along with a top-level domain. Different organizations around the world are responsible for registering and administering the domain-naming system.

▶ IP addresses consist of a unique 32-bit number that identifies the network to which a computer belongs. IP addresses are allocated based on the size of the network in use at a site.

▶ Domain addresses are converted (resolved) to IP addresses by a DNS server. Thousands of these servers are available throughout the world, and each is responsible for its own small part of the Internet.

▶ Windows NT Workstation understands the TCP/IP network protocol, which must be used on the Internet.

▶ To configure the protocol, you need to know information about both your domain and how IP addresses are allocated on your network.

▶ The ping command is used to discover whether a remote computer is actively connected to the Internet.

▶ The nslookup command is used to reveal information that is stored in DNS servers. It can help in troubleshooting addressing problems at a site.

▶ The tracert command is used to find the route that is followed by a message when traveling from your site to a remote site.

▶ You can use the ftp command to transfer files to and from remote sites. The ftp client program that is supplied with Windows NT Workstation is used to connect with an ftp server running on another computer system.

▶ The telnet command enables you to connect to another computer system — over the Internet — as if you were a terminal on that system.

▶ The Internet Explorer is Microsoft's World Wide Web browser. You can use it to view millions of documents that are stored at thousands of sites around the world.

▶ You can add elemental Internet services to your workstation by using the Peer Web Services that are supplied with Windows NT Workstation.

Chapter 15

Personal Communications Tools

In This Chapter

In the last couple of chapters, you learned quite a bit about data communications. Windows NT includes many features and tools that enable you to make the most of your modem and your phone line.

In this chapter, you learn about several additional tools. These tools build on the telephony features of Windows NT as well as on the Internet information that you learned about in Chapter 14. In particular, you gain insight on the following items:

▶ How you can use the Phone Dialer to interface with your personal telephone

▶ How HyperTerminal can be used to connect to remote computer systems and share information

▶ How to install Microsoft Exchange and configure it for your needs

▶ How to send, receive, and manage messages using Microsoft Exchange

Using Phone Dialer

One of the simplest communications tools that is included in Windows NT is the Phone Dialer accessory. This tool is intended to be used much like a speed-dialer — you can use it to dial numbers for you, after which you pick up the phone and start talking. The Phone Dialer takes complete advantage of the TAPI features described in Chapter 13.

Note

Remember that the Phone Dialer is used to make calls for you; this means they are voice calls. Thus, the Phone Dialer is only useful if you have a voice telephone attached to your modem. Most modern modems come with two phone cord jacks. One of these is intended to connect the modem to a wall jack and the other to connect with a telephone set; you need both connected for Phone Dialer.

To start the Phone Dialer, follow these steps:

STEPS

Starting the Phone Dialer

Step 1. Choose the Programs option from the Start menu. This displays the Programs menu.

Step 2. Choose the Accessories option from the Programs menu. This displays a menu of accessories that are installed on your system.

Step 3. Click on the Phone Dialer option from the Accessories menu. This displays the Phone Dialer, as shown in Figure 15-1.

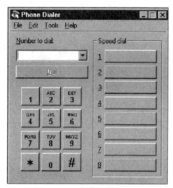

Figure 15-1: The Phone Dialer is used to make speed-calls on your system.

The Phone Dialer consists of three major parts besides the normal program menu. In the upper-left corner is a field where you can enter a phone number to dial, in the lower-left is the phone keypad, and on the right is the speed-dial list. How you use each of these areas is described in the following sections.

Secret

If you need to change your dialing properties (such as selecting a different dialing location) or change the modem that you are using, use the selections from the Tools menu.

Dialing a number

There are several ways that you can dial a phone number with the Phone Dialer. The method that you use to dial depends entirely on you. You can pick any of the following methods:

- Type the phone number in the <u>N</u>umber to Dial field, and then click on the <u>D</u>ial button.

- Click on the phone keypad numbers, which causes the number to appear in the <u>N</u>umber to Dial field. When you are ready, click on the <u>D</u>ial button.

- Use the drop-down arrow on the <u>N</u>umber to Dial field to select one of your recently dialed numbers. When you are ready, click on the <u>D</u>ial button.

- Click on a button in the speed-dial list.

Regardless of which way you choose, the number is dialed by the modem. When the connection is made, a dialog box appears, as shown in Figure 15-2, that instructs you to pick up the phone and click on <u>T</u>alk.

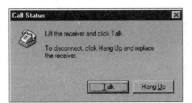

Figure 15-2: You need to pick up the phone and click on <u>T</u>alk when you are ready to talk.

If you don't click on <u>T</u>alk, the individual at the other end of the connection cannot hear you. You can also click on the Hang <u>U</u>p button to terminate the call.

At this point, you can continue your call as normal. When you are done talking, simply hang up your phone.

Secret

After you pick up the phone and click on the Talk button, Phone Dialer leaves a dialog box on the screen indicating that it is dialing. As long as you have picked up the phone, you can click on the <u>H</u>ang Up button in the dialing dialog box with no ill effects on your call.

Programming a speed-dial button

The purpose of a speed-dialer is twofold: to remember phone numbers for you and to dial them quickly. Phone Dialer excels at both tasks. Notice that, at the right side of the Phone Dialer dialog box, there are eight buttons.

Each of these can be programmed with a phone number that you commonly dial. To program one of the blank buttons, simply click on it. This displays the Program Speed Dial dialog box, as shown in Figure 15-3.

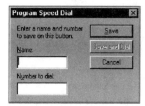

Figure 15-3: Programming a speed-dial button is easy.

In the Name field, enter the name that you want to appear on the speed-dial button. In the Number to Dial field, enter the number that you want to have dialed when this speed-dial button is clicked.

After entering the information, you can either click on the Save or Save and Dial buttons, depending on what you want to have done. The name that you entered then appears on the speed-dial button.

Note that this method of programming a speed-dial button only works for those buttons that are blank. If you want to change a button that already has a number on it, you must use the editing feature described in the following section.

Editing your speed-dial buttons

Another way that you can change the names and numbers on speed-dial buttons Is to use the editing feature of Phone Dialer. You access this feature by choosing the Speed Dial command from the Edit menu. This displays the Edit Speed Dial dialog box, as shown in Figure 15-4.

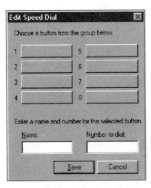

Figure 15-4: You can edit any name or number on your speed-dial list.

When you click on one of the eight speed-dial buttons, the current name and number appear in the fields at the bottom of the dialog box. You can then edit the current information or replace it. When you are done, click on another button to continue editing or click on Save to save your changes and exit the Edit Speed Dial dialog box.

Using HyperTerminal

One of the most common uses for a modem is to connect to dial-up services on other computers and access information on that service. The HyperTerminal program, provided with Windows NT, is a powerful, capable program that allows you to call other computers and perform routine tasks such as transferring files, sending messages, or anything else you would normally do with a communications program.

To start the HyperTerminal program, follow these steps:

STEPS

Starting HyperTerminal

Step 1. Choose the Programs option from the Start menu. This displays the Programs menu.

Step 2. Choose the Accessories option from the Programs menu. This displays a menu of accessories that are installed on your system.

(continued)

Starting HyperTerminal

Step 3.   Click on the HyperTerminal option from the Accessories menu. You should shortly see the Connection Description dialog box, as shown in Figure 15-5.

Figure 15-5: The first time that you use HyperTerminal you must create a connection definition.

Creating a connection definition

HyperTerminal works through the use of connection definitions. You can think of these as shortcuts to another computer system through your modem. Within HyperTerminal, these definitions are also referred to as *sessions.*

A definition or session contains everything that HyperTerminal needs to make the call and establish the connection. Because these definitions are required to make any calls, whenever you start HyperTerminal, you have the opportunity to create a new connection description.

With the Connection Description dialog box visible, you can create a new definition by following these steps:

STEPS

Creating a new session definition

Step 1.   In the <u>N</u>ame field, enter the name by which you want this connection know.

Step 2. In the Icon area, select an icon that you want to have saved with the definition.

Step 3. Click on the OK box to progress to the next step. The Connect To dialog box is displayed, as shown in Figure 15-6.

Figure 15-6: While creating a description, you need to supply a phone number and other connection information.

Step 4. Make sure that the country, area code, and phone number all match those of the service that you are dialing with this description.

Step 5. Make sure that the modem listed in the Connect drop-down list is the one that you want to use to dial this service.

Step 6. Click on the OK box to proceed to the next step. The Connect dialog box should appear, as shown in Figure 15-7.

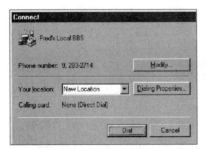

Figure 15-7: You are done defining and are ready to make a connection.

(continued)

Creating a new session definition

Step 7. Double-check everything in the Connect dialog box to make sure that it reflects how you want to make this call.

Step 8. Click on the Dial button to connect to the remote system.

The connection with the remote system should now be established. When you are connected, you can see information from the other services in HyperTerminal's terminal window, as shown in Figure 15-8. You can now use HyperTerminal to do any work on the remote system that you require.

Figure 15-8: HyperTerminal makes it easy to connect to another system and do your work.

When you are finished working on the remote system, you can disconnect by either clicking on the hang-up tool or by choosing <u>D</u>isconnect from the <u>C</u>all menu.

Saving your connection definition

Just because you were successful in connecting to a remote system does not mean that HyperTerminal saves your connection definition. If you call the remote site often, you should save the definition so that you can reuse it again at a later date.

There are three ways that you can save your connection definition:

- Break the connection with the remote system by choosing Disconnect from the Call menu. You are automatically asked if you want to save your session. If you answer Yes, the session is saved.

- Exit the HyperTerminal program. Again, you are automatically asked if you want to save your session. If you answer Yes, the session is saved.

- Choose Save from the File menu, and the session is saved.

Regardless of which method you use, the session is saved in the name that you supplied when you first defined the connection. Using the same name, you can later recall the connection.

Note

Don't think that saving a session involves saving all of the transactions or communication that took place during your time on-line. Saving a session only involves saving the connection definition that you created.

Changing session properties

Just like any other object in Windows NT, your connection session has its own set of properties. Besides the basic connection information (phone number, name, and so on), these properties control how HyperTerminal behaves while connected to the remote site.

To change the properties, choose the Properties option from the File menu. (You can also click on the Properties tool on the toolbar, the last one on the right.) This displays the Properties dialog box, as shown in Figure 15-9.

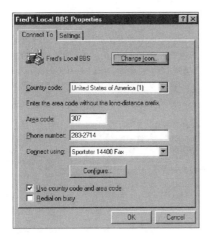

Figure 15-9: You can change the properties of your connection session.

There are two tabs in the Properties dialog box. The information in this first tab, Connect To, should look familiar — it is the same information that you supplied when you first created your connection definition. There is one item of interest on the tab, however.

At the bottom is a check box entitled <u>R</u>edial on Busy. If you check this option, then you can greatly automate your connection time. When HyperTerminal tries to contact the remote computer but isn't able to because the line is busy, it keeps redialing until it can get through.

If you click on the Settings tab, you can change the terminal configuration of HyperTerminal. With the Settings tab selected, the Properties dialog box looks like what is shown in Figure 15-10.

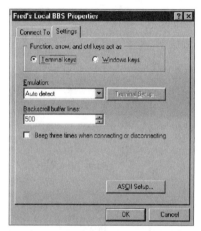

Figure 15-10: The Settings tab allows you to change the terminal configuration.

At the top of the dialog box, you can specify how the special keys on your keyboard should work when connected to another system. Normally, you would want them to work as if you were a terminal connected to the remote system. You can, however, make changes so that the special keys function as they should under Windows.

The first drop-down list on the tab allows you to specify what terminal emulation should be used by HyperTerminal. In most instances, the default of Auto Detect is perfectly acceptable; HyperTerminal does a very good job of detecting what type of terminal the remote system requires.

If you have problems, however, you can always select a terminal type from the drop-down list. HyperTerminal supports the following terminal emulations:

- ANSI
- Minitel
- TTY
- Viewdata
- VT100
- VT52

Secret

If you are having terminal problems with the remote system, try using VT100. (This is one of the most common terminal types on the market.) If you still have problems, contact the system administrator for the remote system.

When you select one of the specific terminal options, you can also click on the Terminal Setup button to configure different characteristics of the emulation. Different terminal emulations provide different setup dialog boxes, but none of them are terribly difficult. In most cases, you don't need to bother with setting up the terminal.

Just below the terminal emulation, you can specify how many lines of text HyperTerminal should retain in its buffer. Retaining lines in the buffer allows you to use PageUp to scroll back through information that may have scrolled off your screen too quickly.

Finally, the check box at the bottom of the tab allows you to indicate if HyperTerminal should make a sound when connecting or disconnecting. Your choice here is obviously your personal preference.

When you are done making changes to the session properties, click on the OK button. The changes take place immediately, even if you are already in the middle of an on-line session.

Sending and receiving files

HyperTerminal supports exchanging files between computers using many of the popular transfer protocols that are on the market. When you transfer a file, one computer is the sender (the uploader) and the other is the receiver (the downloader). If you want to transfer a file between you and the remote system, both of your computers must be using the same transfer protocol.

HyperTerminal supports the following protocols:

- 1K Xmodem
- Kermit
- Xmodem
- Ymodem
- Ymodem-G
- Zmodem
- Zmodem with crash recovery

After you are connected to a remote system, you can send a file by choosing the Send File option from the Transfer menu. This displays the Send File dialog box, as shown in Figure 15-11.

Figure 15-11: Sending a file is easy with HyperTerminal.

Simply enter the name of the file that you want to send. Then, in the Protocol drop-down list, select the same transfer protocol that is being used by the receiver. When you click on the Send button, the file is sent to the remote system. While the file is being transferred, you cannot do anything else with HyperTerminal; the entire attention of the program is concentrated on successfully transmitting your file.

Secret

When sending and receiving files, both the sender and the receiver need to be attempting the transfer at the same time. If this isn't the case, then there may be no one there to receive the file or vice versa.

If you want to receive a file that someone else is sending, you can do so by choosing the Receive option from the Transfer menu. This displays the Receive File dialog box, as shown in Figure 15-12.

Figure 15-12: You only need to pick a folder and a protocol to receive a file.

The Receive File dialog box is very similar to the Send File dialog box. Just pick a folder where you want the received file to be stored, and then pick a transfer protocol. The file is stored using the same name as it has on the remote system, whenever possible. If it is not possible (for instance, if there is a name conflict), then you are asked to provide a filename.

Printing terminal output

You can also print your output with HyperTerminal. There are two ways that you can print information, which are as follows:

- The first is to print information as it is received by HyperTerminal. This means that as soon as you see information from the remote computer on your screen, it is already being sent to your printer. You do this by selecting the Capture to Printer option from the Transfer menu.

    When you select this option, the words *Print Echo* appear in the status bar and a check mark appears next to the Capture to Printer option on the Transfer menu. To turn off printing, simply select the same menu option again.

- The other way to print is to wait until you are done with your session and then choose the Print option from the File menu. This displays prints the contents of the session buffer to the printer, all at one time.

Secret

Printing an entire session at once is great, as long as your session is not too long. Remember that HyperTerminal maintains a print buffer, which is initially set at 500 lines. If your session exceeds the buffer length, then the oldest information is lost. This also means that it cannot be printed.

Using Microsoft Exchange

Microsoft Exchange is a handy receipt-and-delivery system for electronic mail; it is the centerpiece of the messaging system that is built into Windows NT. In Chapter 13, you learned about the TAPI interface that is built into Windows NT.

Another built-in interface is known as MAPI, which is an acronym for Message Application Program Interface. The Microsoft Exchange delivery system uses special MAPI drivers to route messages to their final destination.

Installing Microsoft Exchange

Microsoft Exchange is not automatically installed when you first install Windows NT. However, an Inbox icon appears on your desktop; this is the key to installing and using Microsoft Exchange.

If you double-click on the Inbox icon, you should see a dialog box that asks if you want to install the Windows Messaging System. (This is a fancy name for Microsoft Exchange, as evidenced by the title bar of the dialog box.) If you click on the Yes button, the files are copied from your Windows NT Workstation CD-ROM. (You may be asked to insert the CD-ROM or identify where it is located.)

The appropriate MAPI files, program files, and other drivers are quickly copied to your hard drive. When complete, your system looks unchanged; there is no dialog box announcing completion, nor is there any other signal that the installation has been finished.

Instead, you need to double-click on the Inbox icon again. This time, the Microsoft Exchange Setup Wizard is started, as shown in Figure 15-13.

Figure 15-13: During Setup, you have the chance to specify which Microsoft Exchange services you want to use.

Three services are depicted in the dialog box. These services represent services external to Microsoft Exchange that you can use with the messaging system. You should examine which services you really need, and then select only those that are appropriate.

For the purposes of this chapter, select the Microsoft Mail service as well as the Internet Mail service. When you are ready to proceed, click on the Next button. This displays the dialog box shown in Figure 15-14.

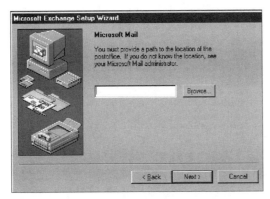

Figure 15-14: If you are installing Microsoft Mail service, you need to specify where the post office is located.

Microsoft Mail uses the concept of a post office, which can be viewed as a centralized clearing house for the mail that is on your network. This post office is typically installed on a server, accessible through your network, which is shared under a directory called WGPO, meaning *workgroup post office.*

To use the Microsoft Mail service with Microsoft Exchange, you need to know where your post office is located. If you cannot find it, check with your network administrator; he or she should be able to tell you the location.

Once you have either located the path to the post office or you have entered it in the dialog box, click on the Next button. This displays the dialog box that is shown in Figure 15-15.

Figure 15-15: You need to have an existing account when using Microsoft Mail.

In this dialog box, you see a list of all the mail accounts on the post office you have selected. You should select your post office account from the list. If your name is not available, then you need to talk to your network administrator about getting an account.

Once you have selected your mail account, click on the Next button to continue. This displays a dialog box in which you are asked for the password for your mail account. Enter the password (again, from your network administrator), and then click on the Next button.

This completes the configuration of Microsoft Exchange for the Microsoft Mail service; now you need to configure it for the Internet Mail service. This is first done with the dialog box that is shown in Figure 15-16.

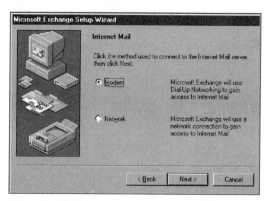

Figure 15-16: You can receive your Internet mail a couple of different ways.

Here you must specify how you receive your Internet mail: through a modem connection (a dial-up connection) or through a network connection (a dedicated connection). If you pick the modem option, then Microsoft Exchange uses Dial-Up Networking, which you learned about in Chapter 14.

Make your choice based on how you get your mail, and then click on the Next button. The dialog box that you see next depends on which choice you made. If you are getting your mail through a dial-up connection, the next dialog box (Figure 15-17) asks you to specify the Dial-Up Networking connection to use. If you are using a network connection, then this dialog box does not appear.

Figure 15-17: You use a Dial-Up Networking connection to retrieve your Internet mail.

If you have multiple connections defined, then you can use the drop-down list to select the proper one for your e-mail. If you haven't defined a connection, you can do so by clicking on the New button. (This allows you to create a Dial-Up Networking connection, as you learned to do in Chapter 14.) When you are done, click on the Next button to continue.

The next dialog box to appear is shown in Figure 15-18. Here you are asked for the address of your Internet mail server. If you have a mail server on your network, then you can get the address from your network administrator. If you are using a dial-up connection with an Internet provider, you can get the information from your provider.

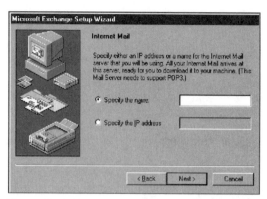

Figure 15-18: You need to enter the location of your Internet mail server.

You can specify the address of your mail server using either the DNS name or the IP address, both of which you learned about in Chapter 14. When you are done, click on the Next button to continue.

At this point, you see a dialog box that asks how you want to have your Internet e-mail retrieved: off-line (which means manually) or automatically. The latter choice is much easier and more efficient, but the choice is really yours.

Make your selection based on how you work with your Internet e-mail. When you are done, click on the Next button to continue. This displays the dialog box that is shown in Figure 15-19.

Figure 15-19: You finally need your Internet e-mail address.

Here you need to enter your Internet e-mail address. This is similar to your user name, followed by an at (@) sign, and your mail server domain name. (You learned all about addressing in Chapter 14.)

For example, my e-mail address is awyatt@dcomp.com; this is what I would enter in the A_ddress field. When you are done, click on the Next button to continue. This displays the dialog box that is shown in Figure 15-20.

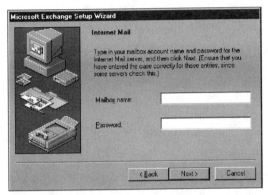

Figure 15-20: Now you need to specify your account information on the Internet mail server.

When you had an account set up on the Internet mail server, there was a mailbox (user) name and password assigned to you. You may know this information, or you may need to check with the administrator of the mail system for your network or your Internet service provider.

In this dialog box, enter both pieces of information. Without them, Microsoft Exchange is not able to retrieve your e-mail from the Internet mail server. When you have entered the information, click on the Next button.

You are now at the end of configuring Microsoft Exchange for your Internet Mail service. There are only a few more questions to answer before you are finished. In the dialog box that is shown in Figure 15-21, you are asked to specify where your personal address book is located.

You can change the path here, but you should only do so if you really have an address book located somewhere on your system or on the network. If you don't have one or are not sure, then click on the Next button to accept the default path and filename.

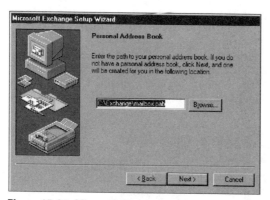

Figure 15-21: Microsoft Exchange maintains a personal address book for you.

Now you are asked to specify the location of your personal folders. These folders are used to store and organize your e-mail. This dialog box looks very similar to the one that is shown in Figure 15-21.

You can, again, change the directory if you have a need to. If you don't already have personal folders, then simply click on the Next button to accept the default. This displays the dialog box that is shown in Figure 15-22.

Figure 15-22: You can add Microsoft Exchange to your Startup group.

Here you are asked whether you want to add Microsoft Exchange to your Startup group. If you do, then Microsoft Exchange is started every time that you log in to your system. If you don't add it there (the default), then you must start Microsoft Exchange whenever you want to check for mail.

In general, if your system has quite a few resources and you are connected to the network, then adding it to your Startup group is no problem. (Resources are an issue because Microsoft Exchange is rather demanding of resources; it takes quite a few of them.) When you are done making your selection, click on the Next button. This displays the dialog box that is shown in Figure 15-23.

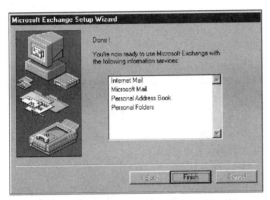

Figure 15-23: You have completed the setup of Microsoft Exchange.

This is the final dialog box for the Setup Wizard; it means that you are done installing and configuring. When you click on the Finish button, the Wizard is closed.

The Microsoft Exchange interface

When you are done installing Microsoft Exchange, its window is left open on your desktop, as shown in Figure 15-24.

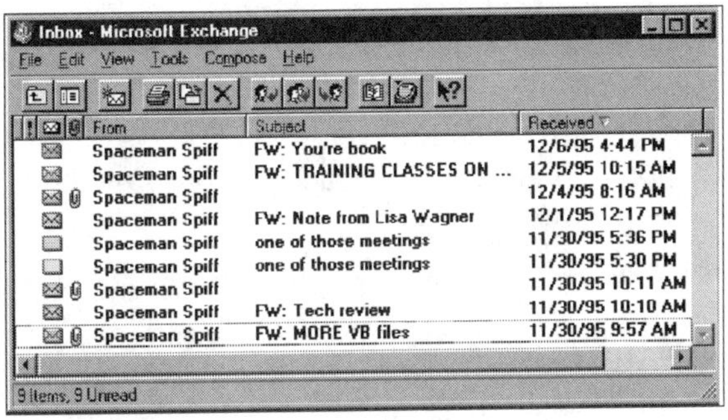

Figure 15-24: Microsoft Exchange includes a familiar Windows interface.

In your version of Microsoft Exchange, mail may or may not be available. This depends on whether there was any mail available for you on the server. If you look at the interface that is used by Microsoft Exchange, it is very similar to interfaces that are used in other parts of Windows NT.

For instance, there are similarities between this interface and those used in both a folder window and in the Printers folder. The interface consists of the following items:

- A menu with six choices

- A toolbar that provides access to most of the commands that are found in the menus

- A mail window that lists information about each pending message

To use the interface, simply select a message on which you want to take an action and then choose a menu command or tool to initiate the action.

Understanding the toolbar

The toolbar includes the majority of commands that you use in managing your mail. While actual management activities are covered later in this chapter, it does not hurt to understand the different tools that are available on the toolbar.

The toolbar is composed of 12 tools, divided into 6 different groupings. These groupings are as follows:

- The first two tools, from the left, are used to control mail folders. The concept of using mail folders is discussed in more detail in the next section.

- The next tool, which is the only one in its group, looks like an envelope. This tool is used to compose a new message that you want to send.

- The next group is comprised of three tools. The first allows you to print a message, the second is used to move the message to a different folder, and the third is used to delete a message.

- The next set of three tools is used to respond to a message that you have received. The first tool is used to respond to the sender. The next tool is used to respond not only to the sender but also to any other recipients of the message. The final tool in this group is used to forward a message to a different recipient.

- The next tool allows you to view your address book; it is followed by a tool to display your inbox.

- Finally, the last tool is used to get help on any other item that you point to and click on.

Working with folders

It seems natural that if you receive mail, you should be able to file it. Microsoft Exchange allows you to store messages in virtually any file structure that you can think of.

When you first use Microsoft Exchange, the directory structure of your mail system is not displayed. You may find it advantageous to display it, however.

You do this by clicking on the second tool from the left, which displays or hides the mail folders. When displayed, your Microsoft Exchange window appears, as shown in Figure 15-25.

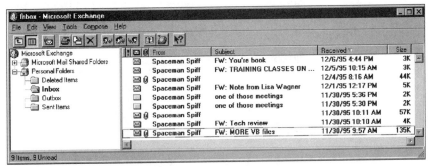

Figure 15-25: You can file your messages in different folders.

Notice that the folder structure now appears as a tree to the left of the message listing. With the folder tree displayed, the Microsoft Exchange window is reminiscent of the Explorer window. You can view the messages that are stored in any folder simply by clicking on the folder.

If you want to add a new folder, you can easily do so. For instance, you may be working on a special project and you need a folder to hold all of the mail that is related to the project.

You can choose the New Folder option from the File menu, and a new folder is created within the folder that you have selected in the folder window. You can then start to move and file mail in the new folder right away.

Managing your messages

The majority of the time that you are using Microsoft Exchange, you are performing actions that can be classified as managing your messages. This includes routine duties, such as sending messages, reading your mail, and responding or forwarding messages.

Each of these activities is covered in the following sections.

Sending a message

Sending a message with Microsoft Exchange involves two steps: composing the message and sending the mail. With the interface that is used by Microsoft Exchange, you typically don't need to worry about these items as separate steps. Instead, you follow a logical progression based on the tools and menu commands that are available.

To send a message, follow these specific steps:

STEPS

How to send a message

Step 1.   Open the Microsoft Exchange window (if it is not open already) by double-clicking on the Inbox icon on your desktop. The window should look similar to either Figure 15-24 or Figure 15-25, as shown earlier.

Step 2.   Click on the New Message tool. (This is the one that looks like 539an envelope.) This displays a message window, as shown in Figure 15-26.

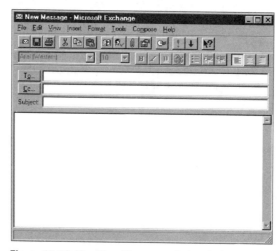

Figure 15-26: The New Message window is (obviously) used to create a new message.

Step 3. In the To and Cc fields, enter the addresses of the intended recipients. You can also click on these buttons to access and retrieve an address from the address book.

Step 4. In the Subject field, enter the subject for your message. Be as concise as possible, without being bland. (You want your message to be noticed, and people typically judge what to read by the subject.)

Step 5. If you feel that your message is important, click the Importance: High button (the exclamation point) on the toolbar. This flags the message as urgent and demands immediate attention from the recipient.

Step 6. Enter your message in the message area at the bottom of the dialog box. Type the message as you want it to appear to the recipient.

Step 7. Use the formatting tools on the toolbar to format your message.

Step 8. Insert files or add attachments to your message, as desired. Attachments allow you to send a file as part of an e-mail message. You can attach a file by clicking on the Insert File tool, which looks like a paper clip.

Step 9. When you are done composing your message, click on the Send tool. This is the left-most tool on the toolbar; it looks like a speeding envelope.

Reading a message

When you open your Inbox, you may notice that there are messages that need to be read. These messages are listed in the Microsoft Exchange window, as shown earlier in Figure 15-24 and Figure 15-25.

The list indicates the subject of the message, when it was sent, who it is from, and other information such as its importance and whether it has attachments. These messages can be read, replied to, or disposed of.

To view a message, follow these steps:

STEPS

How to view a message

Step 1. Open the Microsoft Exchange window (if it is not open already) by double-clicking on the Inbox icon on your desktop. The window should look similar to either Figure 15-24 or Figure 15-25, as shown earlier.

(continued)

STEPS *(continued)*

How to view a message

Step 2.   In the list of available messages, locate the message that you want to read.

Secret

Clicking on one of the column headers in the Microsoft Exchange window causes your messages to be sorted by that column. For instance, clicking on the From column causes the messages to be sorted by the person who sent them.

Step 3.   Double-click on the message subject or on the envelope icon at the left side of the message line. A window containing the message is displayed, as shown in Figure 15-27.

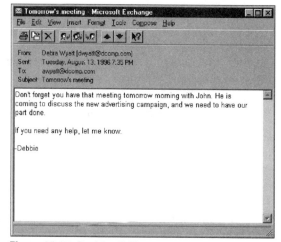

Figure 15-27: Double-clicking on a message opens a window in which the entire message is displayed.

Step 4.   If you want to have a printed copy of the message, click on the Print tool on the toolbar.

Step 5.   To reply to a message, click on one of the Reply tools (there are two of them). The Reply tool with one person on it causes the reply to go only to the sender. The other Reply tool (with two heads) sends the reply to all of the original recipients.

Step 6.   To delete the message, click on the Delete tool (the one with the X on it).

Step 7.   When you are done reading, close the message window.

When you are done reading a message, it remains in your inbox until you explicitly do something with it. You already know how to delete a message (as indicated in Step 6), but you can also file one, as discussed in the next section.

Filing messages

Earlier in this chapter, you learned that you can create custom folders for your messages. A common way to manage your mail is to move messages from the inbox to one of your folders.

You do this in the same way that you move files in the Explorer: simply drag the message (by its envelope icon) to the folder in which you want it stored. When you release the message, it is moved to the folder that you want.

Some messages are placed in folders automatically by Microsoft Exchange. If you look at the folder list, notice that there are four standard folders in your mail box:

- **Deleted Items.** Items are moved to this folder as you delete them. This folder functions similarly to the Recycle Bin on the desktop. Normally, the items in the Deleted Items folder are permanently deleted when you exit the Microsoft Exchange program.

  You can modify this behavior by changing the program properties, as discussed in the next section.

- **Inbox.** This is where you receive your mail and where it waits pending your action.

- **Outbox.** When you create, reply, or forward mail, it is moved to this folder until you connect to a mail service. Thus, this folder is a temporary holding area for your outgoing mail. When you connect to a mail service, the mail in this folder is sent and then deleted.

- **Sent Items.** Items are copied here when they are mailed. By default, this folder contains a record of all the messages that you have sent. You can modify this behavior by changing the program properties, as discussed in the next section.

If you want to work with any of the standard folders or your custom folders, you can do so by simply clicking on the folder. The contents of the folder are then displayed in the message list.

Controlling Microsoft Exchange properties

Microsoft Exchange has been around for a few years and for a couple of versions of Windows NT. In the latest version of Windows NT, it has become politically correct to call any configuration settings *properties*.

Microsoft Exchange does not refer to program settings as properties, however, even though they are. If you want to set the properties for the program, you can do so by choosing Options from the Tools menu.

This displays the Options dialog box, as shown in Figure 15-28.

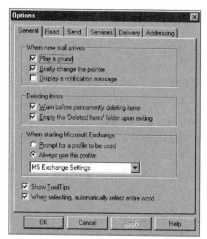

Figure 15-28: Microsoft Exchange allows you to configure the program in quite a few ways.

Six tabs are available in this dialog box, and each is discussed in the following sections.

The General tab

The properties on the General tab are those that do not fit into the other tabs in the Options dialog box. These settings allow you to configure the general operation of the program. The General tab is displayed when you first enter the Options dialog box, as shown in Figure 15-28.

In the top portion of the tab, you can specify what you want the program to do when you receive new mail. Notice that you can choose any (or all) of three options. The different options affect the speaker, the pointer, and the desktop (by displaying a message).

The options are listed in order of least obtrusive (the sound) to most obtrusive (the message). When Microsoft Exchange is first installed, the first two options are the defaults. You should pick the options that best reflect what you want to have happen.

The next group of options allows you to control what happens to items in the Deleted Items folder. You learned earlier in this chapter that items in the Deleted Items folder are placed there automatically when you delete them.

By default, the folder is emptied when you exit the program, and you are warned when the deletion is about to happen. You can modify the settings in this area to match your preferences.

The next portion of this tab controls how Microsoft Exchange begins. Normally, if your workstation is configured for a single person (you), then you don't need to worry about these settings. However, if you configure Microsoft Exchange to receive the mail of multiple individuals, then you can control which user profile is loaded when Exchange is started. (Creating multiple mail profiles is beyond the scope of this book.)

The two check boxes at the bottom of the tab control miscellaneous items. Specifically, you can turn Tool Tips on and off, and you can control how selecting is done when editing a message in the message window.

The Read tab

The information on the Read tab controls what happens when you are reading a message. When you click on the Read tab, the Options dialog box appears, as shown in Figure 15-29.

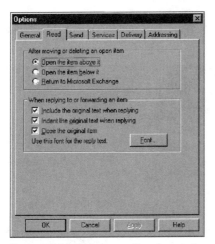

Figure 15-29: There are only a few options on the Read tab.

The first group of radio buttons, at the top of the Read tab, is used to specify what should happen when you delete a message that you are reading. By default, the message window automatically displays the message in the queue right above it. However, you can also cause Exchange to display the message below it or to simply close the message window.

The other group of options controls how a reply message is put together. You can indicate whether you want the original message included in your reply, whether the original text should be indented, and which font should be used for your reply (with the Font button).

The Send tab

Just as the Read tab is used to set properties of mail that you are reading, the Send tab is used to set properties of mail that you are composing. The contents of the tab are shown in Figure 15-30.

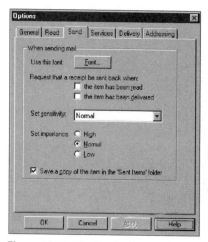

Figure 15-30: The Send tab controls messages that you are creating.

At the top of the tab is another Font button, which you can use to set a default font for your mail. Just below this are two check boxes that control any receipts that you receive on mail that you send. Remember that these are default controls; you can also specify what type of receipts you want on a message-by-message basis.

The next two controls are used to indicate the default sensitivity and importance of the messages that you compose. These, as well, can be changed while you are composing.

Finally, you can specify whether the items that you send should also be saved in the Sent Items folder. By default, messages are saved there. You can change this, however, if you don't want copies of your messages or if you are running low on disk space.

The Services tab

When you click on the Services tab, you have the opportunity to review which mail services are installed on your system. As you can see in Figure 15-31, the list of mail services should match those that you selected when you first installed Microsoft Exchange.

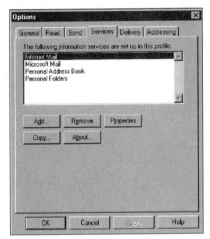

Figure 15-31: The Services tab is used to reconfigure the mail services that are in your system.

As you can tell from the buttons below the Services list, you can also reconfigure your services from this tab. Using the Add and Remove buttons, you can select which services are in your system.

You can also use the Properties button to change the configuration of any of your installed mail services. This button allows you to change the information that you originally provided when you installed the services.

The Delivery tab

The Delivery tab is used to specify where mail should be delivered to you and where your mail should be delivered for outbound processing. When you click on the Delivery tab, the Options dialog box appears, as shown in Figure 15-32.

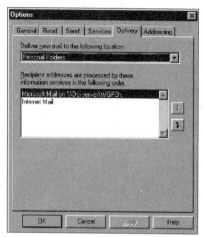

Figure 15-32: The Delivery tab has only two controls on it.

The top drop-down list in this tab allows you to specify where your incoming mail should be stored. The default location is in your Personal Folders, which is fine most of the time. You may want to change it, however, if you have multiple user profiles set up in Microsoft Exchange.

The next list in the tab indicates the order in which outgoing mail is processed. As shown in Figure 15-32, mail on this system is processed by the Microsoft Mail post office first and then by the Internet Mail server. Most of the time, this order is acceptable; however you may want to change it if you find that you are having addressing conflicts. (These happen very rarely, however.)

The Addressing tab

The information on the Addressing tab controls how the addresses that you enter in your messages are checked. As shown in Figure 15-33, the tab contains lists of different address books that are used by Microsoft Exchange.

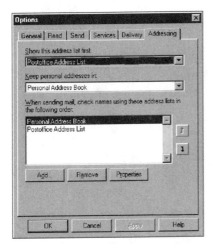

Figure 15-33: The Addressing tab controls how address books are used.

At the top of the tab, you can specify which address list is shown first when you are browsing through addresses. The next drop-down list indicates where your personal addresses should be stored. Finally, the list at the bottom of the dialog box allows you to indicate the order in which address books should be searched.

You can also change the properties of an address book by clicking on the Properties button. For your personal address book, you can change the location in which it is stored as well as how names are listed in the address book.

Summary

Windows NT Workstation includes a number of personal communications tools that you can use to increase your productivity and improve your level of connectivity with the outside world.

In this chapter, you have learned about three of those tools: the Phone Dialer, HyperTerminal, and Microsoft Exchange. In particular, you have learned the following items:

▶ The Phone Dialer is an accessory that allows you to use your computer as a speed-dialer. You use the computer to dial the modem, and then you pick up the phone to conduct your voice conversation.

▶ HyperTerminal is a full-fledged communications program that is included with Windows NT. It allows you to connect with remote systems and share information.

▶ When using HyperTerminal, you define connection descriptions, which control how a connection occurs and communication is established. You can create as many descriptions, or sessions, as you desire.

▶ You can use HyperTerminal as a terminal program, as a file transfer program, or to print information that was gleaned from a session.

▶ Microsoft Exchange can be lengthy to install, but it provides a convenient way to access your electronic mail.

▶ The Microsoft Exchange program is a client program that interfaces with different types of mail servers on your network or in related networks, such as the Internet.

▶ Microsoft Exchange provides a full set of tools that allow you to create mail, read mail, reply to messages, file your messages, and print the messages.

▶ Quite a few properties control the default behavior of Microsoft Exchange.

Making the Most of Your System

Chapter 16

Establishing Security

In This Chapter

Windows NT has always provided ways for it to be a secure operating system. Notice that I did not say it *is* a secure operating system; it is not. It has the potential of being one, however. Windows NT can be only as secure as you want it to be. For instance, if you are using your Windows NT system in a mountain cabin, 20 miles from the nearest neighbor, you are probably not too concerned about computer-based security issues. Your physical location provides adequate security for your needs.

If you are like most people, however, you need to be a bit concerned with how you can apply computer-based security to your system. The two areas of concern are local security and global security. Local security comes into play only if you have multiple users defined for your local system. Global security is a concern if you have made resources on your system available to others on your network or around the world.

This chapter focuses on the security aspects of Windows NT Workstation. Here you learn how to make your system more secure from the ground up. In particular, you learn the following items:

▶ How to develop an effective security strategy for your workstation

▶ How to use the User Manager to create individual and group user accounts

▶ Why you need to set up effective account policies and how to do it

▶ What it means to set user rights for different accounts

▶ How to set file and folder permissions for your workstation

▶ How to control security auditing

▶ How to manage the log files that are created on your system

Effective Security Strategies

Throughout this chapter, you learn many different ways in which you can increase the security of your Windows NT system. For any security measures to be effective, you need to approach the topic from a holistic approach.

This means that you need to examine every facet of how you use your system, brainstorming ways in which you can improve the security of the information that is on your computer and the integrity of the data that are contained on it. In many respects, security is not a condition as much as it is a process; if you are not improving your security, you are allowing security to lapse.

According to some experts in the field, there is no "static condition," no status quo. The way in which you implement security typically represents a fundamental change in how you act and react to the use of your system.

To have a sound strategy for securing your system, you need to examine a few areas. These areas are not intended to be all-encompassing; indeed, they cannot be since security issues are constantly evolving. The next few sections, however, help you understand more of what you need to consider when looking at security.

Written security plans

The first bulwark of any effective security strategy is, unavoidably, written in nature. Your company may have some written guidelines that describe the security plan for your location.

If so, you should read through them and understand exactly what your company expects in the way of security. Such plans are a great starting point for implementing security for your own workstation. (If your company does not have a written security plan, prod managers to get one — it demonstrates a mindset that can help avoid security problems at a later date.)

You may even want to go so far as to create your own written security plan. Such a practice is uncommon in large companies with centralized MIS departments. This is understandable, because overall system security is typically the responsibility of that department. If you work in a smaller company or are self employed, you may want to write down a plan.

In this case, make sure that your plan includes these two items:

- An indication of what you are doing for security
- An indication of what you will do if it doesn't work

These items may seem odd to some people, but if you don't know what you are doing for security, it's doubtful that you have any security at all. Also, you should know what you are going to do if your security is breached.

Will you change passwords? Perhaps institute more detailed log files. Or you may deny external access to your system altogether until the security hole is plugged.

Exactly what you do is up to you, but you are basically setting checkpoints along with a threshold to trigger some remedial action on your part. If the checkpoints are breached and the threshold exceeded, you need to be prepared to carry out your remedial actions.

Reliable backups

Does it sound odd to think about backups as part of a security plan? While they are primarily insurance against losing data, what if the loss of data is instigated by a breach in security? Or, what if someone breaks into your system and installs a virus or a Trojan horse program? In these cases, reliable backups definitely become a security issue.

When you make backups, you should make two types: a day-zero backup as well as routine backups.

Routine backups

Routine backups are those that you make as a matter of course; they are discussed fully in Chapter 11. Most people back up their workstation at least once a week; some do it every day. This is a good practice, but you may not discover a data-related security problem for a couple of weeks. In that case, your backups from last Friday do little good because they are corrupted as well.

Day-zero backup

This is where the *day-zero backup* comes in. This backup is one that you created when you first installed Windows NT Workstation. At that time, you knew you had a clean, reliable system. This is the system that you should make a backup of, and then put the backup in a safe place.

Normally, the day-zero backup is used to restore program files, because you haven't really put data on your system yet. It is invaluable, however, if you discover that someone has corrupted your operating system files or the program files that you use every day.

Using log files

As you already know, Windows NT allows you to automatically create log files. In accounting terminology, log files provide an "audit trail" of what happens on your system. You should use log files whenever possible, because they provide a way for you to discover what happened on your system. Without the log files, you can only guess what someone (or something) did to break your security.

Plan on reviewing your log files periodically. If you get into the habit of reviewing the log files, you can figure out what is going on with your system.

In some instances, you may even be able to head off suspicious activities before they become a security problem. Also, plan on keeping your log files for at least a week before you discard them. This allows you to go back and reconstruct a trail that may have taken days (or longer) to create.

Manageable drives

Most modern workstations come with huge hard drives. It is not uncommon to find 1, 2, or 4GB drives on systems. If you have a huge hard drive, consider how you partition your disk space in light of your security concerns.

Believe it or not, it can hurt your security if you partition the entire hard drive as a single disk drive. The reason is that, when you have a single drive, everyone who has access to your system has access to that drive.

It would be much better to partition your drive into at least two and preferably three drives. In either approach, one partition is large enough for your system files; this is the drive on which you install Windows NT Workstation. You can then protect this drive using directory and file permissions as discussed later in this chapter.

The other partition is used to store files that you want to share with others; this is the drive to which you give others access. Finally, if you have a third partition, you can use it for your own private data.

Password protection

There is a good chance you already know a bit about Windows NT passwords, particularly since you use one to gain access to your system. There are two types of passwords that you should be concerned with:

- Your own domain-access password

- Passwords to your system

After you receive a password to the domain of which your workstation is a part, you need to protect that password. You should change it periodically, even if the network does not force you to change it. And you should *never* give your password to someone else.

If you do, you may as well give him the key to your house or your car as well. Even if it is a coworker whom you know and trust, you don't know if he may leave your password lying about for someone else to discover and misuse.

If you issue passwords to other people to access your workstation, you obviously do so for security reasons. Without the passwords, you cannot be sure who is accessing your system and what they are doing. Understand, however, that the effectiveness of your password security depends on your willingness to enforce it for everyone that has access to your workstation.

As you learn later in this chapter, it is easy to institute password policies requiring everyone to change his password every two weeks. But what if Anne, your closest and dearest friend, comes to you and says that she's tired of changing her password all the time?

If you make an exception in her case and change her account so that her password never expires, you are starting to dismantle your security procedures. You may not think it's a big thing, but someone else may obtain Anne's password and then have a permanent passkey into your system.

Physical security

Even though you may have implemented all of the security precautions that are described in this chapter, and taken advantage of every security feature that is offered by Windows NT, it won't do you much good if people have free access to your computer system.

If they have access to your computer, they can do any of the following things:

- Reboot your system with a floppy disk and take information from your drive.
- Reboot your system with a floppy disk and wipe out your hard drive.
- "Play around" at the log-on screen until they can figure out a password to gain access.
- Access your system when someone forgets to log off.

This is just the tip of the iceberg. People can actually do quite a bit to bypass or foil your security measures if they have physical access to your workstation. In addition, they may be able to get access to the network of which your workstation is a part.

The solution to this, as simple as it sounds, is to make sure that you keep your workstation behind a locked door. Only those who need access to the workstation should have a key to the door.

Working with the User Manager

You may have multiple people using your workstation. Many companies have a workstation pool, in which users have access to whichever workstation is available.

Others may assign you a computer, but when you are not at work, it is being used by other people. In any of these cases, you need to be concerned with how you define different users for your system; this involves the creation of user accounts for your specific computer.

The tool that you use to manage user accounts is called, oddly enough, the User Manager. You start the User Manager by following these steps:

STEPS

Starting the User Manager

Step 1. Choose the Programs option from the Start menu. This displays the Programs menu.

Step 2. Choose the Administrative Tools (Common) option from the Programs menu. This displays a list of system tools that are installed on your system.

Step 3. Click on the User Manager option. This opens the User Manager window, as shown in Figure 16-1.

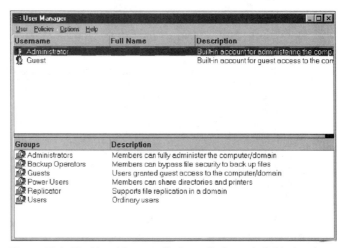

Figure 16-1: The User Manager displays all of your individual and group accounts.

If you open your User Manager, it may appear a bit different from the one shown in Figure 16-1. The biggest difference may be the number of user accounts that are defined in the top portion of the User Manager window.

The User Manager is not limited to working strictly with individual user accounts. As you can tell from the User Manager window, you can also work with user groups.

The individual user accounts are listed in the top portion of the User Manager window, and the group accounts, or user groups, are listed in the bottom portion. Both user accounts and group accounts are covered in the following sections.

Local versus domain accounts

There are two types of accounts on your system — local and domain. The account that you use when logging in to Windows NT determines what you can access on your system and on the network to which you are connected.

When you use the User Manager on your workstation, you are managing and working with local accounts. To use information that is on the net-

work, you must have a domain account. A domain account is set up by your network administrator, because the domain account information is stored on the domain server.

The network administrator uses the same User Manager interface you do when you set up accounts on your local computer.

Working with user accounts

When you first install Windows NT Workstation, two default accounts are established on your system: Administrator and Guest. You are the administrator, so the Administrator account is the one that you use to do your management work on the workstation.

As Administrator, you have access to everything that goes on within your system. The Guest account is used for people to log on to your system temporarily.

The following sections detail the management tasks that you can perform in relation to user accounts.

Creating a user account

From a user's perspective, a user account consists of only a user ID and a password. After all, this is all that is required for access to the computer. Windows NT, however, allows you to maintain quite a bit more information about each user and what he can do on your system.

To create a new user account, simply select the New User option from the User menu. This displays the New User dialog box, as shown in Figure 16-2.

Setting up a new user account is easy, because you don't need to fill in all of the fields in the New User dialog box. The only two fields that are mandatory are the Username and Password fields. (And, of course, the Confirm Password field.) It doesn't take much time to fill in the rest of the information, however.

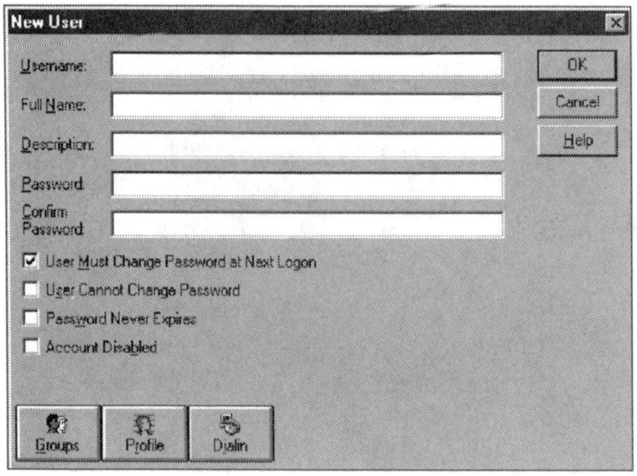

Figure 16-2: Setting up a new user account is easy with the User Manager.

The New User dialog box allows you to also specify additional information about the user that you are adding. In the Full Name field, you can enter the user's full name. This name appears when you are viewing user accounts in the User Manager as well as other Windows NT management tools.

The Description field allows you to provide any descriptive text necessary for the account. This information appears only in the User Manager window.

Near the bottom of the New User dialog box are four check boxes that control the user's password and account status:

- **User Must Change Password at Next Logon.** If this check box is selected, the user must modify his password when he first logs in to the system. This means that the password you provide in the New User dialog box is temporary, good only for logging on the first time. It is a good idea, for security purposes, to select this option.

- **User Cannot Change Password.** If this check box is selected, the user can never change his password; you must do it. If his password expires and he cannot change it, then you must pull up his account in the User Manager and modify the password for him.

- **Password Never Expires.** This check box overrides the account policies, which are discussed later in this chapter.

- **Account Disabled.** This option can be used to temporarily disable an account.

At the bottom of the New User dialog box are some buttons. These buttons allow you to specify additional information for this account. Of the three buttons, the one that you use most often is the Groups button.

You can click on this button to specify the user groups to which this new user belongs. (User groups are discussed later in this chapter.) The Profile button is used to specify a user profile for the new user, and the Dialin button is used to indicate whether the user can connect to your system via a Dial-Up Networking connection. (Dial-Up Networking is discussed in Chapter 13.)

When you are done specifying information for your new user, click on the OK button. This adds the user to Windows NT and returns you to the New User dialog box.

Editing a user account

The easiest way to edit an existing user account is to simply double-click on the account name in the User Manager. This displays the User Properties dialog box, as shown in Figure 16-3.

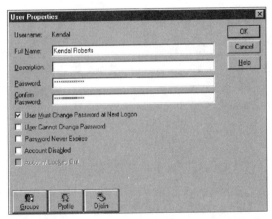

Figure 16-3: You can easily edit the information that is maintained for an account.

The information that is in the User Properties dialog box is the same information that you first specified when setting up the account. There is an additional check box on the User Properties dialog box, however.

At the bottom of the dialog box, there is a grayed-out check box. This check box is only active when you have enabled account locking (in the account policies, as described later in the chapter) and the user has exceeded the threshold of bad logons that you implemented. In that case, the check box is selected, but you can unselect it to grant the user access again.

All of the other fields and buttons on the User Properties dialog box work exactly the same as their counterparts in the New Account dialog box. When you are finished making changes in the account, click on the OK button to save your changes and close the dialog box.

Removing a user account

To remove an existing user account, simply highlight the account name, and then either press Delete or choose <u>D</u>elete from the <u>U</u>ser menu. When you do this, the User Manager displays a warning dialog box, indicating the implications of what you are doing.

To continue deleting the account, simply click on the OK button. The account information is removed, and the user no longer appears in the User Manager.

Secret

If you want to make a user account temporarily unavailable so that someone cannot use it to log in to your system, simply edit the account and click on the Account Disa<u>b</u>led check box. This preserves the internal pointers and security information that you would otherwise lose by deleting the account.

If you later want to reactivate the account, you need to go through the process of adding the account all over again, as described in the previous sections.

Working with group accounts

To aid you in your management of user accounts, Windows NT allows you to define user groups. These groups can then be used for assigning user rights, permissions, and security auditing. (All of these features are described later in this chapter.)

When you install Windows NT Workstation, it includes a number of predefined user groups. These six groups can be a real time-saver for you:

- **Administrators.** Members of this group can manage the local domain and computer system.

- **Backup Operators.** Members of this group can back up any files that are on the domain.

- **Guests.** Members of this group are generally limited user accounts, providing entry-level access to the local domain.

- **Power Users.** This group is the same as the Users group, except that members can share directories and printers.

- **Replicator.** This group is designed for use by the system replicator facilities and not by users.

- **Users.** This group is made up of general, local system users.

If you are able to use one of the groups for your needs, you should definitely do it. The only drawback to the groups is that, because they are predefined, everyone knows what they are.

While this doesn't present an immediate security risk (people log in to user accounts, not into group accounts), it can tell a savvy hacker what to do if he is able to crack an individual account and discover which group he is in. To get around this potential problem and make your system more secure, you may want to create different groups or at least rename the existing groups.

Users can be included in more than a single group. When you do this, the user inherits all of the rights and privileges of both groups. Thus, if a user account is assigned to both the Power Users and Backup Operators groups, then the user can act in either capacity.

If a user is assigned to the Administrators group, there is little sense in assigning him to any other group, because members of this group have the highest available permission level; membership in any other group would be redundant.

Every user account that you establish must belong to at least one user group. When you first set up the accounts, the user account is assigned by default to the Users group. You can then assign the user to additional or different groups, as desired.

Adding a group

Even though Windows NT provides a number of default groups, at some time you may want to create your own group. You do this by choosing the New Local Group option from the User menu. This displays the dialog box that is shown in Figure 16-4.

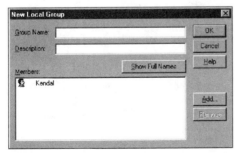

Figure 16-4: Setting up a group involves providing a group name and a list of members.

To define the group, simply provide a name for the group in the Group Name field, and optionally, a description in the Description field. You can also specify which user accounts belong to the group by using the Add and Remove buttons.

When you are done defining the group, click on the OK button. The new group appears in the bottom of the User Manager along with the other groups that are on your system.

Editing group membership

You can take a couple of approaches when editing the membership of a group. First of all, you can simply double-click on the group name in the User Manager. This displays a dialog box that is very similar to the one that you used to create the group in the first place. From this dialog box, you can add and remove users, the same as you did when defining the initial membership.

The other approach is to modify the group information from the user side of the fence. If desired, you can edit a user account and then click on the Groups button. This displays a Group Memberships dialog box, as shown in Figure 16-5.

Figure 16-5: You can add and remove an individual user from different groups.

This approach (from the user side of the fence) is the opposite of working with the group as a whole. This approach is very efficient for moving a single user in and out of a number of groups all at the same time.

Removing a group

Deleting a group is done in the same manner as deleting a user account. You simply select the group to delete, and then press Delete or choose <u>D</u>elete from the <u>U</u>ser menu. Either way, you are asked to confirm your action. After it is confirmed, you are asked to confirm it a second time. After doing so, the group is removed and is no longer listed in the User Manager.

When you delete a group, the members of the group are not affected, other than that they no longer belong to that group. Otherwise, they remain defined as users in the User Manager.

Establishing Account Policies

If you allow multiple people to use your workstation, then you become, by default, the administrator of your system. This means that you decide how people can gain access to your system and under what terms.

You do this by setting up *policies*. These policies determine which rules you want Windows NT to enforce and how it should do it. One of the policies that you can create has to do with user accounts and how they are set up.

Earlier in this chapter, you learned how you can set up user accounts; the account policies determine how that account is initially configured and the rules under which the account is used.

To create your account policies, use the User Manager tool. To open the User Manager, follow these steps:

STEPS

Setting account policies

Step 1.   Choose the <u>P</u>rograms option from the Start menu. This displays the Programs menu.

Step 2.   Choose the Administrative Tools (Common) option from the Programs menu. This displays a list of tools that are installed on your system.

Step 3.   Click on the User Manager option. This opens the User Manager window.

(continued)

STEPS *(continued)*

Setting account policies

Step 4.   Choose the <u>A</u>ccount option from the <u>P</u>olicies menu. This displays the Account Policy dialog box, as shown in Figure 16-6.

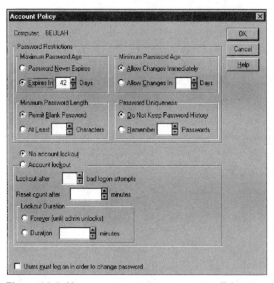

Figure 16-6: You can set up many account policies.

You can see that the Account Policy dialog box is basically divided into two major sections. The top half of the dialog box is used to set password restrictions, and the bottom half is used to set account lockout information.

Setting password restrictions

The top half of the Account Policy dialog box allows you to establish password restrictions. These are the rules that govern user passwords. User passwords are one of the most important security items that you have in any computer system.

They, in conjunction with the user ID, form the basis by which someone gains access to a computer. Because user IDs are typically easy to guess or to oversee, it is the password that becomes the real key.

The policies that you define in the Account Policy dialog box allow you to specify how you want passwords implemented on your system. The information in the Password Restrictions area of the dialog box controls the characteristics of all passwords that are on your system.

The area is divided into four sections, with the upper-left section controlling the maximum age for a password. Here you indicate two possible conditions: the passwords never expire or they expire in a certain number of days.

Setting passwords to never expire is convenient for users, but it is bad for security. The more often that you force passwords to be changed, the less likely that someone has time to break or steal a current password. You can set passwords to expire from 1 day to 999 days.

The upper-right section of the Password Restrictions area controls a minimum age for a password. Here you can specify if the user can make password changes immediately or if he must keep a new password a certain number of days. Again, you can pick a range between 1 and 999 days.

There is some debate on the best setting for a minimum password age. Some people think that changes should be allowed immediately, while others believe that including a minimum age increases security. For example, if someone oversees a person changing a password, then he could use the password and change it later that same day — unless, of course, the minimum age was set to a couple of days. How you implement this criterion is up to you.

In the lower-left corner of the Password Restrictions area, you can set a minimum password length. Here you can specify either that blank passwords are acceptable or that a password must contain a specific number of characters. For security reasons, you should never permit blank passwords; it is tantamount to leaving the door on the bank wide open, with no guard to check IDs.

Instead, set the minimum length to something long enough to make it difficult for someone to guess a password, yet short enough that it doesn't become a burden for users. You can pick any length from 1 to 14 characters. At a minimum, you should select a length of five or six characters.

In the lower-right corner of the Password Restrictions area is the final password configuration item. Here you can specify how unique a password must be. The default value is to not keep a password history; however, you can specify that Windows NT remembers a certain number of passwords for each user.

For instance, if you set the Remember value to four, then Windows NT would remember the last four passwords for each user. When a user changed his password, he would not be permitted to use any of the passwords in that list. For security purposes, it is a good idea to use the password history; you can set it to any value between 1 and 24.

The final password restriction is the check box at the bottom of the Account Policy dialog box. This check box controls when users can make changes to their password. If the check box is clear (the default), then users can change their password from the log-in dialog box; if you select it, they must log in before changing.

Setting account lockout information

The bottom half of the Account Policy dialog box governs how Windows NT treats the misuse of passwords; this is the account lockout information. These settings control how Windows NT reacts to people using passwords incorrectly. By default, account lockout is turned off. You can increase the security of your system by turning it on.

With account lockout turned on, Windows NT automatically disables the ability to log in to a system after a specific number of unsuccessful attempts. The length of this disability can also be specified. The first control in this area is where you specify how many bad log-on attempts should trigger a lockout. You can set it to any value between 1 and 999.

The second counter controls how many minutes the bad-try count should be maintained for. You can choose any value from 1 to 99,999 minutes (69 days, 10 hours, and 39 minutes). Any time that the lockout threshold is reached within this time range, regardless if there have been successful times in between, the lockout is triggered.

For example, you may have set the duration value to four hours, and the threshold is three bad attempts. If there are two unsuccessful log-on attempts followed by two successful attempts, then everything is fine. If the third unsuccessful attempt occurs within four hours from the first unsuccessful log-on attempt, then your system is locked out.

The bottom portion of the Account Lockout area is used to specify how long the lockout should last. You can specify that it should be permanent (until you release the account) or that it automatically resets after a period of time. Again, the time can range from 1 to 99,999 minutes, but it must be at least as great as the duration that you set for the reset duration (the Reset Count field).

When you are finished setting your account policies, click on the OK button to save your changes. This returns you to the User Manager.

Setting User Rights

After you have users defined, you can use Windows NT to expand or limit the rights of those users. This is done by establishing *user rights,* which can be applied to either individual users or to entire groups of users.

The simplest definition of user rights is that they control who can do what on your network. They are different then permissions, which are discussed later in this chapter. Whereas permissions determine what people can access, user rights determine which actions they can take.

As you have learned, Windows NT Workstation already has a large number of user groups that are already defined. These groups already have the applicable user rights assigned to them.

If you use these built-in groups, then those rights are applicable to the members that you place in the groups. However, if you define your own groups, then you must be concerned with which user rights those groups possess. You define user rights by using the User Manager, which you learned about earlier in this chapter. Follow these steps to change user rights:

STEPS

Changing user rights

Step 1. Choose the Programs option from the Start menu. This displays the Programs menu.

Step 2. Choose the Administrative Tools (Common) option from the Program menu. This displays a list of tools that are installed on your system.

Step 3. Click on the User Manager option. This opens the User Manager window.

Step 4. Select the User Rights option from the Policies menu. This displays the User Rights Policy dialog box, as shown in Figure 16-7.

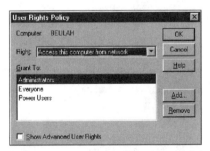

Figure 16-7: Users should be granted rights according to their needs on your system.

The User Rights Policy dialog box is easy to use. Controlling user rights is essentially a two-step process:

1. Select a user from the Right drop-down list.

2. Make sure that the groups and users in the bottom of the dialog box have the selected right.

If you need to change which users or groups possess a certain right, use the Add and Remove buttons to adjust those shown in the list. The following sections describe how you can add and remove users to whom a certain right has been granted.

Adding accounts

As you learned in the previous section, you grant a right to someone by selecting a particular right and then making sure that the correct accounts are listed as those possessing the right. To add an account to the list of those possessing a right, click on the Add button. This displays the Add Users and Groups dialog box, as shown in Figure 16-8.

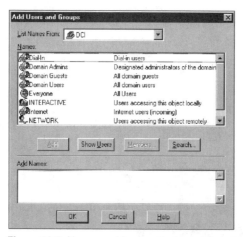

Figure 16-8: You can add accounts from different sources to the rights on your system.

There are three main parts to the Add Users and Groups dialog box. At the top of the dialog box is a drop-down list that indicates where the list of available users was drawn from. In the case of Figure 16-8, the list was drawn from DCI, which is the domain to which the workstation belongs.

You can also use the drop-down list to select a different source for users. You can choose any domain of which you are a part, or you can limit the user's list to the accounts that are defined on your local system.

The second part of the dialog box is the list of users. This list changes as you select a different source for the list. In this list, you select the groups that you want to add to the group possessing the right that you selected in the previous dialog box. The Add Users and Groups dialog box works only with groups by default, although you can change that.

You can cause individual users to be listed by clicking on the Show Users button in the middle of the dialog box. This adds the users that were defined at the source you have selected to the end of the Names list.

After you have selected a group or user name, click on the Add button. The name then appears in the list at the bottom of the dialog box; these are the names that are to be added to the list in the previous dialog box.

For instance, if you wanted to assign the selected right to the Backup Operators group, simply click on the group in the names list and then click on the Add button. The group name appears at the bottom of the dialog box.

When you are satisfied with the groups or users that you want to add to the right, click on the OK button. This closes the Add Users and Groups dialog box, and the names that you selected now appear in the User Rights Policy dialog box as a group or user to whom the right has been granted.

Removing accounts

You can also use the User Rights Policy dialog box (Figure 16-7) to remove an account from those to whom a right has been granted. Select the right, select the account, and finally click on the Remove button. The selected user or group is immediately removed from the list.

After you have removed a user or group from the list of those to whom the right has been granted, you cannot undo your action. The only way to again grant the right is to go through the process of adding the account, as described in the previous section.

Understanding the rights

If you use the drop-down rights list in the User Rights Policy dialog box, you may be surprised by the number of rights that are available. Windows NT includes quite a few different actions that can be taken by an individual or by a program, and each of these actions reflects a right.

The rights that are available, however, are divided into two general categories:

- Regular rights
- Advanced rights

The rights that belong to each category are discussed in the following sections.

Regular rights

Regular rights are those rights that an account needs to conduct its regular activities. On a Windows NT Workstation system, this category consists of 10 rights, which are always available in the drop-down rights list.

Regular rights include the following items:

- **Access this computer from network.** This right allows accounts that are connecting to your system through a network to access resources that are on your system. Normally, this right is assigned to a broad range of users, because resources are routinely shared over the network.

  If you want to shut your computer off from the rest of the network, however, you can simply remove accounts from this right.

- **Back up files and directories.** This right allows accounts to run the backup programs that are provided with Windows NT Workstation. Users with this right can back up information and do whatever they want with it, so the right should not be granted to everyone.

- **Change the system time.** This right allows an account to change the date and time from the Control Panel. Whether this setting is critical depends on whether you have services that rely on the correct time in order to run. (See Chapter 17.)

- **Force shutdown from a remote system.** This right allows an account, if logged on from a remote system, to shut down your computer. This right should be limited to only those people who may have a need to do this. By default, this only includes members of the Administrators and Power Users groups.

- **Load and unload device drivers.** This right allows an account to manage system device drivers. Typically, this right is granted only to the Administrators group.

- **Log on locally.** This right allows an account to log on to the computer when he is physically in front of it. Normally you should grant this right to individuals that must physically use your machine but not to those who access your system through the network.

- **Manage auditing and security log.** This right allows an account to modify the various access logs that are generated by Windows NT, using the Event Viewer.

  By default, this is granted only to members of the Administrators group. Remember that accounts with access to the logs can delete the tracks of their actions.

- **Restore files and directories.** This right allows accounts to restore files from previously made backups. This is a powerful right, because it allows the user to overwrite existing files that are on your system.

- **Shut down the system.** This right allows an account to shut down your workstation when using it locally. This right is essentially given to everyone, because someone sitting in front of the machine can also just turn off the power switch.

- **Take ownership of files or other objects.** This right allows an account to take complete control (ownership) of Windows NT objects. This right is quite powerful, as it means that the user can change who has access to your files.

  By default, this right is only given to members of the Administrators group.

Advanced rights

Besides the regular rights that were discussed in the previous section, Windows NT also maintains a category known as *advanced rights*. These rights are not normally available in the drop-down rights list.

You can make them available by clicking on the Show Advanced User Rights check box at the bottom of the User Rights Policy dialog box. The advanced rights then appear, interspersed with the regular rights in the drop-down list.

Advanced rights are typically used by programmers and when setting up specialized accounts for programs. This last use of advanced rights is the most typical — granting rights to programs.

Thus, as you review the advanced rights, remember that the term *account* may refer not just to individuals but also to programs acting as users of your system. The 17 advanced user rights are as follows:

- **Act as part of the operating system.** This right allows an account (typically a program) to act as a secure, trusted part of the operating system. This right is typically granted to secure programs so that they can operate with the highest clearance possible. This right should be granted only if you are sure that you can trust the program.

- **Add workstations to domain.** This right allows an account to add new workstation definitions to an existing domain. Normally, this right is granted only to those who are doing domain-based management from your workstation. By default, this right isn't granted to anyone.

- **Bypass traverse checking.** This right allows an account to move through directory trees freely. By default, this right is granted to everyone. You should limit the right if you want the user to stay within a particular directory. Normally this right is only modified if you are running POSIX programs on your system.

- **Create a pagefile.** This right allows an account to create page files (swap files). This setting is used primarily for programs that use page files to do their work.

- **Create a token object.** This right allows an account to create access tokens. These tokens are used by Windows NT to represent users or groups of users. If a program is granted this right, it can masquerade as other users or groups.

  This means that it can bypass normal security safeguards by circumventing absolute audit trails. By default, no one has this right granted.

- **Create permanent shared objects.** This right allows an account (typically a program) to create special permanent objects, such as \\Device, which are used elsewhere within the operating system. By default, this right isn't granted to anyone.

- **Debug programs.** This right allows an account to perform low-level debugging of objects such as threads. This right is necessary when developing programs for Windows NT but should not be granted to any other user. Some security features of Windows NT are automatically bypassed by users with this right.

- **Generate security audits.** This right allows an account (typically a program) to add entries to the security audit log. This right isn't granted to anyone, nor should it necessarily be granted.

  The use of this right is, itself, not audited. Thus, security is decreased if programs exercise this right irresponsibly.

- **Increase quotas.** This right is intended to allow an account to increase object quotas. The right isn't currently implemented in Windows NT.

- **Increase scheduling priority.** This right allows an account to raise the priority level that is assigned to a program or process. This right is normally assigned to the Administrators and Power Users groups.

- **Lock pages in memory.** This right allows an account (typically a program) to lock memory pages so that they can't be paged out to the swap file. Locking pages has the effect of limiting a valuable resource (memory) that you may need for other purposes.

- **Log on as a batch file.** This right allows an account to log on to Windows NT by using a batch queue facility. This right isn't implemented in this version of Windows NT.

- **Log on as a service.** This right allows an account (a program) to log on to Windows NT as a system service; this means that it has access to high-level security procedures. This right is also typically granted to programs that must run in the background at all times.

- **Modify firmware environment values.** On some systems, environment variables are kept in nonvolatile RAM so that they are quickly available from one session to another. This right allows an account to modify those variables, provided that it's a feature of the hardware. Normally this right is granted only to the Administrators group.

- **Profile single process.** This right allows an account to use the performance-sampling capabilities of Windows NT on a program or process. This right isn't implemented in this version of Windows NT.

- **Profile system performance.** This right allows an account to use the performance-sampling capabilities of Windows NT on the entire system.

  This right is required to use the Performance Monitor effectively, as discussed in Chapter 18, so it's granted to the Administrators group by default.

- **Replace a process level token.** This right allows an account (a program) to modify the security access token for a process. This right effectively gives a program complete run of your system and shouldn't be granted lightly.

Defining File and Folder Permissions

In Chapter 5, you learned how you can set security permissions on a printer that you are sharing on the network. A printer is not the only resource that you can share, however.

As you have learned, Windows NT allows you to share directories and (by extension) the files that are within those directories. The security features of Windows NT allow you to control who has access to the files and folders that you have made available on the network.

There is one caveat to setting permissions, however. Security permissions can only be set on NTFS drives. Thus, if your directory or file is on a FAT drive, you cannot limit access. Although you can still share the information on that drive, you cannot protect it as effectively as you can on an NTFS drive.

In concept, making permission changes is simple. Simply select the directory or file that you want to protect, and then specify which users or groups can access the directory or file.

To make changes in the permissions for a directory or file, follow these steps:

STEPS

Changing permissions

Step 1. Either browse your desktop or use the Explorer to locate the directory or file whose permissions you want to change.

Step 2. Right-click on the icon for the directory or file. This displays a Context menu for the object.

Step 3. Select the Properties option from the Context menu. This displays the Properties dialog box for the object.

Step 4. Click on the Security tab. This displays three buttons in the dialog box.

Step 5. Click on the Permissions button. A Permissions dialog box appears, as shown in Figure 16-9.

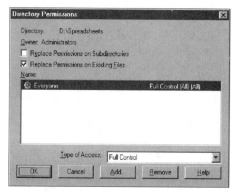

Figure 16-9: You can easily modify who has access to a file, directory, or drive.

Regardless of the object on which you are changing permissions, the dialog box effectively looks the same. There are some minor differences, however:

- **Directory.** The Permissions dialog box looks the same as shown in Figure 16-9.

- **File.** The Permissions dialog box does not include the two check boxes that are shown at the top of Figure 16-9; they are not applicable to files.

- **Disk Drive.** The Permissions dialog box looks the same as for a directory, as shown in Figure 16-9.

If you are working with directories, you use the check boxes at the top of the dialog box to indicate whether the changes that you are making should apply to subdirectories and to existing files in your directories. The default is to affect files but not subdirectories.

The Permissions dialog box may seem somewhat familiar; it is similar to the User Rights Policy dialog box that was discussed earlier in the chapter. (This makes sense, because both user rights and permissions are related to users and groups.)

In the middle of the Permissions dialog box is a list of users who have access to the object that you have selected. Immediately after each name is two sets of parentheses. The first set indicates the directory permissions that are granted to the user or group, and the second indicates the file permissions that are granted.

If you want to change the rights of an individual, you first add the person to the list of names and then modify his permissions. You can add or remove users by using the Add and Remove buttons at the bottom of the dialog box. Adding users or groups is done in essentially the same way as adding users and groups was done with user rights.

Setting permissions for a user or group involves selecting the user or group from the list of names and then changing the permissions for them. Note that Windows NT provides two ways that you can change permissions.

The first involves using the drop-down list of permissions at the bottom of the Permissions dialog box. The seven options in the list are as follows:

- **No Access.** This setting clears all permissions and prohibits access to the object by the selected group or user.

- **List.** This option sets only the Read and Execute permissions for the directory and the Not Specified permission for the files that are in the directory.

- **Read.** This option sets the Read and Execute permissions for both the directory and the files that are in the directory.

- **Add.** This option sets the Write and Execute permissions for the directory and the Not Specified permission for the files that are in the directory.

- **Add & Read.** This option sets the Read, Write, and Execute permissions for the directory, and the Read and Execute permissions for files that are in the directory.

- **Change.** This option sets the Read, Write, Execute, and Delete permissions for both the directory and the files that it contains.

- **Full Control.** This option grants all six of the individual permissions.

As you looked through this list, you may have gotten the idea that these seven options are essentially groups of permissions. For instance, if you look at the Change access option, you can see that it sets four other permissions.

This brings us to the second way that you can change the permissions for an object: by modifying the individual permissions. If you look at the bottom of the drop-down list, there are two additional options:

- **Special Directory Access.** This option allows you to change the individual permissions that are applicable to directories.

- **Special File Access.** This option allows you to change the individual options that are applicable to files.

If you choose either of these options, another dialog box is displayed that allows you to control individual permissions, as opposed to groupings of permissions. Both options present essentially the same dialog box; Figure 16-10 shows the dialog box that is displayed when you select the Special File Access option.

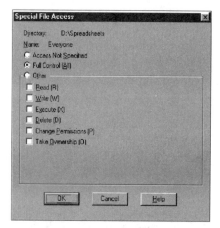

Figure 16-10: Individual permissions are used to control access to an object.

At the top of the dialog box are three radio buttons that can be used to quickly set permissions. The first radio button, Access Not Specified, indicates that the directory permissions don't apply to the files in the directory. Instead, permissions must be granted on a file-by-file basis. (This button is not available on the Special Directory Access dialog box.)

The second radio button indicates that full control is provided to the object; this is the same as selecting every check box in the rest of the dialog box. The third radio button, Other, is selected automatically if you start selecting any of the check boxes that are in the balance of the dialog box.

These other check boxes control the permissions that you want to grant to the selected individual or group:

- **Read.** The user or group can read the file or directory.

- **Write.** The user or group can overwrite the file or save information in the directory.

- **Execute.** The user or group can run a program file.

- **Delete.** The user or group can delete the file or directory.

- **Change Permissions.** The user or group can change permissions on the file or directory.

- **Take Ownership.** The user or group can take complete control of the file or directory.

When you are finished making changes to the permissions, click on the OK button. The modified permissions are now shown in the Permissions dialog box. You can continue to make permission changes, as desired. When you are finished, click on the OK button to close the Permissions dialog box.

Logging Events

One of the features included in Windows NT is the ability to track what happens on your system. This feature, called *auditing,* is an important aspect of any security that you implement at your site.

Using auditing, you can control when information is written into the log files that are maintained by Windows NT. You can then review the log files to see, from a security perspective, what has been happening on your workstation. (How you manage log files is discussed later in this chapter.)

To use auditing, you must first enable it. Then you can determine exactly what should be audited.

To set audit policies for your entire server, follow these steps:

STEPS

Turning on auditing

Step 1. Choose the <u>P</u>rograms option from the Start menu. This displays the Programs menu.

Step 2. Choose the Administrative Tools (Common) option from the Programs menu. This displays a list of tools that are installed on your system.

(continued)

STEPS *(continued)*

Turning on auditing

Step 3.   Click on the User Manager option. This opens the User Manager window.

Step 4.   Select the Audit option from the Policies menu. This displays the Audit Policy dialog box, as shown in Figure 16-11.

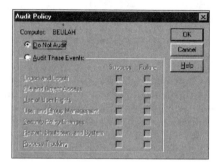

Figure 16-11: The Audit Policy dialog box allows you to control system-wide auditing.

The Audit Policy dialog box contains a series of check boxes that control exactly which types of events are audited. To activate the check boxes, just click on the Audit Test Events radio button.

There are seven categories of events that you can audit:

- Logon and Logoff
- File and Object Access
- Use of User Rights
- User and Group Management
- Security Policy Changes
- Restart, Shutdown, and System
- Process Tracking

To audit a particular category of event, click on the appropriate check box under the Success or Failure column. Clicking in the Success column indicates that you want to audit successful completion of events in the category, and clicking in the Failure column indicates that you want to audit unsuccessful completions.

Each additional check box that you add means that more information is written to the log files, as discussed later in this chapter. When you are done making changes, click on the OK button. This closes the Audit Policy dialog box and implements your new audit policy.

The seven categories that you can set in the Audit Policy dialog box are discussed more fully in the following sections.

Logon and logoff auditing

This event category is used when you want to record when someone enters or leaves your system. When this category is selected, log entries are generated whenever someone logs in or out locally or through the network.

If you select the Success column, then you have a record of when people made it into your system. If you select the Failure column, then you have a record of when people tried to enter your system. Thus, you can tell if there is a problem with someone trying to break into your system.

Secret

If you suspect that someone is trying to break into your system, you can turn on the account lockout feature of Windows NT. This capability is covered earlier in this chapter.

The Failure check box can also be helpful for monitoring new users. Many times a new user has trouble getting into a system, particularly if he is new to computers in general. If you monitor this type of event, you can plan some rudimentary training for your novice personnel.

File and object access auditing

While auditing items at a system level is a feature of Windows NT, auditing access at a file and directory level is a feature of the NTFS filing system. While you can still enable this type of auditing in the Audit Policy dialog box, you cannot take the second step, which is to turn on auditing at the file and directory level. Thus, if you are using the FAT system, it does no good to enable this level of auditing.

Selecting this event category turns on or off all file and directory auditing. After turning it on, you still need to specify how to audit individual files or directories.

To set audit properties on the files and directories, perform the following steps:

STEPS

Setting audit properties for files and directories

Step 1. Browse your desktop or use the Explorer until you locate the file, folder, or drive whose access you want to audit.

Step 2. Right-click on the icon for the object. This displays a Context menu.

Step 3. Choose the Properties option from the Context menu. This displays the Properties dialog box for the object.

Step 4. Click on the Security tab. This displays three buttons in the dialog box.

Step 5. Click on the Auditing button. This displays the Auditing dialog box, as shown in Figure 16-12.

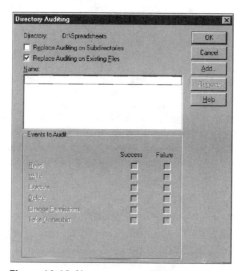

Figure 16-12: You can set auditing properties on drives, files, and folders.

This dialog box should look fairly familiar; it is very similar to the Permissions dialog box that you used when setting directory and file permissions (see Figure 16-9). The same general type of dialog box is used, regardless of whether you are changing auditing properties on a disk, a directory, or a folder.

The differences between the dialog boxes are as follows:

- **Directory.** The Auditing dialog box looks the same as shown in Figure 16-12.

- **File.** The Auditing dialog box does not include the two check boxes at the top of Figure 16-12; they are not applicable to files.

- **Disk Drive.** The Auditing dialog box looks the same as for a directory, as in Figure 16-12.

If you are working with directories or drives, the check boxes at the top of the dialog box are used to indicate whether your changes should apply to subdirectories and to existing files in the directories. The default is to affect files but not subdirectories.

Auditing dialog boxes, regardless of the type, contains two major areas. The first area is in the center of the dialog box, where you specify the users or groups whose actions you want to audit.

You use the Add and Remove buttons to control the list of accounts that you want to have audited. Adding and removing accounts are done the same way as when you managed user rights, as discussed earlier in this chapter.

Secret

If you want to audit all accesses to a file or folder, add the Everyone group to the Name list. This can, however, cause your log files to grow very quickly, especially if it is a popular file or folder.

The second part of an Auditing dialog box is at the bottom, in the Events to Audit area. Here you can use the check boxes to specify which actions you want to have audited on this object and for the selected users.

Notice that you can audit the success or failure of six different actions. The failure side can be particularly helpful, as you can determine who has tried to get into a file and failed.

Tip

When auditing file and directory access, you need to carefully consider what you are trying to achieve. This is because every auditable activity results in a record being written in the Security log file. On an active system, it's possible to overflow the Security log file rather quickly. This implies that you need to actively manage the log file, a process that is discussed later in this chapter. Judicious use of file and directory auditing also enables you to detect security problems more easily.

When you are done changing the audit properties, click on the OK button to save your changes. The auditing is started immediately after closing the dialog box.

User rights auditing

Earlier in this chapter, you learned about setting user rights for different users and groups. The Use of User Rights event category causes Windows NT to record an event log entry every time someone exercises any of his user rights.

Secret

Auditing user rights related to logging on and off your system is not controlled by the User of User Rights category. Instead, these are controlled by the Logon and Logoff event category.

If you have been careful in setting your user rights, you probably don't need to check the Success column for this event category. Doing so could quickly fill your log files, because many programs exercise user rights during the normal course of operation.

Selecting the Failure column can provide more meaningful information from a security standpoint. This allows you to monitor when a person or program is attempting to exercise user rights without success. Because this is a potential security breach area, it is a good exception to always flag.

User and group management auditing

This event category is used to audit when changes are made in any of your users and groups. Log entries are recorded when a user or group is created, deleted, changed, renamed, disabled, or enabled. In addition, a log entry is recorded when a user password is changed. Because you should be the only one making changes in user information, this is a very good event to audit.

Security policy changes auditing

This event category allows you to track when someone modifies your system policies (account, user, or audit). Because these areas are so powerful and control so much of the security of your system, it is always a good idea to audit this category, both for success and failure.

The only problem with this event area is if a user has access to your system, and he knows enough to change your system policies, he probably also knows enough to wipe out the system log files. The only way to solve this problem is to keep your workstation under lock and key.

Secret

You can also audit the directory in which the log files are stored. In this way, you can see if anyone is making changes to the log files. Even when someone wipes out the log file, a record is written in the brand new (empty) log file that indicates who did it.

Restart, shutdown, and system auditing

This event category keeps track of when your system is shut down, started up, or restarted. In addition, if a critical error is generated by the operating system, a record of that is generated in the log file. The value of this event category depends on if you feel this area is a problem.

Remember that this event category comes into play only if someone performs an orderly shutdown. If he turns off the power or unplugs the system, or if the power in your building goes off, the system does not have time to write a log file entry. If this happens, however, a log file event will be generated when the power comes back on and the system is restarted.

Process tracking auditing

Process tracking means the auditing of events at a process-by-process level. This is pretty nitty-gritty stuff and probably isn't necessary for daily operation. The best time to use this type of auditing is if you are writing a program and you want to track exactly what the processes in your program are doing.

Managing Log Files

As you have learned, Windows NT includes the ability to create detailed log files on almost everything that happens in your system. This information is logged in special system log files, which are nothing but journals of what happens on your system over a period of time. Windows NT Workstation maintains three log files, each of which can be managed with the Event Viewer.

You start the Event Viewer by following these steps:

STEPS

Starting the Event Viewer

Step 1. Choose the <u>P</u>rograms option from the Start menu. This displays the Programs menu.

(continued)

STEPS *(continued)*

Starting the Event Viewer

Step 2.   Choose the Administrative Tools (Common) option from the Program menu. This displays a list of tools that are installed on your system.

Step 3.   Click on the Event Viewer option. This opens the Event Viewer window, as shown in Figure 16-13.

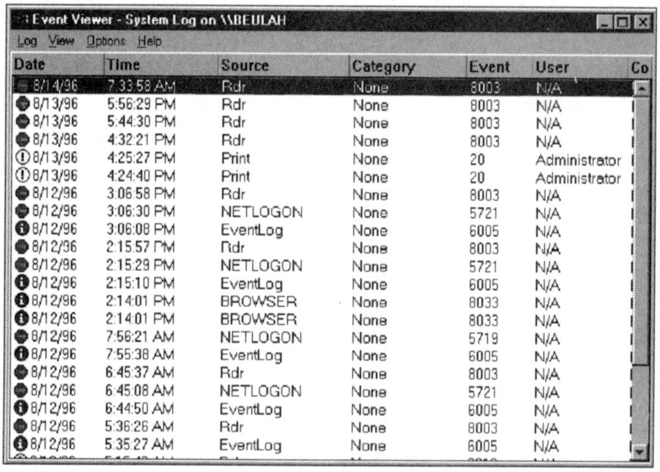

Figure 16-13: The Event Viewer is used to manage the log files that are on your system.

The information that is displayed in the Event Viewer is for one of the three log files on the current system. You can, however, choose to view the event log on a different system on your network if you have the proper permissions on that system.

You do this by choosing the Select Computer option from the Log menu. This displays the Select Computer dialog box, as shown in Figure 16-14.

Figure 16-14: You can use the Event Viewer to manage log files on remote systems on your network.

You can either enter the UNC path for the remote system in the <u>C</u>omputer field or select a computer by browsing through the network tree at the bottom of the dialog box. When you click on the OK button, the log files on the remote system are opened and displayed.

Reviewing event logs

As mentioned earlier, three types of event logs are maintained by Windows NT. When you start the Event Viewer, you specify the log that you want to view by selecting any of the following options from the Log menu.

Each option represents a separate and distinct event log:

- **System.** This log keeps track of events that are generated by the operating system. Examples include device drivers that are not loading, messages about system memory usage, and messages from different system modules.

- **Se<u>c</u>urity.** This log tracks security violations. This includes all of the events generated by the permissions logging and auditing discussed earlier in this chapter.

- **Application.** This log lists events that are generated by your applications. The exact types of events differ from program to program. For example, some programs log when they are started and stopped, while others may only log errors that occur during operation.

Using the Event Viewer, you can work with each log using the same methods and techniques. The only thing different from one log to the next is the information that is contained therein and the way that information is categorized.

From a system perspective, it is undeniable that the most important information in the log files are the contents of the security log. Depending on how you use your workstation, you may want to review the security log every day or two.

Keep the following in mind as you look through the security log:

- Pay particular attention to the contents of the Category and User fields. These fields can help you zero in on potential trouble areas.

- Look for events that appear to be out of line with what you know should be happening. For instance, someone besides you making changes to the user accounts or group assignments could indicate a severe security breach.

- Pay special attention to repetitive events, particularly failed repetitive events. For instance, several unsuccessful attempts at logging on to your system may indicate that someone is trying to break into your system.

The information listed in the log files is simply a summary of the events that have occurred. If you want to see detailed information about a particular event, just double-click on the event. This opens a dialog box with all of the event details, as shown in Figure 16-15.

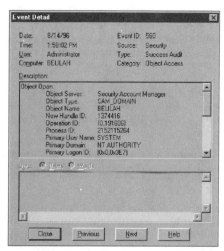

Figure 16-15: The event logs contain detailed information on each event that occurs.

Log file settings

Besides simply looking at log files, you can use the Event Viewer to configure how Windows NT creates the log files. To change how the log files are maintained by Windows NT, choose the Log Settings option from the Log menu. This displays the Event Log Settings dialog box, as shown in Figure 16-16.

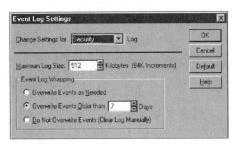

Figure 16-16: You can control how Windows NT maintains log files.

The drop-down list at the top of the dialog box controls which log file you are configuring. When you first display the Event Log Settings dialog box, it assumes that you want to make configuration changes to the log file that you are viewing. You can use the drop-down list to select a different log file, if you want.

The next control in the dialog box is a specification for the maximum size of your log file. You can set the log file to any size that you want, in 64K increments, from a minimum of 64K to a maximum of 4GB. Many workstations would probably never need an individual log file size larger than 512K–1MB.

The last area on the tab controls what happens when the event log reaches the maximum size that you specified. There are three ways in which Windows NT can handle the log file:

- **Overwrite Events as Needed.** This option causes the operating system to overwrite the oldest log file events when it is full.

- **Overwrite Events Older than X Days.** This option causes the operating system to overwrite any event at least *X* days old, where you can specify the time.

- **Do Not Overwrite Events.** This option is used when you don't want to lose anything. When the maximum log-file size is reached, you are notified. You should not select this option if you don't have a large log file.

If your log file fills up and it needs your attention (for instance, if you told Windows NT not to overwrite events), then the messages that keep popping up on your workstation interfere with other work as the operating system waits for you to clear the log file. For this reason, you should establish a fairly large log file and indicate that you want to keep entries for a minimum of seven days.

When you are finished specifying how your event logs should be kept, click on OK to close the dialog box and save your changes.

Archiving and clearing event logs

The Event Viewer can be used to save an event log into an archive file. The log files are saved in a binary format, using a name you specify, along with a filename extension of .EVT. You can later use the Event Viewer to reload and review the archive files. Unfortunately, you cannot set Event Viewer to automatically create the archive files for you; you must do it manually.

To save the current log file as an archive, simply choose the Save As option from the Log menu. This displays a regular Windows NT file selection dialog box, and you can specify a name for the file.

If you choose to clear your log file, Event Viewer also asks you if you want to save the log file in an archive. To clear a log file, simply choose Clear All Events from the Log menu. This displays the dialog box that is shown in Figure 16-17.

Figure 16-17: You have the opportunity to archive log files when clearing them.

To save your log file in an archive, simply click on the Yes button; you are then asked to specify a name to use for saving. If you instead click on the No button, then your information is cleared without saving.

Summary

When you work in a multiuser or networked environment, you need to be concerned about security. Windows NT includes quite a few features and tools that allow you to secure your system from just about every angle that you can think of.

In this chapter, you have learned how you can secure your system. In particular, you have learned the following items:

▶ Before trying to secure your system, you should have a written security plan that indicates what you want to accomplish, how you plan to go about it, and what happens if your security is breached.

▶ The User Manager is the tool that you use to create individual and group user accounts. User accounts are created for everyone using your system, and group accounts are created to aid in management of those users.

▶ Account policies are used to lay the framework from which all of your user accounts are created and in which they operate. Setting effective account policies is a big boon to system security.

▶ Windows NT relies on user rights to define what a group or user can do on the system.

▶ On NTFS drives, your files and folders that are accessible to other people can be protected by changing their permissions.

▶ Windows NT allows you to audit most actions on your system. With auditing enabled, a record is kept (in system log files) of the success or failure of different event categories.

▶ You can use the Event Viewer to manage the system log files that are created on your system. The Event Viewer allows you to review, archive, and configure the log files according to your needs.

Chapter 17

Automating Tasks

In This Chapter

Many tasks are done with a computer that seem very repetitive. While special programs can be developed to take care of some of these tasks, others may not be well-suited for using a single program. Fortunately, Windows NT includes some features that can help you to automate some of the work that you do on a daily basis.

Even though the information on these features is not widespread or readily understood, this chapter provides the information that you need to get started. In particular, you learn the following items:

▶ How to run programs when you first log in to Windows NT

▶ How to create batch files to automate some of your commands

▶ How to schedule tasks so that they run at a given time

Running Programs at Startup

When you first log in to Windows NT Workstation, one of the last tasks accomplished is Windows NT examining the contents of a special folder on your system; it then processes the contents of that folder. This folder, Startup, can contain almost anything: programs, documents, shortcuts, and additional folders.

Exactly how the contents are processed depends on exactly what the item is:

■ **Program.** If the item is a program, then the program is executed.

■ **Document.** If the item is a document, then the program that is associated with the document is started and the document is loaded. If it is a document for which there is no association, then the Open With dialog box appears, as if you double-clicked on the unassociated program yourself.

- **Shortcut.** If the item is a shortcut, it is treated in the same way as if it were the actual item. For instance, a shortcut to a document is handled in the same way as a document.

- **Folder.** If the item is a folder, then the folder is opened, and a folder window appears on the desktop.

Secret

If a file that you place in the Startup folder has the hidden attribute turned on (the file is hidden), then it is not started when you start your system.

In general, you should only place shortcuts in your Startup folder. This stops the folder from getting too cluttered with nonessential files. For example, you may want to start a program when you first start Windows NT.

If you place the actual program file in the Startup folder, that may be fine. What if the program needs a data file? You may then need to move that data file (or more) to the Startup folder.

The next time that Windows NT starts, it runs your program, but it also tries to open each individual data file that is in the folder. It's much better to store the program and its data elsewhere, and simply include a shortcut to the program.

Note

If you installed Windows NT Workstation as an upgrade to an earlier version of Windows or Windows NT, then the contents of your previous StartUp group was automatically transferred to the new Startup folder.

There are two ways in which you can modify the contents of your Startup folder:

- You can use a Wizard that is provided for this purpose.

- You can modify the folder manually.

The following sections examine these methods, starting with the Wizard first.

Changing the Startup folder with a Wizard

One of the Wizards that is included with Windows NT Workstation 4.0 allows you to create shortcuts. This same Wizard can be used to modify the contents of the Startup folder, as shown in the following steps:

STEPS

Adding a shortcut to the Startup folder

Step 1. Right-click on the Taskbar. This displays a Context menu.

Step 2. Choose the Properties option from the Context menu. This displays the Taskbar Properties dialog box.

Step 3. Click on the Start Menu Programs tab. The Taskbar Properties dialog box now appears, as shown in Figure 17-1.

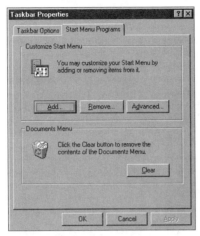

Figure 17-1: The Taskbar Properties dialog box is used to configure the Taskbar and Start menus.

Step 4. Click on the Add button. This starts the Create Shortcut Wizard, as shown in Figure 17-2.

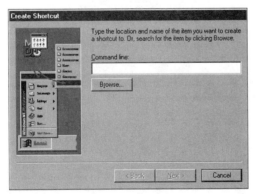

Figure 17-2: You can use a Wizard to create shortcuts for your system.

Step 5. In the Command Line field, enter the name of the program that you want to have started whenever you start Windows NT. You can also use the Browse button to locate the program.

(continued)

STEPS *(continued)*

Adding a shortcut to the Startup folder

Step 6.   After you have specified a program, click on the <u>N</u>ext button. This displays the Select Program Folder dialog box, as shown in Figure 17-3. (The directory tree that is shown on your system may be a bit different.)

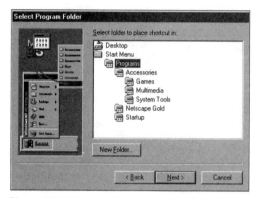

Figure 17-3: You can place your new shortcut anywhere you like.

Step 7.   Double-click on the Startup folder, which is shown at the bottom of the directory tree in Figure 17-3.

Step 8.   Click on the <u>N</u>ext button to proceed to the final step. This displays the dialog box that is shown in Figure 17-4.

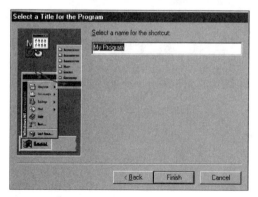

Figure 17-4: You can give your shortcut any name.

Step 9.   Enter the name that you want to have used for your new shortcut. The default name is based on the name of the program that
you selected in Step 5.

Step 10.   Click on the Finish button.

At this point, the new shortcut is added to the Startup folder. The Taskbar
Properties dialog box, shown earlier in Figure 17-1, is still visible, and you
can add more shortcuts, if desired.

The next time you log on to your workstation, the new shortcut is automatically processed by Windows NT.

Wizards: help or nuisance?

Let's face it: Many of the people who are using Windows NT have been using computers for years. Because of this, they find themselves quite comfortable with hardware, operating systems, software, and computing in general. Because of this, many Windows NT users view Wizards as rather condescending. These inter-mediate-to-advanced users understand why Wizards are in Windows 95 (the operating system for the masses), but don't understand why they are in Windows NT (the operating system for the rest of us).

I won't try to defend Microsoft on this one. It seems that their Wizards, instead of being con-verted lock, stock, and barrel to NT, could have gone through some screening. A case in point: the Wizard to create shortcuts, which is used in this section to add items to the Startup folder. In reality, anyone who is comfortable browsing through directories or using the Explorer will have no problem just pulling up the Startup folder for his or her user profile and then making changes.

As for the Wizards that you run into, I suggest that you use them if you want to, but otherwise ignore them. Maybe someday Microsoft will make them an optional installation item, which would please users of all experience levels.

Changing the Startup folder manually

One of the finer points of automatically starting programs, which you may have missed up to this point, is the fact that the Startup folder is just that — a folder. This means that you can open it, just like any other folder, and manipulate its contents. Because you can add, remove, or edit items in the Startup folder manually, this method is much more flexible and powerful than using a Wizard.

You manually change the Startup folder by following these steps:

STEPS

Manually changing items in the Startup folder

Step 1. Right-click on the Start button. This displays a Context menu.

Step 2. Select the Open option from the Context menu. This displays the Start Menu folder window.

Step 3. Double-click on the Programs icon in the Start Menu folder window. This displays the Programs folder window.

Step 4. Double-click on the Startup icon in the Programs folder window. This displays the Startup folder window.

Step 5. At this point, you can make changes in the Startup folder. This includes adding or removing items as well as creating any shortcuts.

When you are done, close the folder windows on your desktop. The next time you log on, your changes are processed as Windows NT is started.

Secret

If you create a folder in the Startup folder, the new folder is opened and displayed when you start Windows NT. The contents of the folder are not executed; the folder is simply displayed.

Running startup programs after starting

There may be times when you need to restart a program after you have started your system. Perhaps a simplistic example can help illustrate this point. Consider adding a shortcut to the Explorer in your Startup folder. When you first log in to Windows NT, the Explorer is started automatically. If you later close the Explorer, you need to restart it by choosing the Explorer option from the Start menu structure.

This may seem like a no-brainer, but you could have shortcuts in your Startup folder that point to programs that are more difficult to find. You can even include programs that don't appear in a menu structure. In these cases, when you exit the program before you intend to, you may be tempted to believe that restarting your system is the easiest way to restart the program.

Fortunately, there is a way that you can relaunch programs that are stored in your Startup folder. To do this, follow these steps:

STEPS

Restarting a Startup folder program

Step 1.   Choose the Programs option from the Start menu. This displays the Programs menu.

Step 2.   Choose the Startup option from the Programs menu. This displays the items in your Startup folder.

Step 3.   Choose the menu item that represents the program that you want restarted.

Creating Batch Files

Those who have been around PCs since the days of DOS may remember *batch files*. These are nothing but ASCII text files, using a .BAT filename extension, that contain a series of DOS commands to be executed.

When you entered the name of the batch file at the command line, each command within the batch file was executed in turn. Batch files were very helpful in accomplishing many of the repetitive tasks that always seemed to pop up on a computer system.

While DOS may be gone (as far as your workstation is concerned), Windows NT includes the command-prompt environment that you learned about in Chapter 9. This environment enables you to create batch files in the same way that you did under DOS.

The batch file can contain any valid command-prompt command. This does not include just the commands that are discussed in Chapter 9 but also most of the commands that were developed for the DOS environment.

As an example, consider a batch file that was comprised of the following five lines:

```
@echo off
pause Press any key to format disk in drive A:
format a: /u
beep
dir a:
```

If you save this in a batch file called FMT.BAT, then to execute all five lines of commands, you enter the following at the command prompt:

```
fmt
```

When Windows NT sees that you have entered this command, it first looks for a file called FMT.COM, one called FMT.EXE, and finally one called FMT.BAT. It looks not only in the current directory but in every directory in your path, until a matching file is located. The result is that you can execute a complex series of sequential steps just by remembering a single command name.

Putting together a batch file

Batch files are nothing but normal ASCII text files. This means that you can create a batch file by using a text editor such as Notepad (in the Windows interface) or EDIT (at the command prompt).

You can use other programs, such as your word processor or WordPad, provided that you save the document as a text file. If you save the document using the program's normal way of saving documents, then the word processor or WordPad puts extra formatting characters in the file. These formatting characters cannot be understood by the command-prompt portion of Windows NT.

Regular tasks that can be boiled down to a series of commands at the command line are prime candidates for batch files. For instance, you may regularly (daily, weekly, monthly, as so on) archive the data files for your accounting software.

Using a program such as PKZip, you can accomplish this easily with a batch file:

```
cd "\programs\accounting"
pkzip -a archive *.dat
move archive.zip "\programs\accounting\backups"
cd\
```

Each line does the following:

- The first line of this batch file changes the current directory (using the CD command) to the directory that is used by the accounting program.

- The second line then runs the PKZip program, using the command line that is required by that program.

- The third line then moves the new archive file to the a storage directory.

- The final line changes the current directory back to the root directory.

The examples that you have seen so far are for batch files that are rather static. While this still opens up some powerful capabilities, you can also use a feature called *replaceable parameters* with your batch files.

This means that you can use parameters with the command line that initiates your batch file, and those parameters can be used by the commands in your batch file. For instance, consider the following variation on the archiving batch file:

```
cd "\programs\accounting"
pkzip -a %1 *.dat
move %1.zip "\programs\accounting\backups"
cd\
```

The only difference between this and the previous version is that the word *archive* has been replaced with the *%1* replaceable parameter. Perhaps the name of the batch file is WEEKEND.BAT.

To run the batch file, you would use the following command:

```
weekend 960823
```

When this batch file is processed by Windows NT, it replaces every occurrence of %1 in the batch file with the first parameter that you used on the command line. Thus, the batch file is translated as follows when it is finally executed:

```
cd "\programs\accounting"
pkzip -a 960823 *.dat
move 960823.zip "\programs\accounting\backups"
cd\
```

You can use more than one replaceable parameter on your command line and access each of them individually in your batch file. For instance, consider the following command line to run a batch file named MYFILE.BAT:

```
myfile one two three four five six seven eight nine
```

This command line includes the name of the batch file along with nine parameters (one through nine). Table 17-1 indicates how the parameters from this command line are referenced in the body of the batch file.

Table 17-1 How replaceable parameters are referenced in a batch file

Parameter	Translation
%0	myfile
%1	one
%2	two
%3	three
%4	four
%5	five
%6	six
%7	seven
%8	eight
%9	nine

As you develop your own batch files, you will most likely use replaceable parameters quite a bit. They make your batch files much more flexible and applicable to a wider variety of situations.

Understanding batch file commands

There are many command-line commands that are used almost exclusively within batch files. Don't get the idea that this means the number of commands that you can use in a batch file is limited.

On the contrary, you can use any valid command that you want in addition to any program name. Table 17-2 simply indicates those commands that are especially applicable to use in batch files.

Table 17-2 Batch file commands

Command	Meaning
@	Causes everything else on the line to not be displayed when the batch file is running
CALL	Runs another batch file and then returns to finish the current batch file

Table 17-2	*(continued)*
Command	**Meaning**
ECHO	Controls the display of information on the screen as a batch file is running
FOR..IN..DO	Repeats a specific command for a specific number of executions
GOTO	Jumps to the line in the batch file that contains a specified label
IF	Permits conditional execution of a command
PAUSE	Displays a message and waits for a key to be pressed
REM	Indicates that everything else on the command line is a remark and should be ignored
SHIFT	Shifts the command-line parameters one position to the left

The major batch file commands are discussed fully in the following sections.

Messages and comments

Normally when you run a batch file, the commands in the batch file are displayed on the screen as they are executed. You can use the ECHO command to modify this behavior, however.

The ECHO command has two uses, which are as follows:

- You can use it to turn on or off the display of command lines. The ECHO OFF command turns off command-line display, and the ECHO ON command turns it back on.

- You can use is to display a message on the screen.

For instance, consider the following batch file command lines:

```
echo This is the first test line
echo This is the second test line
```

When you run this batch file, the output looks a little strange. If you run it from the C prompt, then the output is as follows:

```
C:\>echo This is the first test line
This is the first test line

C:\>echo This is the second test line
This is the second test line
```

Notice that the ECHO command did what it was supposed to do — it displayed the message that appeared on the same line. However, the command lines in the batch file were also displayed, just before they were executed.

To fix this, the ECHO OFF command is placed at the beginning of the batch file, as in the following commands:

```
echo off
echo This is the first test line
echo This is the second test line
```

Now when you run the batch file, it appears like this:

```
C:\>echo off
This is the first test line
This is the second test line
```

This is much closer to the desired output. There is only one other change to make, which brings up the use of the @ command. This command, when used as the first character of a line, suppresses the display of the command on that line only.

Thus, if you include it on the first line of the batch file, it suppresses the display of that command. The batch file then looks like this:

```
@echo off
echo This is the first test line
echo This is the second test line
```

This is the same technique that is used on the batch file examples earlier in this chapter. Now the output looks clean and to the point, without any extra lines confusing the output:

```
This is the first test line
This is the second test line
```

Secret

You can also use the ECHO command to insert a blank line in the output of your batch file. Simply use the ECHO command immediately followed by a period. For instance, you would use the following command:

```
echo.
```

If you simply want to include comments in your batch file (which is always a good idea when the batch file is more than a couple of lines long), then you can use the REM command. This command is a flag to indicate that everything else on the line should be ignored when the batch file is executing. The command name is short for *remark*, which describes its purpose concisely.

Pausing for input

Another way that you can use messages in your batch files is with commands that allow rudimentary interaction with the user. The prime example of this is the PAUSE command. This command is used to halt the batch file until the user presses a key.

For instance, the following example uses the PAUSE command:

```
@echo off
echo Insert a disk, then
pause
```

When you run this batch file, the output is as follows:

```
Insert a disk, then
Press any key to continue . . .
```

The first output line was created by the ECHO command in the batch file, and the second was created by the PAUSE command. When the user presses a key, the batch file continues running with the next line. You cannot use any other message with the PAUSE command like you would with the ECHO command. If you try to, anything else on the line is ignored.

The PAUSE command is a good choice to include in your batch file if the next command does something important, like copy a file, delete a file, or format a disk. This gives the user an opportunity to stop the action if he wants to. A rather standard way of doing this in a batch file is shown in this example:

```
rem Batch file to automatically format a disk correctly
@echo off
echo Insert a disk that you want to format in drive A
echo.
echo Press Ctrl+C to stop this action, otherwise
pause
format a: /u /f:720
```

When you run this batch file, the output is as follows:

```
Insert a disk that you want to format in drive A

Press Ctrl+C to stop this action, otherwise
Press any key to continue . . .
```

If the user presses Ctrl+C, then the batch file is interrupted. (This is the normal way to stop a batch file in progress.) On the other hand, if the user presses a different key, the batch file continues, and the disk is formatted.

Running a secondary batch file

Using the CALL command, you can run another batch file from within your current batch file. (This is often referred to as *nesting*.) When the secondary batch file is done, control is returned to the first batch file, and it continues executing.

As an example, the following is a very simple batch file that you can name ONE.BAT:

```
@echo off
echo Now running the first batch file
call two
echo Still running the first batch file
```

On the third line of this batch file, the CALL command is used to execute a second batch file, called TWO.BAT. This second batch file contains the following two lines:

```
@echo off
echo Now running the second batch file
```

When you run the first batch file (ONE.BAT), the output looks like this:

```
Now running the first batch file
Now running the second batch file
Still running the first batch file
```

The ability to execute secondary batch files is very powerful, as you learn in the next section. It also provides the opportunity to break big tasks down to a few small batch files that you can execute as you need them.

Conditional execution

The IF command allows you to add conditional processing to your batch file. This means that you can test a condition and then take an action based on the outcome of the test. Conditional logic is used in everyday conversation among humans.

For instance, you may say, "If it rains tonight, I will watch a movie." This statement provides the condition (if it rains) and what happens if the condition is met (watch a movie).

The same sort of logic can be used in your batch files. You can test several different types of conditions in your batch file, and then act accordingly. For example, you can test the following conditions:

■ If two strings are equal to each other

■ If a file exists

■ The ERRORLEVEL of a program

You test the equality of two strings by using == (two equal signs) between the two strings, as in the following command:

```
if %1 == BACKUP then call archive %1
```

In this case, a replaceable parameter (%1) is compared against a known value (BACKUP). If the two are equal, then the CALL command is used to run another batch file (ARCHIVE.BAT), passing it the replaceable parameter.

Using the IF command in conjunction with the CALL command, in this manner, provides an effective and powerful combination.

A common use of the equality test is to see if a parameter has been provided by the user. The way that you do this is to use other characters in conjunction with the replaceable parameter. This is what is done in the following example:

```
if "%1" == "" then call dodefault
```

To understand what is happening here, assume that the user starts the batch file and includes a parameter — PARM1. In this case, the code line would then translate as follows:

```
if "PARM1" == "" then call dodefault
```

The equality would not be there, so the CALL command would never be issued. If the user left off the parameter, however, then the code line would translate like this:

```
if "" == "" then call dodefault
```

In this case, the two sides are equal, and the CALL statement is executed. In these examples, I used quotation marks, but only because that seems understandable to me, not because quotation marks are required. You could use any other characters that you wanted.

For example, the following code line would work just as well as the one I used:

```
if %1a == a then call dodefault
```

Besides testing for string equality, you can also use the IF command to check for the existence of a file. This is helpful if you want to avoid error messages for trying to use a command on a nonexistent file. For example, take a look at the following, which is a variation on the archiving batch file that was used earlier in the chapter:

```
@echo off
cd "\programs\accounting"
if exist data.mon pkzip -a archive data.mon
if exist data.tue pkzip -a archive data.tue
if exist data.wed pkzip -a archive data.wed
if exist data.thu pkzip -a archive data.thu
if exist data.fri pkzip -a archive data.fri
if exist data.sat pkzip -a archive data.sat
if exist data.sun pkzip -a archive data.sun
if exist archive.zip move archive.zip "\programs\accounting\backups"
cd\
```

This example uses the IF command extensively. After changing to the directory where the accounting data are stored, the IF command is used to check for the existence of the individual data files.

If they exist, then they are added to the archive. Finally, the IF command is used to check the existence of the archive file itself. If present, then it is moved to its final storage directory.

A variation on checking for the existence of a file is checking to see if it does not exist. You do this by using the NOT modifier in your command line. For instance, the following example line checks to see if a file is missing:

```
if not exist myprog.ini call makeini
```

This example checks for the existence of an initialization file; if it does not exist, then the CALL command is used to run a batch file that presumably creates the file.

The final way that you can use the IF command is to check the ERRORLEVEL of a program. Some command-prompt commands terminate using the ERRORLEVEL system value to indicate the success of the command.

The different commands that use ERRORLEVEL are as follows:

- BACKUP
- DISKCOMP
- DISKCOPY
- FORMAT
- GRAFTABL
- KEYB
- REPLACE
- RESTORE
- XCOPY

In general, an ERRORLEVEL of 0 indicates that the operation was successful. If a higher ERRORLEVEL is returned, then an error occurred. Understanding this allows you to use the IF command as shown in the following command:

```
if errorlevel 1 echo There was an error!
```

The IF command always checks to see if the ERRORLEVEL is equal to or greater than the value that you specify. If so, then the command on the line is executed. It is important to remember that the check is for an ERROR-LEVEL equal to or greater than; if you use the IF command in some other way with ERRORLEVEL, then you don't get your desired results.

Jumping to another location

There may be times when you want to jump to another location in your batch file. This is particularly true when using the conditional IF command that you learned about in the previous section. The GOTO command allows you to jump from the current location to a different location of the batch file.

The following batch file illustrates how this is done:

```
@echo off
if "%1" == "" goto NOPARM
cd "\programs\accounting"
pkzip -a %1 *.dat
move %1.zip "\programs\accounting\backups"
cd\
goto END
:NOPARM
echo You must use the name of the desired archive file
echo as a parameter. Please try again!
:END
```

This example uses the GOTO command in two places. First, on the second line of the batch file, the IF command is used to check if a parameter was provided by the user. If not, then GOTO jumps to the line labeled NOPARM. Later, the GOTO command is used to jump to the label END to skip over the portion of the program that displays an error message.

Notice that, on the lines where the GOTO command is used, a label is used as the target of the jump. There is nothing special about this label; it can be virtually anything that you want.

On the line where the label is used, however, the target must include a colon as a preface to the label. Thus, when using GOTO with the NOPARM label, the batch file jumps to a line with the :NOPARM label (colon included) on the line.

Shifting parameters

Earlier in this chapter, you learned how you can use replaceable parameters with your batch file. There may be rare situations where you need to use more than nine parameters on a line.

Just because you can only use %0 through %9 in your batch file, this does not mean that you cannot access more than nine parameters. This is where the SHIFT command comes into play.

The SHIFT command is used to move all command-line parameters one position to the left. Thus, what would have been %1 is now referenced as %0, %2 is referenced as %1, and so on.

To see how this works, create the following batch file:

```
@echo off
:BEGIN
echo %0
shift
if "%0" == "" goto END
goto BEGIN
:END
```

When you run this batch file, try using it with several different command lines. Each command line should have a different number of parameters. Did you understand the results that you received?

The first line of the batch file turns off echoing, and the second is a label that indicates the start of a loop. The third line displays the first replaceable parameter on the command line, and the fourth shifts all of the parameters to the left. The next line checks to see if the end of the parameters has been reached.

If so, then the GOTO command causes the batch file to skip to the last line of the file. Finally, the sixth line jumps to the beginning of the loop, where everything is repeated again.

Processing lists of information

The final batch command to be discussed is the FOR..IN..DO command. This powerful command allows you to accomplish a number of things with a single step. The syntax of the command is as follows:

```
for %%var in (set) do command
```

The %%VAR specification is similar to the replaceable parameters that you have used so often in this chapter. They represent a variable that is taken from the set of items that you specify in the parentheses.

For example, the following is a simple use of the FOR..IN..DO command:

```
for %%a in (one two) do type %%a.bat
```

In this instance, the TYPE command is issued twice, once for each item in the parentheses. This command line, when executed, shows the following results:

```
type one.bat
type two.bat
```

While this may seem a silly command to use on a short list of items (only two in this case), it is very powerful to use on long lists. For instance, consider the following variation of the previous example:

```
for %%a in (*.bat) do type %%a
```

In this case, every file in the current directory that ends with the extension .BAT is typed, in turn, by the command. It doesn't matter if there is 1 file or 50; each of them is typed in turn.

This same command can be used to shorten the archiving example that was used earlier:

```
@echo off
cd "\programs\accounting"
if exist data.mon pkzip -a archive data.mon
if exist data.tue pkzip -a archive data.tue
if exist data.wed pkzip -a archive data.wed
if exist data.thu pkzip -a archive data.thu
if exist data.fri pkzip -a archive data.fri
if exist data.sat pkzip -a archive data.sat
if exist data.sun pkzip -a archive data.sun
if exist archive.zip move archive.zip "\programs\accounting\backups"
cd\
```

When used with FOR..IN..DO, the batch file can be rewritten as follows:

```
@echo off
cd "\programs\accounting"
for %%a in (mon tue wed thu fri sat sun) do if exist data.%%a pkzip
-a archive data.%%a
if exist archive.zip move archive.zip "\programs\accounting\backups"
cd\
```

The batch file is now much smaller, yet the same amount of work is accomplished. You can probably use the FOR..IN..DO command similarly in many places in your own batch files.

Automatic Programs

In Chapter 9, you learned a little about the AT command. This powerful command is used to schedule programs that you want to run automatically, at a particular time.

Because there may be many programs that you want to execute at a particular time, it is interesting that Windows NT includes AT as a command-line command, but it does not provide a version that uses the Windows interface.

Running the Schedule service

Before you can us the AT command, the Schedule service must be running on your system. The AT command makes use of the Schedule service to fulfill its work.

This service can be run by following these steps:

STEPS

Starting the Schedule service

Step 1. Choose the Settings option from the Start menu. This displays the Settings menu.

Step 2. Choose the Control Panel option from the Settings menu. This opens the Control Panel.

Step 3. Double-click on the Services icon in the Control Panel. This displays the Services dialog box.

Step 4. Scroll through the list of services until you can select the service that is entitled Schedule. The Services dialog box now appears, as shown in Figure 17-5.

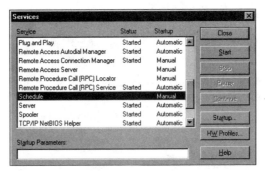

Figure 17-5: The Services dialog box is used to configure how different services are started.

Step 5. Notice that, in the Startup column, there is an indication of how the Schedule service is designed to be started. If set to Manual, then you must manually start the Schedule service each time that you want to use it. If set to Automatic, then it starts for you every time that you start your system. If you want to always start the service manually, skip to Step 10.

Step 6. Click on the Startup button. This displays the Service dialog box, as shown in Figure 17-6.

Figure 17-6: The Service dialog box allows you to specify the startup method that is used for a service.

Step 7. In the Startup Type area, click a radio button to select a method by which you want the Schedule service to begin.

Step 8. Make sure that the service is scheduled to log on with privileges that are sufficient to run the programs that you plan on scheduling.

Step 9. Click on the OK button to close the Service dialog box.

Step 10. Click on the Start button. This starts the Schedule service, and you should see the Status column change to *Started*.

Step 11. Click on the Close button to close the Services dialog box.

Scheduling a command

With the Schedule service started, you are ready to start scheduling your commands. If you want to schedule a task, use the following syntax:

```
AT time "command"
```

In this instance, *command* is replaced with the command that you want to have executed, which must be surrounded by quotation marks. The *time* refers to the time of day at which you want the task to be executed. The *time* is specified in a 24-hour format, as in 17:00 for a command to be executed at 5:00 p.m.

Secret

You can only use the AT command to schedule programs if you belong to the Administrator group on your system. This is done for security reasons, so that nonadministrators cannot run programs that violate system security.

The commands that you schedule can be any program or batch file that you want. You should make sure, however, that the program or batch file is capable of running by itself.

It doesn't do much good to schedule a command that requires user input at 2:00 a.m., if no one is going to be around to tend to it. As an example, the following command can be used to schedule the MYPROG program:

```
at 13:15 "c:\programs\myprog
```

This command schedules the program to be run at 1:15 p.m. on the day that it was scheduled. You can also use the AT command to schedule recurring programs. Simply include one of the AT command switches before the actual command but after the time specification.

There are three switches that you can use, as shown in Table 17-3.

Table 17-3	Scheduling switches for use with the AT command
Switch	*Meaning*
/every:*date*	Indicates that the task should be run on a certain day of the week or a specific day of the month. For days of the week, you can use the abbreviations M, T, W, Th, F, S, and Su. If you indicate a number, then it is taken to be a day of the month. You can specify multiple dates with commas, as in /every:1,16.
/next:*date*	Indicates that the task should be run on the next occurrence of a day of the week or day of the month. For *date*, you can use the same notation as in the /every switch.
/interactive	Allows the task to interact with whoever is using the computer at the time that it is executed.

As an example, you may have a specific program that you want to have run every weekday at 2:00 a.m. In this case, you could use the following AT command to schedule the program:

```
at 02:00 /every:M,T,W,Th,F c:\programs\myprog
```

Now the program is executed Monday through Friday, at 2:00 a.m.

Secret

If you schedule a program to run at a certain time, and the program cannot be run because you typed the wrong program name, or the program was moved or renamed after you scheduled it, then the Scheduler notifies you by placing a message in the System log. You can view the error message by using the Event Viewer, as described in Chapter 16.

Displaying a list of scheduled commands

To see which commands are currently scheduled, use the AT command by itself, with no parameters or switches. Figure 17-7 shows an example of how scheduled commands are listed.

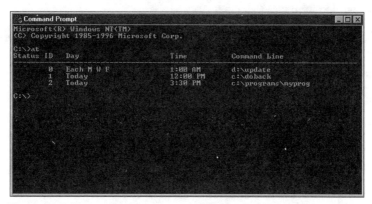

Figure 17-7: You can list the programs that are scheduled on your system.

The listed schedule indicates the following information about each item:

- **Status.** This is the status of the program. Normally this item is blank if the program is still pending. The status changes when the program is being executed by the Scheduler.

- **ID.** This is the schedule ID that is assigned to the item by the AT command.

- **Day.** This is the day or date when the program is scheduled to run.

- **Time.** This is the time of day at which the program is to be run. This time is shown in a.m. and p.m. notation, even though you needed to specify information using 24-hour notation.

- **Command Line.** This is the program's command line as it will be executed at the specified time.

Removing a scheduled command

You can use the /delete switch to remove a program that you previously scheduled. To use the switch, you must also know the ID that is assigned to the program by the AT command. For this reason, you probably want to list the scheduled activities before trying to delete a command.

As an example, you may want to delete a command that was assigned an ID of 1. You would then enter the following at the command prompt:

```
at 1 /delete
```

This causes the specified item to be immediately deleted. You can confirm that the item is indeed gone by using the AT command, by itself, to list the scheduled items.

If you use the /delete switch without an item ID, then AT assumes that you want to delete all of the scheduled jobs. In this case, you are asked to confirm your action. After this confirmation, all of the scheduled items are removed from the Scheduler.

Summary

Many of the tasks that you perform with your computer may seem very repetitive. Fortunately, Windows NT includes several features that allow you to automate the work that you do. These features allow you to automatically start programs, combine commands into special batch files, and schedule commands to be run at a given time.

This chapter has focused on ways that you can automate your system through the use of these features. In particular, you have learned the following items:

▶ Windows NT includes a special Startup folder that is used to indicate which programs you want to have started whenever you first log in. You can add different objects to the folder so that they are automatically started according to your needs.

▶ Batch files are regular ASCII text files, with a .BAT filename extension, that contain command-prompt commands that you want to execute in sequence.

▶ You can use any command-prompt command in your batch files as well as the name of any program that you can run from the command line.

▶ Windows NT includes several special command-prompt commands that are designed for use in batch files. These commands can be used to enhance the flexibility of your batch files.

▶ You can use the AT command, in conjunction with the Scheduler service, to run different commands and programs at a specified, scheduled time.

Chapter 18

Improving Performance

In This Chapter

When you have a system that is running at peak efficiency, you know it. When something slows, you can generally tell that, too. Windows NT includes several tools that you can use to keep your system in peak running condition.

This chapter focuses on how you can make sure that your system is the best it can be. In particular, you learn the following items:

▶ What performance means and what contributes to it

▶ How you can use the Task Manager to get an idea of how your CPU and memory are being used

▶ How to put the Performance Monitor to work to help you check out your system

▶ What areas you can examine on your workstation to improve overall performance

What Is Performance?

When it comes to computers, people define performance in different ways. Some people may think that only the CPU affects overall performance, but this is akin to thinking that the size of a car's engine is the only thing that affects the performance of the car.

Rather, every element of your computer system works together to provide an overall effect. Some people refer to this as *throughput* — the capability to get work done in a certain amount of time. This is the definition that I rely on; all aspects of the computer system must be considered.

When looking at throughput as a measure of performance, you may get more work done with your workstation than someone else does with the same hardware. Does this mean that your system performs better?

As a matter of fact it does, because the hardware alone is not a sole determinant of performance. The purpose for which that hardware is used is also a prime factor. This is why people use different cars for different types of driving. If you are driving over rough terrain, you would use a four-wheel-drive vehicle, whereas for smooth highway driving you may use a luxury car or a snazzy sports car.

In the computer world, you must also examine the uses to which your computer is to be put. For instance, you may use your system to develop multimedia applications, while another person may be doing CAD/CAM work.

You are able to get more done, because your hardware, coupled with your software, provides a better platform for your purposes than it may for a CAD/CAM system. However, by changing the components in the CAD/CAM system, the other person may be able to get just as much performance as you do.

This may leave the issue of performance still a little fuzzy in your mind. It may be helpful to look at the twin components of performance — hardware and software.

Hardware components

From a hardware perspective, many components make up your computer system. Everything from your CPU to your RAM to your CD-ROM to your mouse can affect performance. Fortunately, for raw ability to process data, only a few items affect the overall performance of your system.

These major items are as follows:

- CPU type and implementation
- Bus design
- RAM type and speed
- Video card design
- Hard-drive speed

It is not the purpose of this chapter or this book to provide a detailed discussion of the different technologies that are used in each of these areas. Indeed, there are books on the market that can provide quite a bit of information in these areas. However, you do need to understand a bit about each of these items to understand how you can improve the performance in your present workstation.

Your CPU

The CPU, while not the single determining factor in a computer system, is still quite important. The CPU is the brain of your system; if the brains are not "up to par," there's little hope for the rest of your system. In IBM PC–compatible systems, the CPU is either an Intel chip or a clone of an Intel chip. Entire books could be written on the different CPUs that have been used, along with their capabilities.

Without delving into the long history of Intel CPUs, suffice it to say that, as of this writing, the mainstream CPU type is based on the Intel Pentium chip. This CPU is quite capable, providing computing power that was unthinkable just half a decade ago.

Even though the Pentium is the mainstream processor, it is not the state-of-the-art in Intel CPUs. That honor is reserved for the Pentium Pro, which is a souped-up version of the Pentium that is designed for use with 32-bit operating systems and software.

Both the Pentium and Pentium Pro are more than adequate for running the Windows NT operating system and the software that runs under Windows NT. If you are running any Win16 or DOS programs on your system, then the Pentium is a better choice for CPU than the Pentium Pro.

Due to the architecture of the Pentium Pro, the CPU runs 16-bit software slightly slower than the older Pentium. When it comes to 32-bit software, however, the Pentium Pro can really fly.

Processor speeds have steadily risen over the past few years, regardless of the type of CPU being discussed. The average Pentium system now boasts processor speeds of 133 or 166 MHz (millions of cycles per second).

Faster Pentiums, at 200 MHz, are also starting to appear. The faster 200 MHz Pentium Pros have been on the market for some time, and clock speeds are expected to increase on this product line.

Another way that many computer systems increase speed is to include multiple CPUs. It is not difficult to find systems that feature 2, 4, or more CPUs. Typically this is done with Pentium Pro systems, although it can also be done with Pentiums. This option for improving speed is attractive, especially because Windows NT Workstation automatically supports symmetric multiprocessing.

The system bus design

When you examine CPU speeds, you are looking at how fast the CPU can internally process data. If the design of the motherboard limits how fast information can be delivered to the CPU or how fast information can be accepted from the CPU, the effective system speed is greatly reduced.

The part of the system that controls the transfer of information among components (the CPU is one of those components) is referred to as a *bus*. There are several buses in any computer system, and the efficiency of these buses is determined by two things: the speed at which they operate and the number of bits that they can transfer at a single time. There have been several different bus designs used in PCs over the past two decades.

These are as follows:

- **ISA.** This bus design was introduced when the first PCs were designed and then upgraded when the PC XT hit the market. Even though it is quite old and limited (it only allows transfer of information at a data width of 16 bits), it is still the most used bus design in the world.

- **Micro Channel.** This bus design, originally developed by IBM as a successor to the ISA bus, is difficult to find in any new computer systems. There are many historical and political reasons for this, which space does not permit addressing at this point.

- **EISA.** This bus design was developed in response to the Micro Channel bus by a consortium of computer companies. It permits high performance but has typically only been implemented in servers and other high-performance systems.

- **VESA Local Bus.** This bus design was developed to alleviate the bottleneck in the ISA design regarding high-performance video systems. The VESA local bus is typically found only on 486 systems.

- **PCI Local Bus.** This bus is found on almost every Pentium and Pentium Pro system. It is an add-on to the historical ISA bus, providing the ability to add specially designed high-speed adapter cards.

In general, the PCI local bus provides the best bang for the buck. It is able to transfer data at a width of 64 bits, which matches the needs of both the Pentium and Pentium Pro.

In addition, it operates at a clock speed much closer to that of the CPU than any other bus design. Regardless of your CPU type or speed, or the number of CPUs that you need, you can find a PCI bus system that fits the bill.

Your memory

The type of memory that is used in your computer system can affect the system's overall performance. It would appear that some system developers almost consider RAM an afterthought, however.

While there are many different technical considerations regarding memory, three factors have a huge impact on the typical workstation:

- The speed of your memory
- The type of memory that is used
- The amount of memory that is in the system

Memory speed is measured in nanoseconds (billionths of a second). The speed of the memory chips that are used in a workstation can vary greatly — from 10 to 200 nanoseconds. The lower the number, the faster the RAM chip. In general, RAM chips with speeds below 30 nanoseconds are only used for caching purposes, where high speeds are critical.

In most workstations, system RAM runs between 60 and 80 nanoseconds. In general, you should seek systems that have RAM speeds of 70 nanoseconds or below.

Typically, you cannot improve the performance of an existing system by replacing your existing memory chips with faster chips. The reason is that the timing specifications of the motherboard are set when the board is designed.

Thus, even though you may add RAM chips that are capable of faster speeds, the motherboard is still designed to deliver and access information at the slower speeds. Memory speed is something that you need to check when you first purchase a workstation.

At one time, there was only a single type of memory used in RAM chips for workstations. That has changed in recent years and months, as additional types of RAM have become available.

There are several different types of RAM that you can have installed in a modern system:

- **DRAM.** This is the original type of RAM that was used in most workstations. DRAM is an acronym for *dynamic random access memory.*

  The technology used in these RAM chips is tried and true, and prices are the lowest of all the RAM types. However, if you want blazing speed, you need to check out different types.

- **EDO RAM.** EDO is an acronym for *extended data-out,* which describes how the performance of this RAM type has been improved over the older DRAM chips.

  If you get a system that has EDO RAM, you can expect to pay several hundred dollars more than you would with regular RAM, but you can also expect to see 20 percent performance improvements on memory-intensive operations.

- **SDRAM.** This is a specialized version of the older DRAM memory. SDRAM means *synchronized DRAM.* It gains a performance advantage because of changes in the structure of the chip that allow information to be accessed in a more orderly manner. These special chips can cost about 50 percent more than traditional DRAM chips.

Regardless of which type of memory you get, the motherboard in your system must be designed to handle that memory. Thus, if you want to use EDO RAM, then the motherboard must be designed for EDO RAM.

Another factor relating to memory is how much you should have installed in your system. Most Pentium workstations are available with 4, 8, or 16MB of memory. You probably know right up front that 4 or 8MB is not enough to run Windows NT; you need at least 16MB.

If you can, it is well worth your investment to get a system with 32MB or more of memory. You can notice a huge improvement in system performance just by adding additional memory to your workstation.

Your video card

Over the years, there have been many different types of video cards, each developed to a distinct video standard. For Windows NT Workstation, you must have at least a VGA (video graphics array) card in your system. One of the biggest changes in video adapters in recent years has revolved around their ability to process data quickly while maintaining backward compatibility with the VGA standard.

The changes in video cards have been necessitated by more complex graphics needs from a software perspective. As a rule, the greater the graphics needs of a program, the slower it runs.

This is directly related to the amount of data that must be updated on the video screen. Processing huge amounts of video information puts a high demand on the CPU and on the system bus in your computer

It's not that your computer can't handle it — it can, given enough time. That is why complex video displays can take quite a while to display all of the information that they are asked to process.

The solution to this "video bottleneck" is to use a graphics accelerator. In fact, many SVGA (super VGA) cards on the market are marketed as graphics accelerators, because they provide specialized circuitry that allows them to process information much more quickly than standard VGA cards.

The effect of using these cards is simple — if you speed the video, you speed the entire computer system. This is because you don't need to wait as long for one of the slowest parts of your computer system.

Graphics accelerators achieve their blazing speeds by using any of the three following techniques:

- Wider data width
- Faster video RAM
- A graphics coprocessor

Any of these items can be mixed and matched in an accelerator to provide different performance increases and price points. Most modern graphics accelerators feature wider data paths in one way or another. One way that graphics accelerators increase the data width is to take advantage of the VESA or PCI local buses in your system.

Another way is to increase the data width of the bus that is used on the video adapter itself. There are several 128-bit video cards on the market; this width refers to the internal data width on the card. (The widest local bus is only 64 bits wide.)

Virtually all graphics accelerators use specialized RAM to speed display procedures. Older graphics accelerators use regular DRAM, which you learned about earlier in this chapter.

Most of today's graphics accelerators feature a faster, more expensive VRAM (video RAM). This RAM is different than the RAM that is in your computer system; it can be written to and read from at the same time, thereby increasing throughput.

Finally, a number of different graphics accelerators are starting to include their own specialized video coprocessor. These specialized chips can offload much of the processing from your CPU. Because of this, less data have to travel over the local bus or I/O bus between the video card and the CPU. This means faster overall processing than is otherwise possible.

Your hard drive

Many types of hard drives are on the market, and discussing the technical merits of each is best left to the specialized books that you can find at your bookseller. Essentially, when you consider a hard drive from a performance perspective, you need to pay attention to two items: drive type and speed.

The following are the most common types of drives that are currently on the market:

- **IDE.** This is actually a category of disk drive, describing a drive in which the controller electronics are actually on the drive itself. IDE is an acronym for *integrated drive electronics,* and the EIDE upgrade (which allows larger disk capacities) refers to *enhanced integrated drive electronics.* (In reality, any IDE drive over 538MB in size is actually an EIDE drive. The terms are used almost interchangeably.)

  IDE drives first started appearing in the mid-1980s, and the latest models feature capacities in excess of 2GB. Because of the high degree of electronics integration and other refinements of hard-drive technology, IDE drives can be small in physical size, low in cost, and very easy to install. Most new computer systems come with IDE drives installed unless you specify a different type.

- **SCSI.** This is a generic term referring to an entire family of drives. SCSI is an acronym for *small computer system interface*. The interface is actually used for many types of devices in addition to hard drives, including scanners, tape drives, and CD-ROM drives.

  SCSI drives are typically very fast, high-performance devices, and many have very large capacities. Single SCSI drives capable of storing more than 9GB are available and are often are used on network servers. In some situations, SCSI drives have a performance advantage over IDE drives. For this reason, they are typically favored by those wanting the most performance from their systems.

The speed of your hard drive affects the performance of your system quite a bit, especially for disk-intensive programs. Hard-drive speed is typically measured in many ways.

Several terms are used in relation to hard drives, and each has a bearing on speed:

- **Seek Time.** This is the average amount of time that is necessary to move the read/write heads from their current position to another random position that is not on the same track.

- **Latency.** This has to do with the average amount of time that is necessary to locate a sector after the read/write heads have positioned themselves over the proper track. This is purely a function of the rotational speed of the hard drive.

- **Access Time.** This is the average amount of time that is necessary to find a given sector on the disk, starting from any other sector. In reality, it is the sum of the seek time and the latency.

- **Transfer Rate.** This is a measure of how much data can be transferred per second by the disk drive to the computer. Typically, this is provided in millions of bits per second (Mbps). The higher the transfer rate, the better your system performance is.

When you look through advertisements for disk drives, the speed referred to is generally the access time. If you compare the access time from one drive to that of another, you are comparing apples to apples, and you can make a rough estimate of the relative performance of the drives.

If you see an advertisement that specifies seek time instead of access time, you should temper this by looking at the rotational speed of the drive (measured in RPM, or revolutions per minute). The faster the drive spins, the lower the latency and thus the lower the access time. For the best performance, you want a drive that has high RPM, low seek time, and (in all cases) a high transfer rate.

Software components

The software components that you use in your system include both your operating system and the software that you use. I assume that you are using Windows NT Workstation 4.0 as your operating system, because that is the focus of this book. The software that you use under Windows NT can greatly affect your overall performance, based on how the software is developed.

In Chapter 8, you learned about the different operating modes of software and the different standards to which it can be developed. If you use software that is designed for the Win16 standard, then that software runs slower and is less stable under Windows NT than a comparable program that is written to the Win32 standard. Why?

There are two reasons for this:

■ The internal operations of Windows NT are optimized for 32-bit software. This means that the operating system subroutines and functions that are used to support 32-bit software run faster and with a lower system overhead requirement.

■ 32-bit software can process information up to twice as fast as 16-bit software. Because 32-bit software inherently uses larger internal registers to move and process information, it is faster than programs that only access 16 bits at a time.

The net result is a greater ability to complete a larger amount of work in a given period of time. Thus, you can improve your system performance simply move updating your software to the newest 32-bit versions.

Measuring Your Performance

Now that you understand the different components that contribute to system performance, you are ready to take a look at how that performance can be measured on your system. Windows NT includes two major tools that you can use to keep tabs on performance. The first is the Task Manager, but the primary tool is the Performance Monitor.

Both tools are discussed in the following sections.

The Task Manager

Technically, the Task Manager is the portion of the operating system that enables you to control exactly what is being worked on at any given time. Typically, you use the Task Manager to switch between programs or to terminate errant programs. With the introduction of Windows NT Workstation 4.0, there is a new use for the Task Manager — evaluating the level at which your CPU and memory are operating.

To use the Task Manager for this purpose, follow these steps:

STEPS

Using the Task Manager to measure performance

Step 1. Right-click on the Taskbar. This displays a Context menu.

Step 2. Choose the Task Manager option from the Context menu. This displays the Task Manager, which contains three tabs.

Step 3. Click on the Performance tab. The Task Manager now appears as shown in Figure 18-1.

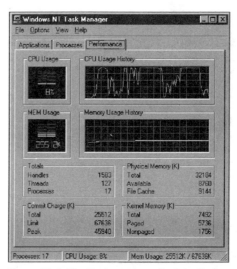

Figure 18-1: The Performance tab of the Task Manager displays CPU and memory usage in your system.

The Performance tab of the Task Manager allows you to analyze the performance of your system in relation to the two heaviest-used resources in your system: your CPU and memory.

The gauges and graphs at the top of the dialog box are beneficial in determining the current load on your system. At the bottom of the dialog box there is also a summary of other memory usage information.

If you double-click anywhere on the Performance tab of the Task Manager, the Task Manager window changes to display a larger representation of your CPU usage, as shown in Figure 18-2.

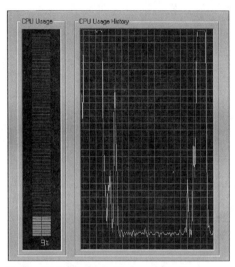

Figure 18-2: The Task Manager can display larger graphs showing the use of your CPU.

To return the Task Manager to the regular view, as shown in Figure 18-1, simply double-click on the graph again.

You may not have noticed it, but when you opened the Task Manager, a small green square appeared at the right side of your Taskbar, just to the left of the system time. This block is a small gauge that indicates your CPU usage.

This gauge comes in handy when the Task Manager is not displayed in an open window. For instance, if you minimize the Task Manager, then you can keep an eye on the gauge to see how your CPU is doing.

Secret

You can choose Hide When Minimized from the Options menu to hide the Task Manager. When you minimize the Task Manager, it disappears, but the small gauge on the Taskbar remains visible. You can redisplay the Task Manager by double-clicking on the gauge.

By keeping an eye on the Performance tab of the Task Manager while you are working, you can get a general idea of how your resources are holding up. If you want more in-depth information or analysis, then you need to use the Performance Monitor, as described in the following section.

The Performance Monitor

While the Task Manager allows you to glimpse the level at which your CPU and memory are operating, the Performance Monitor is a diagnostic tool that allows you to measure the performance of many different parts of your system.

Tip

Using the Performance Monitor and then acting on the information that it reports, you can make your system run at peak efficiency. Unfortunately, the Performance Monitor is often overlooked, despite its capabilities.

To start the Performance Monitor, follow these steps:

STEPS

Starting the Performance Monitor

Step 1.   Choose the Programs option from the Start menu. This displays the Programs menu.

Step 2.   Choose the Administrative Tools (Common) option from the Programs menu. This displays a list of tools that are installed on your system.

Step 3.   Click on the Performance Monitor option. This displays the Performance Monitor window, as shown in Figure 18-3.

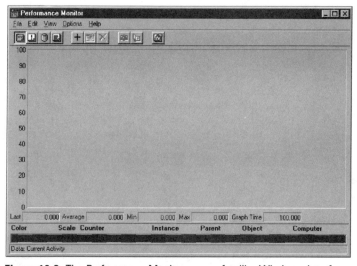

Figure 18-3: The Performance Monitor uses a familiar Windows interface.

At first glance, the Performance Monitor does not look that exciting. However, the usefulness of the Performance Monitor becomes clearer after you learn about the interface and begin using its features.

The user interface

The Performance Monitor window is divided into several parts, and each can be used to customize the information that is displayed by the program. At the top of the program window is a menu, which looks much the same as the menu on other Windows programs.

Each of these menus choices represents a series of options that allow you to control the information that is displayed in the rest of the Performance Monitor window, along with how it is displayed. This menu includes the following choices:

- **File.** The choices on this menu are used to create a new Performance Monitor window, load a file from disk, save your Performance Monitor settings, save your entire workspace, export the information in the Performance Monitor, and exit the program.

- **Edit.** The choices on this menu allow you to add items to or remove items from the Performance Monitor window, change an item, change the axis settings, and clear the display.

- **View.** The choices on this menu allow you to change which window is viewed in the Performance Monitor. (The available windows are discussed shortly.)

- **Options.** The choices on this menu control how information is derived, stored, or displayed by the Performance Monitor. In addition, you can control which parts of the Performance Monitor window are visible at any time.

- **Help.** The choices on this menu allow you to access the Windows NT Help system.

Below the menu is a toolbar that you can use to accomplish many of the same actions that are accessible through the menus. The ten tools on the toolbar are divided into four groups.

These groups are as follows:

- The leftmost group, consisting of four tools, controls which window is currently shown in the Performance Monitor. The first tool displays the Chart window, the second the Alert window, the third the Log window, and the fourth the Report window. (Again, these windows are discussed shortly.)

- The second group of tools provides a way to quickly modify items that are added to the windows. The first option is for adding an object, the second for editing the object, and the third for deleting an object.

- The third group of tools consists of only two tools. The first tool is used to update (refresh) the information in the Performance Monitor window, and the second is used to set a bookmark in a log file.

- The final group consists of a single tool. Clicking on it displays the options that are available for the current Performance Monitor window.

Performance Monitor windows

As you may have surmised by this point, the Performance Monitor allows you to view four different windows of information. These windows are simply different ways in which you can view the performance characteristics of your system.

Although there are subtleties between windows, by and large they all function in the same way, particularly from a menu and toolbar standpoint. The four windows are as follows:

- **Chart.** This window is preferred when you want to graphically see the performance of your system. It displays information by plotting performance results in a graph format.

- **Alert.** This window is preferred when you want to perform a specific action or sound a warning when the performance of an item falls above or below a certain threshold.

  The information that is in the Alert window consists of instances when the performance surpassed the threshold that you established.

- **Log.** This window is preferred when you want to write your performance measurements to disk for analysis at a later time. The information is stored on disk and can later be replayed in the Performance Monitor.

- **Report.** This window is preferred when you want a written report of performance statistics. The information displayed is pretty much the same as that in the Chart window, except that the information is shown numerically instead of graphically.

Each Performance Monitor window is shown in the display area after you select the window type from the <u>V</u>iew menu or the toolbar. When you are viewing one window, the performance of the objects in the other windows is still being tracked.

Observing objects in the Performance Monitor

The Performance Monitor works by examining how various objects are doing from time to time. For instance, the Performance Monitor can be configured to sample how heavy a load the CPU is carrying at certain intervals, such as every second or two.

The Performance Monitor can sample a variety of objects, including the following ones:

- Browser
- Cache
- Logical Disk
- Memory
- Objects
- Paging File
- Physical Disk
- Process
- Processor
- System
- Thread
- Printers

In addition, there may be a whole range of network-related objects that the Performance Monitor can sample. Objects can be monitored in any of the four windows that makes the most sense for your purposes. In addition, you can add the same object in more than one window so that you can track it in different ways.

To add an object to the current window, click on the Add tool on the toolbar to display the Add To dialog box. The exact appearance of the dialog box differs, depending on the window that is currently displayed.

For example, if you're working in the Chart window and you choose to add an object, the dialog box appears as shown in Figure 18-4.

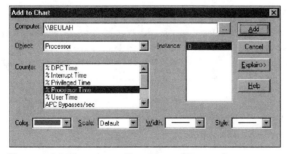

Figure 18-4: You can easily add an object to the Performance Monitor window.

Notice that the dialog box allows you to select a Computer, an Object, a Counter, and an Instance. These items are hierarchical in nature. When you select a computer, that determines the actual objects from which you can choose what you want to add. Likewise, selecting an object affects the counters that are available, and the counter affects the instances.

Note

The Computer field allows you to specify which computer on your network you want to monitor. You can select your own system or any other system for which you have the proper security permissions.

The objects that are available on a particular computer system are, to a degree, dependent on what's installed on that system. Different system components provide different Performance Monitor objects.

In addition, different applications may add their own objects that the Performance Monitor can access. For instance, if you install the Peer Web Services that are described in Chapter 14 or the RAS Server that was described in Chapter 13, then additional objects are added to the Performance Monitor.

Within objects, you can monitor different counters or instances of counters. The counters vary depending on the object that you have selected. For example, if you choose the processor object, you can monitor counters such as processor time or interrupt usage. If you pick an object such as threads, you can monitor counters such as thread state or thread wait reason.

If you want to know what a specific instance within an object represents, click on the Explain button in the Add To dialog box. This action displays an explanation area at the bottom of the dialog box.

As you can imagine, the number of items that you can monitor in the Performance Monitor is astounding. On my Windows NT Workstation system, 19 objects were available in the Performance Monitor. The number of counters that are available for that group was well over 400, and when you look at the number of instances, the number goes higher still.

Refresh rate

One of the items that is most often changed when using the Performance Monitor is the refresh time. This value determines how often the Performance Monitor samples the values that are necessary to update the information that you are tracking.

The default update time varies, depending on the window that you are using. In the Chart window, it is updated once per second; in the Alert log, once every 5 seconds; in the Log file, once every 15 seconds; and in the Report window, once every 5 seconds.

To change the refresh rate, click on the Options tool on the toolbar. This displays the Options dialog box, which again can vary based on the window that you are viewing. For instance, Figure 18-5 displays the Options dialog box for the Alert window.

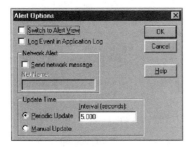

Figure 18-5: An Options dialog box allows you to change the refresh rate, among other items.

At the bottom of the Alert Options dialog box is the refresh information, in the Update Time area. This is the same position for the information on every other Options dialog box as well. Setting the refresh rate in one window, however, does not affect the refresh rate in the other windows.

To change the refresh rate, make sure that the Periodic Update radio button is selected, and then change the value in the Interval field to reflect the number of seconds that you want between each sample.

You can also choose the Manual Update radio button. If you do so, information is not updated on a regular basis. Instead, you must click on the Update tool on the toolbar to manually sample the performance information.

Printing reports

Unfortunately, the Performance Monitor doesn't allow you to print results. If you want printed output, you are forced to use one of two options to circumvent the lack of printing capability.

While these options are workable, it would have been nice for Microsoft to provide some sort of printing capability. The two methods you can use are described in the following sections.

Printing with a graphics program

The first option is to use the Clipboard and a graphics program to produce your output. (This option is particularly well suited for the information that is in the Chart window.)

The following steps produce output using the Paint accessory that is
included with Windows NT:

STEPS

Producing output using the Paint accessory

Step 1. Start and use the Performance Monitor as described earlier in
this chapter.

Step 2. Make sure that the Performance Monitor contains the information
that you want to print.

Step 3. Press Print Screen. This moves a copy of your desktop to the
Clipboard.

Step 4. Open the Paint accessory.

Step 5. Choose the Paste option from the Edit menu. The copy of the
your desktop (including the Performance Monitor window)
appears in the Paint window.

Step 6. Using the Page Setup option from the File menu, indicate how you
want your printout to appear.

Step 7. Choose the Print option from the File menu. This opens the Print
dialog box.

Step 8. Click on OK. Your printout is sent to the printer.

Step 9. Close the Paint accessory.

Remember that these steps provide a simple way to print the contents of
your Windows desktop. If you want, you can use a different graphics program, but the end-result should still be the same.

Printing raw data

The other option for printing Performance Monitor information is to export
the raw data that are generated by the Performance Monitor to another program and then use that program to print the information.

For instance, you may use your spreadsheet or database programs to produce output using Performance Monitor data. Using this method of printing
allows you to add additional information to your report. You can also change
the format or appearance of the information using the capabilities of your
spreadsheet or database program.

To export the information from the Performance Monitor, follow these steps:

STEPS

Exporting information from the Performance Monitor

Step 1. In the Performance Monitor, display the window containing the information that you want to export.

Step 2. Choose the Export option from the File menu. This opens the Export As dialog box, as shown in Figure 18-6.

Figure 18-6: You can pick a filename when you export information from the Performance Monitor.

Step 3. In the Save as Type drop-down list at the bottom of the dialog box, select TSV or CSV. (TSV stands for tab-separated values; CSV is for comma-separated values.)

Step 4. In the File Name field, specify the name to be used for your export file.

Step 5. In the appropriate places, specify the drive and directory in which the export file should be saved.

Step 6. Click on the Save button. The file is created, as you specified.

After you have created the export file, you can use your spreadsheet or database program to load the data and manipulate them. When loaded in your program, you can then format and print the information according to your needs.

Improving Your Performance

Using the tools that are provided in Windows NT, you can measure the performance of your system. This is the first step in making your workstation the best that it can be.

When you know where performance is lacking, you can take actions to correct the deficiency. If your workstation is used for very demanding programs, then it becomes critical to make sure that it is operating at peak efficiency so that you can be as productive as possible. By actively monitoring how your workstation performs under day-to-day operations, you can come up with ways to make your system run even better.

When should you start to check your performance? Typically, you should do so at the first sign that your system is running slow. If your workstation seems sluggish, then you need to find out why.

Of course, if you have a brand new workstation and you don't know if it is operating at top efficiency, you cannot determine if it is operating sluggishly unless you use the Performance Monitor to check it out.

On the hardware front, experience has proven that the cause of a sluggish workstation is typically due to the amount of memory that is in your system or to your CPU. Before you run out and add more memory, upgrade your CPU, or add another CPU to your system, you should use the Performance Monitor to check out the problem.

You do this by applying the information that is covered in this chapter, along with the guidelines in the following sections. If you monitor the proper system counters, you can make sure that a decision to spend additional money is a good one.

Evaluating memory usage

From information that is provided in various places in this book, you already know that Windows NT Workstation uses a concept called *virtual memory*. This means that your system uses as much RAM as you have installed in your system.

If this is not enough, Windows NT swaps information to and from the hard disk in a page file. With this understanding in mind, you can monitor the performance of several counters to see how well your system is performing in the memory area.

First, examine the Pages/Sec counter of the Memory object. This counter indicates how many pages are being swapped to disk every second by Windows NT. The Pages/Sec counter is the primary way that you can determine whether your workstation is paging information to disk excessively. (In technical terms, excessive paging is sometimes referred to as *thrashing*.)

As the value of the Pages/Sec counter increases, your workstation responsiveness is reduced. This is because your workstation must spend a greater part of its time reading and writing the page files from disk.

The highest acceptable value for the Pages/Sec counter can vary from system to system. One way to determine if your workstation is spending too much time paging is to observe whether processor activity (as evidenced by the % Total Processor Time counter of the System object) drops significantly as the Pages/Sec counter increases.

If it does, this indicates that your system is more occupied with swapping pages than with processing instructions. You can also compare the Pages/Sec counter to the Avg. Disk Sec/Transfer counter of the Logical Disk object. If both counts are high, your system is spending quite a bit of time swapping information to and from the disk.

If analysis of the counters indicates that your system is spending excessive time paging information to and from disk, then your memory is acting as a bottleneck to your system. In such a condition, adding more memory can help increase system performance dramatically.

Evaluating CPU performance

You already know that the CPU is the heart of your system. The Performance Monitor allows you to perform a checkup on the CPU to determine if it is slowing your overall performance. You can examine a couple of counters in this regard.

First, take a look at the % Processor Time counter of the Processor object. Add this to the Chart window, and then add the % Disk Time counter from the Physical Disk object. If the processor time is consistently high (over 75%) and your disk time is low (under 10%), you would probably benefit from an upgraded or additional CPU.

On the other hand, if your disk time is high, you may benefit from a faster hard drive more than an upgrade to your CPU. If your hard drive has an access time of 10 ms or greater and your disk time is high, then start considering a faster hard drive of 8 ms or less. After you have replaced the hard drive, you can then repeat the monitoring to see if the CPU performance improves.

If you really want to make sure that you have a bottleneck with your CPU, take a look at the Processor Queue Length counter of the System object. If the queue length is greater than 2 for extended periods, the rest of your system is waiting inordinately long on your CPU. In a situation like this, you definitely need to add another CPU or upgrade the one that you have.

Evaluating your video system

Unfortunately, the counters that are available in the Performance Monitor do not include a way to measure the performance of your video system. Instead, you need to rely on some old-fashioned horse sense.

Using your current workstation as a guide, answer the following questions:

- When you issue a redraw command in a program, does it take a long time to refresh the screen?

- When you use the print preview feature of your software, does it take quite a while to display the image on the screen?

- When you configure your system to use a higher resolution, does your video performance drop drastically?

- Does the software that you use rely heavily on video, including full-motion video or full-color graphics?

- When you are using Windows NT (not your software), do screen refreshes take quite a while?

If you can answer yes to any of these questions, then you are a candidate for an upgraded graphics accelerator. Looking for an accelerator that features all of the technology that was discussed earlier in the chapter can result in faster overall system performance.

Note

If you are considering a new graphics accelerator, make sure that the resolutions it supports are also supported by your video monitor. If not, then you may either need to put up with the slow video or purchase a new monitor as well.

Summary

Many times it seems that keeping your system operating at optimal performance is a never-ending battle. (And many times it seems like a losing battle.) As you change and adapt the ways in which you use your system, the performance characteristics of your system can also change.

In this chapter, you have learned what elements determine your system performance, what tools are available to monitor those elements, and specific areas where you can test your system. In particular, you have learned the following items:

▶ System performance is best measured by the amount of work that you are able to accomplish within a given time; the better your throughput, the better your system performance.

▶ Many elements contribute to your overall system performance. The major elements are your CPU type and implementation, the bus design of your motherboard, the type and speed of RAM in your system, your video card design, and your hard-drive speed.

▶ You can use the Performance tab of the Task Manager to view a snapshot of how your CPU and memory are performing. The information that you glean from here can be your first indicator that you need a more thorough analysis of your system performance.

▶ The Performance Monitor can be used to track and analyze a wide array of system objects. These objects can be included in any of four different windows, each offering a different way to view performance information.

▶ The most common cause of poor system performance is either the CPU, system memory, or the video system. The Performance Monitor enables you to analyze the first two, but the final element must be deduced without the aid of a system tool.

Appendix

✦ ✦ ✦ ✦

In This Part

The Companion
CD-ROM

✦ ✦ ✦ ✦

Appendix

The Companion CD-ROM

As you have undoubtedly noticed, *Windows NT Workstation 4.0 Bible* includes a CD-ROM. This CD-ROM contains quite a bit of 32-bit software designed to help you increase your productivity on Windows NT. I encourage you to use the software on the CD-ROM and put it to work on your workstation. Please see the readme file on the CD-ROM for late-breaking information.

Types of Software

Many types of software are available, but the companion CD-ROM contains three distinct kinds: freeware, shareware, and demos. Each of these types is explained in the following sections.

What is freeware?

Freeware refers to programs that require no registration fee. Some freeware programs are also called public domain programs. This means that the software author has released the copyright to the program, and anyone may use the software for any purpose. Most freeware, however, is not in the public domain, and you should not assume you can use a freeware program for a commercial purpose, such as bundling it with commercial software. In these instances, you need to contact the program's author for explicit permission.

What is shareware?

Shareware refers to software that you can try, for a limited time, before you decide to buy. The software is typically limited in some way until you register it. For instance, the program may only work for a specific period of time, or it may have some features disabled. In either case, the author of the shareware gives you the right to use his or her program for a specific length of time. After that time, you are requested to register the software and pay a registration fee. Each program has its own accompanying file explaining how to register the software.

Shareware is copyrighted software that is owned by the software author. You should understand that you did not purchase a license for the shareware programs on the CD-ROM when you purchased this book. Indeed, you are still required to register the programs with their respective authors if you find them useful. The companion CD-ROM represents a way to distribute to you, the reader, the best in Windows NT shareware at the time this book was written.

What are demos?

Many times the publisher of a commercial software program creates a demonstration version, or *demo*, of its software. This demonstration version can typically be downloaded electronically or distributed through some other means (such as the CD-ROM with this book). The demonstration software is designed to show the capabilities of a full commercial software program. If you like what you see in the demonstration, you are encouraged to contact the vendor and purchase the full commercial version of the software.

What About Technical Support?

When a program does not function as expected, it is natural to seek technical support on fixing the problem. Most shareware authors (but not all) provide technical support to users *after* they register their shareware. Some shareware authors provide limited support to unregistered users if they have problems installing the software. In either case, the best way to get technical support is to look in the text file or help file that accompanies each program and send electronic mail to the e-mail address listed there.

Freeware programs come with no technical support. If a program does not work properly or do what you expect, you should try out a different program until you find one that does fit your needs.

The author and publisher of this book are not familiar with the details of every program and do not provide any technical support for the programs on the CD-ROM; the programs are supplied as-is. Allen Wyatt, Discovery Computing Inc., and IDG Books individually and collectively disclaim all warranties, expressed or implied, including, without limitation, the warranties of merchantability and of fitness for any particular purpose, and assume no liability for damages, direct or consequential, which may result from the use of the programs or reliance on the documentation. See the IDG Books Worldwide End-User License Agreement at the back of the book for a complete description of the uses and limitations of the CD-ROM and the programs it contains.

What Do You Get If You Register?

The author and IDG Books strongly encourage you to register any shareware you use past the initial evaluation period. Registration brings you a variety of benefits. Each program has its own set of registration benefits, which are described in the accompanying text or help files. Depending on the specific program, you may receive one or more of the following:

- At the very least, you receive a permanent license to use the program on your workstation.

- In most cases, you receive the capability to upgrade to a future version of the program, with features that may significantly enhance the version you have.

- In most cases, you are entitled to receive technical support to configure the software for optimum performance on your system.

- Sometimes you receive a printed manual with more detail or better illustrations than can be provided in the shareware version. If you register multiple copies for your company, you may be able to receive a copy of the printed materials for each user in your company.

- In a few cases, you may receive a diskette that contains additional shareware programs, along with the registered version of the program you licensed.

In all cases, when you register shareware, you help finance the development of new Windows shareware programs. This helps to bring new "killer apps" to the shareware marketplace — a real benefit to us all.

A Word on Operating Systems

Windows NT 4.0 is a brand new version of the operating system. Many of the software programs provided on the CD-ROM take advantage of the Windows NT 4.0 interface. Other programs were originally developed for previous versions of NT but have yet to be updated to NT 4.0. This does not mean they are not powerful programs or that they won't work. On the contrary, they should still work with your version of Windows NT 4.0 just fine. Contact the program's author for additional information on updated versions for NT 4.0.

When you use some of the software on the CD-ROM, you may notice that it states it is for use with Windows 95. This is not unusual; for many, many programs, a single version works just fine for both Windows 95 and Windows NT 4.0. In fact, this signifies that the software is a 32-bit version that should work on your workstation.

What Is on the CD-ROM?

As mentioned earlier, the companion CD-ROM contains a wide variety of Windows NT programs. You can put these programs to work right away. The programs are divided into categories which can help you understand what the programs do. These categories include the following:

- **Accessories.** These programs augment the built-in Windows NT accessories. They help accomplish specific tasks that you may need to perform every day.

- **Business.** These programs are designed to help a small business accomplish its work. They include planners, organizers, and other business tools.

- **Desktop.** These programs include screen savers and cursors. They are used to enliven your desktop and help customize the look of your workstation.

- **Disk Tools.** These programs are used to help manage the files on your disk drives or the disk drives themselves. They include compression programs, file managers, and the like.

- **Games.** These programs are self-explanatory. They are used to provide rest and relaxation from the normal grind of everyday work.

- **Graphics.** These programs are used to work with or develop graphics files. They may include complete graphics development programs or simple utilities used to manage existing graphics files.

- **Internet.** The Internet is an exciting and dynamic area. The tools in this category are used to make your Internet experience more productive.

- **Security.** You already know that Windows NT can be a secure system. These tools help you manage the security features or augment them for greater security.

- **System Tools.** These programs help you perform general maintenance and upkeep on your system. Typically these are well-focused utilities that help you accomplish a task that is not done easily with existing Windows NT tools.

Table A-1 provides an overview of the various programs on the CD-ROM and where you can find them. In all cases, you should refer to the documentation and help files supplied with each program for detailed information.

Category	Program Name	Version	Type	Author	Directory	Comments
Accessories	Astronomy Clock 2		Shareware	Eric Bergman-Terrell	\Access\Clock2	Program to display universal time for any location on earth

Category	Program Name	Version	Type	Author	Directory	Comments
Accessories	Clockz	v1.1a	Shareware	Starfire Software, Inc.	\Access\ClockZ	Shows current time in up to four time zones
Accessories	DiscPlay	v3.31	Shareware	Matt Jensen	\Access\ DiscPlay	32-bit CD player with Internet access, printing, and more
Accessories	Expression Calculator	v2.26	Freeware	Daniel Doubrovkine	\Access\ ExpCalc	Multithread scientific calculator
Accessories	Math Expression Calculator		Freeware	Hyperionics	\Graphics\ MathExp	Calculator program using the command prompt
Accessories	Net Toob	v2.6	Shareware	Duplexx Software, Inc.	\Access\ NetToob	The Ultimate Multimedia Player for Windows
Accessories	Reverse Polish Notation calculator		Shareware	Eric Bergman-Terrell	\Access\ RPNCalc	Great calculator program
Accessories	Turbo Browser	v5.1	Demo	Pacific Gold Coast Corp.	\Access\ Turbo	Provides enhanced Visual File Management for Windows 95/NT 4.0. It safely manages, archives, and cleans up your data. Views and prints most popular file formats without native applications.
Business	Quote Ticker Bar	v3.51	Shareware	Starfire Software,	\Business\ QTB	Shows scrolling stock ticker information, derived from the Internet
Business	Visual Day Planner	v5.0	Shareware		\Business\ DayPlan	Day planner, calendar program
Desktop	Animated Cursors		Freeware	Daniel Goldwater	\Desktop\ Cursors	Huge collection of animated and regular cursors
Desktop	NT Logo Screen 1		Freeware	Daniel Goldwater	\Desktop\ Logos	Windows NT wallpaper or log-on logo
Desktop	NT Logo Screen 2		Freeware	Daniel Goldwater	\Desktop\ Logos	Windows NT wallpaper or log-on logo

(continued)

Category	Program Name	Version	Type	Author	Directory	Comments
Desktop	NT Logo Screen 3		Freeware	Daniel Goldwater	\Desktop\ Logos	Windows NT wallpaper or log-on logo
Desktop	Psychedelic Screen Saver	v3.0	Shareware	Michael Irvine	\Desktop\ Psych	Awesome screen saver
Disk Tools	DumpDisk	v1.0 build 8	Freeware	Bertrand Velle	\Disk\ DumpDisk	Program to edit physical disk sectors, even on NTFS volumes
Disk Tools	File Monitor System	v1.03	Shareware	George Spafford	\Disk\FileMon	Monitors paths, sends SMTP mail with changes detected. Great for monitoring upload directories.
Disk Tools	JCS NT Backup Scheduler		Freeware	Rene A. Parsell	\Disk\JCSBack	32-bit NT backup scheduler
Disk Tools	ScanNT	v1.1	Demo	Midwestern Commerce, Inc.	\Disk\ ScanNT	Attempt to pinpoint security problems by cracking existing passwords on your network
Disk Tools	WinZip		Shareware	Niko Mak Computing	\Disk\ WinZip	The definitive compression/decompression utility for Windows NT
Game	Arasan Chess	v3.1	Freeware	Jon Dart	\Games\ Arasan	Good, easy-to-use chess program
Game	Bog 2		Shareware	Eric Bergman-Terrell	\Games\ Bog2	Word game, similar to Boggle
Game	Bomb Squad 2		Shareware	Eric Bergman-Terrell	\Games\ Bomb2	You need to defuse a bomb by working out the proper code
Game	Hangman 2		Shareware	Eric Bergman-Terrell	\Games\ Hang2	Computerized version of the traditional hangman game
Graphics	FracView 2		Shareware	Eric Bergman-Terrell	\Graphics\ FracView	Program to view fractals
Graphics	HyperSnap	v2.70	Shareware	Hyperionics	\Graphics\ HyperSnp	Screen capture program

Category	Program Name	Version	Type	Author	Directory	Comments
Graphics	PaintShop Pro	v3.12	Shareware	JASC, Inc.	\Graphics\ PSPro	A powerful graphics tool; must-have for every serious system
Graphics	PolyView	v2.60	Shareware	Larry Reeve	\Graphics\ PolyView	Graphics viewer, converter, and printing tool
Graphics	SmartDraw Pro 95	v2.07	Shareware	SmartDraw Software Inc.	\Graphics\ SmartDrw	Business graphics
Graphics	Wright Design		Demo	Wright Technologies Pty Ltd.	\Graphics\ Design	A design tool combining the functionality of imaging systems with that of page layout programs
Graphics	Wright Image		Demo	Wright Technologies Pty Ltd.	\Graphics\ Image	A full-featured image editor for high-resolution work
Graphics	Wright Texture	v1.0	Demo	Wright Technologies Pty Ltd.	\Graphics\ Texture	Tool for creating textures and patterns
Internet	Eudora Light	v3.0 beta 11	Demo	Qualcomm	\Internet\Eudora	E-mail client
Internet	HTMLed 32-Bit	v1.5f	Shareware	Peter Crawshaw	\Internet\ HTMLed	HTML editor
Internet	Internet Explorer	v3.0	Freeware	Microsoft	\Internet\ Explorer	One of the most popular Web browsers available
Internet	Pegasus Mail	v2.42a	Freeware	Pegasus	\Internet\ Pegasus	Full-featured e-mail client
Internet	Web Media Publisher Pro	v11	Shareware	Steve Jackson	\Internet\PubPro	HTML editor
Internet	WS Gopher 32-Bit	v 2.0	Shareware	Dave Brooks and Ken Brown	\Internet\ Gopher	Gopher client
Security	NT Command Line Security Utilities		Shareware	Keith Woodard	\Security\ Utility	Utilities for modifying NT file security
Security	NT File Monitor	v1.1	Shareware	Mark Russinovich and Bryce Cogswell	\Security\ NTFMon	Monitors and displays activity on major system files
Security	Somarsoft DumpAcl	v2.7.7	Shareware, crippled	Somarsoft, Inc.	\Security\ DumpACL	Program to dump the ACL and other security information of an NT system. Useful for tightening security.

(continued)

Category	Program Name	Version	Type	Author	Directory	Comments
Security	Somarsoft DumpEvt	v1.5.2	Shareware, crippled	Somarsoft, Inc.	\Security\ DumpEVT	Program to dump the event logs in a format suitable for using with database programs
System Tools	Somarsoft ACTS	v1.8	Shareware, crippled	Somarsoft, Inc.	\System\ ACTS	Program to call standardized time sources and update system clock
System Tools	Somarsoft DumpReg	v1.1	Shareware, crippled	Somarsoft, Inc.	\System\ DumpReg	Program to dump the Registry in a highly useable manner
System Tools	XReplace 32	v1.57	Freeware	Daniel Doubrovkine	\System\ Xreplace	Allows you to replace information in text files. Great program with a Windows interface.

Using the CD-ROM Software

The majority of the programs on the companion CD-ROM come with installation programs. In order to use the software, you need to run the installation program. The installation programs typically set up the software to work on your system, as well as configure your system as required by the software. For instance, the installation program may add information to your Registry, or it may create INI files on your hard drive.

Most of the programs on the companion CD-ROM are stored in an uncompressed format. This means you can copy the programs to your hard drive and run them just fine, or you can install them directly from the CD-ROM without any problem. When you examine the directories for some of the programs, you may see a single executable file. Typically these are self-extracting programs that install themselves on your system. In that case, all you need to do is run the executable file, and the installation will occur. If you cannot determine exactly how to install a particular piece of software, try these two tips:

- Look in the documentation or readme file for the program you want to install. Many times it will include detailed installation instructions.

- Look for a setup program (such as SETUP.EXE or INSTALL.EXE) in the CD-ROM directory where the program is stored. Run this program to install the software.

I wish you success in using your software and in exploring how to better use Windows NT 4.0 Workstation.

INDEX

Symbols

@ (at sign)
    batch file command, 602
    in separator file commands, 157, 159
\ (backslash), in separator file commands, 156
+ (plus sign), in Explorer, 60
/ (slash), in command-line switches, 297
\n command, 156

A

access time, 626
accessories, 211–255
    Calculator, 213–217
    CD Player, 225–228
    Character Map, 217–219
    Clipboard Viewer, 219–221
    Clock, 221–222
    games, 212
    HyperTerminal, 521–529
    Imaging, 222–225
    Internet Explorer, 504–510
    Media Player, 235–237
    Notepad, 238–239
    overview, 211–212
    Paint, 240–246
    Phone Dialer, 517–521
    Sound Recorder, 231–235
    Volume Control, 229–231
    WordPad, 246–253
Account Disabled check box, 560
account policies, 565–568
    account lockout information, 568
    auditing changes, 584–585
    password restrictions, 566–568
    setting, 304–305, 565–566
    user rights, 568–575
    See also User Manager

Account Policy dialog box, 566–568
Action field, 123–124
active dragging, 81
Adapters tab, Network, 410–411, 415–416
Add Printer Wizard, 41–42, 143–150
    manufacturer and model selection, 146–147
    naming your printer, 147–148
    network printers, 149–150
    port configuration, 145
    printer location selection, 144–145, 149
    sharing your printer, 148–149
Add RAS Device dialog box, 449
Add/Remove Programs Wizard, 268–270, 286–287
adding. See creating; installing
address resolution protocol, 324–325
addresses
    arp command, 324–325
    DNS domain names, 132, 472–476, 481–482
    domain names, 420–421
    Internet addressing, 471–478, 480–483
    IP addressing, 476–478, 480–481
    memory, 182
    Microsoft Exchange properties, 549
    resolution, 478
    for TCP/IP configuration, 478
    UNC (universal naming convention), 130, 131–132
    URL address, 506–507
    WINS configuration, 482–483
Addressing tab, Options (Microsoft Exchange), 549
adjusting bindings, 418–419
Administrator folder, 69
Administrators group, 562
Advanced Connection Settings dialog box, 439–441
Advanced tab
    document properties, 173
    Find, 119–120
    Print Server Properties, 138–139

(continued)

(continued)

(continued)

R

(continued)

X

Title	Author	ISBN	Price
The Internet For Macs® For Dummies® 2nd Edition	by Charles Seiter	ISBN: 1-56884-371-2	$19.99 USA/$26.99 Canada
The Internet For Macs® For Dummies® Starter Kit	by Charles Seiter	ISBN: 1-56884-244-9	$29.99 USA/$39.99 Canada
The Internet For Macs® For Dummies® Starter Kit Bestseller Edition	by Charles Seiter	ISBN: 1-56884-245-7	$39.99 USA/$54.99 Canada
The Internet For Windows® For Dummies® Starter Kit	by John R. Levine & Margaret Levine Young	ISBN: 1-56884-237-6	$34.99 USA/$44.99 Canada
The Internet For Windows® For Dummies® Starter Kit, Bestseller Edition	by John R. Levine & Margaret Levine Young	ISBN: 1-56884-246-5	$39.99 USA/$54.99 Canada

MACINTOSH

Mac® Programming For Dummies®	by Dan Parks Sydow	ISBN: 1-56884-173-6	$19.95 USA/$26.95 Canada
Macintosh® System 7.5 For Dummies®	by Bob LeVitus	ISBN: 1-56884-197-3	$19.95 USA/$26.95 Canada
MORE Macs® For Dummies®	by David Pogue	ISBN: 1-56884-087-X	$19.95 USA/$26.95 Canada
PageMaker 5 For Macs® For Dummies®	by Galen Gruman & Deke McClelland	ISBN: 1-56884-178-7	$19.95 USA/$26.95 Canada
QuarkXPress 3.3 For Dummies®	by Galen Gruman & Barbara Assadi	ISBN: 1-56884-217-1	$19.99 USA/$26.99 Canada
Upgrading and Fixing Macs® For Dummies®	by Kearney Rietmann & Frank Higgins	ISBN: 1-56884-189-2	$19.95 USA/$26.95 Canada

MULTIMEDIA

Multimedia & CD-ROMs For Dummies® 2nd Edition	by Andy Rathbone	ISBN: 1-56884-907-9	$19.99 USA/$26.99 Canada
Multimedia & CD-ROMs For Dummies®, Interactive Multimedia Value Pack, 2nd Edition	by Andy Rathbone	ISBN: 1-56884-909-5	$29.99 USA/$39.99 Canada

OPERATING SYSTEMS:

DOS

MORE DOS For Dummies®	by Dan Gookin	ISBN: 1-56884-046-2	$19.95 USA/$26.95 Canada
OS/2® Warp For Dummies® 2nd Edition	by Andy Rathbone	ISBN: 1-56884-205-8	$19.99 USA/$26.99 Canada

UNIX

MORE UNIX® For Dummies®	by John R. Levine & Margaret Levine Young	ISBN: 1-56884-361-5	$19.99 USA/$26.99 Canada
UNIX® For Dummies®	by John R. Levine & Margaret Levine Young	ISBN: 1-878058-58-4	$19.95 USA/$26.95 Canada

WINDOWS

MORE Windows® For Dummies® 2nd Edition	by Andy Rathbone	ISBN: 1-56884-048-9	$19.95 USA/$26.95 Canada
Windows® 95 For Dummies®	by Andy Rathbone	ISBN: 1-56884-240-6	$19.99 USA/$26.99 Canada

PCS/HARDWARE

Illustrated Computer Dictionary For Dummies® 2nd Edition	by Dan Gookin & Wallace Wang	ISBN: 1-56884-218-X	$12.95 USA/$16.95 Canada
Upgrading and Fixing PCs For Dummies® 2nd Edition	by Andy Rathbone	ISBN: 1-56884-903-6	$19.99 USA/$26.99 Canada

PRESENTATION/AUTOCAD

AutoCAD For Dummies®	by Bud Smith	ISBN: 1-56884-191-4	$19.95 USA/$26.95 Canada
PowerPoint 4 For Windows® For Dummies®	by Doug Lowe	ISBN: 1-56884-161-2	$16.99 USA/$22.99 Canada

PROGRAMMING

Borland C++ For Dummies®	by Michael Hyman	ISBN: 1-56884-162-0	$19.95 USA/$26.95 Canada
C For Dummies® Volume 1	by Dan Gookin	ISBN: 1-878058-78-9	$19.95 USA/$26.95 Canada
C++ For Dummies®	by Stephen R. Davis	ISBN: 1-56884-163-9	$19.95 USA/$26.95 Canada
Delphi Programming For Dummies®	by Neil Rubenking	ISBN: 1-56884-200-7	$19.99 USA/$26.99 Canada
Mac® Programming For Dummies®	by Dan Parks Sydow	ISBN: 1-56884-173-6	$19.95 USA/$26.95 Canada
PowerBuilder 4 Programming For Dummies®	by Ted Coombs & Jason Coombs	ISBN: 1-56884-325-9	$19.99 USA/$26.99 Canada
QBasic Programming For Dummies®	by Douglas Hergert	ISBN: 1-56884-093-4	$19.95 USA/$26.95 Canada
Visual Basic 3 For Dummies®	by Wallace Wang	ISBN: 1-56884-076-4	$19.95 USA/$26.95 Canada
Visual Basic "X" For Dummies®	by Wallace Wang	ISBN: 1-56884-230-9	$19.99 USA/$26.99 Canada
Visual C++ 2 For Dummies®	by Michael Hyman & Bob Arnson	ISBN: 1-56884-328-3	$19.99 USA/$26.99 Canada
Windows® 95 Programming For Dummies®	by S. Randy Davis	ISBN: 1-56884-327-5	$19.99 USA/$26.99 Canada

SPREADSHEET

1-2-3 For Dummies®	by Greg Harvey	ISBN: 1-878058-60-6	$16.95 USA/$22.95 Canada
1-2-3 For Windows® 5 For Dummies® 2nd Edition	by John Walkenbach	ISBN: 1-56884-216-3	$16.95 USA/$22.95 Canada
Excel 5 For Macs® For Dummies®	by Greg Harvey	ISBN: 1-56884-186-8	$19.95 USA/$26.95 Canada
Excel For Dummies® 2nd Edition	by Greg Harvey	ISBN: 1-56884-050-0	$16.95 USA/$22.95 Canada
MORE 1-2-3 For DOS For Dummies®	by John Weingarten	ISBN: 1-56884-224-4	$19.99 USA/$26.99 Canada
MORE Excel 5 For Windows® For Dummies®	by Greg Harvey	ISBN: 1-56884-207-4	$19.95 USA/$26.95 Canada
Quattro Pro 6 For Windows® For Dummies®	by John Walkenbach	ISBN: 1-56884-174-4	$19.95 USA/$26.95 Canada
Quattro Pro For DOS For Dummies®	by John Walkenbach	ISBN: 1-56884-023-3	$16.95 USA/$22.95 Canada

UTILITIES

Title	Author	ISBN	Price
Norton Utilities 8 For Dummies®	by Beth Slick	ISBN: 1-56884-166-3	$19.95 USA/$26.95 Canada

VCRS/CAMCORDERS

Title	Author	ISBN	Price
VCRs & Camcorders For Dummies™	by Gordon McComb & Andy Rathbone	ISBN: 1-56884-229-5	$14.99 USA/$20.99 Canada

WORD PROCESSING

Ami Pro For Dummies®	by Jim Meade	ISBN: 1-56884-049-7	$19.95 USA/$26.95 Canada
MORE Word For Windows® 6 For Dummies®	by Doug Lowe	ISBN: 1-56884-165-5	$19.95 USA/$26.95 Canada
MORE WordPerfect® 6 For Windows® For Dummies®	by Margaret Levine Young & David C. Kay	ISBN: 1-56884-206-6	$19.95 USA/$26.95 Canada
MORE WordPerfect® 6 For DOS For Dummies®	by Wallace Wang, edited by Dan Gookin	ISBN: 1-56884-047-0	$19.95 USA/$26.95 Canada
Word 6 For Macs® For Dummies®	by Dan Gookin	ISBN: 1-56884-190-6	$19.95 USA/$26.95 Canada
Word For Windows® 6 For Dummies®	by Dan Gookin	ISBN: 1-56884-075-6	$16.95 USA/$22.95 Canada
Word For Windows® For Dummies®	by Dan Gookin & Ray Werner	ISBN: 1-878058-86-X	$16.95 USA/$22.95 Canada
WordPerfect® 6 For DOS For Dummies®	by Dan Gookin	ISBN: 1-878058-77-0	$16.95 USA/$22.95 Canada
WordPerfect® 6.1 For Windows® For Dummies® 2nd Edition	by Margaret Levine Young & David Kay	ISBN: 1-56884-243-0	$16.95 USA/$22.95 Canada
WordPerfect® For Dummies®	by Dan Gookin	ISBN: 1-878058-52-5	$16.95 USA/$22.95 Canada

10/31/95

"A lot easier to use than the book Excel gives you!"

Lisa Schmeckpeper, New Berlin, WI, on PC World Excel 5 For Windows Handbook

**Official Hayes Modem
Communications
Companion**
by Caroline M. Halliday

ISBN: 1-56884-072-1
$29.95 USA/$39.95 Canada
Includes software.

**1,001 Komputer Answers
from Kim Komando**
by Kim Komando

ISBN: 1-56884-460-3
$29.99 USA/$39.99 Canada
Includes software.

BESTSELLER!

**PC World DOS 6
Handbook, 2nd Edition**
*by John Socha, Clint Hicks, &
Devra Hall*

ISBN: 1-878058-79-7
$34.95 USA/$44.95 Canada
Includes software.

**PC World Word
For Windows® 6 Handbook**
*by Brent Heslop
& David Angell*

ISBN: 1-56884-054-3
$34.95 USA/$44.95 Canada
Includes software.

BESTSELLER!

**PC World Microsoft®
Access 2 Bible,
2nd Edition**
*by Cary N. Prague
& Michael R. Irwin*

ISBN: 1-56884-086-1
$39.95 USA/$52.95 Canada
Includes software.

**PC World Excel 5
For Windows® Handbook,
2nd Edition**
*by John Walkenbach
& Dave Maguiness*

ISBN: 1-56884-056-X
$34.95 USA/$44.95 Canada
Includes software.

**PC World WordPerfect® 6
Handbook**
by Greg Harvey

ISBN: 1-878058-80-0
$34.95 USA/$44.95 Canada
Includes software.

**QuarkXPress
For Windows® Designer
Handbook**
*by Barbara Assadi
& Galen Gruman*

ISBN: 1-878058-45-2
$29.95 USA/$39.95 Canada

NATIONAL
BESTSELLER!

**Official XTree
Companion, 3rd Edition**
by Beth Slick

ISBN: 1-878058-57-6
$19.95 USA/$26.95 Canada

NATIONAL
BESTSELLER!

**PC World DOS 6
Command Reference
and Problem Solver**
*by John Socha
& Devra Hall*

ISBN: 1-56884-055-1
$24.95 USA/$32.95 Canada

SUPER STAR

**Client/Server
Strategies™: A Survival
Guide for Corporate
Reengineers**
by David Vaskevitch

ISBN: 1-56884-064-0
$29.95 USA/$39.95 Canada

**"PC World Word
For Windows 6
Handbook is very
easy to follow with
lots of 'hands on'
examples. The
'Task at a Glance'
is very helpful!"**

Jacqueline Martens, Tacoma, WA

**"Thanks for publish-
ing this book! It's
the best money I've
spent this year!"**

*Robert D. Templeton,
Ft. Worth, TX, on MORE
Windows 3.1 SECRETS*

For scholastic requests & educational orders please
call Educational Sales, at 1. 800. 434. 2086

FOR MORE INFO OR TO ORDER, PLEASE CALL ▶ 800. 762. 2974

For volume discounts & special orders please call
Tony Real, Special Sales, at 415. 655. 3048

Macworld® Mac® & Power Mac SECRETS,™ 2nd Edition
by David Pogue & Joseph Schorr

This is the definitive Mac reference for those who want to become power users! Includes three disks with 9MB of software!

WINNERS 1994-95 TECHNICAL PUBLICATIONS AND ART COMPETITIONS OF THE SOCIETY FOR TECHNICAL COMMUNICATION

ISBN: 1-56884-175-2
$39.95 USA/$54.95 Canada

Includes 3 disks chock full of software.

NEWBRIDGE BOOK CLUB SELECTION

Macworld® Mac® FAQs™
by David Pogue

Written by the hottest Macintosh author around, David Pogue, *Macworld Mac FAQs* gives users the ultimate Mac reference. Hundreds of Mac questions and answers side-by-side, right at your fingertips, and organized into six easy-to-reference sections with lots of sidebars and diagrams.

ISBN: 1-56884-480-8
$19.99 USA/$26.99 Canada

Macworld® System 7.5 Bible, 3rd Edition
by Lon Poole

ISBN: 1-56884-098-5
$29.95 USA/$39.95 Canada

NATIONAL BESTSELLER!

Macworld® ClarisWorks 3.0 Companion, 3rd Edition
by Steven A. Schwartz

ISBN: 1-56884-481-6
$24.99 USA/$34.99 Canada

NATIONAL BESTSELLER!

Macworld® Complete Mac® Handbook Plus Interactive CD, 3rd Edition
by Jim Heid

ISBN: 1-56884-192-2
$39.95 USA/$54.95 Canada

Includes an interactive CD-ROM.

BMUG SPRING 1995 CHOICE PRODUCT

NEWBRIDGE BOOK CLUB SELECTION

Macworld® Ultimate Mac® CD-ROM
by Jim Heid

ISBN: 1-56884-477-8
$19.99 USA/$26.99 Canada

CD-ROM includes version 2.0 of QuickTime, and over 65 MB of the best shareware, freeware, fonts, sounds, and more!

Macworld® Networking Bible, 2nd Edition
by Dave Kosiur & Joel M. Snyder

ISBN: 1-56884-194-9
$29.95 USA/$39.95 Canada

WINNER

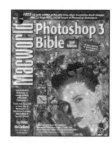

Macworld® Photoshop 3 Bible, 2nd Edition
by Deke McClelland

ISBN: 1-56884-158-2
$39.95 USA/$54.95 Canada

Includes stunning CD-ROM with add-ons, digitized photos and more.

WINNERS 1994-95 TECHNICAL PUBLICATIONS AND ART COMPETITIONS OF THE SOCIETY FOR TECHNICAL COMMUNICATION

NEW!

Macworld® Photoshop 2.5 Bible
by Deke McClelland

ISBN: 1-56884-022-5
$29.95 USA/$39.95 Canada

NATIONAL BESTSELLER!

Macworld® FreeHand 4 Bible
by Deke McClelland

ISBN: 1-56884-170-1
$29.95 USA/$39.95 Canada

Macworld® Illustrator 5.0/5.5 Bible
by Ted Alspach

ISBN: 1-56884-097-7
$39.95 USA/$54.95 Canada

Includes CD-ROM with QuickTime tutorials.

For scholastic requests & educational orders please call Educational Sales, at 1. 800. 434. 2086

FOR MORE INFO OR TO ORDER, PLEASE CALL ▶ 800. 762. 2974

For volume discounts & special orders please call Tony Real, Special Sales, at 415. 655. 3048

IDG BOOKS WORLDWIDE ™

Order Center: **(800) 762-2974** *(8 a.m.–6 p.m., EST, weekdays)*

Quantity	ISBN	Title	Price	Total

Shipping & Handling Charges

	Description	First book	Each additional book	Total
Domestic	Normal	$4.50	$1.50	$
	Two Day Air	$8.50	$2.50	$
	Overnight	$18.00	$3.00	$
International	Surface	$8.00	$8.00	$
	Airmail	$16.00	$16.00	$
	DHL Air	$17.00	$17.00	$

*For large quantities call for shipping & handling charges.
**Prices are subject to change without notice.

Ship to:

Name _____

Company _____

Address _____

City/State/Zip _____

Daytime Phone _____

Payment: ☐ Check to IDG Books Worldwide (US Funds Only)

☐ VISA   ☐ MasterCard   ☐ American Express

Card # _____ Expires _____

Signature _____

Subtotal _____

CA residents add
applicable sales tax _____

IN, MA, and MD
residents add
5% sales tax _____

IL residents add
6.25% sales tax_____

RI residents add
7% sales tax_____

TX residents add
8.25% sales tax_____

Shipping_____

Total _____

Please send this order form to:

**IDG Books Worldwide, Inc.
Attn: Order Entry Dept.
7260 Shadeland Station, Suite 100
Indianapolis, IN 46256**

*Allow up to 3 weeks for delivery.
Thank you!*

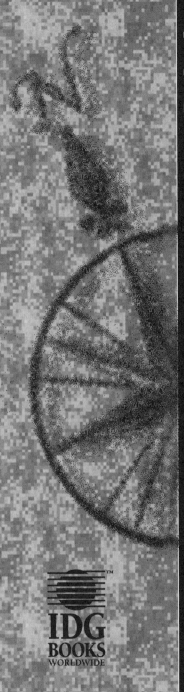

IDG BOOKS WORLDWIDE, INC.
END-USER LICENSE AGREEMENT

<u>Read This</u>. **You should carefully read these terms and conditions before opening the software packet(s) included with this book ("Book"). This is a license agreement ("Agreement") between you and IDG Books Worldwide, Inc. ("IDGB"). By opening the accompanying software packet(s), you acknowledge that you have read and accept the following terms and conditions. If you do not agree and do not want to be bound by such terms and conditions, promptly return the Book and the unopened software packet(s) to the place you obtained them for a full refund.**

1. <u>License Grant</u>. IDGB grants to you (either an individual or entity) a nonexclusive license to use one copy of the enclosed software program(s) (collectively, the "Software") solely for your own personal or business purposes on a single computer (whether a standard computer or a workstation component of a multiuser network). The Software is in use on a computer when it is loaded into temporary memory (i.e., RAM) or installed into permanent memory (e.g., hard disk, CD-ROM, or other storage device). IDGB reserves all rights not expressly granted herein.

2. <u>Ownership</u>. IDGB is the owner of all rights, title, and interest, including copyright, in and to the compilation of the Software recorded on the disk(s)/CD-ROM. Copyright to the individual programs on the disk(s)/ CD-ROM is owned by the author or other authorized copyright owner of each program. Ownership of the Software and all proprietary rights relating thereto remain with IDGB and its licensors.

3. <u>Restrictions on Use and Transfer</u>.

(a) You may only (i) make one copy of the Software for backup or archival purposes, or (ii) transfer the Software to a single hard disk, provided that you keep the original for backup or archival purposes. You may not (i) rent or lease the Software, (ii) copy or reproduce the Software through a LAN or other network system or through any computer subscriber system or bulletin-board system, or (iii) modify, adapt, or create derivative works based on the Software.

(b) You may not reverse engineer, decompile, or disassemble the Software. You may transfer the Software and user documentation on a permanent basis, provided that the transferee agrees to accept the terms and conditions of this Agreement and you retain no copies. If the Software is an update or has been updated, any transfer must include the most recent update and all prior versions.

4. <u>Restrictions on Use of Individual Programs</u>. You must follow the individual requirements and restrictions detailed for each individual program in "The Companion CD-ROM" section of this Book. These limitations are contained in the individual license agreements recorded on the disk(s)/ CD-ROM. These restrictions may include a requirement that after using

the program for the period of time specified in its text, the user must pay a registration fee or discontinue use. By opening the Software packet(s), you will be agreeing to abide by the licenses and restrictions for these individual programs. None of the material on this disk(s) or listed in this Book may ever be distributed, in original or modified form, for commercial purposes.

5. <u>Limited Warranty</u>.

(a) IDGB warrants that the Software and disk(s)/CD-ROM are free from defects in materials and workmanship under normal use for a period of sixty (60) days from the date of purchase of this Book. If IDGB receives notification within the warranty period of defects in materials or workmanship, IDGB will replace the defective disk(s)/CD-ROM.

(b) IDGB AND THE AUTHOR OF THE BOOK DISCLAIM ALL OTHER WARRANTIES, EXPRESS OR IMPLIED, INCLUDING WITHOUT LIMITATION IMPLIED WARRANTIES OF MERCHANTABILITY AND FITNESS FOR A PARTICULAR PURPOSE, WITH RESPECT TO THE SOFTWARE, THE PROGRAMS, THE SOURCE CODE CONTAINED THEREIN, AND/OR THE TECHNIQUES DESCRIBED IN THIS BOOK. IDGB DOES NOT WARRANT THAT THE FUNCTIONS CONTAINED IN THE SOFTWARE WILL MEET YOUR REQUIREMENTS OR THAT THE OPERATION OF THE SOFTWARE WILL BE ERROR FREE.

(c) This limited warranty gives you specific legal rights, and you may have other rights which vary from jurisdiction to jurisdiction.

6. <u>Remedies</u>.

(a) IDGB's entire liability and your exclusive remedy for defects in materials and workmanship shall be limited to replacement of the Software, which may be returned to IDGB with a copy of your receipt at the following address: Disk Fulfillment Department, Attn: Windows NT Workstation 4.0 Bible, IDG Books Worldwide, Inc., 7260 Shadeland Station, Ste. 100, Indianapolis, IN 46256, or call 1-800-762-2974. Please allow 3-4 weeks for delivery. This Limited Warranty is void if failure of the Software has resulted from accident, abuse, or misapplication. Any replacement Software will be warranted for the remainder of the original warranty period or thirty (30) days, whichever is longer.

(b) In no event shall IDGB or the author be liable for any damages whatsoever (including without limitation damages for loss of business profits, business interruption, loss of business information, or any other pecuniary loss) arising from the use of or inability to use the Book or the Software, even if IDGB has been advised of the possibility of such damages.

(c) Because some jurisdictions do not allow the exclusion or limitation of liability for consequential or incidental damages, the above limitation or exclusion may not apply to you.

7. **U.S. Government Restricted Rights.** Use, duplication, or disclosure of the Software by the U.S. Government is subject to restrictions stated in paragraph (c) (1) (ii) of the Rights in Technical Data and Computer Software clause of DFARS 252.227-7013, and in subparagraphs (a) through (d) of the Commercial Computer—Restricted Rights clause at FAR 52.227-19, and in similar clauses in the NASA FAR supplement, when applicable.

8. **General.** This Agreement constitutes the entire understanding of the parties and revokes and supersedes all prior agreements, oral or written, between them and may not be modified or amended except in a writing signed by both parties hereto which specifically refers to this Agreement. This Agreement shall take precedence over any other documents that may be in conflict herewith. If any one or more provisions contained in this Agreement are held by any court or tribunal to be invalid, illegal, or otherwise unenforceable, each and every other provision shall remain in full force and effect.

IDG BOOKS WORLDWIDE REGISTRATION CARD

RETURN THIS
REGISTRATION CARD
FOR FREE CATALOG

Title of this book: **Windows NT™ Workstation 4.0 Bible**

My overall rating of this book: ❏ Very good [1] ❏ Good [2] ❏ Satisfactory [3] ❏ Fair [4] ❏ Poor [5]

How I first heard about this book:

❏ Found in bookstore; name: [6] _____

❏ Advertisement: [8] _____

❏ Word of mouth; heard about book from friend, co-worker, etc.: [10] _____

❏ Book review: [7] _____

❏ Catalog: [9] _____

❏ Other: [11] _____

What I liked most about this book:

_____

_____

What I would change, add, delete, etc., in future editions of this book:

_____

_____

Other comments: _____

Number of computer books I purchase in a year: ❏ 1 [12] ❏ 2-5 [13] ❏ 6-10 [14] ❏ More than 10 [15]

I would characterize my computer skills as: ❏ Beginner [16] ❏ Intermediate [17] ❏ Advanced [18] ❏ Professional [19]

I use ❏ DOS [20] ❏ Windows [21] ❏ OS/2 [22] ❏ Unix [23] ❏ Macintosh [24] ❏ Other: [25]_____
(please specify)

I would be interested in new books on the following subjects:
(please check all that apply, and use the spaces provided to identify specific software)

❏ Word processing: [26] _____

❏ Data bases: [28] _____

❏ File Utilities: [30] _____

❏ Networking: [32] _____

❏ Other: [34] _____

❏ Spreadsheets: [27] _____

❏ Desktop publishing: [29] _____

❏ Money management: [31] _____

❏ Programming languages: [33] _____

I use a PC at (please check all that apply): ❏ home [35] ❏ work [36] ❏ school [37] ❏ other: [38] _____

The disks I prefer to use are ❏ 5.25 [39] ❏ 3.5 [40] ❏ other: [41]_____

I have a CD ROM: ❏ yes [42] ❏ no [43]

I plan to buy or upgrade computer hardware this year: ❏ yes [44] ❏ no [45]

I plan to buy or upgrade computer software this year: ❏ yes [46] ❏ no [47]

Name: _____ Business title: [48] _____ Type of Business: [49] _____

Address (❏ home [50] ❏ work [51] /Company name: _____)

Street/Suite# _____

City [52] /State [53] /Zipcode [54]: _____ Country [55] _____

❏ **I liked this book!** You may quote me by name in future
IDG Books Worldwide promotional materials.

My daytime phone number is _____

**IDG
BOOKS**

THE WORLD OF
COMPUTER
KNOWLEDGE

 # YES!

Please keep me informed about IDG's World of Computer Knowledge.
Send me the latest IDG Books catalog.